The Making of the Modern Jewish Bible

How Scholars in Germany, Israel, and America Transformed an Ancient Text

Alan T. Levenson

ROWMAN & LITTLEFIELD PUBLISHERS, INC.
Lanham • Boulder • New York • Toronto • Plymouth, UK

Published by Rowman & Littlefield Publishers, Inc.
A wholly owned subsidiary of
The Rowman & Littlefield Publishing Group, Inc.
4501 Forbes Boulevard, Suite 200, Lanham, Maryland 20706
http://www.rowmanlittlefield.com

Estover Road, Plymouth PL6 7PY, United Kingdom

Copyright © 2011 by Rowman & Littlefield Publishers, Inc.

Chapter 3 appeared as "Samson Raphael Hirsch's Bible Project" by Alan T. Levenson in *CCAR Journal: The Reform Jewish Quarterly* vol. LVII/IV (Fall 2010). Copyright © 2010 Central Conference of American Rabbis and is under the copyright protection of the Central Conference of American Rabbis and reprinted for use by permission of the CCAR. All rights reserved.

All rights reserved. No part of this book may be reproduced in any form or by any electronic or mechanical means, including information storage and retrieval systems, without written permission from the publisher, except by a reviewer who may quote passages in a review.

British Library Cataloguing in Publication Information Available

Library of Congress Cataloging-in-Publication Data

Levenson, Alan T.
  The making of the modern Jewish Bible : how scholars in Germany, Israel, and America transformed an ancient text / Alan T. Levenson.
      p. cm.
  Includes bibliographical references and index.
  ISBN 978-1-4422-0516-1 (cloth : alk. paper) — ISBN 978-1-4422-0518-5 (electronic)
  1. Bible. O.T.—Criticism, interpretation, etc., Jewish—Germany. 2. Bible. O.T.—Criticism, interpretation, etc., Jewish—Israel. 3. Bible. O.T.—Criticism, interpretation, etc., Jewish—United States. I. Title.
  BS1186.L476 2011
  221.6088'296—dc22
                                                                    2011018085

∞™ The paper used in this publication meets the minimum requirements of American National Standard for Information Sciences—Permanence of Paper for Printed Library Materials, ANSI/NISO Z39.48-1992.

Printed in the United States of America

וּשְׁמַרְתֶּם, וַעֲשִׂיתֶם כִּי הִוא חָכְמַתְכֶם וּבִינַתְכֶם, לְעֵינֵי הָעַמִּים אֲשֶׁר יִשְׁמְעוּן, אֵת כָּל-הַחֻקִּים הָאֵלֶּה, וְאָמְרוּ רַק עַם-חָכָם וְנָבוֹן, הַגּוֹי הַגָּדוֹל הַזֶּה. כִּי מִי-גוֹי גָּדוֹל, אֲשֶׁר-לוֹ אֱלֹהִים קְרֹבִים אֵלָיו, כַּיהוָה אֱלֹהֵינוּ, בְּכָל-קָרְאֵנוּ אֵלָיו. וּמִי גּוֹי גָּדוֹל, אֲשֶׁר-לוֹ חֻקִּים וּמִשְׁפָּטִים צַדִּיקִם, כְּכֹל הַתּוֹרָה הַזֹּאת, אֲשֶׁר אָנֹכִי נֹתֵן לִפְנֵיכֶם הַיּוֹם.

Observe them faithfully, for that will be proof of your wisdom and discernment to other peoples, who on hearing of all these laws will say, "Surely that great nation is a wise and discerning people."

—Deuteronomy 4:6, Jewish Publication Society, Tanakh

Contents

Acknowledgments   xi

Introduction   1

1. Spinoza as *Jewish* Bible Critic   9

Part I: The Emergence of Modern Jewish Bible Studies in Germany

Introduction: Starting with Germany   26

2. Mendelssohn's Bible: The Ideal of Jewish Self-Sufficiency   29

3. Samson Raphael Hirsch: The Chimera of Self-Explanatory Scripture   45

4. Benno Jacob and the Call for a "Jewish" Bible Scholarship   65

5. The Martin Buber–Franz Rosenzweig Bible: Culture or Religion?   81

Part II: Zionism and the Creation of a National Bible

Introduction: The Bible in Modern Israel   96

6. Early Zionism and the Bible: Ahad Haam and His Opponents   103

7. The Bible as National Linchpin: David Ben-Gurion and His Opponents   115

8. Nehama Leibowitz's Bible: Returning Tradition to the Text   133

Part III: The Flowering of Jewish Bible Studies in North America

Introduction: America and the Jewish Bible   152

9   Finding a Jewish Voice: Nahum Sarna and Robert Alter   157

10   Seeking an American Jewish Bible   181

Conclusion: Is There a "Jewish School" of Modern Bible Study?   209

Notes   215

Selected Bibliography   233

Name Index   241

Subject Index   245

About the Author   247

Acknowledgments

Since I have been thinking about the topic of modern Jewish Bible scholarship for many years, I will no doubt forget to thank many people whose comments and criticisms at various points helped me formulate this project. My greatest debt is to the students of Siegal College in Cleveland, Ohio, who signed up for three different versions of Making of the Jewish Bible over the course of a decade. The very last version of this class included students from Houston, Birmingham, and Atlanta as well as locals; this group was particularly good at pushing back on the claims I have made in this book. So many Cleveland students, colleagues, and friends read parts of this manuscript that it is impossible to thank them all. Special gratitude, however, is due Ms. Karen Spector and Mr. Eric Kisch, who commented on the entire manuscript. Dr. Moshe Berger gave my chapters on Hirsch and Leibowitz a thorough going-over; Dr. Roger Klein shared his appraisals of American Jewish Bible scholarship. Mr. Sid Good decided that he would spoil me with his hospitality whenever I returned to Cleveland. For eighteen years, Jean Loeb Lettofsky and the librarians at Siegal College served as unofficial research assistants, and I remain grateful for their help. Although I cannot ask the librarians at the University of Oklahoma to track down and photocopy references in *Encyclopedia Mikrait*, the interlibrary loan department here at OU has delivered many gems from faraway places, including Nehama Leibowitz's 1931 doctoral dissertation.

My mentor, Professor Marc Lee Raphael, invited me to the College of William and Mary as a Bronfman Distinguished Visiting Professor during an early formulation of this project. The students treated me to an engaged hearing and asked some great questions. In Williamsburg (Virginia, not

Brooklyn), Professor Julie Galambush, a scholar of both the Hebrew Bible and Jewish-Christian relations, provided me with many bibliographic suggestions. Professor Susannah Heschel, midway through this project, urged me to aim for the audience I actually taught (undergraduates and educated laypeople), and I am glad that I listened to her advice. Professor David Biale urged me toward a more inclusive approach to defining the modern Jewish Bible. The suggestion was liberating and allowed me to abandon my historicist tendencies, which were mainly a remnant from too much uncritical reading as an undergraduate.

Moving to the University of Oklahoma was a culture shock, but one that continues to generate unforeseen benefits. I have found several OU colleagues, most especially in history, Judaic studies, and religious studies, who have been extremely encouraging. History department chair Professor Rob Griswold and Judaic studies director Professor Noam (Norman) Stillman have been extraordinarily solicitous of me and of my family as we "transition" to the Bible Belt. My colleague Professor Carsten Schapkow generously took time away from his own work to review my German translations and citations. Professors Shmuel Shepkaru, Ori Kritz, and Leah Reches, the rest of our core Judaica faculty, shared their experiences as students and teachers of Bible in Israel. Ms. Jan Rauh, Judaic studies administrator, was kind enough to format this book, written in many different fonts and with many different reference styles. Fortunately for me, her mind, not to mention her desk, is better organized than mine. The young, overwhelmingly Christian students at the University of Oklahoma who sign up for my classes could not be much more different demographically from the Jewish adults whom I taught in Cleveland. But I have found them to be motivated, intellectually curious, and religiously open-minded; my East Coast prejudices have been rebuked by their attentiveness. I would also like to thank the University of Oklahoma for its general support of this project and my ongoing research.

Quite a few "electronic" colleagues shared their wisdom: Professor David Sorkin offered his candid opinions about scholarship on Moses Mendelssohn; Rabbi Walter Jacob shared his intimate knowledge of sources produced by and about his grandfather, Rabbi Benno Jacob. Dr. Shlomo Chertok shared the findings of his important study of Samson Raphael Hirsch, *Kankan Yashan male Chadash*. Dr. Avi Bernstein-Nahar told me I better take a second look at postmodern discussions of Buber's hermeneutics—he was, of course, correct. Professors Steve Zipperstein and Yossi Goldstein answered several questions regarding Ahad Haam. The chapter on Leibowitz benefited from the comments of a number of her former students, including professors Ben Hollander (z"l), Ron Brauner, and Walter Herzberg, as well as some observations and references by Dr. Mira Ofran, Nehama's niece. In the section dealing with American Jewish Bible scholarship, Professor Frederick Greenspahn and Professor

S. David Sperling shared unpublished materials and graciously took an interest in this interloper's foray into their field. The anonymous readers' reviews of previously published pieces of this book in *Journal of Reform Judaism*, *Journal of Jewish Education*, and *Shofar* helped with the disposal of much extraneous material. I thank these reviewers and these journals for allowing me to reproduce parts of these earlier efforts. Although this much help ought to have resulted in an immaculate text, I am aware that I have not produced one. Any and all remaining errors are, obviously, my own responsibility.

The Memorial Foundation for Jewish Culture supported this project, as did Dr. David S. Ariel, now president of the Oxford Centre for Hebrew and Judaic Studies, who granted me a sabbatical from Siegal College. I was so pleased with the job that Rowman and Littlefield did with the second edition of *An Introduction to Modern Jewish Thinkers* (2004) that I did not consider shopping this book around. Ms. Sarah Stanton and her colleagues, always a pleasure to deal with, shepherded this book with great skill, and I am indebted to them as well.

Finally, I thank Hilary, my wife of twenty years, for her constant love and encouragement. My mother, Doris Hettmansberger, will notice that I have once again failed to write a best seller, though I appreciate her irrational conviction that someday I will. Ben, please read the epigraph; it is as true as anything else you are likely to hear.

Introduction

The title of this book—*The Making of the Modern Jewish Bible: How Scholars in Germany, Israel, and America Transformed an Ancient Text*—may strike the general reader as an extended oxymoron. First, how can the Bible, a work stemming from the ancient Near East, possibly be modern? Second, why would the Bible need to be "made," when everybody knows that the Jews are the "people of the book," who have never ceased reading the Bible? Even the word *Jewish* might raise an eyebrow. With the Bible having been bequeathed to Christianity and Islam and Western culture in general, can the Bible still be "Jewish"?

Although it will take me this entire book to answer these three questions adequately, I need to suspend your disbelief long enough to turn the page. Here is a simple answer to the first question: The Bible is modern because the reader also determines the meaning of a text. Even if some ancient Israelites heard some of the words later written in the Bible recited aloud, it is clear they did not perceive them as being THE BIBLE.[1]

Even canonization of the Bible was only one dividing line, though maybe the clearest, in its reception. When Ezra the Babylonian (fifth century BCE), Rashi (eleventh century CE), and the contemporary Jew read the text, they all read it differently. This claim applies to all modern readers of the Bible. Reflecting on the Bible in post-Reformation Germany and England, Jonathan Sheehan writes, "No longer tied to God's Word, the Enlightenment Bible became authoritative by virtue of its connection and relevance to human morality, aesthetics and history. Instead of theology, culture would be the new rock atop which the legitimacy of the Bible was built."[2]

Ask a contemporary Jew *why* she or he reads the Bible and you will probably receive a variety of answers: It is a commandment, but only according to rabbinic tradition. There's no commandment in the Bible to read the Bible, unless you happened to be the king of Israel. It is our national history, but this means something quite different to Israelis than to Americans. It was the centerpiece of premodern education—a misapprehension, since boys quickly graduated to rabbinic literature in most times and places.

Ask an average American Jew *how* she or he reads the Bible, and you may receive the following answers: In a book, except for that small subpopulation of American Jews comfortable enough to read Torah from a scroll. In English translation, none of which are value-neutral. In synagogue, usually from a Chumash, a peculiarly Jewish book comprised of the Torah, broken up into weekly portions, prophetic readings, commentary, and more. Most revealingly, the contemporary Jew is just as likely to read about the Bible, often in beautiful books with charts, time lines, and illustrations. We are modern readers; we read a modern Bible. In the words of the Zionist thinker Ahad Haam, "The Holy Scriptures are not immanently holy. The book exists forever, but its content is changed by life and learning."[3]

Of course, the Bible is also an ancient text, but how ancient? Jewish tradition considered the Five Books of Moses (the Torah) to be Mosaic, although this was less a dogma than a governing assumption. Early rabbinic and medieval scholars knew that certain verses, such as those describing the death of Moses (Deuteronomy 34:1–12), were better ascribed to his successors, and certain narratives, such as Balaam the Moabite prophet's, did not seem Mosaically authored—despite the insistence of the Babylonian Talmud. Beyond the Torah, the attitude toward the Bible was still more relaxed, with the rabbis asking, for instance, if the story of Job was real or a parable. Jewish tradition reflected similar latitude toward the issue of canonization: the question of when the Bible became the Bible. Jewish tradition tended to credit Ezra the Babylonian (fifth century BCE) with standardizing the Torah text and Hebrew alphabet we now recognize, but also recorded debates, as late as the third century CE, over those books of the Bible whose inclusion some contested, such as Ecclesiastes, Esther, and the Song of Songs. While all the contested books came from the third triad of Tanakh (Writings), the rabbis also acknowledged contradictions between the Torah and one of the major prophets (Ezekiel 40–48).

For modern scholars, the antiquity of the Bible has been a matter of considerable dispute. Beginning in the seventeenth century, scholars proposed a variety of dates for the composition and canonization of the Bible. Nineteenth-century Bible scholars differentiated four main authors of the Torah (J, E, D, and P), which were also correlated to different eras in Ancient Israel. Even the earliest of these sources (J and E) were presumed to have been written down no earlier than the time of David and Solomon, and the latest of these authors (P) as late as the Babylonian exile.

The findings of source criticism clashed with the traditional premise of Mosaic authorship. The Jewish responses often reflected a dual loyalty: to progressive scholarship on the one hand, and to adherence to traditional Judaism on the other. For a long time, the undeniable antisemitism of many source critics sharpened this internal conflict; in the end, it has proven possible to disentangle these earlier prejudices from the validity of source-critical procedures. Ironically, the most widely disseminated account of source criticism, among Christians and Jews alike, remains Richard Eliot Friedman's *Who Wrote the Bible?*

What is it about the Bible that is Jewish? To begin with, it is not Christian, as reflected in Rabbi Benno Jacob's complaint about the fruits of a century of Protestant Bible scholarship: "The Bible is no longer our Bible." From Moses Mendelssohn until today, Jewish scholars resisted the biases of the Protestant-dominated world of Bible study, and showed kinship with Jewish efforts. Franz Rosenzweig commented that the Bible translation produced by the Orthodox Samson Raphael Hirsch was closer in spirit to his own avant-garde efforts than to any Christian translation. At the risk of being circular: a modern Bible that was not also a *Jewish* Bible would not have satisfied modern Jewry. At the surface level, this is not problematic. One expects a Chumash, a Jewish study Bible, or a nondenominational Torah commentary to be informed by Jewish traditions. The "Jewish" aspect of the Bible becomes problematic when we turn to academic works, what one scholar has tried to differentiate as "Bible research" rather than "Bible study." Since modern scholarship purports to be objective and bias-free, why should works undertaken in this framework nevertheless reflect a Jewish sensibility? I started pondering this question while reading the preface to *Judaic Perspectives on Ancient Israel*. Jacob Neusner, one of the editors, attempted to isolate three Jewish characteristics of Jewish Bible scholars:

> First, they take up texts neglected by others, or treated by others in a quite different context.... Second, they draw upon a corpus of exegetical traditions that has been neglected up to now.... And third, at some very specific points, Judaic perspectives on ancient Israel lead to a distinctively and particularly Judaic inquiry into a biblical text or problem. That is self-evident in the theological papers presented here. Clearly, then, Jewish biblical scholars can be defined as a distinct group.[4]

Prompted by Neusner's claim, which once seemed to me obviously true, I started collecting examples of modern Jewish Bible scholarship. Eventually, subjected to some rigorous questioning, I came to see Neusner's description as too essentialist. It is easy to find Bible scholarship by Jews that evidences nothing particularly Jewish in any way. It is also easy to find non-Jewish Bible scholars who display mastery of scholarship produced in modern Hebrew by Israeli scholars, knowledge of rabbinic traditions, and theological independence from Christian biases regarding Judaism and the relationship of the "Old" and "New" Testament, language which many colleges and universities have abandoned in their course titles. As in any profession, how a scholar has been trained has an enormous impact. When it comes to Bible study, purely disciplinary considerations (Is one a source critic? A form critic? A rhetorical critic? A canonical critic?) or ideological considerations (Is one a feminist? A secularist? A liberation theologian?) prove to be the controlling factors, more important than the Jewish dimension. Readers of S. David Sperling's *Students of the Covenant*, a discussion of North American Bible scholars of Jewish descent, may conclude that where and with whom somebody did his or her PhD has more influence than any other factor. In other words, Neusner's claim that "Jewish biblical scholars can be defined as a distinct group" is not true today, even if it were closer to being true in 1987.

Academics generally oppose the suspect concept of "essentialism" with the concept that cultural realities are "constructed," that is, an agreed-upon agenda or set of premises that give a group or society self-definition. This will be my approach to describing the modern Jewish Bible, but I am conservative in my use of the term. The modern Jewish Bible may be constructed, but not arbitrarily. The Bible itself exerts enormous gravitational pull, so when Zionists put a secularized, historicized Bible at the center of their national ideology, they invested it with a significance that can only be called—biblical. Similarly, Jewish tradition, especially rabbinic exegesis, drew modern interpreters down certain pathways and excluded others. Alongside this ongoing dialogue with the past, I have also tried to pay attention to the encounter with the surrounding, usually Christian, culture. By treating the modern Jewish Bible as constructed, I am claiming that this Bible did not just happen, it has been "made."

The scope of this book may strike the reader as hubristic. How can one author pretend to tell the story of the role of the Bible in modern Jewish culture, when this role is ubiquitous? To examine the making of the modern Jewish Bible in Germany, Israel, and North America would not only require expertise in these three distinct histories, it would also require knowledge of the field of Bible studies in general. There are, indeed, many scholars whom I would consider more competent to write this book. Why this has not happened, other than scholars having a healthy regard for their reputation, I would attribute mainly to an academic division of labor which defines the Bible as one realm, modern Jewish thought as a second realm, and modern Jewish history as a third. For most of my career I taught what most colleagues considered an oppressive workload (four-four-two). The downsides of this arrangement can be easily imagined; the upside was that even though I was trained as a modern Jewish historian, I got to teach Bible every semester for twenty years. Mainly, I am motivated by the conviction that the making of the modern Jewish

Bible is too momentous to leave alone. This book is *not* an original piece of scholarship: I have merely tried to translate the findings of the academy for a wider audience.

A few scholarly works emboldened me to write this book and have guided my inquiry. Jonathan Sheehan's *The Enlightenment Bible* discusses the means by which the Bible, understood as a fundamentally religious document before the Reformation, became a cultural centerpiece in Germany and England over the course of the sixteenth through eighteenth centuries. Sheehan explores the complexity of transforming the Bible for a more secular era. Yaacov Shavit and Mordechai Eran, in *The Hebrew Bible Reborn: From Holy Scripture to the Book of Books*, detail the Jewish resistance to nineteenth-century German Protestant Bible scholarship in Germany and the land of Israel. As the subtitle suggests, Shavit and Eran focus on a phenomenon similar to that described by Sheehan: the transformation of the Bible from Holy Writ into cultural icon. In Germany, Shavit focuses especially on the Babel Bible controversy, a protracted exchange in which the Bible scholar Friedrich Delitzsch impugned the originality of the Bible and German Jews defended it. The authors also treat the role of the Bible in the formation of Israeli culture: a development taken for granted in Israel, and virtually unacknowledged by American Jews, who tend to see Israelis as either "secular" or "religious." A third book, Naomi Seidman's *Faithful Renderings*, employs translation theory to range over the history of Jewish Bible translations from the Greek Septuagint to Buber-Rosenzweig, exploring the politics of translation and the dynamics of Jewish-Christian difference. I am encouraged that the use and abuse of the Bible in the modern world has recently become of great interest, and I apologize to those scholars whom I did not have time or space to integrate into this study.

I am using a couple of terms in this book more casually than is standard academic practice, including the central one, Bible. None of the alternatives seemed workable. For some of our authors, Torah meant the first five books of Moses only; for others, the entire Written Bible; and for still others, the Written Torah and the Oral Torah together. Some of our figures used the term Torah as a claim of divine authorship, by no means equivalent to the academic term Pentateuch. As I will explain, a Pentateuch is not a Chumash, although both have the number five as a root meaning. Chumash, a term only lightly attested in early rabbinic parlance, has become synonymous with a Bible produced for synagogue use. Using Torah throughout would have created a different problem: the term itself, from the Hebrew root meaning "instruction" or "teaching," was used mainly in a Jewish context, and much of this book deals with polemics and apologetic directed at the Christian world. The same objection applies to Tanakh, the acronym for the triad of Torah, Neviim (Prophets), and Ketuvim (Writings). Scripture implies a divine origin for the books under discussion, which would not work for the several figures, principally Zionist, who specifically reject that premise. And, as Martin Buber noted, while the Hebrew equivalent Mikra contains the sense of out-loud declamation, the word *scripture* lacks it. The very plasticity of the term Bible attracted me, and since I will be dealing exclusively with the Hebrew Bible (excluding the Greek New Testament of the Christian Bible), adding *Hebrew* throughout the manuscript seemed cumbersome. Obviously, where I am quoting others, I will use the term that they themselves used.

Naturally, no text as heavily freighted as the Bible can ever be approached from a value-free perspective—neither Archimedes nor anyone else could have a lever that long. In this book, the reader will so easily perceive my own predilections that I have no need to detail them here. In a stunning reading of Jeremiah 31, the philosopher Emil Fackenheim lucidly distinguished medieval, modern, and postmodern readings. The medieval reader was frankly polemical, certain he had the truth; the modern reader pretended to objectivity, but consistently failed to reach it; the postmodern reader tries to be reflective about his or her bias and seeks to avoid misrepresenting the text, but knows that objectivity is an elusive goal. Accepting Fackenheim's criteria, my own starting point becomes postmodern, and it may be preferable to describe many of the characters I have discussed as "postmodern" rather than "modern."[5] Many of the scholars in the American part of the book use literary theory to argue the indeterminacy of the biblical text, or cite rabbinic midrashim even while dissenting from midrashic premises about the Torah, or acknowledge the variation in Genesis 1 and Genesis 2, but treat this account as a reflection of the contradictory nature of humanity, rather than as authorial competition within the Bible. All of these interpretive stances might be called "postmodern." I have stuck with the title of this book for a simple reason: I think that there are more interesting issues to discuss than whether a particular interpreter is postmodern or simply modern.

Not all ages in Jewish history have accorded equal importance to the study of the Bible. Sometimes the Bible has been scrutinized and at other times it has been put on a pedestal inside an ark. The early rabbinic period saw a profusion of legal and narrative midrashic works with the Bible as their basis; the twelfth century saw an explosion of scholarship bringing philological and mystical perspectives on the Bible to bear. But one could argue that even in these periods the truly revolutionary advances lay elsewhere. As Lawrence Schiffman concludes in his standard textbook of early rabbinic Judaism: "By the amoraic period, the rabbis were openly asserting the superiority of the oral law . . . Scripture had been displaced by Talmud."[6] Similarly, Ephraim Karnafogel, surveying Bible study in medieval Europe, writes, "Independent Bible study was advocated in medieval Ashkenaz only by small, unrelated groups of scholars and religious leaders."⁷ Relatively speaking, the periods described by Schiffman and Karnafogel were golden ages of Bible study. In other periods, such as the century before Moses Mendelssohn's epochal translation, the Hebrew Bible suffered even greater neglect. Contrary to assumptions about the poverty of modern Jewish thought, I would argue that this era has been the golden age of Jewish Bible study.

My office is crammed with translations, publishers' catalogs, commentaries, and varied books on the Bible, almost all of them written within the last quarter century. Shortly before I left Cleveland for the University of Oklahoma, I was presented with *The Torah: Women's Commentary*, a book whose title and contents would have been unimaginable when I was born. (Elizabeth Cady Stanton published *A Women's Bible* in the 1890s, but this feminist classic was controversial in its own day and full of the regnant anti-Jewish bias.) Living in the Bible Belt, I am reminded daily that America is a very religious country and that American Protestantism is very biblically oriented. This makes the American Jewish obsession with the Bible less surprising. We will need to ask why this was also so for modern German Jewry and for the prestate Zionists. A prior question: When did the Bible start to become modern? One possible answer: in the generation of Benedict (Baruch) Spinoza, Judaism's favorite heretic.

After an initial look at the inadvertent Jewishness of Spinoza as a Bible critic, this book divides into three sections, each preceded by a brief orientation for the nonexpert reader. The first section deals with Germany, focusing on the translations and commentaries of Moses Mendelssohn, Samson Raphael Hirsch, Benno Jacob, and Buber-Rosenzweig. For all their differences, these works developed a religious humanism that typified the German-Jewish striving to be fully modern and authentically Jewish. The second section treats prestate and modern Israel, focusing on the writings of Ahad Haam, the state-sponsored biblicism of David Ben-Gurion, and developments in Zionist-Orthodox Bible studies as represented in the work of Nehama Leibowitz. All of these efforts aim at an appropriation of the Bible as relevant for a modern nation. The third section deals with our contemporary American Jewish renaissance, which emerged after World War II. The works of Nahum Sarna and Robert Alter will be the central focus of "Finding a Jewish Voice"; the modern Chumash and the rise of feminism, the focus of "Seeking an American Jewish Bible"; the question of whether there is a Jewish school of Bible studies serves as my brief conclusion. I argue that Jewish Bible scholarship in America cultivates an ethnic identity, defined by contemporary Jewish diversity, opposition to exclusive Christian ownership of the Bible, and a desire to connect to the Jewish past. My generalizations invite many exceptions, some that I am aware of, and others, no doubt, that will be brought to my attention. My claims are heuristic—that is academese for, right or wrong, I hope this book provokes further discussion.

1

Spinoza as *Jewish* Bible Critic

Regarded by all as a European philosopher of the first rank, Baruch (Benedict) Spinoza (1632–1677) was probably the most original mind produced by the Jewish people since Moses Maimonides. The basic outlines of Spinoza's life are well known: He descended from Portuguese conversos (secret Jews) who found refuge in seventeenth-century Amsterdam. Spinoza's mother, Hannah, died while he was still a child; his father, Michael, a merchant, died while Spinoza was in his early twenties. Spinoza grew up in Amsterdam's enlightened Jewish community, whose schools taught Bible and Hebrew, both grammar and composition, and had rabbis well versed in non-Jewish culture. How far Spinoza proceeded in his education remains a matter of some debate. Whether or not Spinoza advanced to the study of Talmud and other rabbinic literature, his Hebraic skills proved more than adequate for the task of attacking the authority of the Bible, the one item on his agenda that I will try to explain here. Thanks mainly to Steven Nadler's biography, *Spinoza: A Life*, we know that Spinoza befriended a variety of freethinkers and religious nonconformists and developed into a first-class heretic at an impressively young age. The Amsterdam Jewish community excommunicated Spinoza on July 27, 1656. Unlike other conversos such as Uriel D'Accosta and Dr. Juan De Prado, Spinoza made no attempt to win reinstatement. He spent the rest of his life in a variety of Dutch cities, actively carrying on correspondence with leading European thinkers, eyeing political developments in the Dutch Republic carefully, and living modestly on the benefaction of admirers. (Spinoza also ground glass lenses, but this seems to have been motivated more by an interest in optics than a source of income.) He passed away on February 21, 1677. Within a year, his posthumous works appeared in Latin and in Dutch translation, and within a short period of time appeared the first of many biographies.

RECLAIMING A JEWISH SPINOZA

Spinoza became a hero to many subsequent rebels and won laurels as the most personally admirable of modern philosophers. Even Bertrand Russell, who had something negative to say about almost everybody, wrote, "Spinoza is the noblest and the most lovable of the great philosophers. Intellectually, some others have surpassed him, but ethically he is supreme. As a natural consequence, he was considered, during his lifetime and for a century after his death, a man of appalling wickedness."[1] Spinoza's reputation in philosophy, until recently, rested with the posthumously published *Ethica Ordine Geometrico Demonstrata* (the *Ethics*), 1674. The *Ethics* deployed axioms, theorems, proofs, and corollaries to grasp God, the mind, good and evil, and bondage and freedom. The boldness and self-contained nature of Spinoza's venture prompted the French philosopher Henri Bergson to quip that every philosopher has two systems—his own and Spinoza's. The *Ethics* has nothing obviously Judaic about it, and the format owes much more to the French Catholic René Descartes and to the English Protestant Francis Bacon than to any Judaic traditions. Spinoza's audience, limited in those days to fellow freethinkers, was certainly not Jewish. And none of Spinoza's preserved writings are in a Jewish language, though Spinoza knew Hebrew and was working on a Hebrew grammar when he died. Spinoza's main philosophic works were in Latin, with some occasional letters in Dutch. Clearly, the usual criteria of what makes Jewish philosophy Jewish—language, audience, subject matter, and ultimate loyalties—disqualify the Spinoza of the *Ethics*. The ingenious and oft-cited argument by the Jewish Marxist Isaac Deutscher that even in his general philosophy Spinoza belonged to a special type, alongside Karl Marx and Sigmund Freud, that Deutscher termed "The Non-Jewish Jew," seems, in retrospect, a claim too circular to lead anywhere worth going, although that has not stopped several authors from trying.

But Deutscher's essay underscored a definite desire on the part of modern Jews (present author included) to treat Spinoza as a Jewish figure—a genre recently lampooned as "the Spinoza defense."[2] This interest in reclaiming a Jewish Spinoza hinges on the relative weight accorded the *Ethics* and the *Tractatus Theologico-Politicus* (1670), Spinoza's two greatest works. The *Ethics* (1674) contains Spinoza's unique philosophical system; the *Tractatus* contains his great statement on religion and politics. While the *Ethics* continues to provoke reconsideration, especially as brain research lends increasing support to Spinoza's strictly deterministic outlook, a veritable flood of works has appeared on the *Tractatus*. The heightened interest in this latter work can be best demonstrated by noting the number of new translations—translation being a notoriously tedious and difficult task. The mathematician R. H. M. Elwes translated Spinoza into English in 1853 and, after more than a one-hundred-year hiatus, no fewer than three translations of the *Tractatus* into English have appeared in the last twenty years![3]

The desire to reclaim a Jewish Spinoza goes back to before this recent translational activity. In Weimar Germany, Leo Strauss, now known mainly as a University of Chicago professor who influenced many founders of neoconservatism, completed a doctoral dissertation. This dissertation became a book, *Spinoza's Critique of Religion*, which called attention to the magnitude of Spinoza's challenge to religious orthodoxy, personified for Strauss by Moses Maimonides. Although Strauss lavished attention on Spinoza's challenge to John Calvin, too, he staged the battle between Spinoza and Maimonides as the true heavyweight championship. Who won the contest? In Strauss's view, Spinoza had failed to dislodge his medieval adversary:

> The genuine refutation of orthodoxy would require the proof that the world and human life are perfectly intelligible without the assumption of a mysterious God; it would require at least the success of the philosophic system: man has to show himself theoretically and practically as the master of his life; the merely given world must be replaced by the world created by man theoretically practically. Spinoza's *Ethics* attempts to be that system, but it does not succeed . . . it remains fundamentally hypothetical.[4]

Around the same time Strauss's work appeared in English, Harry Wolfson, a Jew from Poland who achieved a professorship at Harvard University, wrote an elegant study called *From Philo to Spinoza*. Wolfson had written academic tomes on both these figures previously, but tied them here together most revealingly. By marrying reason and revelation, Wolfson argued, Philo had inaugurated the Middle Ages; by divorcing reason from revelation, Spinoza marked their conclusion. Thus two diaspora Jews, one living in first-century Alexandria and the other in seventeenth-century Amsterdam, provided the true bookends to medieval thought. In Wolfson's own words:

> Perhaps this reinstatement of Greek philosophy is all one could expect of Spinoza or of any other philosopher. For on all these religious issues there are only two alternatives. One was stated in the Hebrew Scripture, and the other in the various writings of Greek philosophers. Thereafter, the great question in the history of religious philosophy was whether to follow the one or the other, or to combine the two. And in the history of religious philosophy, so conceived, two figures are outstanding, Philo and Spinoza. Philo was the first to combine the two; Spinoza was the first to break up that combination.[5]

While Strauss and Wolfson differed on many points, they agreed that Spinoza played a pivotal role in Western thought. Strauss's view of Spinoza as an esoteric thinker who hid his true opinion that religion and the Bible were little more than vehicles for cajoling the vulgar masses into political obedience has had enormous influence—many have rejected Strauss's view and inclined to a view that "truth" and "meaning" each have a role in Spinoza's thinking, a position more congenial to Wolfson's analysis.

The Jewish context, particularly the Marrano/converso experience, also held the key to Spinoza's thought for a third philosopher, the Israeli Yirmiyahu Yovel. In a wide-ranging two-volume work, *Spinoza and Other Heretics*, Yovel argued that Spinoza's converso background helped explain his remarkable ability to think outside the box. Among Spinoza's many tantalizing insights was his early articulation of the possibility of secular Jewish existence, voiced near the end of the third chapter of the *Tractatus*. Having demolished the idea of divine national election (i.e., the chosenness of the Jews, or of any other people), Spinoza imagined the revival of a modern Jewish nation:

> Furthermore, I think that the sign of circumcision has such great importance as to persuade me that this thing alone will preserve their nation for ever and in fact, were it not that the principles of their religion weaken their courage I would believe unreservedly that at some time, given an opportunity, since all things are changeable, they might reestablish their state and God will choose them again.[6]

Earlier readers had noted this passage with excitement as a charter of modern Jewish secularism. Certainly most readers of Spinoza understood his phrase, "God will choose them again," to mean something like "fortune will smile upon them." David Ben-Gurion, whose views on the Bible we will examine in detail, idolized Spinoza and tried to get his ban of excommunication formally rescinded by the Israeli rabbinate. For Ben-Gurion and other Zionists, Spinoza was a forerunner who arrived too early on the scene of history. But Yovel recognized that Spinoza could actually be claimed as an advocate for a number of mutually inconsistent positions, including national assimilation, Reform, Zionism, or even Jewish nationalism in a diaspora setting. To simplify Yovel's point, Spinoza, a Jew in bad standing, did not care about the Jewish future one whit.[7] Contemporaries saw Spinoza as Jewish, but he did not:

> Spinoza, as an adult, did not see himself as a Jew; in no way was his self-identity bound up with his Jewish birth and upbringing. The clearest indication of this can be found in the *Treatise* itself, where the Jews are always referred to in the third person: it is "they" who have nothing to boast about in terms of God's election over and above other peoples. Spinoza belonged to no confessional religion and had no intention of joining any "sect."[8]

Writing in Schocken's Jewish Encounters series, Rebecca Goldstein in *Betraying Spinoza* (2006) acknowledges the central irony: "By what right is Benedictus Spinoza included in this series, devoted as it is to Jewish themes and thinkers?"[9] Goldstein answers her own question largely by amplifying her subtitle. If a Jew "gave us modernity," a widely held view about Spinoza, then surely modern Jews can take a little tribal pride in the matter. A host of academic reasons for the renewed interest in Spinoza's *Tractatus* could be cited: the recognition of Spinoza's role in the radical Enlightenment; the creation of a counternarrative designed to demonstrate Jewish centrality to the general culture; the growing interest in the relationship of state and religion, fueled by worldwide political developments, including those in the United States; a postmodern desire to claim ethnic kinship with a thinker who may be otherwise uncongenial to us, and so on. Speculating on the wherefores and whys of Spinoza's contemporary comeback as a Jewish icon is probably more fun than fruitful. Rather than pursuing these elusive motives, I want to revisit the *Tractatus* as a piece of Bible scholarship, and suggest that there are elements of this work that do indeed suggest a Jewish sensibility. This will require more discussion of both the *Tractatus* and the Bible than the well-versed reader would require, but I see no alternative.

THE REVOLUTIONARY NATURE OF THE *TRACTATUS*

The *Tractatus* is in some ways a Jewish text; it is in every way a revolutionary text. While Spinoza stands alongside other contemporary pioneers in the modern study of the Bible, including the great Thomas Hobbes, his contributions were astounding. To Spinoza, the Bible was a humanly produced document, subject to the same rules of observation and analysis that apply to an astronomical or a meteorological event. As Spinoza baldly stated in chapter 7 of the *Tractatus*, "the method of interpreting Scripture does not differ widely from the method of interpreting nature—in fact, it is almost the same." In early chapters dealing with prophecy, miracles, and Israel's election (i.e., "chosenness"), Spinoza uses his rationalism to cut the Hebrew Scriptures down to human size, while being sufficiently veiled in his formulations to avoid persecution. A careful reader will nevertheless recognize that prophecy, miracles, and the doctrine of Israel's election are divested of their usual meaning and radically reinterpreted along natural as opposed to supernatural lines. Spinoza's Bible was not the Bible of traditional Judaism, then or now. To Judaism, the Torah's meaning always went beyond the text, into the living life of the Jewish community. For Jewry, the Torah provided the liturgical calendar, the basis of laws, the religious vocabulary (e.g., covenant, blessing, and commandment), the vocabulary and content of many rabbinically ordained prayers, the centerpiece of the literary canon, the ultimate court of appeal in academic debates, the primer of human morality, and more. Spinoza wished to dislodge the Bible from this venerated position.

Armed with this agenda, a superb Jewish education, and one of the most penetrating minds Western civilization has ever produced, Spinoza set out to demonstrate that the Bible is a human document written for one people (ancient Israelites), in one place (ancient Israel), and at one time (before the exile of 70 CE). The Bible, therefore, unlike philosophy, has no claim to eternal or universal truth. And here, perhaps, is the most extraordinary thing about the *Tractatus*: Spinoza's revolutionary Bible scholarship intended principally to clear the ground for a political state in which people are left unmolested in their religious ideas. As the last chapter of the *Tractatus* puts it: "That in a free state every man may think what he likes, and say what he thinks." Proclaiming that "the true aim of government is liberty," and living his adult life as a true religious independent, possibly the first European who belonged to no religious community, it is no wonder that Spinoza ultimately came to be regarded as a hero to dozens of young Jews in the nineteenth century who sought to break the bonds of traditional Jewish community without lapsing into another orthodoxy such as the majority Christian culture offered. The Hebrew Commonwealth, in which heresy was tantamount to treason, since God was the recognized head of state, was for Spinoza a one-time occurrence that could not and should not be reproduced in seventeenth-century Europe.

In Spinoza's day, biblical criticism was in its infancy. The fields of archaeology and ancient Near Eastern philology that have illuminated the Bible by placing it in its ancient Near Eastern context did not yet exist. The tools Spinoza had at hand, therefore, were not much different from those of more than a millennium of traditional interpreters. Given the Bible's preeminent role in medieval culture, we could hardly expect Spinoza to notice things that predecessors—Jewish and Christian—had not seen as well. In a spirited defense of a literary as opposed to a historical reading of the Bible, Alan Cooper observed that Augustine of Hippo raised most of the questions Spinoza would pose twelve hundred years later in the former's *De doctrina christiana*, an important fourth-century-CE work synthesizing the Bible and the Greco-Roman tradition as Europe was turning Christian and as the Roman Empire fell apart. Augustine faced many challenges, including marauding Vandals who would conquer his North African home. One of Augustine's greatest challenges, relevant to Spinoza's day and our own, was demonstrating the Bible's literary quality in comparison to the Greco-Roman classics.[10]

A reader of Augustine's Bible commentaries, or rabbinic midrash, will likely conclude that every question that could have been asked of the Bible had been asked. Spinoza's concept of the purpose of Bible scholarship and the bluntness with which he stated his conclusions, more than the questions he posed, made the *Tractatus* revolutionary. In terms of method, Spinoza advocated techniques of Bible scholarship that have become accepted practice in the secular academy. Spinoza analyzed editorial measures, earlier and later traditions, the social conditions in which texts were originally produced, manuscript variations and corruptions, and so on. Spinoza grasped the importance and interlocking roles of linguistics, literary analysis, historical criticism of the era and circumstances of individual authors, and settings. He attended to changes in meaning of vocabulary and doctrine, editorial revisions of earlier traditions, order of narratives, arrangements, and genre of biblical books relative to each other. He tried to be scrupulous about not importing subsequent interpretation, whether Jewish or philosophical, into Scripture. He opposed all interpretations of Scripture that attempted to "rescue" the Bible's apparent primitivisms. Spinoza's version of "Scripture alone," however, bore scant comparison with the Protestant understanding of that battle cry, which presumed a divinely authored text and the role of faith as an interpretive key to unlock that text, two propositions that Spinoza rejected. Spinoza may have believed the message of Scripture "divine," but the text itself was a human artifact. Regarding the role of faith as necessary for true understanding, Spinoza's words ooze sarcasm:

> I shall consider those who hold that the natural light of reason does not suffice to interpret the Scripture and that for this a supernatural light is absolutely essential. What this light is which is beyond nature, I leave to them to explain. I, for my part, can only surmise that they have been trying to admit, in very obscure terms, that they are generally in doubt about the true sense of Scripture; for if we examine their interpretations, we find they contain . . . nothing more than mere conjectures.[11]

Spinoza's conception of how one might interpret the Bible on its own terms receives its clearest formulation in chapter 7:

> Firstly, such a history must include the nature and properties of the language in which the biblical books were composed and which their authors were accustomed to speak . . . and the writers of both the Old and New Testament were Hebrews and undeniably the history of the Hebrew language is more essential than anything else not only for understanding the books of the Old Testament . . . but also those of the New Testament.
> Such a history must gather together the opinions expressed in each individual book and organize them by subject so that we may have available by this means all the statements that are found on each topic.
> Finally, our historical enquiry must explain the circumstances of all the books of the prophets whose memory has come down to us: the life, character and particular interests of the author of each individual book, who exactly he was, on what occasion he wrote, for whom and in what language. Then the fate of each book, who exactly he was, on what occasion he wrote, for

whom and in what language. Namely how it was first received and whose hands it came into, how many variant readings there have been of its text, by whose decisions it was received among the sacred books and finally, how all the books which are now accepted as sacred came to form a single corpus. All this, I contend has to be dealt with in a history of the Bible.[12]

To reiterate, earlier Jewish and Christian scholars were aware of these issues, including that of authorship, but the *Tractatus* resolved these issues in a novel fashion. While Abraham Ibn Ezra and others may have regarded several verses as having been composed by a different hand than Moses's, none of these sages considered the sanctity of the Torah impugned by this recognition. If Moses did not scribe a particular verse, then Joshua did, and if not Joshua, then another one of the Prophets deserved credit. All medievals accepted that God's word stood behind the text and that Torah represented the way of life for Jewish society. When the Torah scrolls were read in synagogue Ibn Ezra stood up and affirmed along with the rest of the congregation, "This is the Torah that Moshe placed before Israel by the word of God." Spinoza, on the contrary, drew stunningly radical conclusions from similar literary investigations. After the review of Deuteronomy addressed above, Spinoza concludes: "From all this it is plainer than the noonday sun that the Pentateuch was not written by Moses, but by someone else who lived many generations after Moses."[13] By the standards of his day, Spinoza had truly earned his heretic status.

THE JEWISHNESS OF THE *TRACTATUS*: HEBRAICA VERITAS

Cribbing a question from Steven Smith's *Spinoza, Liberalism and the Question of Jewish Identity*, let us ask: how Jewish is the *Tractatus*?[14] If the *Ethics*, once considered Spinoza's magnum opus, has nothing explicitly Jewish about it, the *Tractatus* qualifies him, at the very least, as a formidable critic of the Judaic tradition. Throughout the *Tractatus*, Spinoza subjects the Hebrew scriptures to historical critical analysis. Spinoza took many of his hints from early and medieval Jewish exegetes who were well aware that Moses did not write every word of the Torah. Rabbi Abraham Ibn Ezra (eleventh-century Spain), for instance, clearly did not believe that the last few verses of Deuteronomy, which describe Moses's death and unknown place of burial, were actually written by Moses. What to do with that observation depends on one's premises. One midrash imagines Moses writing the last verses of Deuteronomy, describing his own death, "with tears in his eyes." This piece of midrashic lore, however, was not stated as a dogma. In chapter 8, Spinoza noted Ibn Ezra's cagey implications that Moses had not written every line of the Torah. But Spinoza proceeded beyond Ibn Ezra's six passages, citing more decisive arguments against Mosaic authorship. Among other anomalies, Spinoza noted: (1) that many passages of Deuteronomy presume that Israel already was dwelling in the land of Canaan, not the plains of Moab, (2) that Deuteronomy refers to Moses in the third person, and (3) that Moses refers to himself as "the most modest of men." Curiously enough, while many pioneers of a source critical approach (ultimately known as the Documentary Hypothesis; or "J, E, P, D," or source criticism), focused on the opening of Genesis with its two stylistically different creation narratives and its alternating divine names (God/Elohim versus Lord/Yahweh), Ibn Ezra and Spinoza found the most striking evidence of multiple authorship in Deuteronomy. Is this a coincidence? While the difference in vocabulary between Genesis 1:1–2:4 and Genesis 2:5–2:25 can be demonstrated, any elementary student of Hebrew will recognize a great difference in style and vocabulary between Deuteronomy and the first four books of the Torah. There remains something suggestively Jewish about Deuteronomy, nicknamed "the book of the covenant" in the rabbinic tradition, becoming the battleground for Spinoza's assault.

If this assertion goes too far, no one could argue that Spinoza's Bible was a Hebrew Bible, a simple observation obscured by translations which do not reproduce the Hebrew typeface found in Spinoza's original manuscript—Yaffe's translation is a notable and praiseworthy exception. While some American Protestants insist that the King James Bible supersedes the version given at Sinai, I would claim the Hebrewness of the Bible for all Jews is a cultural given. Intellectually, Spinoza's reliance on and citation of a Hebrew text is evident at every turn: he relied on Jewish translations and takes issue with the tenth-century-CE Masoretes who standardized the vocalizations of the vowelless Hebrew text. He followed medieval exegetes who led him to contradictions in the text—which Spinoza exploited rather than midrashically resolved. Spinoza was simply obsessed with the manifold problems of arriving at a clear understanding of biblical Hebrew, returning to these problems numerous times in the *Tractatus*. From his references to the disagreements between rabbis and the observation of Rashi regarding blatantly conflicting texts in Chronicles, a book the rabbis said was given for the making of midrash, it is clear that Spinoza had his rabbinic Bible at hand while composing the *Tractatus*. We should not judge a book by the cover, especially since the *Tractatus* appeared anonymously with a false publisher name and false place of publication, but we are surely entitled to form an impression. To one casually leafing through it, looking at the notes and the names, the *Tractatus* feels Jewish.

No chapter exemplifies this Jewish "feel" better than the hodgepodge chapter 9, "Further queries about the same books, namely whether Ezra made a definitive version of them, and whether the marginal notes found in the Hebrew MSS are variant readings." The items that Spinoza treats therein reflect issues more readily articulated by a lapsed Jew than a Christian Hebraist: the matter of truncated spaces in the Torah scroll; the question of why the Traditional Text frequently offers two variant readings, what is read in synagogue (*keri*), and what is written in the scroll (*ketiv*); the existence of Hebrew letters easily mistaken for others; the existence of Hebrew letters of emphasis, direction, and modification; the testimony of tractate Soferim (dealing mainly with the scribing of Torah scrolls); and differences between the early rabbis of the Talmud and the later Masoretes. Alongside the "lower critical" examples given in chapter 7 (e.g., duplicate letters, uncertainty of Hebrew verb tenses, and absence of punctuation and vocalization), this chapter gives the unmistakable impression of a reader entirely at home with the Hebrew text who finds his touchstones—both positive and negative—in the Jewish tradition. Revealingly, the non-Jewish sources that Spinoza cited frequently in the *Tractatus* were pagan poets such as Virgil and Terence. He did not seem overly impressed with the slew of contemporaries who shared his view on Mosaic authorship (including John Lightfoot, Simon Patrick, John Richardson, Samuel Fischer, or Isaac La Peyrere) or with the venerable tradition of Christian Bible commentary. "Spinoza cited none of the standard commentaries by Christian scholars that were read by almost everyone in the Republic of letters. In his library, he had grammars and dictionaries by the Christian Hebraists, but not their expositions or explanations of Scripture."[15] Jay Harris sagely observed that the remarkable facet of Spinoza's uncompleted Hebrew grammar was his desire to compose such a work independent of rabbinic understanding—and his failure to do so. I am *not* suggesting a covert desire on Spinoza's part to celebrate rabbinic erudition, merely the difficulty he had in freeing himself of its influence.

THE JEWISHNESS OF THE *TRACTATUS*: IF NOT MOSES, EZRA

For Spinoza, Ezra was the principal author of the Bible, heterodoxy from the standpoint of the Judaism of Spinoza's day. Like all his contemporaries, Spinoza accepted the fundamental historicity of the Bible. While he had harsh words for subsequent interpreters, he did not regard the text as a "pious fraud," to invoke the famous judgment of Wilhelm De Wette on Deuteronomy. Spinoza did not see the Bible as a malignant document of patriarchy or orientalism or white supremacism. Spinoza saw the Bible as fundamentally benign, or at least capable of being put to social benefit (*Tractatus*, chapters 12–14). Whether Spinoza admired Jesus more than Moses, he admired both men. He directed his ire not against the message of the biblical text, but against the many abuses which grew out of it: clericalism, casuistic interpretation, and bibliolatry.

Given that nobody learned Bible in an ecumenical environment before the last few decades, it should come as no surprise that certain books, figures, and doctrines elicited different responses from scholars raised in different religions. One figure likely to divide readers is Ezra, judged by precontemporary scholars as either a reformer or a bigot. It can hardly be overstated how deeply the rabbis venerated Ezra as reestablishing the Torah after it had been forgotten by Israel. Conversely, it can hardly be overstated how deeply German Protestant scholarship despised Ezra as the father of Judaism and the deadener of prophetic spirit. For many founders of source criticism, Ezra codified the law and killed the biblical spirit. Spinoza does not share this bias. Spinoza's main interest in discussing Ezra seems to be threefold: (1) Determining the most important biblical author, "The foremost of these is Ezra whom I will continue to regard as their author until someone demonstrates a more certain candidate." (Like Hobbes, Spinoza rejected the mere designation of a book, "Joshua," for instance, as adequate proof of authorship.) For Spinoza, Ezra arranged all the books from the distant past to his own day; although he did not write every word, he most deserves the title author. (2) Finding the logical terminus for the long stretch of biblical writing that extends from Genesis to II Kings, often called the "primary history" or "Dodecateuch" by contemporary scholars. Spinoza, in fact, anticipated this scholarly verdict: "the author of Chronicles borrowed his account from other chroniclers and not from the twelve books [e.g., Genesis–II Kings] we attribute to Ezra." (3) Casting someone in the role of what later scholars would call the Redactor, did Ezra "produce a definitive version of this work and complete it as he intended to do"? Spinoza's tenth chapter answers his question negatively: Ezra did not have a chance to finish the editorial project he commenced. Nevertheless, Spinoza's attribution of Ezra as the principal architect of Torah reminds us most of all of the rabbinic dictum "Had Moses not preceded him, Ezra would have been worthy of receiving the Torah for Israel" (BT, Sanhedrin, 21b). Is this reading of Ezra's importance a consciously Jewish move on Spinoza's part to rescue the Jewishness of the Bible? Surely not, as this would conflict with Spinoza's overarching goal to transcend both Jewish and Christian application of biblical authority in a contemporary setting. Does this reading nonetheless reflect a Jewish education that shades Spinoza's reading? I think so.

A JEW FOR JESUS? JEWS, CHRISTIANS, AND THE *TRACTATUS*

Given Spinoza's overall political goal, the limiting of biblical influence on contemporary European politics, he ought to have dealt with both testaments. Therefore, the absence of sustained analysis of the New Testament is more striking than the mere absence of Christian commentators, already noted. Since his target audience was freethinking Christians, why was only one of the *Tractatus*'s twenty chapters devoted principally to the New Testament? Spinoza explains:

> Now it should be time likewise to examine in the same manner the books of the New Testament. However, I am well aware that this has already been done by men expert in the relevant fields of knowledge and especially the languages whereas I myself do not have so accurate a knowledge of Greek that I would dare enter this field; on top of which we lack the originals of the books originally composed in Hebrew.[16]

Steven Smith reads Spinoza's reticence to treat the New Testament in a Straussian mode: Spinoza wanted to avoid persecution at the hands of Calvinist zealots, thus his demurral is mere pretense. But given the importance Spinoza places on an accurate knowledge of Hebrew, evident not only in his *Tractatus*, but in his unfinished Hebrew grammar, I think Smith makes too little of Spinoza's demurral. I prefer to take Spinoza at his word. He feels qualified to interpret the Jewish Bible, but not the Christian Bible. While Spinoza expresses a preference for Christianity's universalism, for Jesus over Moses, for the rituals of the Church over those of the synagogue, not everybody would grant Spinoza's sincerity on this point. Nancy Levene describes this characterization as a "familiar platitude."[17] But on this point I side with Smith in seeing that Spinoza placed Jesus "who knew God with his mind" on a higher level than Moses, who heard God "with a real voice." Moreover, as a champion of one-world, one-substance monism, one could suspect Spinoza had a natural affinity with a religion that professes to be universalist.

Smith says, sensibly, that Spinoza had to know that the presentation of Judaism as carnal, superstitious, particularistic, and ritualistic relative to Christianity recapitulated traditional prejudices against the mother religion. This "betrayal" of his former people, in fact, was what the great philosopher Hermann Cohen found so distasteful about Spinoza personally. Smith, like Leo Strauss before him, acknowledges that some of this supersessionist rhetoric should be attributed to Spinoza's fear of persecution and good salesmanship. After all, Spinoza had much to fear from Calvinist zealots and nothing to gain by trying to win professing Jews over to his cause.

Smith suggests another reason for Spinoza's apparent preference for Christianity over Judaism: Christianity was a smaller impediment to his desire to forge a new, privatized, civil religion based on the few irreducible premises of the Bible. I think that Spinoza's New Testament neglect has another dimension. I have already cited Spinoza's intriguing statements in chapters 7 and 11 that "the writers of both the Old and New Testament were Hebrews and undeniably the history of the Hebrew language is more essential than anything else not only for understanding the books of the Old Testament . . . but also those of the New Testament," and "on top of which we lack the originals of the books originally composed in Hebrew." What are we to make of these claims? Spinoza's scholarship regarding early Christianity may or may not be correct. Many modern New Testament scholars doubt the existence of Hebrew- or Aramaic-language Gospels. Whatever the earlier sources, Mark, writing in Greek, appears to have created the genre "Gospel narrative." Moreover, not only is Luke generally considered non-Jewish, but the "Jewishness" of any first-century-CE figure needs to be defined to be useful. (How helpful would it be today to know that an American author is Jewish without knowing anything more about his or her education or orientation?) The key thing is that Spinoza considered the New Testament comprehensible *only as a Jewish document*, a claim that mainstream nineteenth-century scholarship resisted mightily. This seems to me to undercut the preference Spinoza shows for Christianity over Judaism along ethnic lines—even if we conclude Spinoza preferred Christianity to Judaism as a religious teaching, he still seems to consider the New Testament a Jewish book. But I do not think that a preference for Christianity over Judaism (everyone agrees that Spinoza prefers his own system to either religion!) ends the discussion of Spinoza's *Tractatus* as Jewishly inflected. Recall what Spinoza thinks the Bible actually constituted: a human document produced in one place, in one era, and for one people. Christianity thus emerges as superior to Judaism and Jesus as superior to Moses only because they are already less biblical! While the Old Testament and New Testament taught compatible doctrines, Spinoza thought the Hebrew Bible the more "biblical" of the two testaments, as did Nietzsche.

IMAGINING A CHRISTIAN *TRACTATUS*

What would the *Tractatus* have been like had it been written by a Christian? This question has been asked by historian Adam Sutcliffe, though less crudely than I just did. Examining fellow freethinkers in Spinoza's embattled Dutch Republic (Lodowijk Meyer and Adriaan Koerbagh), Sutcliffe concludes that even though it was neither conscious nor intentional, Spinoza's works reflected his Jewish upbringing, and represent a secularist's claim on Jewish history. I believe there is yet another way to imagine a non-Jewish *Tractatus*, namely, by comparison with Thomas Hobbes's *Leviathan*. After all, here we have another first-rank thinker, also committed to cutting the Bible down to human dimensions and freeing up the state from clerical influences. What do we find? The *Leviathan* is a work of monumental importance in the history of political science, and is relatively unimportant in the history of biblical criticism. Although Hobbes devoted an entire section of *Leviathan* to an analysis of the Bible, his interests appear to be dictated by his political ends. Hobbes dealt with the question of canonization at length, but only from the point of view of how political authority is constituted, not how the Bible is constituted.[18] Hobbes noted that Deuteronomy, as the name denotes, repeats the laws of Genesis–Numbers, but made little of this fact as a question of authorship.[19] Hobbes invoked Ezra twice; first, to indicate that the antiquity of the Scriptures is not that impressive, and a second time to note "that the Scriptures of the Old Testament, which we have at this day were not Canonicall, nor a Law unto the Jews, till the renovation of their Covenant with God at the return of their captivity, and the restoration of their Common-wealth under Esdras (Ezra)."[20] While Hobbes engaged in the same kind of crafty attack on major principles of theology as Spinoza, there is no programmatic statement about how one would read the Bible scientifically, were one so inclined. When Hobbes undertook exegesis, such as his reading of the famous proclamation in Exodus 19:1–5 that Israel should be a "Kingdome of God," there is no real engagement with what the threefold charge to be a "treasured people, holy nation, kingdom of priests" actually means. Hobbes skillfully compared the King James and the French and Latin Vulgates, concluding, "but the truest Translation is the first, because it is confirmed by St Paul himself."[21] Greek is as close as Hobbes gets to the original; he did not know Hebrew. Who can doubt it: had Hobbes gone to *heder*, he too could have written the *Tractatus*.

SPINOZA'S BIBLE: A SUMMING UP

What did Spinoza *really* think about the Bible? This seems to me an obvious question, but one which the great scholars have not yet resolved. All agree that Spinoza sought to limit the Bible's influence and to prove that the Bible was humanly produced, and imperfectly so. All agree that the various interpretive traditions committed a categorical error in stretching an ancient text to fit contemporary circumstances, and in refusing to acknowledge that textual discrepancies and conflicts were real, resolvable neither by hyperingenious midrashic methods (e.g., Jews, symbolized by Maimonides) nor recourse to professions of mysteries that surpass human understanding (e.g., Christians, symbolized by Calvin). But is the biblical message coherent and is it beneficent in Spinoza's eyes? From a Straussian perspective on Spinoza, the answer seems to be that as means of teaching the masses obedience, the Bible can be put to good use. It has no philosophical validity, but it does have political utility. Spinoza could not get rid of the Bible altogether—that would have been a cultural-historical impossibility—so he did the best he could with flawed material. An opposing way to look at this question would be to insist on the sincerity of chapters 12 through 14 of the *Tractatus*, in which Spinoza tried to find the irreducible positive teachings of the Bible. Harry Wolfson, Alan Donagan, and Nancy Levene all incline to this view, although these scholars would concede that Spinoza means something very particular about "God," "forgiveness," "lost/saved," and "sin/salvation," the list of seven doctrines which culminates Spinoza's discussion of the universal religion truly represented in the teachings of the Bible. I tend to agree with this less cynical school. Spinoza's assertion that "the worship of the Supreme Being consists in the practice of justice and love toward one's neighbor" sounds sincere, as do Spinoza's praises of Moses and Jesus, once stripped of any supernatural elements. Most of all, though, I incline to the anti-Straussian school because I find it difficult to imagine any thinker grappling with a text so forcefully while secretly considering it a mere artifact. Like many modern readers, I believe, Spinoza considers the Bible neither divine nor dispensable.

Nancy Levene has recently argued that Spinoza deserves to be considered a Jewish religious thinker. I think so, too, but I would not go as far as Levene, who likens Spinoza's God to the God of the Hebrew Bible.[22] I prefer Adam Sutcliffe's formulation, "Spinoza's Jewish origins thus subtly but crucially mark his philosophy apart from the arguments of his closest intellectual collaborators."[23] In this chapter, I have argued that we may consider Spinoza's Bible criticism in the *Tractatus* as Jewishly inflected—Spinoza was hostile to rabbinic tradition, but marked by his Jewish upbringing. Spinoza's focus on the Hebrewness of the text, the reliance on the Jewish interpretive tradition, his assumption of a historical kernel to the Bible, his belief in the Bible's moral utility, his interest in the passage from biblical to rabbinic Judaism, will be found again and again in modern Jewish Bible critics. However, much of what I consider to be typical of modern Jewish Bible criticism emerges in Spinoza despite himself. The huge gap between the "descriptively" and "prescriptively" Jewish, what Yovel called our attention to in assessing Spinoza's attitude toward the Jewish future, applies to his Bible criticism, too. Spinoza did not try to give Jews as Jews a distinct path forward, politically or biblically. In the story of the *Making of the Modern Jewish Bible*, Spinoza represents a fascinating false start.

Part I

THE EMERGENCE OF MODERN JEWISH BIBLE STUDIES IN GERMANY

INTRODUCTION: STARTING WITH GERMANY

One thing everyone knows about German Jews is that they were "more German than Jewish." Unfortunately, that one thing is not true.

The German Jews created the Jewish Enlightenment (Haskalah) which was the critical turning point in the creation of a secular culture and a prerequisite for all modern Jewish movements. German Jews played the pivotal role in pioneering modern, critical scholarship of Jewish sources: Wissenschaft des Judentums. The German Jews created the theological and institutional bases for the three largest denominations within Judaism (Reform, Orthodox, and Conservative). By the start of the twentieth century, when most German Jews had become liberal Jews, they created innovative adult education opportunities and a host of secular institutions dedicated to forwarding philanthropy, self-defense, Jewish welfare, and education. German Jews pioneered the modern Jewish journal and can lay claim to many of the most creative minds in Western Jewry during the long century in between the French Revolution and World War I. Most pertinently, German Jews were Bible translators par excellence.

We will consider only three Bible translations (Mendelssohn's, Hirsch's, and Buber-Rosenzweig's), but there were at least another twenty, including Julius Fürst's *Prachtbibel*, the greatest coffee-table Bible ever produced; Leopold Zunz's successful rendering, which clung to the Hebraic roots of the original; Ludwig Philippsohn's Bible, Philippsohn being the publisher of a widely read Jewish newspaper; and the Bible of Harry Tur-Sinai (also called the Berlin Bible) which, like the Buber-Rosenzweig effort, was completed only in Israel, narrowly escaping destruction by the Nazis.

German Jews produced and consumed Bible translations at a furious rate. Naomi Seidman has called the German Jews a "translation culture," and she does not exaggerate. Hans-Joachim Bechtoldt, in *Jüdische deutsche Bibelübersetzungen*, devotes almost seven hundred pages to this phenomenon. Even this tribute to translation does not take in the whole picture, as many of these Bibles went through several editions, and the Mendelssohn Bible, though originally printed in Hebrew characters, was soon available in German script. Beyond translation, German Jews also responded to Protestant Bible scholarship in many ways. Some major figures in German-Jewish scholarship responded hesitantly to applying historical critical methods to the Bible, especially the Five Books of Moses. Others were less diffident; Rabbi Siegmund Maybaum, for instance, adopted the source critical approach, although he dissented from some of its conclusions. At the end of the nineteenth century David Zvi Hoffmann and Benno Jacob addressed the Protestant biases of Bible scholarship aggressively. Jacob's incredibly detailed Genesis and Exodus commentaries were not translated into English for years, and are only now being translated into Hebrew, thus reaching the two largest living Jewish communities.

Objectively speaking, German Jews in the modern era were bibliocentric—although in a way quite different from bibliocentric Israelis and bibliocentric Americans. Why? The simple answer seems to be that German Jews perceived in the Bible the keystone to their own identity, both halves of which they treasured. Perhaps the question of why a book called *The Making of the Modern Jewish Bible* should begin with German Jewry has already been answered. But let me be even more explicit: the recovery of the Bible as a national centerpiece in Israel and the celebration of the Bible as an ethnic touchstone in contemporary America are inconceivable without the efforts of German Jews.

2

Mendelssohn's Bible
The Ideal of Jewish Self-Sufficiency

Moses Mendelssohn (1729–1786) was the most famous European Jew in his lifetime and remained in Alexander Altmann's words "the patron saint of German Jewry," until the Nazis exterminated this remarkable Jewish culture. Mendelssohn symbolized the successful acquisition of European culture, the possibility of amicable Jewish-Christian social relations, sincere loyalty to the national culture, and, not least, continued fidelity to the Jewish tradition. True, some of Mendelssohn's followers and family converted to Christianity, but they did so after his death. Mendelssohn defended Judaism publicly on numerous occasions, both in philosophical exchanges and in more practical matters such as Jewish court oaths and burial practices. Mendelssohn observed the commandments. When these required bending, such as when Mendelssohn was summoned to Frederick the Great's palace at Potsdam on Shemini Atzeret, a Jewish holiday, he made certain that his halachic flexibility would not be seen as countenancing violation of the law. Although various late-nineteenth-century Jewish figures expressed hostility toward Mendelssohn's legacy, especially as full participation in general society proved so costly to maintaining the interests of the Jewish community, few impugned Mendelssohn's personal piety or observance. The earliest biographies of Mendelssohn celebrated him most of all as a figure of modernity, and tended to emphasize his philosophical and belletristic accomplishments. For a couple of decades, Alexander Altmann's monumental biography *Moses Mendelssohn: A Biographical Study* (1973) seemed destined to be the final word on Mendelssohn. Altmann, a German-born rabbi and philosopher who served in Manchester, UK, and then at Brandeis University, represented in his own person the religiosity and intellectual achievement of Mendelssohn himself. But important figures tend to provoke reconsideration, and, like Spinoza, Mendelssohn has reemerged as a focus of scholarly attention. His literary contributions to the German Enlightenment have been reassessed, the agenda of his Jewish philosophy has been debated, and most of all, his Bible project has finally received the attention that it is due.[1]

David Sorkin's *Moses Mendelssohn and the Religious Enlightenment* (1996) warns against overemphasizing the modern flavor of Mendelssohn's contributions. Sorkin reminds his readers how much of Mendelssohn's work was in Hebrew rather than German, and just how much he was influenced by medieval thinkers such as Nachmanides and Yehuda Halevy. Although I will be concentrating only on Mendelssohn's Bible translation, Mendelssohn also produced a range of philosophical works in Hebrew that set a standard for the Jewish Enlightenment. Mendelssohn stands as an innovator in Hebrew prose too, an intermediary between late medieval rabbinic style and the direct, matter-of-fact Hebrew of the late nineteenth century, epitomized by Ahad Haam. In Sorkin's view, the Mendelssohn myth of "the patron saint of German Jewry" served the needs of two centuries of Jews validating the modernity project, but failed to encompass Mendelssohn's Jewish legacy. Even while evaluating Mendelssohn as an Enlightenment figure, Sorkin demonstrates that Mendelssohn was most influenced by German philosophers active in the 1730s and 1740s, than by his more radical contemporaries. Typical of Mendelssohn's conservatism was his defensive response to the revelation that his good friend, the philosopher Gotthold Ephraim Lessing, who had helped propel Mendelssohn to Europe-wide fame in the former's play *Nathan the Wise*, had embraced Spinozism late in life. Mendelssohn simply refused to believe the evidence of the "Jacobi Fragments," and continued to view Lessing as a pillar of enlightened piety. Sorkin, ultimately, presents Mendelssohn as a transitional figure between medieval and modern Judaism, and, like many transitional figures, negotiating his way tentatively through uncharted terrain. Sorkin argues against overinterpreting Mendelssohn's last and longest philosophical statement on Judaism, *Jerusalem, or on Religious Power and Judaism* (1782). In subsequent works, Sorkin has sharpened his criticism further, suggesting that only an English-language anthology stands a chance of redressing the serious underestimation of Mendelssohn's Hebrew oeuvre. This call for a reassessment also touches the question of Mendelssohn's overall originality, for his prestige as a general philosopher has certainly not fared well in recent scholarship, which tends to see him as a second-rank figure. That estimation would need qualifying were it known that Mendelssohn also stands as the first great modern Jewish Bible commentator.[2]

Coming to a very different conclusion about Mendelssohn, Allan Arkush's *Moses Mendelssohn and the Enlightenment* agrees with Sorkin that *Jerusalem* does not represent Mendelssohn's all-inclusive philosophy. *Jeru-*

salem contains both a general statement on religion and power and specific application of that relationship to Judaism. In this second, more widely read section, Mendelssohn defends halachic (legal) observance, but noticeably diminishes its theological, psychological, and cosmic significance. God intended all humans to attain felicity through the exercise of reason, gave all peoples a historical tradition of their own to engender that quest, and reserved for the Jews an additional set of prescriptions. Inescapably, the commandments at Sinai rank only third in line of the prerequisites of human happiness. This conclusion, patent to readers of *Jerusalem* then and now, must have been clear to Mendelssohn too. Consequently, Arkush argues that Mendelssohn's defense of Judaism was "more rhetorical than real," designed to confirm his credentials as an Orthodox Jew while giving him free rein "to transform his ancestral religion into something radically new and different."[3] Mendelssohn knew exactly what he was doing: reforming Judaism for a socially acculturated, politically liberal future. For Arkush, it is highly significant that in the final paragraph of *Jerusalem*, Mendelssohn admonishes the newly formed United States of America for considering religious qualification for office, prohibited by article 6 of the Constitution. Arkush translated *Jerusalem* from German to English and annotated it brilliantly—Mendelssohn appears in these endnotes primarily as a battler with Spinoza, and as a central figure in the European Enlightenment. Was Mendelssohn a bold, forward-thinking progressive or a hesitant traditional Jew coming to terms with changing times? Did Mendelssohn display an intellectual inconsistency, roughly paralleling his use of German and Hebrew?

This debate over Mendelssohn's internal coherence may remind learned readers of a similar debate regarding Moses Maimonides (1135–1204). Was the latter fundamentally a great philosopher who diverged from traditional Judaism, as a reader of the Arabic-language *Guide of the Perplexed* might conclude? Or, does Maimonides's *Mishneh Torah*, a monumental Hebrew law code, eviscerate any suspicion of heterodoxy, leaving the philosophical opus a majestic cart that nevertheless follows the halachic horse? For the academy, Maimonides is best known as a medieval philosopher, a Jewish Thomas Aquinas. For the world of traditional Judaism, Maimonides is simply the Rambam, the author of *Mishneh Torah*, a Mishnah commentary, and the first to coordinate the 613 commandments and the Torah verses from which they are derived. In Altmann's magisterial biography, the question of Mendelssohn's internal consistency remains unresolved; his scholarly successors have tried to resolve the tension. Does one look forward with Arkush and read Mendelssohn as a fairly radical reformer? Or, does one look backward with Sorkin and see Mendelssohn with at least one foot firmly planted in medieval Jewish thought?

Sorkin was not the only scholar to rediscover the importance of the Mendelssohn Bible and his Hebrew writings. A complementary approach to Sorkin's may be found in Edward Breuer's *The Limits of Authority*. For Breuer, the most important context for Mendelssohn's translation and commentary was not the "higher critical" scholarship, which focused on macro questions of authorship and authority, but the "lower critical" school, which questioned the integrity of the biblical text. To Mendelssohn, the work of the ninth- to tenth-century Masoretes, who supplied the vocalization, punctuation, and cantillation of the text, accurately reflected an ancient oral tradition. Mendelssohn knew that leading non-Jewish scholars, including the founder of the historical critical school Johann Gottfried Eichhorn (1753–1827), rejected a traditional concept of the biblical text, as had Hobbes, Spinoza, and several others. But Mendelssohn affirmed the absolute reliability of the Traditional Text.

Unless we regard Mendelssohn as duplicitous, and I think we should not, he seems to have believed that God spoke to Moses at Sinai, voicing the Torah out loud, with proper intonation, and with unmistakable emphases. That some contemporary Christian scholars were willing to emend the biblical text based on their conjectures as to how the text ought to read demonstrated only their impiety and Hebraic incompetence. With specific reference to Eichhorn, Mendelssohn wrote: "I do not know in fact when we will get to the end of this audacity. In the meantime, so long as the fashion has the charm of novelty, one must allow it to take its course. In time people will lose their taste for it; and then it will be time to redirect them to the path of healthy reason."[4] Here, Mendelssohn clearly dissented from the historical critical school of Bible studies, but also the radical Enlightenment of the 1770s–1780s and its general hostility toward religion. Mendelssohn was keenly aware of radical alternatives to his pious, traditional approach to the Bible. He rejected them. Breuer's Mendelssohn, like Sorkin's, emerges as an ardent defender of the internal Jewish traditions of exegesis.[5] Although Mendelssohn's Bible contained far more than a translation, the latter has long been the focus of controversy. Early readers both criticized and praised Mendelssohn's willingness to make the Bible a passport to German culture, depending on their own proclivities. W. Gunther Plaut best summarized the project's nature: "Far from engineering Jewish assimilation, Mendelssohn, with his Bible translation, initiated a golden age of Jewish life which in scholarship was the equal of the vaunted Spanish model, but which in many ways surpassed it in lasting influence."[6]

Recently, Seidman's *Faithful Renderings* focuses on the common denominator among all these German-Jewish translations—hybridity. No matter whether the translator focused more on the source language (Hebrew, in the case of Buber-Rosenzweig), or on the target language (German, in the case of Mendelssohn), all translations, by definition, are linguistic hybrids. Mendelssohn drew a hard and fast line between the use of Yiddish in speech or in letters, as, for instance, to his fiancée Fromet Guggenheim, and the use of Yiddish in an scholarly context. Mendelssohn joined his Enlightened circle in considering only "pure" languages such as Hebrew or German suitable for scholarly purposes. But Seidman thinks that in practice Mendelssohn owed much to the highly colloquial Yiddish-language Bibles mass-produced for women, often bearing the title *Tsena U'renah*. In the eyes of later critics, both Orthodox and Zionist, "Mendelssohn's recruitment of Hebrew to the service of German is both a class demotion and a sexual degradation of the Jewish male. . . . If Mendelssohn had hoped to construct a proper Jewish masculinity in the face of the corrupt notions of gender in traditional Jewish society, he had ended merely by emasculating again in his deference to German norms."[7] Would Mendelssohn have been disconcerted to learn that his translation was used in *Zena U'renah Benot Zion*, published in 1822 in Basel? Would Mendelssohn have responded to characterizations of his Bible translation's "Yiddishized" and "feminized" element with his patented ironic grin? On a simplistic level, it is certain that German Jews needed a German translation more than Germans needed to master the Hebrew original—a measure of subordination, as Seidman suggests, was probably inherent in the project. Jonathan Sheehan deftly captures the elusiveness of Mendelssohn's linguistic task in his Psalms and Pentateuch translations, which "were supposed to give largely *Yiddish-speaking* Jewish children a subtly rendered *German text* in order that they might access to the *Hebrew original*."[8]

For Abigail Gillman, the traditional appearance of the original Mendelssohn Bible deliberately masked its revolutionary content. Knowing that a translation into "modern" German and an "Enlightened" commentary would arouse rabbinic ire, and that only a text of traditional appearance would find a reading audience in the Jewish world, Mendelssohn wheeled in a biblical Trojan horse. Without question, the Mendelssohn Bible, arranged in four columns of Hebrew letters, two in Rashi script, approximated the appearance of the medieval rabbinic Bible. But there is no smoking gun, such as a letter to his publisher or friend, to prove Gillman right. An alternative way of looking at the format of the text is to conclude that Mendelssohn and his collaborators simply never considered that a Jewish Bible commentary should look any other way. Gabriel Josipovici's wonderful *The Book of God* noted that until Christianity grew and introduced the widespread use of the codex, Jews had remained quite content with reading from scrolls. Indeed, reading of Torah from a scroll in Hebrew has remained the norm in Jewish worship services of every denomination. A natural conservatism exists in religious matters, extending to sacred places, calendar dates, ritual items, and the use of texts. I conclude that this too is a viable explanation for the appearance of the Mendelssohn Bible. The appearance of ornamental/illustrated Bibles, Bibles with a profusion of maps and charts, and Bibles with learned essays became part of Enlightenment culture. Just like translation into the vernacular itself, all played a role in modernizing the Bible. But Mendelssohn's Pentateuch work appeared from 1779 to 1783, at the beginning of the process by which Jewish-produced Bibles became objects of culture as well as religion. Steven Lowenstein's supposition that the first Mendelssohn Bible in a German script edition was intended for Christian readers supports this view: Latin letters were suitable for non-Jews; Jews were meant to read the Bible in Hebrew characters, even in a German translation.[9]

Lowenstein uncovered an interesting fact: Mendelssohn's Bibles succeeded best as commercial enterprises in traditional garb. Mendelssohn Bibles sold better in Hebrew-only script than they did in Gothic script, and found a wide readership for the first half of the nineteenth century. Even for those editions printed in preunification Germany, only six editions of his Pentateuch appeared exactly as Mendelssohn intended. Changes eliminated the innovative dimension of the project. A scholar of Jewish languages, Werner Weinberg, compiled a list of twenty-seven Bible editions found in the Hebrew Union College Library in Cincinnati that used all or parts of the Mendelssohn Bible. Weinberg observed various ways and means of enhancing the traditional aspect of Mendelssohn's Bible:

> In most cases, the Mendelssohn Pentateuch was reprinted for synagogue use. The worshipper could, as always, follow the weekly Torah and prophetic readings through traditional explanations, the Targum of Onkelos and also the German translation of Mendelssohn. This appeared in still many other editions with the Prophetic readings, the five holiday scrolls, the translation of Onkelos, with Rashi, and thus the unity of the Mendelssohn Bible no longer existed.[10]

Steven Lowenstein's painstaking examination of later editions indicates that Mendelssohn Bibles fared best of all in German lands in the nineteenth century, where the traditional "enhancing" detailed by Weinberg above combined with use of a German translation, which no longer stirred fears of heterodoxy, since most German Jews, including Orthodox ones, had switched to that vernacular. By contrast, Lowenstein demonstrates, the Mendelssohn Bible in eastern Europe continued to be controversial: championed by the Jewish Enlighteners (Maskilim), it provoked suspicion on the part of the traditionalists. Lowenstein, a social historian, concludes: "The judgments passed in the different times and places on the translation and the very different readerships done at different places and times, were more closely connected with the positions of the various forces within the Jewish community than with actual nature of Mendelssohn's work itself."[11]

Ironically, then, even if Gillman's supposition about the intent of his Bible were correct, Mendelssohn's initially radical Bible got "koshered" by subsequent publishers. This would not be a first in the history of the Jewish book. Yosef Hayim Yerushalmi demonstrated that a very similar fate occurred to *Shevet Yehuda*, a cutting-edge, nontraditional analysis of the Spanish Expulsion by the sixteenth-century scholar Solomon Ibn Verga which was "transmuted perceptually into a standard piece of edifying folklore."[12] I am not convinced that Mendelssohn's Bible had such radical aims, but Gillman makes an important point that goes back to the debate between Sorkin and Arkush. By turning her glance to the Bible project rather than Mendelssohn's *Jerusalem*, Gillman suggests that the forward-looking Mendelssohn emerges in Hebrew as well as German. It seems, then, that there are both conservative and reformist elements not only within the Mendelssohn opus in general, but even within the Mendelssohn Bible project. The task of the historian is rarely to choose between "either" and "or." More frequently, the historian looks for preponderance of evidence and judges as best as she or he can. Leaving Mendelssohn's *Jerusalem* and his other philosophic writings to the side, what can we conclude from the evidence of the Mendelssohn Bible itself?

WHAT IS THE MENDELSSOHN BIBLE?

We have to address this question, although the reader has certainly come to some conclusions regarding the debates that swirled around it, then and now. The Mendelssohn Bible, which appeared under the name *Sefer Netivot ha-Shalom*, contains: (1) the Bible itself, specifically, the Traditional Text; (2) a German translation (*Targum ashkenazi*) written in Hebrew characters, by Mendelssohn himself and by other collaborators; (3) a commentary (the *Biur*), written in Rashi script, again inspired by Mendelssohn and written by Mendelssohn and others; and (4) notations on the Traditional Text (*tikkun sofrim*), also in Rashi script, written by Solomon Dubno, an early collaborator of Mendelssohn's. Even with help, Mendelssohn's project took approximately fifteen years to complete and generated some interesting side notes along the way, most famously *Alim L'Trufah* (Leaves of healing), a prospectus and promotional piece for the new work, and *Or L'Netivah* (A light to the path), a lengthy introduction to the Bible project. I think the human element of this massive undertaking needs mention. Mendelssohn engaged collaborators, corresponded with them, and dealt with their agendas. Dubno resigned from the undertaking in a pique; Wessely sought to link Mendelssohn to his own program of radical reform. Mendelssohn promoted the Bible project and paid for its publication through subscriptions. The financial aspect should not be overlooked. Mendelssohn grew up poor and became comfortable, but never independently wealthy. He was also a husband and a father and an employee of a silk manufacturer. Moreover, translating is a painstaking and terribly time-consuming task. I conclude that it cannot make sense to regard the Bible project as anything other than one of Mendelssohn's greatest legacies. Mendelssohn wrote his response to Johann Lavater's tasteless public attempt to convert him to Christianity in a matter of weeks, *Jerusalem* in a matter of months. The Bible project occupied Mendelssohn for over a decade. I can only second Sorkin's complaint: the scholarly neglect of the Mendelssohn Bible relative to his German-language works cannot be justified.

Considering the arduous nature of this task, Mendelssohn gave various motives, including his dissatisfactions with other efforts both Jewish and Christian, the education of his sons, the advancement of the European Jews ("I have clearly seen how our Jewish brethren have abandoned Hebrew and I am deeply grieved"),[13] and his incapacity for serious philosophical work, following an unpleasant philosophical exchange (the Lavater affair). The first motive, involving a defense of rabbinic understandings of the Bible, probably has been underestimated in comparison with the others (Breuer). Most of these motives reappear frequently in the century-long fixation of German-Jewish thinkers with Bible translation and commentary. Although all parts of the Mendelssohn Bible were seen as critical by Mendelssohn himself, the translation itself has received the most attention, and for good reason. Mendelssohn's *Sefer Netivot ha-Shalom* (The paths of peace) constituted the first distinguished translation of the Bible into a vernacular language in the modern era carried out by Jews, though preceded by an influential trio of non-Jewish translations: Luther (in German), Calvin (in French), and Tyndale–King James (in English). Mendelssohn found previous Ashkenazic translators inadequate on several grounds, including their use of Christian Bibles![14]

Mendelssohn's *Sefer Netivot ha-Shalom* provided everything the German-Jewish reader needed (e.g., Hebrew original, translation, commentary, textual notes). As in a medieval rabbinic Bible, the tools of Bible study lay at hand. For all Mendelssohn's indebtedness to the medieval Masoretes who standardized the text and the medieval Andalusians who explicated it along rational lines, *Sefer Netivot ha-Shalom* remains a remarkably self-contained text. Some have seen Mendelssohn's production of this Bible and his emphasis on Bible-based education as distinctly Protestant. After all, did not Protestantism elevate the Bible above Church traditions? The always provocative poet-essayist Heinrich Heine put it thus:

> As Luther overthrew the papacy, so Mendelssohn the Talmud, and in the same sense, in that he rejected Tradition, declared the Bible as the source of religion, and translated its most significant part, He destroyed therein, Jewish Catholicism, as Luther destroyed Christian Catholicism.[15]

For Heine, and many others, Mendelssohn appears as the Jewish Luther. In addition to being a great poet and satirist, Heine was also a member of the short-lived Society for the Culture and Scholarship of Judaism. Heine belonged to the generation of German Enlighteners succeeding Mendelssohn's, even as the momentum of this movement moved eastward. Rather than seeing Mendelssohn as a radical eighteenth-century Enlightener (*Aufklärer*), maybe it is preferable to see him, as Heine did, as a Jewish Luther—revolutionary, yet medieval? But the adjective *Jewish* here modifies the noun *Luther* too much to leave Heine's ingenious idea intact. Heine was half right: Mendelssohn did seek to elevate the role of Bible in Jewish life and learning, but he was guided by Jewish tradition in this effort. Not only did Mendelssohn provide a commentary (named *Biur*), and a set of notes on the text (*tikkun sofrim*), but he used the Jewish tradition, not his own pneumatic judgment, to guide his explication of the Bible. Mendelssohn was no Luther. Rather, Mendelssohn created a bibliocentric handbook of Jewish life, as would Samson Raphael Hirsch, the subject of my next chapter.

JEWISH SELF-SUFFICIENCY I: MENDELSSOHN'S RELIGIOUS VOCABULARY

Scholars have noted the careful attention that Mendelssohn placed on those Bible passages of especial theological significance. The long discussion of God's mysterious self-revelation at the burning bush (Exodus 3:14) has been a favorite example, adduced by both Altmann and Sorkin. This scene, pivotal to Moses's role as prophet and instrument of national salvation, prompted Mendelssohn's unusual rendering of the Tetragrammaton. The Tetragrammaton, the special, four-letter name of God (YHVH), that Jews euphemistically pronounce as "Adonai," Mendelssohn translated as *der Ewige*, a departure from contemporary Judeo-German versions and from Luther's *Der Herr* (e.g., "LORD"), a term with a distinct Christian overlay. Although Mendelssohn's rendering *der Ewige* was presumably suggested by John Calvin's rendering "The Eternal" (*L'Eternel*) in his Bible translation, Mendelssohn justified his choice via Jewish tradition. In a lengthy explanation, Mendelssohn traced competing views of God's essence through the ages, with focus on both the early rabbinic period (Onkelos, midrashim) and the medieval literalists (*pashtanim*). Both Altmann and Sorkin stress the philosophical implications of Mendelssohn's choice—eternity was judged by Mendelssohn to stand in nicely for necessity and providence, too—a case of philosophical *pars pro toto*.

For Sorkin, this rendering exemplifies what he considers the genius of Mendelssohn's efforts: the Bible as the source of "practical knowledge," a veritable handbook of proper living that can be deduced from the biblical text and the rabbinic understanding of the same. As conceived and executed by Mendelssohn, *Sefer Netivot ha-Shalom* becomes nothing less than a modern rabbinic Bible. It is worth mentioning that on such a fundamental issue as the name and nature of God, the Jewish tradition emerges as wholly self-sufficient. Mendelssohn may have been prompted by Calvin, but he justified his choice via the sages. For this reason, Franz Rosenzweig, often a harsh critic of Mendelssohn's, praised this rendering of *Adonai* as "the Eternal" rather than "the Lord" as Mendelssohn's single greatest legacy to subsequent Jewish Bible translators. Sorkin gives several other examples of this Mendelssohnian "practical knowledge," including adherence to dietary laws, nonmixing of clothing types (*sha'atnez*), and so on.

It goes without saying, then, that some of this kind of "practical knowledge" is incumbent on all humanity and some of it is incumbent only on Israel. But even theological terms in Genesis, by definition pre-Sinaitic, are translated in a Jewish manner. In Genesis 15:6, a famous crux in Paul's understanding that faith precedes law, and that Abraham trumps Moses, Mendelssohn rendered Abraham's faith (*emunah*) to emphasize its relational, covenantal aspect, rather than something subjective and internal. ("Treue," for Mendelssohn, not "Glaube," as for the very Pauline Luther.) In other words, for Mendelssohn, Genesis 15:6 anticipated the Mosaic covenant; it did not render it unnecessary. With respect to God's hardening of Pharaoh's heart, another time-honored object of skeptical anti-biblicists, Mendelssohn relied on the Nachmanidean free will defense to respond that God allows the evildoer license to follow his natively bad inclination. Following Nachmanides again on the Binding of Isaac (Genesis 22), Mendelssohn emphasized that Abraham's physical actions and willingness to follow God's commands to the utmost honed his character. Mendelssohn thus emphasized that actual performance of acts makes the man—there is a practical dimension to Abraham's deeds leading up to the moment God interceded and stopped the sacrifice. The key word in Genesis 22:1, "God tried (*nisah*) Avraham," had at times been linked by Jewish exegetes to the word *nes* (a public miracle), and at times to the word *nisayon* (real-world experience). Mendelssohn decisively opts for the latter. In Genesis 26:5, a rare reference to the Binding of Isaac but also a rare Genesis formulation of the necessity of observance (*mitzvotai/hukotai/toratai*), Mendelssohn followed rabbinic tradition by taking "laws, statutes, and commandments" as really anticipating later, distinct categories of commandments and mandating obedience to the same. Abraham, long before Sinai, intuited a knowledge of the entire Torah and observed it. Thus, Mendelssohn's translations and his commentaries provided readers with a distinctly Jewish understanding of verses and terms that would not have emerged clearly from other Yiddish translations and not at all from Luther's Bible. Through these means, Mendelssohn supplied his Jewish contemporaries a theological vocabulary to carry with them in the wider world.[16]

JEWISH SELF-SUFFICIENCY II: HISTORY AND HISTORICISM

We have already mentioned Mendelssohn's contempt toward the lower critics who would emend the biblical text. Mendelssohn was aware of the higher criticism as well, and dismissed it out of hand. Mendelssohn's conservatism here is twofold. There were certainly many Enlighteners, Voltaire for instance, who regarded the biblical legacy as pernicious. Their rejection of the Bible stood less on careful scrutiny of the text than on the judgment that biblical literature was vastly inferior and inimical to Greco-Roman literature, and also the source of contemporary intolerance, a view anticipated in Spinoza. Even some of Mendelssohn's most ardent Christian admirers thought his Bible project a waste of time for an Enlightened man. Then again there were early Bible scholars such as Spinoza, Simon, and Eichhorn, all of whom doubted the Mosaic authorship of the Bible and all of whom saw it as a composite text. Mendelssohn rejected these judgments. In his defense of the Bible's historicity, Mendelssohn enjoyed an advantage not shared by subsequent Jewish Bible scholars and translators: while some contemporaries doubted the unity of the Pentateuchal text, few doubted the basic historicity of the Bible. Following Sorkin's helpful distinction, Mendelssohn was historical without being a historicist. He agreed with a correspondent that one needed to know the "author, times and circumstances" of biblical books, but did not think that historical inquiry into the Bible should be a principal endeavor. Naturally, he believed in the basic reality of historical events: God's call to Abraham (Genesis 12), the Exodus (Exodus 12–15), and Sinai (Exodus 19–24). This belief in the fundamentals was not fundamentalist: Mendelssohn was open to considerations of the "author, time and circumstances." But something happened—it was not just the human report of a mythical event. Throughout the nineteenth and twentieth centuries, Jewish Bible commentators and scholars would follow this general compromise: not every last detail was historically true, but the basic story line was. Even Buber, so often abused for his heterodox attitude toward Revelation and Mitzvot, vigorously denied that the events of Sinai could be dismissed as myth. More than a century separated Buber from Mendelssohn; the latter could proffer traditionalist answers more plausibly, and he did.

Or L'Netivah, his general introduction to the Bible, insisted that Moses wrote every word of the Torah, rejecting the idea that Joshua penned the words relating to Moses's death. Likewise, Mendelssohn acknowledged the shift from first-person narrative voice (Genesis–Numbers) to third person in Deuteronomy, noted by Ibn Ezra and employed by Spinoza to cast doubt on unified authorship. Mendelssohn dwelt on the differences between the Torah as written and the Torah as read, orthographic issues, and the standardization of the text under Ezra the Babylonian. The process of reading and rendering the Torah, as described in Nehemiah 8, was seen by Mendelssohn as establishing the fundamental practices of reading, translating, and expounding Torah that Jews had engaged in from that point in the mid-fifth-century BCE onward. Naturally, Mendelssohn's evaluation of Ezra's accomplishment was more generous by far than Spinoza's (see chapter 1). Mendelssohn did not shrink from the question of how we got the Bible in the form we have it today, but rather found it adequately captured by the claim of perfect transmission in Mishnah, Pirkey Avot 1. The heart of his prospectus *Alim L'Terufa* (Leaves of healing) dwelled on the Jewish commitment to Hebrew from the earliest biblical times through the entire biblical period: "Also there [in Egypt] we never forgot our language," "Our Holy Tongue remained among us and our language with us," and the like. Mendelssohn continued his argument for the actual use of Hebrew as a common tongue, bringing proof from the endless examples of Hebrew wordplay in the Bible, from the folk etymologies of Hebrew names, and from biblical tales of interactions with ethnic others (Canaanites, Philistines, Aramaeans) that Hebrew remained the language of the common Israelite until the expulsion of 587/586 BCE. In this same essay, Mendelssohn entered into a history of Jewish translations of the Bible into various languages (Aramaic, Greek, Arabic, Persian), all of which raise potentially embarrassing questions of transmission. That Mendelssohn discussed these matters at all reflects his profound confidence in the reliability of the Traditional Text.

JEWISH SELF-SUFFICIENCY III: THE NATURE OF HEBREW

Yet a third area of Jewish assertiveness needs addressing: Mendelssohn's lofty view of Hebrew, somewhat ironic, as all agree that Mendelssohn was keenly interested in rendering the text into good German. Too good, in the opinion of Rabbi Ezekiel Landau of Prague, the most insightful critic of the translation's likely pedagogical impact. Landau, renowned as a halachic authority, considered the Mendelssohn translation suitable for highly advanced students, but disastrous for beginners. Rather than mastering Scripture, students would exert their energies learning German grammar. As Landau put it, "Our Tora is thereby reduced to role of a maidservant to the German tongue."[17] What Landau put so pungently in this refusal to issue a rabbinic approbation (*haskamah*), despite his personal admiration for Mendelssohn, the latter's first major biographer, Moritz Kayserling, applauded. Kayserling shared Landau's view of the German translation as highbrow, but praised this dimension: "Mendelssohn's translations of the Pentateuch and the Psalms were epoch-making for the cultural history of his people and exercised the most potent and lasting influence of the entire cultural development of his co-religionists. The translation became the educator of the German Jews not just for the comprehension of Scripture itself *but also principally for the German language.*"[18]

Martin Buber and Franz Rosenzweig agreed that Mendelssohn focused on the target language, German, at the expense of the source language, Hebrew. As Rosenzweig famously quipped, a letter from a friend in Turkey should always sound Turkish, even if it has been translated into German! In the long history of Jewish translations, Mendelssohn lands on the side of those who believe that every thought in the Hebrew Bible can be successfully expressed in a different language. Unlike Scholem, who praised the Buber-Rosenzweig translation for leaving what was difficult, the rationalist Mendelssohn thinks the Bible always makes sense. For Mendelssohn, fidelity to units of meaning takes precedence over a word-for-word approach. This can be shown most clearly in Mendelssohn's use of *vav*, the most notorious in the twenty-two-letter Hebrew alphabet. Among the many difficulties *vav* presents as a conjunction—when it is not converting verse tenses, another *vav* function—is that it can mean at least *and*, *or*, *if*, and *but*.[19] Mendelssohn carefully renders his *vavim* into German according to their context, perfectly defensible unless one is committed to consistently translating a single word a single way. Another example of Mendelssohn's confidence was noted by Zev Weintraub in his study of Bible translations from Hebrew to German. Earlier Yiddish renderings generally left words like *shofar*, *aron hakodesh*, *mizbeach*, and other proper nouns untranslated. Mendelssohn translated them all, and even the choice to render YHVH, rather than just leave these four letters as they appear in the text, demonstrates a verdict that the Bible may speak in all human tongues—surely an Enlightenment view, and in tension with Mendelssohn's views toward the sacred nature of Hebrew.[20]

Mendelssohn affirmed an ancient view, upheld also by the early sages and by the medieval philosopher Yehuda Halevy, that Hebrew alone was the divine language and the one spoken by Adam and Eve at the beginning of history. Moreover, the very unvocalized nature of Hebrew made the original speaking of the Torah by God to Moses critical to the Bible's comprehension and the patent of reliability for the Traditional Text. While Mendelssohn affirmed "Oral Torah" in the general sense of relying on rabbinic tradition as the binding authority on how the "Written Torah" should be observed, he affirmed Oral Torah in this specific sense too. As several scholars have shown, Mendelssohn maintained that this orality was a safeguard against idolatry, abuse, and misunderstanding. All this amounted to supreme confidence in the Masoretic text, out of tune with most of his philosophic contemporaries. Christian Hebraists harbored similar views about the Traditional Text in the seventeenth century, but as Adam Sutcliffe has shown, that view ebbed away long before Mendelssohn's Bible project. In this, as in most matters regarding the Bible translation, Mendelssohn took his cues from fellow Jews, most of them from medieval Spain.[21]

JEWISH SELF-SUFFICIENCY IV: THE BIBLE AND THE RABBIS

Mendelssohn's self-sufficiency, turned inward, appears on first glance as biblical self-sufficiency. Heine was not the only one to liken Mendelssohn to Luther as a liberator of the Bible from prior tradition. There is no doubt that this value coheres with the Haskalah's very high regard for the Bible versus the Talmud and other rabbinic literature. Educationally, there is no doubt that Mendelssohn wanted the Bible to occupy center stage, rather than rabbinic literature (e.g., Mishnah and Talmud) as in the preceding centuries of European Jewish life. In a famous letter to the Christian Enlighteners Auguste and Sophie Hennings, Mendelssohn justified a bibliocentric focus as a way of placing Judaism on a basis that could be shared with other people. After all, in the wide world of Jewish literature, the Bible is the only sacred text that Jewish scholars share with other traditions. Non-Jewish scholars have studied other Jewish texts, most famously the Talmud, but more often with polemical rather than pious motives. Mendelssohn's bibliocentrism notwithstanding, Heine's verdict on Mendelssohn as a Jewish Luther is fatally flawed. Mendelssohn wanted the Bible to take precedence over rabbinic literature, but he saw the Bible through the eyes of traditional Jewish commentators. Here is Mendelssohn's comment to the weekly portion Judgments (Exodus 21–24), the first great legal portion in Torah, called by most modern scholars the Covenant Code. Mendelssohn's comment responded principally to the twelfth-century exegete Rashbam, famous as a champion of *p'shat* and a trailblazer in "critical" Bible scholarship. In Sorkin's translation:

> Therefore in every passage in which the discoveries of the literal meaning (*p'shat*) apparently contradict the traditions of our rabbis of blessed memory with regards to rules and laws, it is the duty of the commentator to leave the path of literal meaning and to follow the road of true tradition or to mediate between them, if possible. This is the covenant that we have made for our commentary and we will preserve it, just as the good hand of the Lord protects us.[22]

Here is Mendelssohn's clear declaration that the literal meaning of Scripture should be followed only up to the point that it challenged actual Jewish practice. For all of Mendelssohn's dedication to the literal meaning (*p'shat*), if it had the possibility of disrupting Jewish practice, living Jewish custom would cast the decisive vote. Heine, Graetz, and others likened Mendelssohn to Luther as an innovator linguistically and an enlightener of the nation. The Protestant goal of making Scripture independent of its traditional interpreters would have been completely foreign to Mendelssohn. However much Mendelssohn wanted to enhance Jewish understanding of the Bible and make the Bible a more central part of Jewish education, he had no intent of undoing the binding nature of Jewish laws, all of which, it must be noted, were rooted in the Hebrew Bible by rabbinic exegetes. Not only that, Breuer has shown that Mendelssohn applied, when appropriate, the rabbinic doctrine of a fourfold sense of every Scriptural verse: simple, allusive, homiletical, and mystical. While scholars have searched *Jerusalem* to judge where Mendelssohn accepted and dissented from Spinoza, this radical rejection of Spinoza's understanding of Scripture seems to have been overlooked: scriptures were not obscure or simplistic (Spinoza), but rather, profound and multivalent (the sages). In Leo Strauss's dichotomy, Mendelssohn sided with Maimonides against Spinoza.

CONCLUSION: MEDIEVAL AND MODERN AND RELIGIOUS

Recent scholarship confirms Franz Rosenzweig's intuition regarding the significance of the Mendelssohn Bible. In an appreciation of Mendelssohn published in 1929, Rosenzweig wrote:

> Mendelssohn's important commentary , the so-called *Biur*, which, situated just at the threshold of our century of biblical criticism—already that is, in the modern spirit of and yet still naïve, equally distant from biblical criticism and from neo-orthodoxy—takes up once again the torch of the great medieval exegetes and kindles it anew.[23]

What strikes me most about the Mendelssohn Bible, despite his difficult Hebrew which presupposes familiarity with rabbinic discourse, is Mendelssohn's "modern" confidence that the Jew can live a religiously rich life guided principally by the Bible and its Jewish interpreters. Certainly, Mendelssohn and the other members of the Haskalah wanted Jews to enter modern European society, and preferred an education based on Bible rather than Talmud. Certainly, Mendelssohn held a lofty view of the aesthetic qualities of the Scriptures, Psalms in particular. Nevertheless, I think it is mistaken to describe the goal of Mendelssohn's Bible as bringing the German Jews "from religion to *Kultur*."[24] German Jewry—indeed, Europe in general—secularized in the ensuing decades, but this has little to do with *Sefer Netivot ha-Shalom*. Naturally, secularization exerted an enormous impact socially and intellectually as well as in the realm of religiosity. We turn to the Bible translation of Samson Raphael Hirsch, composed in the 1870s, when most of German Jewry had ceased to be halachic Jews. As a model of personal behavior, Moses Mendelssohn's combination of cultural openness and strict observance of the halachah was correctly pegged by historian Michael Meyer a generation ago as an "ephemeral solution."[25] The same judgment extends to Mendelssohn's philosophy of observance in *Jerusalem*. With respect to propelling the Bible to the center of Jewish life, however, Mendelssohn's legacy seems more normative than ephemeral. When the Bible project is placed foremost in an assessment of Mendelssohn, he emerges as the initiator of a vibrant tradition, voiced by Ismar Elbogen, "This translation has given the Bible back to the Jews."[26]

3

Samson Raphael Hirsch

The Chimera of Self-Explanatory Scripture

To scholars engaged in the modern study of the Bible, my choice to write about the neo-Orthodox Samson Raphael Hirsch (1808–1888), instead of his Reform counterpart, Abraham Geiger (1810–1874), might seem misguided, if not perverse. The two men cofounded a sermonic club for aspiring rabbis at Bonn University and maintained a relationship until their opposing views clashed. Geiger's historical methods were more compatible with nineteenth-century scholarship; he ranks as a founder of Wissenschaft des Judentums, whereas Hirsch opposed this endeavor as heretical. Though also a practicing rabbi, Geiger privately acknowledged the largely mythical nature of the Torah. In an 1836 letter to his friend Joseph Derenbourg, written in the same year that Hirsch exploded on the scene with a vigorous defense of traditional Judaism, Geiger wrote:

> For the love of Heaven how much longer can we continue this deceit, to expound the stories of the Bible from the pulpits over and over again as actual historical happenings, to accept as supernatural events of world import stories which we ourselves have relegated to the realm of legend, and to derive teachings from them or, at least to use them as a basis for sermons and texts.[1]

Geiger's scholarly intuitions have proven to be correct on many particulars. His view that precanonical editions of the Bible displayed considerable variety has proven right, as has his analysis of the Samaritan Pentateuch, an ancient and valuable manuscript. The tie that Geiger saw between Sadducees and Karaites, two antirabbinic groups separated by centuries, has merit, and his critique of fellow Jewish historians that they either failed to apply their insights from rabbinic literature to the Bible, or did not follow out the logical implications of their own insights, cannot be denied. After Leopold Zunz's *Concerning Rabbinic Literature*, the early masters of Wissenschaft des Judentums turned to rabbinic, rather than biblical, texts. Geiger himself focused on the later books and on the process of revision and canonization, leaving the earlier, more controversial periods to German Protestants. In a different letter to Derenbourg, Geiger indicated he had no intention of opening up his *Scholarly Journal for Jewish Theology* to biblical criticism, which Geiger knew was divisive.[2]

Nahum Sarna argued that Geiger, at heart a practical reformer of Judaism, felt source criticism had already done the critical work of demolishing the Mosaic origins of the Torah, and therefore, the divine origins of halachah. For Sarna, this practical consideration drove Geiger to research the early rabbinic period, where his early training in a traditional Jewish environment made him far more competent than Christian contemporaries to treat material that cast light on the formation of rabbinic Judaism and Christianity. The early rabbinic period was a subject about which many Protestant scholars felt free to generalize on the basis of the New Testament alone, without real awareness of the New Testament's polemical aspects. Moreover, most nineteenth-century Protestant scholars lacked expertise in reading the rabbinic texts—Mishnaic, midrashic, Talmudic. Moore, Küsche, Klein, Sanders, and, most recently, Susannah Heschel have thoroughly exposed the biases of this scholarship. With a few notable exceptions, not much written until twenty or thirty years ago on Second Temple Judaism can be trusted.[3]

Geiger's monumental work *The Original Text and Translations of the Bible* (1857) met with nearly universal rejection among Christian contemporaries. As Heschel has demonstrated, Geiger's reconstruction of formative Judaism tried to preempt the categories of "reform" and "progressive" for figures such as Hillel and the other liberally minded Pharisees of his era. Far from being an ossified religious system awaiting a rejuvenator like Jesus, first-century Judaism appears in Geiger's pages as a dynamic faith successfully negotiating changing times. Indeed, in Geiger's description of Christianity, it is that faith which seems stuck in the first century CE, always holding up as its highest ideal a figure (e.g., Jesus) and a circle (e.g., the apostles) of the remote past. Geiger's narrative, explains Heschel, was a classic case of forwarding a counterhistory, one intended to break Protestantism's colonialist hold on the German academy. Naturally, Geiger failed miserably, because to acknowledge what he was proposing would have unsettled the most fundamental assumption of the scholarship: namely, that Christianity was patently superior to Judaism in every respect, and that Jesus stood incomparably far above his Jewish contemporaries.[4]

Geiger had a huge impact on Reform theology, the Reform prayer book, the periodization of Jewish history, and the history of halachah. But Geiger was unable to move non-Jewish scholars in Bible studies. Unlike the contemporary American Jewish Bible scholars that we will address in later chapters of this book, Geiger's audience remained unreceptive. This statement will be obvious to academics, but it needs underscoring for the general reader. The ability of Jewish scholars in contemporary America to shape the direction of biblical research far exceeds what would have been possible in the days of Geiger and Hirsch. Even professional advancement in German universities, especially in value-sensitive humanities disciplines, proved nearly impossible for Jews.[5]

Geiger voiced opinions about the Bible that would be congenial to fellow Jews, but even these ideas tended to be ahead of their times or addressed to the wrong audience. For instance, the idea that the Torah text was the product not of God's revelation, but of the genius of the Jewish people, would have long legs. Like many modern Jews, Geiger believed in inspiration, but not dictation; in Geiger's day, however, denying Mosaic authorship of the Torah still violated Jewish norms. The interplay between the Bible and its readership as the true generator of meaning would be movingly voiced by Ahad Haam and Martin Buber. Geiger beat them to this insight. In the introduction to the second edition of *The Original Text and Translations of the Bible* he wrote:

> The Bible is now and has always been an ever-living Word, not a dead letter. It has spoken to all generations and imparted its teachings to them.... This is the reason why every age, every movement, and every personality in history has brought its own ideas to bear upon the Bible; hence the multitude of elaborations, interpretations, and typical and symbolic attempts at explanation. All efforts notwithstanding, it seems impossible to achieve an objective interpretation of the Bible, and even the non-believer will infuse his own feeling of aversion into his attempts to explain this work. This may result in a good deal of instability in exegesis, but at the same time it points up all the more clearly the significance of the Bible as all things to all men. In the days before the final redaction of the Bible, however, that which in later eras was accomplished by exegesis was achieved by means of textual revision.[6]

The Bible was an "ever-living Word," a product of the Jewish genius and a prompt to the same. Curiously, the Bible scholar Yehezkel Kaufmann, and the first prime minister of Israel, David Ben-Gurion, voiced this view of a Bible created by the nation at large and reflective of its genius. But Kaufmann and Ben-Gurion were Zionists who despised Geiger's view of Judaism as purely religious. Western-style reform was anathema to them, and Geiger occupied a special place in their rogue's gallery as a purely destructive scholar—this was Scholem's damning verdict, and it mirrored the attitude of early Zionism toward Reform.[7]

Geiger, though denying Mosaic authorship, championed the superiority of the Traditional Text. Geiger reacted angrily to the radical emendations proposed in the traditional text and pointed to the traditionalist Samuel

David Luzzato (1800–1865) as an appropriate model of emendation.[8] As we will see, the preference for the Traditional Text is a strong tendency within Jewish Bible scholarship, and a dogma in the case of translations undertaken for the Jewish community. The modern Jewish Bible uses the Traditional Text as its point of departure, for critical editions, translations, or commentaries; this was also Geiger's viewpoint. But at the mid-nineteenth-century mark, this attitude won Geiger no allies. The German-Jewish community felt more comfortable with a more absolute defense of the biblical text (e.g., Mendelssohn, Philippsohn, and Hirsch) or with those who remained circumspectly silent. The viewpoint of non-Mosaic authorship of the Torah text was shared by several German-Jewish scholars, including Jost, Zunz, Herzfeld, Einhorn, Maybaum, Kohler, and Popper. But the Jewish community displayed obvious discomfort with this acknowledgment. Kaufmann Kohler, for instance, wrote a doctoral dissertation on Jacob's blessing that virtually disqualified him for a rabbinic post in his homeland. As the president of the Reform rabbinical seminary in Cincinnati, Hebrew Union College, Kohler allowed source criticism to be taught at the seminary, but not as part of the religious school curriculum. At the Jewish Theological Seminaries in Breslau and in New York, arguably the capitals of Jewish scholarship, nobody taught Torah on the basis of non-Mosaic authorship or the documentary hypothesis until after World War II.[9]

Ironically, Geiger has become mainly a chapter in the history of nineteenth-century scholarship, while Hirsch remains widely read and appreciated. Some of Hirsch's abiding popularity has to do with personality. Geiger was by nature a professor who perforce worked the pulpit. Hirsch, by contrast, was an educator by nature, who stepped into the breach for modern Orthodoxy as theologian, polemicist, and community builder. His publications evidence a desire to shape the Jewish world rather than the academic agenda. Beginning in 1854, Hirsch edited *Jeschurun: A Monthly for the Furtherance of Jewish Spirit and Jewish Life in Home, Community and School*, a journal whose subtitle indicates that it was more tailored to the rank and file than Geiger's lofty *Zeitschrift für Theologie*. Scholars consider Geiger's *History of Judaism*, his most popular work, more methodologically sophisticated than Graetz's *History of the Jews*, but the latter has a naive charm that exerted a much greater impact. Hirsch's genres included a traditional commentary to the Pentateuch (1867–1878) and Psalms (1882) still cited in popular "weekly Torah portion" columns, including in various Israeli newspapers, and by subsequent commentators, including Nehama Leibowitz.

Even without agreeing with Hirsch's theological assumptions, it is possible to warm to the psychological insight with which Hirsch illuminated biblical characters and events. Passion has its advantages, and Hirsch brought his to virtually every discussion. His polemical desire to validate and justify every word of Torah translated into empathetic readings: whether these reflect the biblical authors' intended characterizations or Hirschian eisigesis may not be clear, but to the lay reader, it may not matter very much. To put it another way, one does not need to be Orthodox to benefit from Hirsch's commentary. Hirsch also founded a community in Frankfurt am Main (Israelitische Religionsgesellschaft, IRG) that flourished in Germany until the rise of the Nazis and still exists in diminished form in New York and Israel. Hirsch's IRG became a model for other Orthodox groups wishing independence from the Jewish mainstream, and Hirsch's many descendants and followers provided the people power for quite a few of these endeavors. To put it a little crassly, Hirsch created his own readership. Hirsch's Torah commentary appeared in several editions and has been translated into Hebrew, French, and English (twice). Hirsch played an active role in the day school of this secessionist community, and thus ensured that his style of Torah-based education prevailed. Jacob Rosenheim, an important leader of German Orthodoxy, recalled: "I knew comprehensively, not from Talmud and not from Rashi's commentary, but rather from having studied Hirsch's *Commentary on the Torah*, the whole order of the offerings, the laws of *metzora* [skin disease] and ritual purity and the laws of custodians and damages, with all their manifold details, *more clearly and comprehensively than any yeshiva student*" (my italics).[10]

Finally, Hirsch's legacy remains in dispute, and controversy generally works in favor of an author. Some insist that Hirsch championed a modern Orthodoxy that was very open to general culture and upheld secular learning as an inherent value. Others insist that Hirsch adopted this position as a necessary response to a temporary crisis. Awareness that Hirsch remains a live issue for Orthodox Jewry probably encourages people to look into his writings, as does the accessibility of Hirsch's Bible in most university and synagogue libraries that I have visited. From a purely academic point of view, Geiger was the greater Bible scholar, and accordingly, has received greater attention from the academy. I could justify my focus on Hirsch rather than Geiger for that reason alone, but that would be disingenuous. Who played a greater role in making the modern Jewish Bible? I think the answer is clear: Hirsch did.

HIRSCH'S BIBLE PROJECT: THE RELATIONSHIP OF WRITTEN TORAH AND ORAL TORAH

To explain each verse of Scripture based on the verse itself, drawing the explanation in all its facets from an analysis of the literal text of the Torah, in accordance with the meanings of the words as they are found in the lexicon of *Lashon Hakodesh*; to describe, according to these linguistic explanations and according to the halachic and aggadic explanations that have been handed down to us from the early days of our nation along with the text of Tanach, those truths from which the view of the world and of Jewish life have been derived, which comprise the laws by which the life of the Jew is eternally guided.[11]

The Hebrew Bible has played a central role in modern Judaism—that is the simplistic claim of this book. In Hirsch's case, this requires emphasis, since his biblical work can be seen as an adjunct to a defense of rabbinic Judaism. Scholarly literature has focused mainly on Hirsch's dogged defense of the Oral Torah as equal to, if not greater than, the Written Torah, and his insistence on comprehensive observance of the commandments. The crux of the argument over religious authority in Judaism in the nineteenth century, according to Jay Harris, was over the derivation of halachah.[12] As Harris explains, Hirsch developed a novel view of the relationship between the Written and Oral Torahs. Previous commentators regarded the Oral Torah as an explication of the Written Torah, thus tacitly assigning pride of place to the latter. Hirsch, Harris argues persuasively, reversed this relationship at the intellectual level. For Hirsch, the Written Torah provided the CliffsNotes to the Oral Torah, which God taught Moses directly at Mount Sinai and which Moses then transmitted perfectly to the sages from Joshua onward. For a full forty years then, the Oral Torah existed as living Judaism without the Written Torah at all! Even after the Written Torah was given to Israel before Moses's death, it in no way supplanted the Oral Torah. In Hirsch's own words:

> The Torah *sh'biktav* [Written Torah] is to be to the Torah *sh'ba'al peh* [Oral Torah] in the relation of short notes on a full and extensive lecture on any scholarly subject. For the student who has heard the whole lecture, short notes are quite sufficient to bring back afresh to his mind at any time the whole subject of the lecture. For him a word, an added mark of interrogation, or exclamation, a dot, the underlining of a word, etc., is often quite sufficient to recall to his mind a whole series of thoughts, a remark, etc. For those who had not heard the lecture from the Master, such notes would be completely useless.[13]

Harris's insight deserves our applause. It is truly ironic that a self-conceived defender of traditionalism should introduce such a novelty. Harris's insight also confirms what any historian would suspect: despite Hirsch's self-consciously antihistoricist view of the Bible, he is very much the product of his age and imports commentary, perspectives, and an agenda into his Bible project. Hirsch argues that times change and cultures progress, but Torah is timeless. Hirsch's quest for a Torah that can be explained on its own terms must be chimerical—every explanation of every text will always involve the interpreter and his or her biases.

Several specific conclusions follow from Harris's analysis. First, Hirsch made rabbinic literature the *only* legitimate prism through which the Bible should be interpreted, which puts him at odds with modern Bible scholarship. After all, this view implies that Christians cannot understand the Bible properly, "For those who had not heard the lecture from the Master, such notes would be completely useless," or that ancient Near Eastern analogues could never explain a biblical text. This position is incompatible with two key premises of Bible scholarship: one, that scholarship is an objective endeavor, and two, that the biblical text can be analyzed as a humanly produced, historical document. Second, when Hirsch discusses legal cases, the acquisition of the Hebrew slave in Exodus 21, for instance, he claims that this text cannot represent the entire law of slavery. However, for Hirsch, the entirety of ancient Israelite law on any and every point can be reconstructed by looking at the rabbinic literature, which is inerrant, to borrow a term from Protestant fundamentalists. Bible scholars would agree that the Hebrew Bible does not contain all the laws of ancient Israel—from the Bible alone we know how to initiate a divorce (Deuteronomy 24) but not a marriage. Bible scholars may even agree with Hirsch that the Written Torah deals with exceptional cases or those requiring emphasis. However, Bible scholars today would say that most laws were customary and taken for granted, and therefore were never recorded. The details have simply been lost in the sands of time. That degree of agnosticism, of course, would be unacceptable to Hirsch.

HIRSCH'S BIBLE PROJECT: THE EVIDENCE OF *HOREB* AND *THE NINETEEN LETTERS*

One might be tempted to ask: Was the Written Torah all that important to Hirsch? To follow his own metaphor, if a student really knows the course material (read: the rabbinic tradition), does that student really need the CliffsNotes? The answer is a resounding yes. Aggadically, we need Written Torah to teach; halachically, we need Written Torah to teach meaning of prescribed acts. Hirsch contended that all of Judaism can be found in the Hebrew Bible itself. Hirsch arrived at this basic conclusion early on and even hoped to write a philosophy of Judaism based on the Tanakh, titled *Moriah*. Hirsch wrote to his friend Z. H. May, "This book bearing the title *Horeb* represents an independent work; and only after the appearance of the book called *Moriah* will the *Horeb* form its second part. . . . The book *Moriah*, however, which will contain the fruit of my own study of Tanakh, is intended to present a general conception of the essence of Jewish nationhood." By the mid-1830s, Hirsch believed that *Horeb*, his modern, comprehensive law code for Israel's "thinking young men and women," as the title page reads, required a biblically based theological companion work.[14] Hirsch felt the Bible required more emphasis and attention than it had received in the immediate past, a viewpoint reinforced by his critique in *The Nineteen Letters* of the excessive educational focus on *pilpul*, a target of Mendelssohn and the entire Haskalah. Hirsch was Orthodox: he did not wish to turn back the hands on the clock to sixteenth-century Poland. Hirsch came from a household he called religiously enlightened; like other Jewish Enlighteners, Hirsch also wished to promote the centrality of the Hebrew Bible.[15]

The books that brought Hirsch to fame, *The Nineteen Letters* (1836) and *Horeb* (1837), appeared when Hirsch was only in his twenties. *The Nineteen Letters* emerged from the publisher's suggestion to provide a short, epistolary introduction/companion to *Horeb*, an imposing, two-volume law code. Hirsch's *The Nineteen Letters* is best known for its embrace of Emancipation and modernity from a traditionalist perspective (chapters 16–19), and from the German romantic presentation of God, humanity, and the world (chapters 1–6). The heart of *The Nineteen Letters*, however, judging by its role as guide to the *Horeb*, was Hirsch's highly original classification of the commandments into six categories and their explication (chapters 7–15). Isidore Grunfeld wrote as follows: "Hirsch seems to have been the first of our legal philosophers to try to classify the Commandments of the Torah by exclusively using the terms used by the Torah (toroth, edoth, mishpatim, chukim, mitzvoth, avodah), and to interpret them in the manner set out at the beginning of this section."[16] What a remarkable statement on Grunfeld's part! Why did Hirsch try to do what earlier codifiers avoided? Conversely, one might ask, why did his predecessors avoid Hirsch's procedure? The latter answer seems patent: the Torah's use of these terms is inconsistent and fails to visualize distinct legal categories into which the 613 commandments fall. Indeed, Moshe Greenberg and others have emphasized exactly this point: the distinctions between ritual and ethical, rational and irrational, and moral and ceremonial all derive from nineteenth-century theology. This speculation underscores the radical nature of Hirsch's organizational decision, but it coheres with his view of Torah as a revelation that can be fully explained symbolically. As Noah Rosenbloom explains:

> The classical Jewish codifiers avoided in their works any rationalization of the precepts. Even Maimonides, who devoted a considerable portion of the *Moreh Nevukim* to this subject, refrained from it in the *Mishneh Torah*. Not so Hirsch. He set two objectives for himself in *Horeb*, one normative, one philosophic. This first aimed to familiarize the reader or would-be teacher with the wide range of commandments and prohibitions; the second was to analyze and reflect upon the commandments, to gain some insight into their meaning and significance.[17]

In *Horeb*, these goals of "familiarity" and "reflection" are structured to flow from the Bible. In every section of *Horeb*, Hirsch began nearly every discussion with relevant biblical quotes, and expounded their significance mainly through discussion of biblical passages. This procedure, in my view, differs from the earlier law codes, which focused more on rabbinic literature. No code that I know of assigned centrality to the Hebrew Bible in the way that Hirsch did. Let us look at Hirsch's discussion of circumcision (*brit mila*), the first commandment given to Abraham as opposed to the entire human race, and one which is expressly called symbolic: "sign of the covenant" (*ot ha-brit*). "First let us consider the appointed act of circumcision and its detailed laws. Let us look at it in the entire legal connection of circumstances and expressions under which it has been decreed. From there we proceed to search for the scope of ideas which must lie within its meaning, *and then we find out whether the metaphorical meaning of this act itself and its linguistic designation can be found already expressed in the language of Scripture.*"[18]

For Hirsch, unpacking the symbolic language of Scripture yields the theological significance of the details of the halachah. One might consider this procedure backward. After all, did not halachah always develop over time, under historical pressures? Not in Hirsch's view: the halachah is a given, the inevitable detailing and incarnating of what was implicit in the Torah. Reading *Horeb*, it emerges that the simple dictum to Abraham, "Walk before me and be perfect" holds the key to the entire practice and meaning of circumcision. Do all of the "Torot" (fundamental principles of Judaism) Hirsch identified in *Horeb* center around a discussion of the biblical basis? Yes, they do. Do all of the "Edut" Hirsch identified in *Horeb* begin with a biblical verse? All but one: mourning. I am at a loss to explain this singular gap in Hirsch's symbolic method. Perhaps the discrepancy between rabbinic mourning practices and the Bible's struck him with special force, though the differences between biblical and rabbinic practices are often blatant. Perhaps it is because most of the mourning laws (*hilchot aveilut*) are largely customary. In any case, witness Hirsch's determination to bring Jewish mourning practices back to their biblical roots: "This [set of mourning laws] is based upon inferences in the Torah and the prophets in connection with the deaths of Nadav and Avihu and the wife of Ezekiel.... But it is just from these historical events and legal enactments that our sages realized the task of making allowances for the feeling of bereavement by ordaining set observances in connection with this state of mourning, observances evidence of which they already found in Tanakh."[19]

What made Hirsch's *Horeb* unusual? Some law codes explained their procedures explicitly; others did not. Some were scrupulous about citing their rabbinic sources; some were not. Some included dissenting views; some did not. Some attempted to be comprehensive; others did not.

But all previous law codes were mainly focused on rendering halachic clarity, and that is where much of their creativity lies: *codification was an outcome-driven enterprise.* Hirsch, on the contrary, was mainly content to refer readers to the relevant parts of the *Shulchan Aruch.* His achievement, rather, was to make the halachah familiar, by rendering it into German, and meaningful, by connecting it back to Scripture. Tellingly, the halachic work most similar to *Horeb* is *Sefer ha-Chinuch,* not a law code at all, but a guide to the commandments and their biblical sources traditionally bestowed as a bar mitzvah present.[20]

Hirsch's rationale for organizing and explaining the commandments in light of Tanakh, rather than the *Shulchan Aruch,* was anticipated in his scathing critique of both Moses Maimonides and Moses Mendelssohn in *The Nineteen Letters.* In a footnote to this eighteenth letter, which Hirsch explicated later in his essays on Jewish symbolism, he proposed an alternate procedure to that of Moses Maimonides and Moses Mendelssohn and their tendency to intellectualize, rationalize, and minimize the commandments' full meaning:

> One word here concerning the proper method of Torah investigation [*Thauroforschung*]. Two revelations are open before us; this is, nature and the Torah. In nature, all phenomena stand before us as indisputable facts, and we can endeavor a posteriori to ascertain the law of each, and the connection of all. Abstract demonstration of truth, or rather, the probability of theoretical explanations of acts of nature, is an unnatural process. The right method is to verify our assumptions by the known facts. . . . The same principles must be applied to the investigation of the Torah. In the Torah, as in nature, God is the ultimate cause. In the Torah, even as in nature, no fact may be denied, even though the reason and the connection may not be understood. . . . Its ordinances must be accepted in their entirety as undeniable phenomena, and must be studied in accordance with their connection with each other, and the subject to which they relate. Our conjectures must be tested by their precepts, and our highest certainty here also can only be that everything stands in harmony with our theory.[21]

Of course, the claim of an ancient text being a perfectly objective fact with no prehistory and liable to a scientific investigation like a cloud formation or a tornado is not one that many skeptics would grant. When Hirsch likened "Torah" to "Nature" in this way, he meant almost exactly the opposite of Spinoza's similar-sounding phrase in chapter 7 of the *Theological-Political Treatise,* "The means of interpreting Scripture are not much different from those of interpreting nature." For Spinoza, this statement implied that one engages in a scientific dissection of the ancient text, assessing authorship, transmission, inclusion, and error. For Hirsch, what is in the text cannot be questioned: if we have three narratives regarding a patriarch going down to Egypt and thereby imperiling the chastity of his wife (Genesis 12, 20, and 26), the answer cannot be that very ancient multiple sources are being preserved by a somewhat less ancient editor.[22] Similarly, if Deuteronomy reexplains or amplifies certain teachings in Genesis–Numbers, it cannot be that Deuteronomy comes from a seventh-century-BCE milieu reflecting a more developed society. These examples could be multiplied a thousandfold: explaining such cases constitutes the process of modern biblical scholarship. But for Hirsch, the text as we have it is profoundly factual—Torah literally embodies God's word, as surely as this world embodies God's creation.

(RE)PLACING HIRSCH AS GERMAN-JEWISH BIBLE COMMENTATOR

Hirsch has been grouped with Orthodox stalwarts such as Jacob Zvi Mecklenburg (1785–1865) and Meir Liebush Malbim (1809–1879), who rejected critical Bible scholarship and unified Written and Oral Torah. But Hirsch may also be compared to Mendelssohn, who unlike the former was both a translator and a commentator. Hirsch's translation differed from Mendelssohn's greatly. Mendelssohn freely rendered "units of meaning"; Hirsch's symbolic method, on the contrary, demanded that he stay very close to each Hebrew word, as his commentary was generated by listing verbal roots similar to the scriptural word and then deducing a theological teaching. Mendelssohn cared equally deeply about the translation and the commentary. Not so Hirsch, for whom the translational choices mainly provided a platform for his theology. Nobody has captured the contrasting styles of their commentaries better than Hirsch's descendant Mordechai Breuer: "A comparison with Mendelssohn is very instructive here. Mendelssohn's Bible commentary had, throughout, a coolly rational and often apologetic tone, whereas Hirsch's Commentary on the Pentateuch expressed an aggressively affirmative joy and enthusiasm for tradition and duty."[23]

Yet Hirsch's attitude toward Mendelssohn's achievement was fundamentally ambivalent, not negative. Like most German Jews, Hirsch venerated Mendelssohn as a model German Jew. Breuer tells us that Hirsch's admiration extended even to Mendelssohn's *Biur*, which had been condemned by Rabbi Raphael Kohen of Hamburg, the voice of tradition in Hirsch's hometown.[24] Rosenbloom believes that the roots of Hirsch's symbolism came from Mendelssohn's discussion of the ceremonial law as "a kind of living script." For Mendelssohn, the ceremonial law provided a good guard against idolatry; for Hirsch, it provided grounding in everyday service to God. Rosenbloom locates other possible sources for Hirsch's theory of symbolism, but sensibly concludes that Mendelssohn was both more proximate and indigenous. It would have been very peculiar for any mid-nineteenth-century German-Jewish thinker not to have been deeply imprinted with Mendelssohn's thought.[25]

Mendelssohn's influence is most evident in Hirsch's Bible commentary as counterexample. In Genesis 2:4, for instance, Hirsch blasts Mendelssohn's choice of rendering the Tetragrammaton as *Eternal*. So Hirsch: "A metaphysical transcendental conception which has scarcely any practical application to anything else certainly not to our own lives and existence. . . . The thought Eternal leaves our hearts cold, contains nothing for our lives and hence has no relationship whatsoever with *midat ha rahamim* (the attribute of mercy)."[26] Mendelssohn's choice of *Eternal* was well known, and while Hirsch's criticism has merit, his own choice—to italicize the God name when it represented *Adonai*, to not italicize it when it represented *Elohim*, and to leave a doubling of the God name (i.e., when both God names are used) unremarked except by the use of two Hebrew letters—strikes me as an equally poor translational solution. But, unlike Mendelssohn, demonstrating the Scriptures' ability to speak in any language meant less to Hirsch than making sure we step in as symbolic interpreters of Hebrew word. Weintraub and Becholdt noted Hirsch's dissent from Mendelssohn with respect to God names, and Hirsch distanced himself from Mendelssohn in other ways too. Stylistically, Hirsch stuck very closely to rendering the Hebrew text, with attention to preserving Hebrew word choice, verb form (*binyan*), and verb tense. Mendelssohn was more committed to a text that read well in German, which Hirsch's often does not. In the long history of Jewish Bible interpreters there are minimalists and maximalists. In this dichotomy, Hirsch stood firmly on the maximalist end of the spectrum, Mendelssohn on the minimalist.

Nevertheless, Mendelssohn's Bible project, with its use of good German in the translation, attention to grammar, Orthodoxy regarding both the lower and higher criticism, and fundamental reliance on Jewish sources, set the model for subsequent German-Jewish Bibles, Hirsch's included. As we have seen, Mendelssohn championed a heteronymous view of the commandments, sought to sequester discussions of the Bible from a full-throttled historical-developmental model, and had nothing but contempt for modern biblical scholarship. Hirsch's own 1841 essay expressed his view that the Bible critics simply missed the point of the Bible—that it was a religious text. His son-in-law's three lengthy articles in *Jeschurun*, "The Hypothesis of the Bible Critics and the Genesis Commentary of Rabbi S. R. Hirsch," exceeded Mendelssohn's acerbic criticism of the impiety of Eichhorn and his followers. While Gugenheimer placed much of the blame for the source criticism with Spinoza, he made it clear that those who upheld Moses as a redactor, rather than as a divine vehicle, were no closer to true Judaism. While Gugenheimer attacks gentile and Jewish transgressors, radical reformer David Einhorn's *The Principles of Mosaism* comes in for some special venom. Gugenheimer claimed that, unlike the source critics' speculative procedure, Hirsch's commentary was built "on the ground of a strictly rational scholarly exegesis."[27]

Like Mendelssohn, Hirsch placed enormous importance on the Hebrew Bible as an oral/aural, sounded text. The Bible was meant to be in Hebrew and meant to be heard. For Buber-Rosenzweig, the repetition of theme words (*Leitwörter*) provided a key to interpretation; for Mendelssohn, the fact that Moses heard everything on Sinai with full intonation and emphasis created a shield against misinterpretation. Hirsch incorporated Mendelssohn's view into his symbolic interpretation. For Hirsch, the interrelationship of sounds, what he called *Laut-Verwandschaft*, and his belief that Hebrew was the original language of mankind, a view first voiced by Midrash, repeated often in the medieval world, and affirmed by Hirsch in his comments to Genesis 11:7, led him to form a web of associations with any given biblical word. For instance, and quite typically, Hirsch connected the second word of the Torah, *bara* (create), with *barach*, *barah*, *perach*, *pereh*, and *perah*, all of which, according to Hirsch, connote a striving to get out or bring out. Etymologically, this is dubious, but such wordplay, visible in Hirsch's handwritten notebooks, offered him an opportunity to make the most of soundalike verb roots. The importance of Hebrew as the Bible's language, I believe, was something that has impressed most Western diaspora Jews. In Israel, of course, this is taken for granted, contemporary "Hebrew lite" versions of the Bible notwithstanding. In eastern Europe, commentators continued to write in Hebrew, confident that their target audience could understand them. But in nineteenth-century Germany, as in America today, congregations remain committed to reading Torah in the original. As early as the *Nineteen Letters*, Hirsch insisted:

> We must read the Torah in Hebrew—that is to say, in accordance with the spirit of that language. It describes but little, but through the rich significance of its verbal roots it paints in the word a picture of the thing.... It is as it were a semi-symbolic writing. With wakeful eye and ear, and with soul aroused to activity, we must read; nothing is told us of such superficial import that we need only, as it were, accept it with half roused dreaminess; we must strive ourselves to create again the speaker's thoughts to think them over or it will escape us.[28]

THE HIRSCHIAN BIBLE PROJECT COMPLETED: THE TORAH COMMENTARY

Hirsch's Pentateuch, written in Frankfurt am Main from 1867 to 1878, was the product of decades of teaching, sermonizing, and writing; hardly an Orthodox home was found without it. These years overlapped momentous events, including the unification of Germany and the secession of

Hirsch's community from the Jewish mainstream. Robert Liberles gives several examples of Hirsch's reading the Bible against the backdrop of current events. Liberles notes that the narrative of Pinchas's zealotry in Numbers 25, where he skewers an Israelite (Zimri) who consorts with a Midianite woman (Kosbi), shows Hirsch applauding an "activist" approach, where others find themselves paralyzed. Hirsch apparently read Exodus 1:8, "And a new Pharaoh arose who knew not Joseph," in light of the Prussian takeover of Frankfurt am Main in 1866. Hirsch, like many Frankfurters, expressed reservations about Prussian domination, and wove this concern into his comment. Prior commentators had read in Exodus 1:8 a regime change, and many, linking it back to Joseph (Genesis 37–50), assumed that a native dynasty had taken control. Hirsch, according to Liberles, was unique in seeing the takeover in the opposite direction: a foreign dynasty (Prussia) conquered and paid no heed to local history or custom (Joseph's service to the Egyptian nation).[29]

The remainder of this chapter offers a brief sampler of Hirsch's Pentateuch and an indication of why it has had such enthusiastic readers. Quite a few comments in the first *sidra* of Genesis reveal Hirsch's method. Hirsch held a hard-line view of creation out of nothing, not merely preexisting matter. Hirsch: "The contrary belief, that matter always existed, and only ascribes to God the Creator a formative function, which is equally the foundation stone of heathen conception to this very day is not only a metaphysical lie which robbed the theories of mankind as to the origins of the world of truth . . . which undermines all morality. If the material was there, was given to the world-framer, He could only make the best possible out of that material but not the absolute best world. All physical and moral evil would then unavoidably lie in the imperfection of the material." Hirsch diverged from Rashi's view of creation, which lacks philosophical sophistication; from Rambam's hyperphilosophical view, which explicitly triangulated a rabbinic view with Plato and Aristotle; and from Ramban, who employed the idea of preexistent matter. For Hirsch, any compromise regarding the perfection of creation (Nature) would imply doubt about the perfection of the Torah and could not be countenanced.[30]

The creation of humanity in Genesis 1:26–28 has generated considerable commentary through the ages, but Hirsch's reading is original. He takes each word of the phrase "Be fertile and increase and fill the earth and subdue it as follows" to refer to some specific human institution. So, *fertile* = marriage; for Hirsch, marriage, being inseparable from the production of the next generation, connects *p'ru* to fruitfulness; *increase* = parenthood, child-rearing connecting the Hebrew *rav* to discipline; *fill* = society, seeing others engage in the same acts of family formation as yourself; *subdue* = property and acquisition, but only, says Hirsch, basing his assertion on the fact that this divine injunction comes last, when the other provisos of Genesis 1:28 have been fulfilled. This reading will not pass muster in the eyes of academic scholarship. The injunction "Be fertile and increase" (*p'ru u'rvu*) would be considered by most scholars a typical hendiadys—a doubling of the verb for emphasis. It is a stretch to equate the three-letter verbal root *kvsh* (subdue) to "property acquisition," as Hirsch does. The primeval history, as scholars call Genesis 1–11, seems to have etiology as its main purpose, and these verses most likely explain why humans are to be differentiated from both the animals and the Almighty. To read into this string of verbs an ordering of descending priorities, as Hirsch does, strains logic. Just because "be fertile" comes first in the sentence and "subdue" comes last, does that make "subdue" less important? One can think of too many biblical sentences that violate that principle. Hirsch's reading is forced, but it is also great midrash. Hirsch's reading of every word for maximal meaning places him in the Akivan versus Ishmaelian school, as does his readiness to interpret cantillation notes (he does so frequently), differences in the read text (*keri*) versus the written text (*ktiv*), the scribal breaks on the Torah scroll usually corresponding to paragraph breaks in English (the *petuchah* and *setumah* marks), and the instances where letters are written smaller or larger than ordinary.

To take another example of Hirsch's unique and original mode of commentary, let us look at his discussion of "Hear O Israel!" known as the Shma, and generally acknowledged as Judaism's central affirmation. The Shma contains two cases of enlarged letters in its best-known verse, "*Shma Yisrael Adonai Eloheinu, Adonai Ehad.*" Hirsch explained: *Ehad* is written with a large *dalet*, probably to prevent it being changed for a *resh*, which would make it *Aher* (another), just as in Exodus 34:14. This is a very apt citation on Hirsch's part, since this earlier Torah verse, Exodus 34:14, also concerns idolatry. But Hirsch continued, "The *resh* is the polytheistic thought and is accommodatingly round. The *dalet* of the Jewish truth is sharply angular. With the loss of this little sharpness, the *ehad* becomes *aher*." This extreme position—that the actual shapes of letters contain theological teachings—is also found in Jewish tradition, very famously in midrash Genesis Rabbah with respect to the question of why God created the world with second letter (*bet*) not the first (*aleph*). Still, it is a bit shocking to find this kind of analysis in a modern writer, and I am reminded of the Lenny Bruce classic comic routine: "Jewish and Goyish." Is *resh* really a "goyish" letter and *dalet* a Jewish one? I cannot believe that Hirsch meant this literally. Regarding the teaching of Torah to one's children, in the first line of the *V'ahavta*, the Israelite is enjoined to "teach them to one's children and talk about them." Once again, Hirsch takes a presumed hendiadys and breaks it down: teach them/*shinantem* = Written Torah, while *dibarta bam*/talk about them = Oral Torah. Hirsch goes even farther with this verse, using it to explain the historical-educational development into a threefold injunction to study: Scripture, Mishnah, and Gemara. This threefold division was occasioned only by the reluctant writing down of the Mishnah; originally, it was but twofold, Written Torah and Oral Torah.

Like many German-Jewish commentators, Hirsch resists Christian readings of the "garden narrative" in Genesis 2–3. As was his wont, Hirsch connected the (in)famous line "I shall make him a fitting helpmate" to several cognate verbs, which Hirsch thinks share the property of limiting, restricting, and confining. This indicates the kind of help that the woman will give the man. Hirsch goes in a decidedly egalitarian direction with this thought. Here is Hirsch on Genesis 2:18: "And 'helpmeet' expresses no idea of subordination but rather complete equality, and on a footing of equal independence. Woman stands 'k'negdo,' rendered alternately: 'against,' 'parallel to,' 'on one line,' or 'at his side.'" Later on in this narrative, Hirsch follows older commentators to note that the ground, not the man himself, is cursed by God, which leads Hirsch to a full-throttle rejection of original sin: "One consideration does seem to us of the utmost importance. In the whole of this verdict of God, the curse is pronounced only against the ground and the animal, but in no wise over man. Mankind is in no way placed under the ban for his first disobedience. In all that was said not a single syllable altered Humanity's high calling or ability to reach and fulfill it."[31] A certain resistance to Christian readings is to be expected: most Jewish Bible scholars in the modern era have shown this tendency. Yet one finds no anti-Christian dicta where one might expect them: Genesis 15:6, Genesis 26:5, and even Genesis 49:10, all typical flash points of disagreement in Jewish-Christian exegesis. Hirsch's strong sense of Israel's role within the nations emerged often in his commentary. This comes as no surprise to the reader of *The Nineteen Letters*, where Hirsch went remarkably far, for a traditional Jew, in minimizing the nationalist elements in Judaism. Such phrases as "pure humanity," "where the Torah emanates there is my Israel," "Land and soil were never Israel's bonds of union," and "Summon up before your eyes a nation dispersed" populate this work and give an accurate flavor of Hirsch's diasporic orientation.

Hirsch reflects a profound universalism. Commenting upon the three sons of Noah, Shem, Ham, and Japheth, Hirsch makes them eternal archetypes. Ham represents appetitive instincts; Japheth represents aesthetic beauty; Shem, recognition that service to God is the highest calling. Here is Hirsch on Genesis 9:27:

> When we look around in historical facts we can say: the stem of Japheth reached its fullest blossoming in the Greeks; that of Shem in the Hebrews, Israel who bore and bears the name of God through the world of nations. Right to the present-day it is only these two races, the descendants of Shem and Japheth, the Greeks and the Jews, who have become the real educators and teachers of humanity. . . . Japheth has ennobled the world aesthetically. Shem has enlightened it spiritually and morally. Hellenism and Judaism have become the great active forces in the educational work on mankind, and the rest of the world has been merely the passive material on which they worked.[32]

Hirsch's theme of Jewry's special calling toward "the nations" is further developed with Abram's transformation into Abraham, the model of "Mensch-Jisroel," Hirsch's term for the ideal modern Jew. He writes, "This fact that Abram was ninety-nine when God announced Isaac's birth is important from two aspects. Some people say: 'As long as one has satisfied the moral and humane demands of life one has satisfied God's demands too.' Others think 'to be a Jew is something different from being an ordinary man, it is a substitute for it.'"[33] Hirsch, however, found it very significant that only after a normal life as a righteous man did God come to Abraham and say, in Genesis 17:1, "walk before me and become perfect." Abraham does this, according to Hirsch, primarily through his fulfilling the commandment of circumcision, which Hirsch, not accidentally, considered the model of a symbolic commandment lacking direct rationale. Submission to God's covenant, for Hirsch, defined the Jew, "To be as kind, benevolent, humane, forgiving, unselfish un-grasping as Abraham has shown himself hitherto is no more than the ideal of what every man, every Noahide should be."[34]

Hirsch's universalism and psychological acuity shine in his discussion of Rebecca and Isaac. Hirsch addressed antisemitism directly with respect to Rebecca's deception of Isaac: "The worst antisemite or antibibliologist will want to find some reasoning, some sense, or if you prefer it some cunning in her action. The worse, the more artful such a person would make the Jewish Ancestress appear the less would that attribute to her the most complete imbecility, the most childish stupidity. And even if her intention had been nothing more than, by her trickery, to manage to turn the paternal blessing on to the head of her beloved Jacob, what possible result could she have expected from that."[35] Hirsch continued by explaining that the goal of the deception was not merely to ensure that the right son received the paternal blessing, but also that Isaac would finally realize that Esau posed a danger to a continuation of the value system of Abraham and Sarah, epitomized, for Hirsch, by Esau's willingness to marry Hittite women. Midrash portrays them as struggling in the womb—locked in combat. Hirsch's view that Isaac suddenly had the character of Esau revealed to him is supported in Midrash, not by the biblical text; this reliance on Midrash is typical of many Hirschian comments. The most interesting dimension of this gloss, however, is on Rebecca's and Isaac's parenting skills. Hirsch saw the couple as quite fallible and thought that a better assessment of the merits of both Esau (pagan Rome and then Christianity) and Jacob (ancient Israel and then subsequent Jewry) could have averted much misunderstanding and hostility:

> Had Isaac and Rebecca studied Esau's nature and character early enough, and asked themselves how can even an Esau, how can all the strength and energy agility and courage that lies slumbering in this child, be won over to be used in the service of God . . . then Jacob and Esau with their totally different natures could still have remained twin-brothers in sprit and life; quite

early in life Esau's "sword" and Jacob's spirit could have worked hand in hand, and who can say what a different aspect the whole history of the ages might have presented.[36]

The reunion of Jacob and Esau in Genesis 33:4 ("And Esau ran to meet him and embraced him, and fell on his neck and kissed him and they wept") divided Jewish commentators, some accepting Esau's forgiveness as sincere, and others denying it. Hirsch has no doubt: "The allusion to weeping is a sure sign that what we have here is a revelation of genuine humanity."[37] All in all, a very charitable discussion of Esau emerges from Hirsch's reading compared to numerous traditional commentaries.

Hirsch cited Midrash Rabbah by name in his Pentateuch, often by the sage to whom a particular dictum is directed, but never negatively. I believe Hirsch's debt to the early rabbinic masters has not been stressed sufficiently. While some scholars have cast doubts on Hirsch's acumen as a Talmudist, he clearly had an eye for important rabbinic traditions—I cannot imagine anyone thinks Hirsch's Pentateuch lacks erudition. If he knew Tanakh and rabbinic traditions less intimately than Shmuel David Luzzato (1800–1865) or eastern European contemporaries, that is to be expected—they had not been educated at public schools in Hamburg, as had Hirsch. Similarly, with the exception of barbs directed at Reform contemporaries like Geiger,[38] which are explicit, Hirsch rarely stated his opposition to previous traditional commentators outright, although his dissent may be inferred, as in his comments to Genesis 1. I agree with Grunfeld that Hirsch relied greatly on medievals such as Halevy and Nachmanides and moderns such as David Nietto, Mecklenburg, and the Malbim. Having said that, Hirsch's dependence on the early sages is very great, as is his debt to earlier German Jews. Most of all, Hirsch's originality as an exegete should not be minimized.

CONCLUSION

Hirsch's Pentateuch appears as the culmination of a lifetime's engagement in understanding the message of Torah. While he is justly evaluated as someone who went further than anyone in seeing the Oral and Written Torah as indivisible, I have argued that this implies no disparagement of studying the Written Torah. In his early writings (*The Nineteen Letters* and *Horeb*) Hirsch promised a Jewish theology based on Tanakh (*Moriah*), insisted on the study of Tanakh in Hebrew, and used terms in Torah to organize a legal classification of the commandments. In his own words, and through those of his son-in-law, Joseph Gugenheimer, Hirsch showed his contempt for contemporary Bible critics, Jewish and Christian, who would impugn the sanctity of the Torah. Going further than Mendelssohn, who reserved his explicit disdain to the prologue of his *Sefer Netivot ha-Shalom*, Hirsch did not even permit such *"treyf"* thoughts, though his Deuteronomy commentary (1878) appeared the same year as Wellhausen's grand synthesis. One might imagine Hirsch as midway between Mendelssohn, who could still regard this criticism as ephemeral, and the next generation, who had no choice but to engage source critics directly. Although some ultraorthodox have tried to claim him as one of their own, a focus on his Bible project shows that Hirsch stands in the German-Jewish tradition of elevating the Bible and its religious teachings.[39] Hirsch appears as a vital link connecting the Bible projects of Mendelssohn and those of Benno Jacob and Buber-Rosenzweig.

4

Benno Jacob and the Call for a "Jewish" Bible Scholarship

By the first years of the twentieth century, source criticism had triumphed decisively. Julius Wellhausen's *Prolegomenon to the History of Ancient Israel*, an accessible book notwithstanding its title, had synthesized a century of Bible scholarship. Linking the authors (J, E, D, and P) with the eras of biblical history, and with distinct stages in Israel's religious development, Wellhausen's works divided Bible readers into two camps: the academic mainstream, which accepted the purely human development of the Bible, and dissenters, including those who upheld divine or even Mosaic authorship. The complaints against Wellhausen's presentation have been lodged often: too Hegelian, too Protestant, atomistic, often arbitrary in assigning verses to a particular author, and anti-Judaic. This last criticism includes a whole sublisting: hostile to the Law, hostile to priests and temple service (his synthesis was anti-Catholic too), hostile to Ezra, hostile to postbiblical Judaism, and so on. When Stephen Geller wrote that Wellhausen provided the necessary foil for Yehezkel Kaufmann, he could have been speaking for an entire generation of Jewish Bible scholars.[1]

An additional prompt to a Jewish defense of the Bible came from a controversy in 1902, occasioned by a series of well-publicized lectures by Assyriologist Friedrich Delitzsch, which eventually appeared as a book, *Babel and Bible*. Delitzsch claimed that most of the Bible's "material" could be found in earlier ancient Near Eastern civilizations. Delitzsch impugned not only the divinity, but even the originality, of the Bible. Ironically, the author's father, Franz Delitzsch, was both a Conservative Old Testament Bible scholar of outstanding reputation and a defender of the Jews against antisemitic canards. With some help from a brilliant but erratic Jewish Bible scholar named Arnold Bogumil Ehrlich, Franz Delitzsch even produced the first Hebrew translation of the New Testament. (I own a copy published in Haifa in 1968 with the traditional acronym for "may his memory be for a blessing" after Delitzsch's name, no doubt a tribute to his role as defender of Jews.) Delitzsch the elder may have been a missionary, but he had a deep sympathy with Jews and Judaism. Not so the younger Delitzsch, whose works showed an animus toward things Biblical and/or Jewish, quite similar to many contemporary biblical minimalists.

The details of this Bible-Babel controversy have been well told by Yaacov Shavit. Suffice it to say, the Delitzsch controversy placed a second challenge before Jewish scholars: namely, how to deal with the many parallels between the Bible and the ancient Near East. Today, most Bible scholars find this a nontroubling issue. After all, would not one expect the Bible to reflect many aspects of its historical environment? Is it surprising that Solomon's Temple looks like other temples in the region, especially given that the biblical narrative itself stresses Solomon's foreign affairs? For the decades immediately following Delitzsch, however, the story was different. Schechter's main target in "Higher Criticism—Higher Antisemitism," in fact, was Delitzsch, not Wellhausen. *Babel and Bible*, for Schechter, compromised the Jews' claim to having endowed Western civilization with its foundational document, and consequently threatened Jewish political status. Russian pogromchiks neither knew nor cared much about Delitzsch, but given the outbreaks of violence that descended upon the Jews from 1881 onward, and his own upbringing, one can understand Schechter's defensiveness. Newer "scholarship" in race, religion, history, and Bible seemed to be fueling the rise in antisemitism—Jewish protagonists felt this intuitively. As Benno Jacob wrote, "Has anybody considered what share in the immense suffering brought recently on mankind and on the Jewish people in particular has to be accredited to the modern German-Protestant science of the Old Testament?"[2]

Jewish Bible scholarship lagged far behind the rest of the Jewish scholarly agenda, which had produced landmark works in law, midrash, poetry, philosophy, and history. Jewish scholars, on the whole, continued to avoid the Pentateuch as an area of critical research, although some major figures (e.g., Max Dienemann, Ismar Elbogen, Caesar Seligmann, and Siegmund Maybaum) wished that this situation would change. Despite this stunted development in Bible, German Jews continued their translational fecundity. The midnineteenth century had seen the Zunz, Philippsohn, and Hirsch Bibles, and the closing years of the nineteenth century would see a slew of others. Even these efforts would pale in comparison with efforts in the Weimar Republic, which saw the Berlin Bible of Harry Torczyner (Tur-Sinai), Lazarus Goldschmidt's *PrachtBibel*, and the fabled Buber-Rosenzweig Bible, the focus of the next chapter. Nevertheless, there was at least one figure who blazed a trail in Jewish Bible scholarship, Benno Jacob.[3]

PLACING BENNO JACOB AS MAKER OF THE MODERN JEWISH BIBLE

Benno Jacob (1862–1945) was a colorful figure.[4] Trained at the Breslau university and Jewish theological seminary, he served as rabbi to a very Reform community in Dortmund that met on Sundays. An organizer of Viadrina, a seminal Jewish student organization, he engaged in dueling and displayed a consistently militant attitude toward the burgeoning antisemitism of his time. He publicly confronted the vile antisemite Liebermann von Sonnenberg in 1911, at a public meeting, demonstrated that von Sonnenberg could not read a single line of the Talmud text he was besmirching, and then went on and harangued the audience with his bona fides as German patriot. An ardent anti-Zionist (his wife was not), Jacob engaged in debate with Franz Rosenzweig (a non-Zionist) and Martin Buber (a pro-Zionist). He fled the Nazis at the end of his life for London, and the end of his still to be translated Genesis prologue bears the chilling coda "Hamburg, 13 December 1933," alongside the Hebrew date, the first night of Hanukkah.[5] Unlike the celebrated Freud, who also fled to London and with whom Jacob shares many character similarities, the latter's last years remained difficult. As a figure outside the biblical guild, Jacob's criticisms of German-Protestant *Bibelkritik* did not receive much of a hearing from his non-Jewish contemporaries. The appearance of Jacob's commentaries overlapped the rise of Nazism (*Genesis*, 1934) and World War II (*Exodus*, 1940/1943). His grandson, Rabbi Walter Jacob of Temple Rodef Shalom in Pittsburgh, acknowledged another impediment to the reception of Jacob's two massive Bible commentaries—the sharp criticism he had levied at others and the academy's tendency to keep count of such slights. Were it not for the efforts of his grandson, Jacob might have remained an intriguingly frequent scholarly footnote. Fortunately, Walter Jacob has translated his grandfather's commentaries on both Genesis and Exodus, and every reader of Nehama Leibowitz will appreciate her debt to Jacob. His literary remains, containing his notebooks for a never completed commentary on Leviticus, reside in the American Jewish Archives in Cincinnati, Ohio.[6]

Jacob's delayed impact also owes something to the nature of his works. Neither commentary is a suitable guide for the general reader. Both commentaries, rather, offer Jacob platforms for long discourses on every nuance of Scripture. The Genesis commentary, in its original German, runs almost 1,100 pages, and the Exodus commentary tops one thousand pages. The layout and sheer erudition of these works would have been sufficient to ward off the casual reader. Jacob's commentary on Judah and Tamar, for instance, ran fourteen single-spaced, small-font pages, with very few paragraph breaks, even by German standards. Jacob left many words in Hebrew script and cited numerous contemporaries, whom he generally rebutted, and a slew of rabbinic and medieval Jewish references. His commentaries were not user-friendly, although his short entries in the *Jewish Encyclopedia* give a good indication of his positions. Jacob did not provide German Jews with a simple linear commentary, as Rosenzweig had implored, nor an accessible Chumash brimming with Jewish pride, as did Joseph Hertz. I am thankful that the translators presented Jacob's works in an abridged fashion, and without the scholarly apparatus, much of which would have been dated by the time these publications saw light.

Not a popular author in any sense of the word, Jacob was deeply appreciated by some of his more discerning contemporaries. Buber and Rosenzweig owed Jacob a great debt in their own translation. Even before that, Rosenzweig had approvingly read Jacob's analysis of the Joseph narrative, *Source Criticism and Exegesis* (1915), and declared that Jacob must provide a modern Torah commentary for German Jewry. Jacob's combativeness pervaded his scholarly work. He attacked the methods of contemporary Bible scholars directly in *In the Name of God* (1903), *The Pentateuch: Critical and Exegetical Studies* (1905), and, finally, in a one-hundred-page excursus to his Genesis commentary, *Das Erste Buch der Tora: Genesis*, to name the most extended examples. Jacob had a twofold mission: He believed that the Bible needed to be rescued from hostile non-Jewish hands, and he sought to reverse the neglect of Bible in the Wissenschaft des Judentums.[7]

Both parts of Jacob's mission deserve explication. Jacob appreciated conservative Christian critics and cited them freely in both commentaries. Although he was no doubt aware of Jewish scholarly contemporaries in Bible studies, he did not, apparently, consider them pioneers of a Jewish Bible study. Siegmund Maybaum, despite his resistance to the higher critics on the dating of the Priestly Code (P), seems to have conceded too much in Jacob's view—Maybaum's *Development of Israelite Priesthood* and *Development of Israelite Prophecy* do not even appear in Jacob's indexes. Indeed, Maybaum chaired the conference on Wissenschaft des Judentums in 1907, at which Jacob unleashed his most critical comments on the lack of a Jewish Bible scholarship. Since Jacob also acknowledged the work of Samson Raphael Hirsch, Abraham Kahana, Baruch Halevi Epstein, and Meir Malbim, all of whom were Orthodox and either predecessors or contemporaries of Jacob, this silence on the efforts of his fellow liberals speaks volumes. David Zvi Hoffmann, who combined a mastery of rabbinic sources, enormous animus toward the source critics, and enormous independence, came closer to Jacob's approach. Hoffmann, who taught at the Orthodox seminary on Berlin's Artilleriestrasse, penned a Leviticus commentary, resembling Jacob's on Genesis and Exodus. Nevertheless, Jacob's view that the Torah probably took initial shape in the period of King David could hardly be consistent with Hoffmann's view that the Torah was Mosaic.[8]

Placing Benno Jacob in the history of modern Jewish Bible has been made more difficult by the failure to see the making of the modern Jewish Bible as a persisting project. For instance, Yaakov Elman, a very fine scholar, places Jacob among a slew of nineteenth-century commentators who sought "omnisignificant meaning from the text." As Elman suggests, there was definitely a nineteenth-century trend toward a maximalist posture toward the Hebrew Bible, prompted partly by a Reform tendency to minimize the importance of details versus the big message, and in part by the Bible critics who refused to treat the received text as the necessary exegetical point of departure. The problem with this grouping is that every other example Elman names besides Jacob is Orthodox. Elman acknowledges this: "To that august company I wish to add another name, denominationally distinct, but exegetically similar, Benno Jacob."[9] As much as I appreciate Elman's latitudinarianism, that difference cannot be passed over so lightly. Jacob accepted the non-Mosaic authorship of the Torah, and considered the actual author (*Verfasser*) equivalent to the Redactor. He accepted historical development within the Bible and within Judaism (e.g., Jacob stated that Rosh Hashanah became the Jewish New Year in the late Seleucid period). He became increasingly convinced of the superiority of the Traditional Text, "Die Richtigkeit unseres Hebräischen Textes," but he neither opposed emendation in principle, nor ignored other versions, the Septuagint version of Esther being the subject of his doctoral dissertation. Jacob acknowledged ancient Near Eastern parallels, though he did not deploy them as fully as his successors. All of this would have been anathema to the camp of "omnisignificance" that Elman identifies. Most importantly, all of these figures had an additional goal: to show the Written Law and Oral Law as either compatible or identical. While Jacob had great respect for traditional Jewish commentary, and insisted that it be part of a Jewish Bible scholarship, he did not think any part of that tradition, from Midrash to Rashi, necessarily understood the biblical sense better than he did. To Jacob exegesis might have been the most important thing, but not the only thing. Elman correctly senses the enormous resistance and animosity that Jacob showed toward those who held a cavalier attitude toward the Traditional Text—but this also unites Jacob with figures like Mendelssohn and Geiger, who could not be called champions of "omnisignificance."

If Jacob cannot be placed in the camp of the Orthodox "defenders of the faith," he cannot so easily be placed alongside those for whom translation itself was the vehicle of mediating culture. Seidman does not mention Benno Jacob at all, and mentions S. R. Hirsch only in passing. She is justified: as translators, neither Hirsch nor Jacob advanced a novel approach. For both Jacob and Hirsch, the translation was a way of highlighting aspects of their commentaries, though Jacob was more scrupulous than Hirsch (or Buber-Rosenzweig) in not "cooking the books"—Jacob's translations always had a sound philological basis, which was not necessarily true either of Hirsch or of Buber. Tellingly, the English translators of Hirsch (Isaac Lewy) and Jacob (Walter Jacob) did not make much of the translation itself in their respective introductions. Even Walter Jacob hardly mentions that the translation provided is based on his grandfather's, an indication that the commentaries of Hirsch and Jacob constitute their greater contributions. Similarly, Michael Brenner mentions Benno Jacob only as an advocate for the Buber-Rosenzweig translation: "I know no other translation which so very much replaces the original and text so very much yet presses one to learn the original itself."[10] Jacob does not fit any of these narratives comfortably: as a Bible scholar, he was too Jewish; as a German Jew, his translation is unremarkable; as a rabbi whose main scholarly interest was Bible, his contributions seemed marginal to the mainstream of Jewish Wissenschaft, even in the Weimar period.[11]

Christian Wiese has illuminated one indisputable dimension of Jacob's work: anticolonialism and resistance to Protestant discourse. Like Rabbi David Zvi Hoffmann, Jacob clearly perceived Wellhausen's anti-Jewish animus. In a moving call for a Jewish Bible scholarship, Jacob sounds a note similar to Schechter's "Higher Criticism—Higher Antisemitism." I mention this because the creation of the modern Jewish Bible included resistance to Protestant-dominated Bible studies that crossed denominational lines (Jacob, Reform; Schechter, Conservative; Hoffmann, Orthodox) and also national ones (German Jews, American Jews, and immigrants to prestate Israel all took an oppositional stance). The scope of this phenomenon has not received the attention it is due, once again, because the project of making a modern Jewish Bible has not been put into focus. In the venerable *Allgemeine Zeitung des Judentums* (1898), liberal Jewry's journal of record, founded by Ludwig Philippsohn, yet another German-Jewish Bible translator, Jacob wrote:

> The sole thing that Israel produced in terms of an immortal contribution to the world, the basis of its 3,000 year old spiritual life, its highest possession, its most precious sanctuary, is torn away from it. Our Bible is no longer our Bible. We must return the Bible back to its appropriate place in Judaism as a leader and judge, as the text of our life, which makes us the heralds of its eternal truth for the centuries thirsting for salvation. The Bible must enter the center of Jewish scholarship and Jewish education in order to enter the Jewish house.[12]

Wiese justifiably sees Jacob as a polemicist for the creation of a Jewish Bible studies. But that alone cannot explain why we can still read Jacob's commentary with such profit. Niehoff summarizes Jacob's innovation:

> In summary the notion Wissenschaft was important to Jacob's work and self-image. He identified with its ideals and produced the first purposefully

academic and distinctly Jewish commentaries on the Pentateuch. While Jacob emulated the ideological ethos of the nineteenth-century Wissenschaft, he embraced its rationalism, emphasis on ethical monotheism, and appreciation of the literal, nonmystical meaning of texts. Rather than focusing on the great scholars of the Middle Ages, as nineteenth century scholars had done, Jacob applied these priorities to the study of Scripture itself. The result was a rational, apologetic commentary that is based on the literal meaning and is deeply rooted in traditional Jewish exegesis. The significance of this pioneering effort lies in the fact that it represents an important bridge between religious engaged readings of Scripture and fully critical Bible studies from a specifically Jewish perspective.[13]

Can "Bible studies" be from "a Jewish perspective" without being "religiously engaged"? The second and third parts of this book seek to answer that question affirmatively. The "bridge" between religious and critical that Niehoff invokes has been crossed time and again, in both directions.

BENNO JACOB'S EXEGETICAL STYLE I: HOLISM[14]

Armed with solid university training in philology, a mastery of traditional Jewish commentary, and certainty that the Bible constituted a coherent text, Jacob was well equipped for his role as defender of the faith and champion of modern Jewish Bible studies. It would be difficult to summarize the contributions of a forty-year career of sustained Bible exegesis, especially because the scholarly world has appreciated Jacob only recently, unlike many of the figures discussed in this book. Still, I believe four elements of his exegesis deserve special mentions: (1) his holistic approach to the text, (2) his attention to genealogies and number patterns, (3) his Jewish take on ancient Near Eastern analogues, and (4) his view of the Bible as Jewish turf. It goes almost without mentioning that Jacob shared the German-Jewish belief that the Bible constituted its own best point of reference and that a Tanakh and a concordance were the most reliable implements in the exegete's toolbox—Rashi and the sages were fallible, the Bible was not.

Jacob took special delight in vindicating passages and chapters that the higher critics considered extrinsic, incidental, or pasted on to the main story. As he wrote, "Genesis is a unified work put forth in a single spirit, thought through and worked throughout."[15] And again: "Exodus is even more unified than Genesis."[16] But how does one go about proving this unity, especially in the face of source critics who considered the Torah a patchwork? One response that has proven attractive to the makers of the modern Jewish Bible has been to focus on chapters that, on first glance, fit oddly. No better example of this tendency can be found than Jacob's treatment of the story of Judah and Tamar (Genesis 38), a target of

Protestant animus from Martin Luther to Gerhard von Rad. Jacob wrote: "Tamar has been described as a woman who wants a child at any price, disregards custom and law, even commits incest, and risks life and honor for her purpose. Actually, this story, often regarded as objectionable, is the crown of the book of Genesis and Tamar one of its most admirable women."[17] Whereas many Jewish commentators insinuated that Tamar was not really a Canaanite, and even Mendelssohn followed the Aramaic translator Onkelos in rendering Canaanite (*k'nani*) as "merchant," Jacob considered her Canaanite identity the key to the whole chapter: "Tamar stands even higher as she was originally a stranger. Her descent is not mentioned, only her name. This is intentional in contrast to Judah's wife. Undoubtedly Tamar too was the daughter of a Canaanite, because Judah lived among Canaanites and had taken a wife for himself from them. . . . Nobility of mind is more than nobility of family. Tamar represents the triumph of the spirit over blood, and the attraction of Israel's national-religious ideas of its faith."[18]

Needless to say, Jacob's reading provided a stirring counterpoint to the Nazi racial ideology of his day. But Jacob perceived Tamar as one of a long line of righteous gentiles, and devoted a paragraph to explaining why "Ruth is the worthy successor of Tamar." Perhaps this connection is obvious: both are foreigners who take the sexual initiative for a holy purpose, and both forward the messianic line of Judah/David. But Jacob is original, as far as I know, in recognizing this chapter (Genesis 38) as a counterpoint to the negative examples of exogamy and intermarriage in Genesis 34 and Genesis 36. Moreover, Jacob did not content himself with a "merely" literary explanation, such as that offered by Leopold von Ranke; namely, that Genesis 38 provides a necessary literary pause in the action between Joseph being thrown into the pit (Genesis 37) and his being brought down to Egypt (Genesis 39). Now, as Erich Auerbach, Robert Alter, Meir Sternberg, and others have successfully argued, not all literary arguments are "merely literary." But some clearly are: von Ranke ignored the powerful symbolism of the seeds of redemption (Peretz and the line of Judah) being planted before the bondage begins (Joseph's and Israel's). Benno Jacob, invoking the Midrash, connected Genesis 38 with what comes before and after; his reading is literarily acute, but ultimately theologically driven. Unlike contemporary Jewish proponents of a literary reading, who leave open the possibility of an animating author, an inspired text, and a religiously coherent message, Jacob asserted it without qualification. Sweeping aside claims of Genesis as a patchwork, Jacob stated, "The 'Redactor' is no other than the Author himself."[19]

Although Jacob argued hard that Genesis 38 belonged to the Joseph cycle, he acknowledged the obscurity of the other problematic chapter of the Joseph story (Genesis 49), which includes Jacob's valedictory words to his sons. Often misnamed "Jacob's Blessing," since quite a bit of the content of Genesis 49 is harshly critical, Jacob noted that ten of twenty-three verses of this passage deal with Joseph and Judah, echoing this dual emphasis of the Joseph narrative as a whole. While Jacob acknowledged that a thorough reconstruction of this chapter is impossible because the author wished to avoid anachronism, he maintained that Genesis 49 was a fitting transition from Genesis to Exodus 4.[20] Jacob's holistic defenses of a unified text involved attacking more central pillars of the source criticism than the placement of Genesis 38. On the contrast between Sinai and Horeb, for instance, Jacob argues that Sinai refers almost always to the mountain, while Horeb refers, almost always, to the region. Deuteronomy does not avoid the word *Sinai* out of an ignorance of another source, but out of awe—preferring the term "the mountain" (*ha-har*) for the place of revelation. Is this argument convincing? Possibly not, but it reveals Jacob's desire to emphasize a holistic, noncontradictory reading.

BENNO JACOB'S EXEGETICAL STYLE II: GENEALOGIES AND NUMBER PATTERNS

Benno Jacob's holistic style often relied on paying careful attention to genealogies and counting—verses, weekly portions, scroll breaks, and so on. Jacob was no proponent of pseudoprophetic neofundamentalism—his *Genesis* (1934) was not *The Bible Code*, nor did he engage in *gematria*, relying on the numeric value of Hebrew letters and words. On the contrary, Jacob considered these numerological and genealogical structures exoteric not esoteric, obvious to ancient Israelites, and unjustifiably neglected by modern scholars. Jacob paid close attention to lists, formulas, and numbers as a narrative key. The division of Exodus into two parts—which is suggested by the commonsensical observation that most of the first part of Exodus is narrative and most of the second half legal and tabernacular—Jacob further divided, concluding that there were six equal sections (three in each major part), demonstrable by each having the exact same number of verses. Jacob often did this: take a commonsensical observation about the Bible and see if tabulation of verses or careful scrutiny of same could illuminate an underlying structure and, finally, offer exegetical direction. Thus Benno Jacob rejected the idea that the Bible contains a hopeless contradiction in the number of years of Egyptian exile, given as 430 in Exodus 12:40, and seemingly irreconcilable with other genealogical narratives. For Jacob, "the proper solution was provided by Saadia, Bekhor Shor and Ibn Ezra, who state that the years must be reckoned from the time in which Abraham moved with his father Terah, from Ur to Haran."[21] Genesis 11:31–32, in my own teaching experience, is not a carefully read text, students being eager to start the next weekly portion and the story of Abram proper. But this passage contains the vital information that Terah, not Abram, initiated the migration and that Terah, not Abram, or God, had selected Canaan as a destination. Jacob deployed this passage to indicate that the Samaritan and Septuagint texts were mistaken when they added the phrase "and in Canaan" to Exodus 12:40 in order to reconcile that verse. On the contrary: "The Masoretic text is absolutely clear and unambiguous, and no Israelite reader with any linguistic feeling could have misunderstood it. This has provided us with an excellent example of the misfortune brought about through a mechanical translation without a feeling for the language. One can only regain the lost feeling for language through careful scrutiny of the entire linguistic structure and through precise exegesis."[22] Jacob's preference for the Traditional Text dovetailed with his insistence on internal consistency of the Bible as demonstrated by genealogy, number patterns, and minute differences. Conservative Christians shared this view of Hebraica Veritas, but German-Jewish scholars seem to have taken it as axiomatic. As Henry Wasserman writes:

> [Rudolph] Kittel's original *Biblia Hebraica* [1905–1906] contained no attempts at retranslating the Septuagint, Vulgate and Aramaic translations back into the original. The *Biblia Hebraica* that Kittel offered his colleagues with such bravado was practically identical to the printed Hebrew Bible that conscientious and observant Jews preferred to use, the Jacob ben Chaim version printed in Venice 1524–1525. To the best of our knowledge, with only one exception, German-Jewish periodicals ignored the appearance of *Biblia Hebraica*; this was understandable enough, since it did not constitute a significant advance in biblical scholarship, but only confirmed Jews in their belief that they had been in possession of the authoritative version all along.[23]

To reiterate, Jacob preferred the Traditional Text, but it was not divine nor was it Mosaic. On the structuring of Genesis 1–11, which, obviously occurred before Moses and out of sight or sound of any person, Jacob unambiguously treats the narrative as nonliteral. The genealogies of early Genesis, generally, serve a symbolic function in his view: "The numbers are an artificial construction: this is incontestable regarding the two sets of ten generations from Adam to Abraham. Thus it may be assumed that all such numbers are chosen for certain purposes."[24] Jacob had no problem accepting the modern scholarly unit called the Patriarchal History (Genesis 1–11) in principle. He simply had a healthier regard for the mythopoeic significance of features (number patterns, verb root repetitions, genealogies) that contemporaries regarded as unedifying. For instance, many commentators had noted that the Binding of Isaac (Genesis 22) ended with the seemingly anticlimactic genealogy of Genesis 22:20–24, which included the birth announcement of Rebekah, Isaac's wife. Jacob agreed, sensibly, that Rebekah's birth announcement was the main point of this passage, but also noted that the phrase introducing this paragraph is almost identical to the one introducing the Binding of Isaac narrative as a whole, "achar ha-dvarim ha-eleh" (Genesis 22:1) versus "achar*ei* ha-dvarim ha-eleh" (Genesis 22:20), and also that Milcah's family numbers twelve, as does Ishmael's, and, of course, as do the sons of Jacob/Israel. Jacob's continued this numerological analysis: "The ratio of two to one in the number of children of the main wife, to those of the concubine is similar to the ratio of the children of the wives and concubines of Jacob."[25] All of this, one might object, is picayune, and I would not like to leave the impression that Jacob fails to expound the main part of the Binding of Isaac movingly and with erudition—he does. Jacob's originality can often be found in integrating passages such as these genealogical ones—uninteresting to source critics.

BENNO JACOB'S EXEGETICAL STYLE III: BIBLE AND BABYLON IN JEWISH EYES

Jacob may have been the first modern Jewish Bible scholar to fully acknowledge ancient Near Eastern parallels, while insisting on their inferiority to the biblical version:

> Of foreign creation myths only the Babylonia one is suitable for comparison. It is a poem named "Enuma Elish" according to its opening words. The Biblical story of creation is vastly superior. In the Babylonian myth the creation is only a side theme: its interest is not in the earth, but in the heavens and the gods. Man is created to serve the gods and as the sacrifices naturally go to the priests, this means serving the priests. In the first chapter of Genesis the story of creation does not lead up to Jerusalem, the Temple, and the sacrificial service, but to man as such and his dignity and all creation is encompassed with love.[26]

> The Israelite concept of divinely revealed laws was as radical as the original creation ex nihilo. Just as the latter was not dared by any philosophy or cosmology, so no legal system attempted the former, for it did not have the sanction of God of the Torah.[27]

Jacob's comments constitute more than a response to Friedrich Delitzsch and his ilk. Rather, he recognized the challenge to defend the special nature of the Bible over and against the other ancient Near Eastern texts. The Code of Hammurabi, preserved in many languages and spread out over many lands, was clearly a more important and more ancient text than the Bible—and therefore problematic for any non-Orthodox Christian or Jew. Jacob's solution would satisfy a few generations of Jewish readers: the Egyptians and Mesopotamians may have been first, but we were best. This theme of the presence of ancient analogues that only reinforce the superiority of Torah helped fashion the modern Jewish Bible. Different figures emphasized different aspects: religious, national, and ethical. This move, rightly called supersessionist, served as a means of affirming superiority without affirming divine revelation. It is an apologetic theme, and one that reappears in the works of Cassuto, Kaufmann, Sarna, and Moshe Greenberg.

Jacob's acknowledgment of the newly discovered external controls on the Bible did not mean that Jacob considered it a historicist text. As to the historicity of the patriarchs, Jacob is still far from the Albright-Speiser school of trying to use the ancient Near East analogues to prove specific details about patriarchal society. Like Mendelssohn, Jacob contented himself with the basic historicity of the story. As long as the Bible was preserved from being treated as purely mythological, Jacob did not agonize—the message of the Scripture, not its historicity, gave it ultimate importance. This tendency would come to characterize modern Jewish Bible studies: while a reading of the Bible as straight history was gradually abandoned under the weight of scholarly advances, a distinct desire to hold on to a kernel of historical reality remains, even today, a prevalent Jewish impulse. Consider the scathing attacks on the minimalist school, the defenses of Israelite historiography as in no whit inferior to Greco-Roman, and the resistance to abandoning a kernel of historicity for the Egyptian exodus. Like Moses Mendelssohn, Jacob affirmed biblical historicity without making it the main topic of discussion. Take a look at the difference between the following two passages from Jacob, the first dealing with a historical issue, the second with the overall message of the patriarchal cycle (Genesis 12–36):

> Some have doubted that the Patriarchs were historical. It is not our task to examine this question. The conditions reported however agree surprisingly well with the cultural conditions of the Near East as discovered by archaeology. The patriarchs could indeed have lived in this period.
>
> If the narrative of the patriarchs of the people of Israel is to be understood according to the original intent, it must be viewed with the eyes of a son of this people for whom it was first written. The following main ideas must be remembered while reading it. The ancestral fathers are not the ultimate theme of the stories, but rather the God of the fathers; the God of Abraham who remained the God of Isaac and then became the God of Jacob. He proved himself to three successive generations; therefore their descendents possess the certainty of his unchanging faithfulness and love for all generations in the most remote future.[28]

Jacob accepts the patriarchal cycle as different from what came before the primeval history (Genesis 1–11) and afterward in the Joseph story (Genesis 37–50). On the one hand, Jacob's holism involved rejecting assigning different parts of a single chapter to different authors, rejecting doublets (seeming repetition of narratives or parts of narrative), and stressing the interconnectedness of the parts of Scripture and the overall animating spirit of the author. Jacob proudly trumpeted the fact only Jews still read from a scroll: "which they still today read in the original."[29] On the other hand, Jacob accepted as settled scholarship that Moses did not write the whole Pentateuch: indeed, in Jacob's view, this view was never stated by Torah at all, making it truthful, though not literally a divinely dictated text. Jacob also accepted the major narrative divisions within Genesis, divisions generally unimportant to the exegetical style of rabbinic Judaism. In other words, Midrash evidences no inclination whatsoever to treat Genesis 1–11, Genesis 12–36, and Genesis 37–50 as different kinds/genres of texts requiring different principles of interpretation. Since Torah all came from God via Moses, this position was a given. For Jacob, however, as for the majority of modern scholars, Genesis divides into primeval history, patriarchal cycle, and the Joseph narrative. All of Genesis was bound together, but each of these three major divisions demanded a somewhat different approach. But the canonical coherence of the Jewish Bible as a whole seemed obvious. In a *Jewish Encyclopedia* entry on "Hexateuch" Jacob wrote: "These contentions . . . would not be sufficient to undermine the independence and completeness of the Pentateuch, evident throughout its entire composition, and verified by an uncontradicted tradition which goes back to Biblical times. The Torah has never been connected with the book of Joshua, and has always constituted the first part of the Bible, in contradistinction to the two other parts."[30]

BENNO JACOB'S EXEGETICAL STYLE IV: RECOVERING THE JEWISH BIBLE

While Jacob famously protested that, "Our Bible is no longer our Bible," what he really meant was that contemporary scholarship maliciously engaged in an act of disinheritance. In truth, Jacob believed firmly that our Bible would always be our Bible:

> But for us, the Bible is a book of life, and we, therefore, need our own Jewish Bible scholarship, so that it opens new sources of life to us. We need a Biblical scholarship that does not merely establish what is right, but rather, "refreshes the soul," is not merely true, but "makes the fool wise," is not merely correct, but "gladdens the heart," is not merely pure, "but illuminates the eyes." Only such research is adequate for the true nature of the Bible, and thus without any sidelong glances, only the Jew can understand the Bible. Only the Jew is a spirit of its spirit, only he has remained unwaveringly loyal and has never broken the connection to it.[31]

Jacob believed that Jewishness, manifested in a continuous tradition of reading from the scroll, using Hebrew, avoiding a perspective which regarded the Pentateuch as a springboard for something greater (read: Christianity's use of the New Testament), and feeling part of *b'nei yisrael*, his preferred terminology, conferred a decided advantage exegetically. "[The Bible] must be viewed with the eyes of a son of this people for whom it was first written."[32] Most Christian scholars, to their detriment, had chosen to neglect the Jewish tradition, "so full of fine exegetical traditions." Christianity's break with the Hebrew Bible, in Jacob's eyes, led to exegetical errors. On Genesis 15:6, Jacob wrote, "Abraham is definitely reassured by God's answer to his timid protest. He trusts God who replies, 'I shall remember this.'" Jacob's comment: "The verse has no relation to the dogma of 'justification by faith.'" Every instance of New Testament divergence from the Hebrew Bible's simple sense, every time the New Testament assumes an Old Testament, in other words, everywhere Christianity is itself, it has broken with the Hebrew Bible. Is Jacob's attitude not as unfair as the converse view, that Jews do not fulfill Scripture because they lack Jesus Christ as an interpretive key? To a twenty-first-century monotheist, especially one who accepts multiple covenants, this view is patently intolerant: Jews, Christians, and Muslims all enjoy a covenantal relationship with God grounded in Scripture. In Benno Jacob's point of view, as for many of his Jewish successors, willingness to affirm rabbinic tradition as *a* guide but not *the* guide allowed him to place Judaism closer to the Bible than Christianity. Or at least closer to its "spirit," since the practice of Reform Judaism and ancient Israelite religion could hardly be more different. This differed from the Zionist argument that emphasizes an unbroken historical-national epic, a claim to possess Scripture found in Heinrich Graetz, Ahad Haam, and David Ben-Gurion, among others. But both groups, diaspora and Zionist, wind up in the same place. The Bible belongs first and foremost to the Jew. Biblical language itself favored the familial aspect of Israel's identity, and for this reason Jacob consistently referred to *b'nei yisrael* rather than "Jews."

I conclude by submitting two diametrically opposing views of his biblical contributions. The first, John Van Seters, a pioneer of biblical minimalism, credited Jacob with being one of the fathers of modern Jewish Bible scholarship, but this is damning with faint praise. Van Seters found the Genesis commentary unscientific and colonialist (Van Seters mistakenly considered Jacob to be a Zionist).

> Jacob's method of exegesis may be illustrated by a few examples. Thus in the case of the text in Gen 6:1–4, which deals with sexual intercourse between the "sons of God" and mortal women, Jacob renders the problematic phrase "sons of God" as the "divine ones" and explains that they "were like God in their own eyes, and yet of a very earthly humanity" (p. 45). This leads him

to suggest that the origin of the giants has nothing to do with the divinity of the "sons of God" but with the women who are described as "strong" rather than "beautiful." Furthermore, the age limit of 120 years that is imposed by the deity on the offspring of such a union reminds Jacob of the fact that Moses, "a man of God," lived until 120 years old, so that he becomes one of these "divine ones," and the same applies to Elijah another "man of God," although his age is never specifically given. The whole discussion of this unit becomes a complex interconnection of biblical texts, a fanciful intertextuality that is typical of the rabbinic tradition of midrash.

Van Seters did not mean this last line as a compliment. The whole tone of his review exudes a scholarly doyen's dismissive attitude toward an outsider.

The second verdict on Jacob's legacy, from Wilhelm Schwendemann, agrees with Van Seters regarding Jacob's importance to modern Jewish Bible scholarship, but reverses Van Seters's judgment of Jacob's exegetical worth. Jacob would have been gratified to learn that the minority opinion among Christians in his day regarding Jewish exegetical tradition has become, if not normative, at the least the majority sentiment: "What is special about Jacob's exegesis is the connection of a linguistic-scientific interest with the fact that the First Testament, the belief-basis of ancient Judaism, was equally significant for today's Jewish community and for Christianity alike. Exegesis, that is, the methodological interpretation of the Bible, not only satisfies a scientific, archaeological or historical-critical interest and curiosity, but rather, stands in service of the pronouncement of God's Word in Jewish and Christian community practice and spirituality."[33]

BENNO JACOB'S EXEGETICAL STYLE: NOAH

This note strikes me as an appropriate one to end on: Jacob was a polemical figure, but he had little opportunity not to be, given his correct assessment of the scholarship of his day and his desire to be much more than a traditional *darshan*—a biblical sermonizer. Jacob pursued Jewish biblical scholarship, and if I have emphasized only the negative aspect of that mission, I have inadvertently misled my readers. Jacob believed firmly that one could make objective and demonstrable claims about the biblical text—he was far more positivistic in this regard than were Buber and Rosenzweig, not to mention contemporary Bible scholars. Following the Maimonidean dictum to accept the truth whatever the source, Jacob was quite open to Christian scholarship when it approached the Scripture with the same mix of reverence and acuity that he himself possessed. Let us take a look at Jacob's sympathetic reading of Noah, a flawed figure in rabbinic eyes. Any evaluation cognizant of the Jewish tradition must begin with Genesis 6:9, a verse Jacob rendered, "Noah was a righteous man blameless *in his generations*." Although rabbinic opinion was divided, the majority considered this phrase derogatory: relative to complete sinners worthy of destruction, Noah was blameless; relative to Abraham, he was not impressive. Jacob acknowledged that both perspectives were defensible, but noted that Noah was one of the three famous men who can save sinners by their piety (along with Daniel and Job, as mentioned in Ezekiel 14:14), and that Noah was further distinguished by being the only antediluvian and postdiluvian character worthy of a genealogical list. Most important, in Jacob's eyes, Noah constituted a vast improvement over Adam: "Men righteous before God, did not arise in Israel alone; they are descended from one perfectly righteous man from whom all nations are derived [Noah]. Mankind shall find its higher moral unity not in Adam, the natural man, but in that pious father who by his offering brought about God's gracious resolution to preserve the world."[34] Jacob's approach to Noah and the flood may be termed both maximalist and holistic. Noah is a fully drawn character and the flood is a coherent story. Unlike source critics who consider Genesis 6–9 a composite of J and P, Jacob saw one story. Noah sent the dove out as a messenger, but the raven as a banner of celebration. The dove is the more beautiful bird, but the raven is the more intelligent and faithful—Noah's raven is the ancestor of the raven who will feed the prophet Elijah at the brook of Cherith (I Kings 17:4). The two birds in the Noah story do not result from poor editing of two sources: they are distinct creatures with distinct missions, meanings, and narrative functions. This type of Bible reading, assuming a perfectly constructed text, would not satisfy the source critics. Their type of Bible reading, assuming a terribly patched together text, did not satisfy Jacob.

5

The Martin Buber–Franz Rosenzweig Bible
Culture or Religion?

The intellectual collaboration of Martin Buber (1878–1965) and Franz Rosenzweig (1886–1929) as Bible translators is the most celebrated in modern Jewish thought. For the purposes of this chapter, however, it has seemed simplest for me to introduce Buber first, then the Buber-Rosenzweig Bible, and finally, to add a few words about Rosenzweig. For anyone likely to be reading this book, neither needs a lengthy introduction. Buber was arguably the widest read and most influential Jewish thinker of the twentieth century. Aside from Abraham Joshua Heschel, he is the only Jewish thinker in this era to have exerted a deep impact on Christian theologians. Buber gained fame early as a Zionist activist, interpreter of Hasidism, and the author of *I and Thou*, a classic in modern religious thought. He played a laudable role bolstering German-Jewish morale in the Nazi era, and took an unpopular and controversial left-wing stand on the Arab-Jewish conflict after he moved to Israel. Having grown up in an enlightened but traditional Galician household, Buber wound up as one of the great advocates for creative Jewish religiosity—neither Orthodox nor Reform.

Rosenzweig, whose life was cut tragically short by ALS (amyotrophic lateral sclerosis), traveled in a different direction, beginning life as a son of the acculturated German-Jewish bourgeoisie. Rosenzweig seriously considered conversion to Christianity, but had a conversionary experience in 1913 that drove him to reclaim an unknown intellectual heritage, although most of his family and friends were either Jews or Jews who had recently converted to Christianity. Rosenzweig spent the prewar years advancing his academic and Jewish qualifications, the latter under the guidance of philosopher Hermann Cohen. During World War I, Rosenzweig drafted his *The Star of Redemption* on German army postcards. After the war, Rosenzweig married and turned his efforts to adult Jewish education, creating the Free Jewish Lehrhaus in Frankfurt am Main, which he led until incapacitated by his illness. Among academics, Rosenzweig's writings on culture, translational theory, sickness, and health are seen as a vital link between existentialism and postmodernism. Both figures have generated enormous scholarship and numerous debates. To fully discuss the role of Scripture for either thinker would require books, not paragraphs. What follows is no attempt at a comprehensive or original assessment of either man, but rather simply an attempt to clarify their role in the making of the modern Jewish Bible.

DER MENSCH VON HEUTE UND DIE JÜDISCHE BIBEL

Martin Buber's 1925 address "Der Mensch von heute und die jüdische Bibel," published in 1936, has been translated two ways, both of them problematic. Nahum Glatzer's collection of Buber's essays, *On the Bible*, opted for "The Man of Today and the Jewish Bible." Everett Fox, who retranslated it, included some particularly stunning examples of exegesis. Fox noted that *Mensch* means human—Glatzer had inadvertently introduced a sexist tone the original lacked. But Fox lost on the curve what he gained on the roundabout. His rendering, "*People* Today and the Jewish Bible," turns the singular first word into a plural, thereby blurring Buber's insistence that the Bible calls forth to every individual in his or her uniqueness. Buber delivered his address shortly after the completion of *I and Thou*, and evidences an early application of the powerful insight in that book, which began as a series of lectures titled "Religion as Presence." The dialogical philosophy expounded in *I and Thou* marked a final departure from Buber's early mysticism (*Erlebnismystik*), constituting a clear "before or after" marker in Buber's significant opus. Not coincidentally, the notion of a divine voice which could be heard via an encounter with the biblical text in its immediacy allowed Buber to return to a text he studied as a youth with his learned grandfather but had jettisoned as an adolescent, although Buber never returned to traditional Jewish practice.[1]

I consider Buber's lecture among the most important in the making of the modern Jewish Bible, and teach it whenever I have the chance. It addresses, with admirable frankness, the challenge of reading Bible meaningfully in an era of doubt, when the Bible's sanctity seemed increasingly on the wane. I always begin with this question: Why "the Person" but "the *Jewish* Bible," rather than the "*Jewish* Human" and "the Bible"? My students answer the question of what makes the Bible *Jewish* with a slew of great answers: It is written and read in Hebrew—the original and still-living language used by the Jewish people. It is read from a scroll.

It is read with Hebrew-language commentators. It deals with the Jewish people and contains the most significant chapter of their history. It contains many of the names that the Jewish people still give their children—though not always and not exclusively. It deals with the geography, topography, flora, and fauna of Israel. It contains the core values of Israelite society and subsequent Judaism. It contains the commandments of Israel and Judaism. It is the basis of all subsequent Jewish literature. It mandates Judaism's calendar (Shabbat, holidays, etc.). It is the entire revelation of Judaism and admits of no other testament, that is, the Jewish Bible is not the Christian Bible. All these answers are perfectly correct; none of them are at the core of what Buber meant by "Jewish Bible."

My answer is something like this—the more authentically Jewish, the more authentically human. For many Jews, that which is most distinctive and unlike non-Jewish culture, society, or religion appears the most Jewish. That which is shared by all humanity—let us say, along with Buber, religious yearnings in general—or the particulars of a historical situation, let us say, being middle-class Americans, must be less Jewish. According to this logic, American Jews must be less Jewish than eastern European Jews because they share so much with other Americans. Buber would reject this position. Buber believed in romantic nationalism and the power of roots as forces channeling individual and national development, but the human condition preceded all particulars. For Buber, the Bible contained a power to reach one and all. Buber rejected the idea that one required a particular religious orientation to receive that divine word. Buber, a popularizer of Eastern religion, held the Bible had the power to speak to a Hindu or a Buddhist as well as to a Westerner—whether that Westerner practiced traditional religion or not, since Buber clearly intended to include nonbelievers and agnostics as his targets in this essay. Hence the first part of the title should be human, not Jewish human.

Why then "*Jewish* Bible"? Buber advanced two arguments. First, a singular voice animated the whole biblical corpus. By this, Buber did not mean that the literary differences between prophecy and poetry, narrative and law were negligible. Nor did he mean to take issue with those who insisted that the Bible came from several hands and from several centuries. One of the things that makes this essay, and Buber-Rosenzweig's collaboration, so impressive, is their side stepping of these scholarly debates to grapple with a "live" religious question, to borrow William James's wonderful term: How to hear the voice of God via the hearing of Scripture? Instead of thinking of the direction of Scripture as flowing only from author to reader, they also considered the flow from reader to author. The whole Bible could be the portal for the person who sincerely sought it. Second, everything narrated in the Bible took place within the life of the people—the people Israel. By this, Buber meant that the encounter between God and Israel is narrated as encounter, as history. The Hebrew Bible provided laws, and these dealt with the fleshly, material issues of life: sex, money, relations, religion, and so on. But the Hebrew Bible is not a set of abstract formulas divorced from life, nor is it a triumph of hothouse ethics, of breathlessly awaiting the Messiah by trying to emulate his saintly standard of behavior. For these reasons, then, the Bible was the *Jewish* Bible.

Buber's essay dealt with an eminently practical question: How should the modern person read the Bible? Or, more precisely, can the modern person read the Bible? For Buber, to pick the Bible up and read it as great literature is "merely" literary reading. To read the Bible as history, to pick the Bible up and read it as a great narrative, is "merely" historical reading. To read the Bible for ethical instruction, for pungent proverbs, is "merely" homiletical reading. None of this is reading the Bible as it demands to be read—as the word of the living God. As Everett Fox notes, both the translation and Buber's essays on the Bible are the product of "an essentially religious mentality."[2] Since the modern person, in Buber's view, lived in crisis and alienation, this failure to read the Bible properly meant, "They thus cripple the power that of all existing powers would most likely suffice to deliver them."[3] Reading the Bible properly must mean reading with the intent to hear God's word. But how can the skeptic do this? How can any person in the rational, utilitarian world we inhabit really read the Bible in this fashion? Buber's answer is disarmingly simple: read the Bible as if you have never read it before, as if you do not have a prejudged idea of its contents.

Buber also used this programmatic essay to offer a demonstration of dialogical exegesis. Taking the Hebrew word *ruah*, which first appears in Genesis 1:2, "And the spirit/breath of God hovered over the waters," Buber demonstrated that translating the Hebrew word *ruah* either as "breath" or as "spirit" fails to capture the original sense, which always contains both meanings, though not equally in every case. Buber's solution here (and the Buber-Rosenzweig Bible offers dozens of examples of such neologisms) is to coin a new German word, *Windbraus*, which does contain both ideas, and then use it every time *ruah* appears. This method would alert the reader to the originally oral/aural nature of the text, which was critical to Buber and Rosenzweig, as it had been to Mendelssohn, Hirsch, and Jacob. In each case, this oral/aural nature is conceived somewhat differently. Buber, for instance, was influenced by the Scandinavian school, which likened the development of the Bible to that of Norse myths. This viewpoint has receded in the academy; the later sources (P and D) had earlier *written* texts at their disposal. But that has been a subsequent development: Buber believed the hearing of the text should influence its interpretation, though when breaking up their translations into spoken units, Buber and Rosenzweig felt free to diverge from rabbinic vocalization and from biblical parallelism. The overall effect, in

Seidman's view, was resistance to the separation of consonant and vowel: an agenda that was both intrinsically Jewish and authentically human.[4]

Buber's other exegetical example in this essay, which followed midrashic insights (Buber's grandfather, Solomon Buber, pioneered the modern study of Midrash), read the completion of the Tabernacle in Exodus 39–40 as a sort of re-creation, completed this time by human rather than by divine hands. Buber found honor/weightiness (*kavod*), finished/finishing (*kilah*), and creative work (*malachah*) "theme words" that linked the completion of Creation with that of the Tabernacle. Buber frequently used the repetition of certain words and the similarity of word choice in multiple passages to infer teachings that the Bible offered suggestively rather than explicitly. Buber and Rosenzweig would dub this method of interpretation "theme words" (*Leitwortstil*), and it has exerted tremendous influence on biblical interpreters over the last several decades. In "Abraham the Seer," Buber identified the various forms of the verb "to see" as a key to understanding Abraham's role as the first prophet. To the objection that the most common biblical word for prophet (*navi*) is nowhere used for Abraham, Buber cited I Samuel 9:9b: "Formerly in Israel, when a man went to inquire of God, he would say, 'Come, let us go to the Seer, for the prophet of today was formerly called a seer.'" Seer, *ro'eh*, has the same three-letter root as "to see." This prooftext, to use a term more associated with rabbinic literature than biblical scholarship, served Buber's goal of elevating Abraham to prophetic rank, which, for Buber, stood as the highest exemplar of biblical leadership. Some, such as Harvard's James Kugel, have pointed out how forced this method of *Leitwortstil* can be, but Buber's ultimate goal was not "proving" something in an academic sense, but suggestively teasing out the message of Scripture. As Scholem noted, Buber's Bible reading, at the end of the day, was spiritual, not historical.[5]

James Muilenburg questioned Buber and Rosenzweig's dramatic choice to render the Tetragrammaton with capitalized personal pronouns (YOU, HE, HIM). This choice, the subject of endless scholarly discussion, was animated by their rejection of Mendelssohn's overly philosophical "The Eternal," Luther's overly Christian alternative ("Der Herr"), and, most of all, the desire to make the dialogical moment between God and the reader a continuous possibility. But, as Muilenburg complained, the prophet's use of the Tetragrammaton contains a terrifyingly specific, even tyrannical view of YHVH, not at all compatible with Buber-Rosenzweig's famous translation of Exodus 3:14, "*eheye asher eheye*," "I will be there howsoever I will be there," which emphasized the dialogical nature of the divine-human encounter and the changing nature of God in each and every encounter. Now, as the most influential interpreter of Hasidism in Western Europe, Buber surely knew the mystical traditions which do posit the possibility of human influence on the divine. These traditions, however, were medieval, not biblical, and moreover, were opposed by an equally strong philosophical position that emphasized God's unchanging nature. One can find this tension even in the same worship service: on Friday nights, Jews sing both "Lecha Dodi" (position one) and "Adon Olam" (position two). Everett Fox, his championing of Buber-Rosenzweig notwithstanding, opted for YHWH as the best way to render the Tetragrammaton, to my mind a sensible retreat from the radical position of the 1930 edition of the Buber-Rosenzweig Bible, which used only capitalized pronouns for God's names.[6]

Should one evaluate Buber as a Bible scholar at all? Few German Jews served as professional Bible scholars. Buber had to struggle even to win appointment as a Judaica lecturer/professor at Frankfurt in 1924—when he was thirty-eight years old and world famous. One could legitimately narrow the field of "makers of the modern Jewish Bible" to full-time Bible professionals, but that is not the story I want to tell. On the other hand, unlike Freud, whose foray into Bible led to the disappointing *Moses and Monotheism*, Buber had an impact on other Bible scholars, Jewish and Christian. As Everett Fox sagely noted, Buber's mode of analysis anticipated much of the contemporary modes of literary criticism. As Steven Kepnes has argued, Buber read deeply in the scholarly literature, knew Scripture, and understood Hebrew and Jewish commentary; he was no mere interloper.[7] Muilenburg concluded his tribute to Buber as follows: "He, more than any other Jewish scholar of our time, has opened the Scriptures of the Old Covenant for the Christian community. Without an understanding of and appreciation of the Old Covenant, the Scriptures of the New Covenant must remain forever closed."[8] Ernest Wolf offered yet another perspective: "Under the influence of Buber's biblical humanism and under the impact of the new Bible translation, the study of biblical sources became a major preoccupation of German Jewry, particularly of the youth. Had the young generation of Jews that went through the Buber-Rosenzweig school of Bible reading and interpreting had been permitted to grow up, they would probably have become the most Bible-conscious Jews since the days before the ghetto walls had fallen in Europe."[9]

Is Buber's a Jewish interpretation of the Bible? This question may be superfluous for anyone who considers Jewish upbringing, learning, and demonstrable influence on subsequent Jewry as evidence enough, especially when coupled with an insistence on the unity of the Jewish Bible and a critique of Christianity. Buber, moreover, had a consciously "dissimilationist" agenda in his Hasidic writings, Zionist activism, and Bible works. This dissimilationist tendency in his Bible translation, first identified by Plaut, has been generally reinforced by subsequent scholarship. Like any good countercultural figure, Buber pushes back against his times; like any self-aware member of a colonized people, Buber shows an instinct to resist. Perhaps I am giving the question of Buber's Jewish credentials more credence than it deserves. But since Chaim Potok charged that Buber "spoke" to Christians more than to Jews, a few words of rebuttal may be in order. Potok correctly pegs Buber as a dissenter from traditional Judaism whose view of revelation is not compatible with a normative view of the commandments.[10] Buber may have liberated Judaism from the spell of Kant, as Rosenzweig said in praise, but Buber did not do so in order to champion autonomy over heteronomy, or turn to neo-Orthodoxy. Buber's view of the Bible, which Potok basically ignored, acknowledged that much in Scripture gives offense to modern readers.[11] Yet Buber insisted on the unity of Scripture. "The Bible: such is the name of a book that is the book of books. But it is in reality one book."[12] Rosenzweig elaborated this commitment to one book in a letter to Jacob Rosenheim, an important leader of German Orthodoxy. In the course of reflecting on the affinities between their translation and Samson Raphael Hirsch's, despite their ideological differences, Rosenzweig remarked: "We too translate the Torah as one book. For us too it is a work of a single mind. We do not know who this mind was; we cannot believe that was Moses. We name that mind among ourselves by the abbreviation with which the higher criticism of the Bible indicates its presumed final; redactor of the text: R. We, however, take this R to stand not for the redactor but for Rabbenu. For whoever he was, and whatever text lay before him, he is our teacher, and theology is our teaching."[13] For Buber and Rosenzweig the spoken word (*Mikra*) got recorded as Scripture (*Schrift*), but spokenness (*Gesprochenheit*) came first. Nevertheless, their Scripture—the basis of all exegesis and commentary— was that of the Masoretes. On this point, Buber stands solidly in the line of modern Jewish Bible students, including Mendelssohn, Hirsch, Jacob, and almost all others. Like them, his merits as an academic scholar may be disputed, but not his role as a maker of the modern Jewish Bible. Resistance to source criticism was not the monopoly of Jewish Bible scholars. Conservative Protestants quarreled with it; Catholic scholars generally found it deplorable. But there were particular Jewish tendencies which emerged again and again. These tendencies were conditioned by the particular historical context of German Jews—they were not "essentially" Jewish.

BUBER AND ROSENZWEIG AS TRANSLATORS

The Buber-Rosenzweig original 1925 edition included no commentary and placed tiny chapter and verse notations at the top right of the page, all in an effort to avoid interposing between the reader and the text. The 1930 edition introduced a more traditional chapter and verse notation, as readers found their first edition nearly unusable, but otherwise moved in an even more radical translational direction. Abigail Gillman rightly calls attention to the amount of white on the page, so unlike the traditional rabbinic Bible, with its profusion of words crushed onto the page. Their

Bible was surely not intended as a Chumash, although as Ernest Wolf indicated, it wound up being used that way by a young generation of German Jews. Buber never fully recovered from his youthful goal to extract the true spirit of Judaism from the "rubble of rabbinism." But Buber and Rosenzweig's conscious intention was not denominational—they wished to remove the layers of tradition, which they referred to as a palimpsest, the layers of painting covering an original masterpiece. They wanted the modern Jew to read without Rashi, but also without any translational skewing of the Hebrew original. Their posture was equally antagonistic toward the Aramaic translation Onkelos (assigned a positive religious status in traditional Judaism) and toward the Latin Vulgate of Jerome. As Buber recounted, it was the experience of reading a translation (Leopold Zunz's, also the Rosenzweig family's Bible) that led to his disenchantment with Bible as the living word. Their very hostility toward translation in principle gave the Buber-Rosenzweig translation its motive force. Rejection, then—of translation, of commentary, of rabbinic interjection—all were important. But their rejection of the Luther Bible—even more consequential to German language, culture, and politics than the King James was to English—gave Buber and Rosenzweig their single most powerful push as they commenced their project. As Buber recounted it years later, Rosenzweig had initially insisted that no German translation could be free of Luther; he suggested they begin their work on that assumption, and admitted after one failed attempt that a fresh start was required. Rosenzweig devoted an entire essay, "Scripture and Luther," to their declaration of independence. Luther had successfully fused the Hebrew Bible into a German, Protestant, Old Testament mold—a modern Golden Calf. Buber and Rosenzweig set out to smash it.[14]

A few other unique features of this unique translation bear mention: They titled their original 1925 edition of Genesis "In the Beginning" (*Im Anfang*), following the ancient Near Eastern and subsequent Jewish tradition of calling a book by its opening words, rather than by its major theme (e.g., genesis). They kept the biblical names as close to the Hebrew original as they could, rather than the usual German equivalents (e.g., Moshe/Aharon/Rivka), although it should be noted that they were not the first German-Jewish translators to Hebraize proper nouns—though, of course, *only* Jewish translators did this at all. As mentioned above, they paid careful attention to the oral nature of the text. The Bible was a "calling out" (*Mikra*) before it was Scripture. Also discussed, but worth repeating, they used repeating words (*Leitwortstil*) to draw out spiritual lessons, characterize persons, and link distant chapters, all in a very holistic move that regarded the Bible as one book. While the technique seems literary, in the end the message (*Botschaft*) both men sought should be termed religious, although in a way that transcended the denominational-institutional options of their own day. The Buber-Rosenzweig Bible has found many perceptive analysts, and even in its own day attracted considerable critical attention. Much of it was hostile: the cultural critic Siegfried Kracauer despised its neo-Romantic tones, finding it very much like a Richard Wagner opus without the music. Wilhelm Stapeln, a right-wing scholar, took exception to their penchant for neologisms and, predictably, accused them of Judaizing the German language. On the other hand, many readers, from Orthodox to avant-garde, praised their work. Scholem, who considered their Bible an epitaph to the German-Jewish experience, perceptively acknowledged their achievement in keeping the difficult passages difficult, and the foreign passages foreign, most decidedly one of their goals. Young German Jews, in Michael Brenner's judgment, "were convinced that the Buber-Rosenzweig Bible constituted a document that was particularly theirs. They could understand it because it was written in German, and they could claim that it was essentially Jewish because its German language differed substantially from accepted norms."[15]

We have already cited Ernest Wolf's moving testimony to the impact of the Buber-Rosenzweig Bible on the spiritual seekers of the 1920s to 1930s. Buber and Rosenzweig believed that the Hebrew Bible was the great repository of the ur-Jewish, and that they succeeded in building a bridge from German back to Hebrew. But Maren Ruth Niehoff, adumbrated by Kracauer and Brenner (all native German speakers), thinks too much has been made of the "Hebraic" nature of the translation. She argues that their translation was influenced somewhat by the traditional Jewish exegetical tradition, somewhat more so by contemporary Jewish Wissenschaft and sympathetic Christian Bible scholars, but most of all by German neo-Romanticism. Niehoff convinces more with regard to intellectual origins, less so with regard to intent or impact. Buber's and Rosenzweig's use of Midrash and medieval commentary did not determine their translation to the extent that it determined those of Mendelssohn or Hirsch, but they did give this tradition a voice it did not enjoy anywhere outside the Jewish world. It is clear from Niehoff's own evidence that Buber and Rosenzweig felt reassured when they had rabbinic backing. Their affinity for Hirsch, Jacob, and other dissenters from the source critics also had a Jewish valence, *as they understood it*. Niehoff underestimates their attempt, however faulty, to make the Hebrew word speak from the text. She considers it ironic—but mistaken—that the Buber-Rosenzweig translation is considered a particularly "Hebrew" rendering. But not only did Buber and Rosenzweig think they were deliberately Hebraizing German, so did many of their contemporaries. Niehoff's acute analysis of their translational method, based on the unpublished correspondence of Buber and Rosenzweig, cannot be gainsaid; they were more Germanic than they realized.[16] But this view undervalues authorial intent, audience reception, and subsequent impact: it is difficult to imagine the opening pages of Soloveitchik's *The Lonely Man of Faith*, Nehama Leibowitz's *Studies*, or Robert Alter's *The Art of Biblical*

Narrative, without Buber-Rosenzweig. They were accepted as makers of the modern Jewish Bible—and so they are.¹⁷

FRANZ ROSENZWEIG AND THE RECOVERY OF TRADITION

Having discussed Buber at such length, and having already treated their epochal translation, I am in danger of slighting Rosenzweig's contributions. This risk is magnified by the fact that as a team Buber and Rosenzweig made it only to Isaiah; Buber completed the rest of Prophets and Writings in 1961. Moreover, Buber did the lion's share of the actual translation, though they communicated almost daily by post and Buber visited the incapacitated Rosenzweig weekly to check page proofs. The title pages of their Bible read, "Translated by Martin Buber together with Franz Rosenzweig," a caption that aggravated several of Rosenzweig's admirers. But Buber insisted on Rosenzweig's collaboration when the former was first approached by the innovative publisher Lambert Schneider in April 1924. Schneider had a deep interest in interfaith dialogue and had been impressed by Buber's works in this area, especially *Die Kreatur*, a truly novel effort to publish an interdenominational journal edited by a Protestant, a Catholic, and a Jew. Ironically, then, Schneider, a Christian publisher, initiated the most creative Jewish intellectual collaboration of the modern era. Scholem gave tribute to the fanaticism with which Rosenzweig pursued Jewish learning, and although nobody has contradicted Scholem on that point, more needs to be said about its cognitive dimensions. Scholars have focused on Rosenzweig's spiritual journey and his "hygiene of return" back to an "authentic Jewish life," but not enough on his acquisition of Jewish literacy.

From Mara Benjamin's *Rosenzweig's Bible*, we now know that Rosenzweig developed a view of Bible stretching from his *Star of Redemption* to his last days, including translations from the prayer book, which Rosenzweig had pronounced untranslatable, and from the poet-philosopher Yehuda Halevi, whose writings deeply influenced Mendelssohn, Hirsch, and Rosenzweig. Benjamin rightly identifies his early essay "Atheistic Theology" as an appeal to Scripture as a response to the crisis of historicism. Benjamin writes, "The unapologetic theism of the images and metaphors drawn from the liturgy and the Hebrew Bible implicitly rebuke the 'atheism' of liberal theology."¹⁸ In fact, between "Atheistic Theology" and *Star of Redemption*, we have another excellent example of Rosenzweig's growing interest in Scripture: his educational plan for Jewish youth in German public schools. "It Is Time" (1917) placed an enormous emphasis on learning prayer book and Torah, at the expense of the creedal emphasis found in Reform and at the expense of the rabbinic learning found in traditional Jewish societies. In his rigorously laid out curriculum, Rosenzweig dictated: "The study of the commentary of Rashi will now [year 4] be added to that of the Torah; of course here too, only selections can be taught. Rashi, the great and popular commentator who transmitted to the second millennium of the Exile the vast treasure of the first, will gradually introduce the student into the spiritual world of the Talmud and Midrash—a world which, even in our own times, has greater influence on Jewish character than we know or admit."[19]

Reading the Torah, mastering biblical Hebrew, learning to read from the unvocalized text, and linking Torah with the Jewish calendar all received priority in Rosenzweig's detailed curriculum. Notably, he saw Rashi's commentary on the Torah as a sufficient conduit to Talmud. Rosenzweig meant the aggadic sections of the Talmud—he could not have meant the mastering of Talmudic argument, largely legal-halachic and certainly not learnable from Rashi's linear Torah commentary. Even Haftarot and Psalms take precedent over the Babylonian Talmud, which required "a glimpse" (*Einblick*) before graduation. Anyone familiar with rabbinic literature will find this comment amusing: a glimpse at a page of Talmud is about as meaningful as a technophobe's glimpse at high-level computer program. Unlike Buber, who grew up grounded in Bible and Hebrew, Rosenzweig possessed a convert's fanaticism for acquiring what he previously lacked—in 1913, the year of his Yom Kippur epiphany, Rosenzweig's Greek and Latin were surely better than his Hebrew. Although he studied Talmud with Rabbi Nehemiah Nobel, he did not see it as prerequisite for all. Indeed, it is Rosenzweig's emphasis on Bible and Hebrew which unites his two programmatic educational essays, "It Is Time" and "On Opening the Jewish Lehrhaus," which clash in all other pedagogical respects.[20] Seven years *before* he began the Bible translation with Buber, Rosenzweig had already come to this conclusion: "The German, and even the Jew qua German, can and will read the Bible as Luther, Herder or Moses Mendelssohn read it: the Jew can understand it only in Hebrew."[21]

There is no "Jewish" without "Hebrew." Rosenzweig's conviction—not shared by Walter Benjamin and other German-Jewish intellectuals—only deepened as his Jewish learning progressed. On more than one occasion, Rosenzweig rued the easy Jewish literacy of his predecessors. "The medieval Jew marshals the happy unity of thought and speech in very great degree, and in an exclusiveness dearly paid for. It is not alone lofty thoughts that he casts into chiseled form; any thought that may legitimately call itself a thought moves toward such form. For him, quotation is not a decorative frill but the very warp to the woof of what he has to say."[22] In contrast to this admiring view, consider Rosenzweig's lukewarm assessment of Jacob Klatzkin's translation of Spinoza into modern Hebrew. Klatzkin, a conscious secularist, wanted Jewish nationalism to be devoid of traditional Jewish content. But Rosenzweig was dubious that "Hebrew" and "Jewish" could be separated. Regarding Klatzkin,

Rosenzweig wrote: "The point is: one cannot simply speak Hebrew as one would like to; one must speak it as it is. And it is tied up with the past."[23] But Rosenzweig's most profound statement of the Jewish world we have lost, and what can still be salvaged, may be found in his Bible article in the German-language *Encyclopedia Judaica*, a treasure trove of scholarship unlikely to be translated into the two most used Jewish vernaculars of the twenty-first century, Hebrew and English:

> When dogma and Law cease to be the all-embracing frame of the community and serve only as props from within, the Scriptures must not merely fulfill the task of all Scriptures: to establish a connection between generations; they must also assume another task which is like incumbent on all Scriptures: they must guarantee the connection between the center and the periphery of the community. Thus even if church and synagogue no longer arched the portal on the road to humanity, the Bible would still continue to be at the beck and call, so that humanity could consult it about this very road, "turn its pages again and again" and "find everything in it."[24]

According to Rosenzweig, the Bible always played the task of connecting generations, but that task had been simple in the past. The daily life of a Jewish community, before Emancipation, provided a whole set of connections. Now, in Rosenzweig's day, the Bible would have to serve also as the meeting place between the Jewishly committed and those on the margins of Jewish life. "Center" and "periphery" are recurring tropes in Rosenzweig's writing, and appear most famously in his Lehrhaus address on Jewish adult education. Here, Rosenzweig suggested that the Bible could link center and periphery: Rosenzweig's "It Is Time" and his *Encyclopedia Judaica* placed a large wager on the Bible as a life raft for modern Jewry. To provide the guide for the perplexed for the modern Bible reader, Rosenzweig turned to Benno Jacob; their correspondence will be the last topic discussed in this chapter.

More than Buber, Rosenzweig was open to the readings of the traditional Jewish commentators, and noted on many occasions his debt to the midrashic traditions and to moderns such as Benno Jacob. (In one letter Rosenzweig explicitly cited Jacob as authority against accepting multiple authorship of the first two chapters of Genesis.) Finally, by the end of his life, Rosenzweig joined Jacob's call for a new Jewish Bible scholarship, which would not surrender to modern criticism, but take those insights to further explicate the received text. Rosenzweig's view, and Mara Benjamin deserves credit for pointing this out, would tend toward a holistic, nonatomistic interpretation of the Bible, without recourse to shadowboxing with source criticism. To put it in Nahum Sarna's well-chosen words to his JPS (Jewish Publication Society) Genesis commentary: "The present Commentary is primarily concerned with the completed edifice and only to a minor extent with building blocks. It is not based on the coroner's approach, that is, on dissecting a literary corpse. The Bible is and always has been a living literature and a dynamic force in history, endowed with the ability to move men and transform civilizations."[25]

THE MAKING OF THE MODERN JEWISH BIBLE: THE GERMAN-JEWISH CONTRIBUTION

The role of German Jews in responding to modernity has been thoroughly acknowledged; more recently, the role of German Jews in the making of the modern Jewish Bible has also been appreciated.[26] Moses Mendelssohn consciously and successfully created a Hebrew opus that made the Bible a centerpiece of Jewish religion. This Enlightenment project in no way compromised his Jewishness, and while his translation did ease the way into acquiring German culture, no more authentically Jewish path could be imagined than mastering Torah via the Masoretic text and the medieval *pashtanim*. The casually broached idea that Mendelssohn wanted to move German Jews from "religion" to "culture" needs qualification on three counts: First, this idea overdraws the distinction between religion and culture from a secularist perspective (i.e., it posits religion cannot be aesthetic, beautiful, or refined). Second, this idea takes as the only possible definition of Judaism a rabbinically oriented traditionalism. This critique is itself an essentialist argument that assumes that "Judaism" must relegate the study of the Torah to early education. But Mendelssohn, Hirsch, Jacob, and Buber and Rosenzweig all agreed that the Bible constituted the most important Jewish religious document, and that one's study of it, even as a practical guide to conduct, should continue throughout one's life. Third, the juxtaposition of culture versus religion glides over Mendelssohn's frankly conservative attitude toward the Hebrew Bible, expressed in his many Hebrew writings and verified by the success of Mendelssohn's commentary in traditional quarters in the decades after *Sefer Netivot ha-Shalom* first appeared. Mendelssohn wanted more cultured German Jews: he did not want impious ones.

By the 1830s, Samson Raphael Hirsch had formulated his view that Written Torah and Oral Torah were inseparable. This view animated not only his popular Bible commentaries, but even his earlier works, *Horeb* and *Nineteen Letters*. For all his criticism of Mendelssohn, Hirsch continued the latter's championing of the Hebrew Bible as the repository of Jewish religious teaching. Hirsch was not an old-world *lamdan*, and according to Mordechai Breuer, the authoritative interpreter of German Jewish Orthodoxy, the Frankfurt community that Hirsch led did not produce Talmud scholars of the caliber of eastern European contemporaries. They did, however, know their Bible, through the prism of traditional commentators and that of their own Rav. The many readers of Hirsch's works possessed a clear line linking accepted halachic practice with its biblical basis (*Horeb*) and a refreshingly human picture of religious behavior in the Bible as a guide in the present. Hirsch gave his readers a passionate, uncompromising view of the perfection of Torah, which he treated as a datum as certain as the sunshine.

With the publication of Wellhausen's *Prolegomena to the History of Israel*, source criticism could no longer be ignored. While the Jewish responses, predictably, ranged from acceptance and neutralization of the anti-Judaic elements of the Graf-Wellhausen hypothesis to frontal assault, the enduring responses came from more novel approaches. Benno Jacob championed a close reading of the accepted text that presumed an authorial mind. Jacob illustrated this coherent author by numerous means: the natural breakdown of weekly portions, the use of number patterns and genealogies, subtle inclusions and omissions in biblical narratives, and so on. Jacob also possessed an uncanny mastery of Hebrew language and of rabbinic sources. While he often dissented from traditional Jewish interpreters, he consistently integrated their insights. Jacob polemicized for a consciously Jewish approach, and demonstrated the superiority of the Bible to its ancient Near Eastern counterparts.

Like Jacob, Buber and Rosenzweig did not allow the source critical approach to define their own. Philosophers rather than Bible scholars, Buber and Rosenzweig adopted a dialogical approach to Bible, insisting that meaning emerged from the encounter between reader and text, or better yet, the voice behind the text. But the text itself was the Jewish Bible. Buber did not advocate an encounter with the Enuma Elish or the Septuagint. Rosenzweig, even more emphatically than Buber, insisted on the need for a modern Jewish commentary, nominating Jacob as a new Rashi, and pushed the acquisition of prayer book Hebrew and Bible Hebrew as key to recovering Jewish identity. Israel and the United States remain vibrant centers of Jewish Bible study, while the German-Jewish tradition was brutally exterminated. But by linking the modern Jewish identity to the Hebrew Bible, the German Jews, as so often, hold pride of place.

Part II

ZIONISM AND THE CREATION OF A NATIONAL BIBLE

INTRODUCTION: THE BIBLE IN MODERN ISRAEL

When American university students are told that the majority of Jewish Israelis are secular, I wonder what they think secular means. To be sure, most Israelis do not go to synagogue three times daily, favor a theocracy, or scrupulously observe basic Jewish practices such as Shabbat. On the other hand, the Jewish character of modern Israel strikes American visitors with considerable force. Saturday is the national day of rest (however the individuals spend their free time); holidays are set by the traditional calendar (even if you spend Passover eating pita); and the vernacular language, used for every conceivable purpose, is Hebrew. Most germane to our subject, it is taken for granted by Jewish Israelis that the study of the Bible should form a significant part of their education. Americans, accustomed to a separation of church and state, might be surprised to learn that from the 1890s until today the Hebrew Bible has been part of the school curriculum. To be sure, Israelis in the secular national track learn Tanakh mainly as a historical and literary text, while Israelis in the religious national track learn Tanakh as a religious-spiritual text as well. All Israelis, however, study Bible for about ten years; become familiar with the major commentaries; learn how to read the unvocalized, unpunctuated text from the scroll; and take proficiency exams in high school. While secular Israelis may not be able to chant Friday night blessings or locate specific prayers in a prayer book, one and all display knowledge of the Bible's contents. Much modern Hebrew literature—poetry and prose—relies on biblical familiarity. These facts, I believe, would come as a surprise to my imaginary American university student.

The early leaders of Zionism, most of whom were eastern European Jews who had rebelled against their parents' Judaism, raised the issue of what role Jewishness ought to play in their nationalist movement almost immediately. In response to Theodor Herzl's Zionist vision, expressed in his utopian novel *Old-New Land*, Ahad Haam advanced an alternative vision that would lead to a Jewish state and not just a state of Jews. Herzl, unlike most of the Zionist rank and file, was an acculturated Jew who grew up in Budapest and lived mainly in Vienna. His *Der Judenstaat* (1896) has been translated as *The Jewish State*, but the Hebrew translation *Medinat ha-Yehudim* (The Jews' State) better captures the essentially modern, secular nature of what he proposed: a Switzerland by the sea. Ahad Haam's advocacy of Hebrew language, Jewish milieu, and Jewish values might seem like an uncontroversial tweak, but it was not. Orthodox Zionists, primarily organized in the Mizrahi party, found Ahad Haam's view highly objectionable. Unlike Herzl, who maintained strict neutrality in religious matters, Ahad Haam held that traditional Judaism could not survive in the modern world, and proposed his secularized version of Jewishness as its substitute.

From the Zionist left, figures such as Yosef Micha Berdichevski and Yosef Chaim Brenner found Ahad Haam's views about the retention of Jewishness arbitrary and regressive. Why, they argued, tether a revolutionary movement such as Zionism to the Jewish past? Why retain the ruinous values of the exile? Why spiritualize a nationalistic movement, which needed masculinity, vitality, and physicality? The role assigned to the Jewish past divided Zionists sharply and an evaluation of the Bible seemed central to deciding this question. But Ahad Haam and his opponents regarded the relationship between Zionism and the Bible as obvious—as did his successors. David Ben-Gurion told the Peel Commission that "The Bible is our mandate," and the Israeli Scroll of Independence invoked the Hebrew Bible as a specific Jewish stake to the land and as a universal gift of the Jewish people.

A brief reflection on four paradoxes indicates just how "unnatural" this connection between the Bible and Zionism truly was, and how the centrality of the Bible as national canon should not be taken for granted. First, at the start of the movement few Jews lived in the land of the Bible. The majority of Jews who provided the rank and file for Zionism lived under czarist rule, and their main connection with the land of Israel was in their parents' prayer books—which they had decided to abandon. Few of the early pioneers had visited Israel before "going up" to settle there, and few had a real sense of its topography, geography, or climate. The Israeli emphasis on *yidiat ha-aretz* ("getting to know the land") was driven by practical and ideological motives. Zionism's presentation of Israel as a "natural destination" was derided as utopian by *all* of its Jewish opponents. From the Western Jewish perspective, emancipation and acculturation were working. True, antisemitism remained, but most Jews assumed that reason would triumph over hate. From the eastern Jewish perspective, Jewish-born revolutionaries (e.g., Trotsky, Luxembourg, Zinoviev, etc.) assumed the end of class conflict would bring the end of antisemitism, too. Bundists and Yiddishists accepted the Pale of Settlement as the Jewish heartland, if not homeland; assumed that moving millions of Jews to Palestine was unrealistic; and thought that reform in eastern Europe offered the most realistic possibility of ameliorating the Jewish condition.

The second paradox: Assumptions that the Bible provided a national framework ran afoul of the reality that neither rabbinic nor modern Judaism corresponds to the Temple-based, priestly, sacrificial system described in the Torah and assumed in the Prophets. Judaism is not the religion of the Bible; it was forged by the early rabbis. Nor did the Bible define the political organization of the Jewish people. Since the exile of the first few centuries CE, the rabbinic dictum "the law of the land is the law" relegated Jewry to developing self-governing institutions without the presumption of national or military sovereignty. Finally, the early

Zionists were deeply committed democrats, not would-be restorers of a biblical theocracy or priesthood.

A third paradox: Hebrew, the Bible's language, was not spoken colloquially by any living Jew when Theodor Herzl convened the first Zionist Congress (1897). In eastern Europe, Jews generally spoke Yiddish; in western Europe and America, Jews spoke the vernacular; in Islamic lands, Jews spoke Arabic (and/or Judeo-Arabic, Farsi, or Ladino). Hebrew had not been a vernacular language for some time. Even in the biblical period, scholars agree that Aramaic displaced Hebrew some time following the destruction of the First Temple. That Hebrew was the literary language of the Bible was and is true, but, it could also be argued, this was totally irrelevant to the needs of late-nineteenth-century Jewry.

A fourth paradox: From the Zionist point of view, the largest part of the Jewish past was useless. Zionism rejected the medieval legacy of persecution, exile, and martyrdom (there was much more to medieval Jewish history than this catalog of woes—but not in the Zionist perspective). The modern legacy of political emancipation and integration, however, ran counter to Zionism's central claim: that Jewry would never win general acceptance, and that a Jewish future could only be imaginable in a national context. Given this disjuncture, how did modern Zionism link back to the Bible and its national past? This question will require some explanation.

Why did Zionism need a workable past at all to forge a nation? The answer seems terribly simple: the movement lacked most of the obvious tools for modern nation building, such as common language, common birthplace, a recognized governing class, or even a shared religious practice. Herzl grandly proclaimed, "We are a people, one people," but the Zionist movement ultimately relied on two claims: (1) Jews shared the unfortunate fate of being on the receiving end of gentile aggression, and (2) Jews shared a common past. And, since most of that past was useless, only the distant, biblical past could serve as a linchpin. This partly explains why Zionism turned to the Bible at all, given the frankly secular nature of the enterprise.[1] In this cultivation of a usable past, as well as its cultivation of a national language and defined geography, Zionism bore close kinship with other emerging nationalisms. As numerous scholars have explained, the creation of a national identity did not just happen: it required conscious cultivation from above and receptivity from below. The creation of dictionaries, maps, vernacular newspapers, social clubs, sports teams, and heroes is to be found in most examples of nationalist movements and on all continents.[2]

One question above all concerns us: How did Zionism connect the Bible of ancient Israel to the creation of a modern state in 1948? The three chapters that comprise this section (centered on Ahad Haam, David Ben-Gurion, and Nehama Leibowitz) wrestle with this issue. Two additional elements intimately connected with the Zionist appropriation of the Bible have been dealt with extensively, and I will refer to them only to shed some preliminary light on this process: (1) the revival of Hebrew as a living language, and (2) the Israeli infatuation with archaeology. Readers very familiar with these stories may safely skip the next couple of pages.

Most Israelis would find the linkage between Hebrew language and the Bible absolutely natural. Hebrew was the language of the Bible, aside from a few passages in Aramaic; it was a spoken language in ancient Israel; of Jewish languages, it always enjoyed the highest prestige, whether religiously or even literarily. Zionist ideology, however, not logic, dictated the need to speak Hebrew. After all, one could read Bible in Hebrew and discourse in the language of one's choice—*the proof being that for two millennia most Jews did exactly that*. Even Theodor Herzl imagined his Judenstaat as a linguistic Switzerland with everyone speaking the language of his or her birth. Herzl observed that nobody could buy a railway ticket in Hebrew; the language lacked not only vocabulary but everyday idioms. Haim Hazaz's celebrated short story "The Sermon" poked fun at his fellow pioneers' tortured use of an ancient tongue: "Well, then it's well known that we're all ashamed to speak Yiddish, as though it were some sort of disgrace. I intentionally said 'ashamed.' Not that we dislike, or fear, or refuse, but we're ashamed. But Hebrew, and none other than Sephardic Hebrew, strange and foreign as it is, we speak boldly, with a kind of pride or vanity even though it isn't as easy and natural as Yiddish, and even though it hasn't the vitality, the sharp edge and healthy vigor of our folk language. What's the meaning of this? What's the reason for it?"[3]

Hazaz sarcastically answered his own question by maintaining that Zionists' move to Hebrew language and Hebrew names, many drawn from the Bible, though rarely used in diaspora Jewish culture, evinced a desire to be less Jewish. As lampooned by Hazaz, Zionism sought something fundamentally different from the Jewish culture that had developed in the preceding two thousand years of diaspora: different in language, name, occupation, body type, and worldview. An avalanche of recent scholarship has shown that the cultivation of Hebrew both in Zionist circles in the Pale of Settlement and in Ottoman Palestine was an act of will, symbolized by, but by no means limited to, that Hebrew-language zealot Eliezer Ben-Yehuda (1858–1923). Ben-Yehuda, the subject of popular songs and street names in Israel, forbade his wife to speak to their son in any other language, although they could not freely converse in modern spoken Hebrew.[4]

Many of the early Alliance Israelite Universelle–sponsored schools spoke French; German seemed like the progressive language of technology and science; the major pioneers of the First and Second Aliyah shared Yiddish as a native tongue. The victory of Hebrew over Yiddish, French, and German took a good twenty years. Only with the language debate of 1913, in which Hebrew was chosen over German as the language of instruction in Israel's premier technical college, the Technion in Haifa, did Hebrew became the quasi-official language of the nation-to-be. This domination of one language over others, or at least one standardized language over regional variations, characterized modern nationalism. In the words of Benedict Anderson, "Thus English elbowed Gaelic out of most of Ireland, French pushed Breton to the wall, and Castilian reduced Catalan to marginality."[5] Hebrew posed a more extreme case than these others, but the political dynamic was the same—one nation, one language.

This victory of Hebrew had a fateful consequence Jewishly, which the stridently antireligious Ben-Yehuda did not fully appreciate. The choice of Hebrew as the primary language of Israeli Jews ensured ready accessibility to the biblical text, even to those most removed from Orthodox Judaism. Every tour guide to the Shrine of the Book in the Israel Museum will proudly announce that even Israeli high school schoolchildren can read the Dead Sea Scrolls. True. They can also read the Hebrew of the Mishnah, and have a serious advantage over American Jews should they desire to become literate in the sea of Talmud, since Aramaic is a cognate language. Whatever Hazaz's fictional character assumed, as a means of escaping Jewish identity, German would have been a better choice.

Like Hebrew, the field of archaeology only seems to be obviously wedded to the Bible. From a contemporary archaeologist's perspective, field work may take place quite independently of the biblical text, even independently of a preconceived notion of what is Israelite. In a celebrated essay, "What Is Israelite and What Is Canaanite?" William Dever argues that from material artifacts alone, there is scant difference between the material cultures of Israelites and Canaanites, although the Bible presents the two nations as archenemies. The thrust of contemporary archaeology is to determine settlement patterns and living conditions, and only secondarily to date eminent artifacts.[6] To overstate the point: Syro-Palestinian archaeology (Dever's preferred term) and the Hebrew Bible are not inextricably linked, although only an interest in the latter drove the development of the former.

As with the modernization of Hebrew, the development of modern archaeology does not appear so parochially Jewish on second glance. In 1871, a German businessman and impresario named Heinrich Schliemann (1822–1890), armed mainly with the poems of Homer, began a dig at ancient Troy. His spectacular finds, epitomized by the "Mask of Agamemnon," initiated what might be called the "big game" phase of archaeology. In this game, one took a classical text (e.g., Homer, the Bible) and began digging, looking for confirmation of historical places, events, personalities, and even specific artifacts. Applied to biblical lands by professional archaeologists like the American Protestant William Foxwell Albright (1891–1971), scholars invariably concluded that the Bible had the basic history right. To take one typical comment of Albright's: "As a whole, the picture in Genesis is historical and there is no reason to doubt the general accuracy of the biographical details and the sketches of personality which make the patriarchs come alive with a vividness unknown to a single non-biblical character in the whole vast literature of the ancient Near East."[7]

I cannot think of a single scholar today who would agree with Albright's claim. If literary brilliance were proof of historicity, we would have to conclude that Captain Ahab lived, breathed, and harpooned white whales. Most of the verities of mid-twentieth-century "biblical archaeology" have been discredited: It turns out the Philistines, contrary to their dictionary reputation, had a vibrant and creative material culture. Likewise, while there were certainly enslaved Asiatic peoples toiling in Egypt, there is no physical evidence attesting to the Exodus, not to mention a forty-year sojourn in the desert of six hundred thousand souls. Joshua's military conquest of Canaan, inspirational to early leaders of the State of Israel, was probably an inflated version of Israelite-Canaanite tensions constructed by much later authors.

Schliemann may have been motivated mainly by fame and wealth, whereas biblical archaeologists were also motivated by a religious desire to validate the Bible by modern, scholarly means. Christian archaeologists such as Edward Robinson (American), Jean-François Champollion (French), and Gustav Dahlmann (German) and, above all, Albright, played an important role in encouraging parallel methods and parallel conclusions on the part of the new Israelis. Even Reform Jews in America in this period expressed much enthusiasm about excavating places with particular Jewish resonance.[8] In the view of Amos Elon, the Israeli archaeology craze began precisely in 1928 when kibbutzniks found a beautifully preserved sixth-century-CE synagogue mosaic floor at Beit Alpha, where I spent a year harvesting grapefruit and avocado. After some hesitation both practical (e.g., excavation would delay an irrigation ditch) and ideological (e.g., the kibbutz was adamantly secular), the dig went forward. The leader of the Beit Alpha dig was Eliezer Sukenik, who would later acquire the famed Dead Sea Scrolls on the brink of Israel's war for independence. His son, General Yigael Yadin, led even more famous digs, culminating in the excavation of Herod's desert fortress, Masada. In these decades (1930s to 1960s), find upon find seemed to be making the Zionists' case for them.[9]

Under Yadin's guidance, an impressive cast of archaeologists, Israeli and foreign, painted the following picture: Israel had entered the land as conquerors, and using military stratagems worthwhile of emulation in the present day, overthrew Canaanite cities such as Jericho, Hazor, and

Gezer; the kingdom of David and Solomon left impressive archaeological records culminating in Yadin's excavations at Megiddo. Everybody's neighborhood, or so it seemed, had a mound worth shoveling into and looking for a treasure—Moshe Dayan, a major "collector" of antiquities, had more resources at his disposal than most, but his interest was symptomatic. Thousands of amateur archaeologists spent their Shabbats combing the ground for pottery shards, coins, and other goodies. For Yadin, as Neil Asher Silberman observes, "Archaeology would always be a profoundly patriotic activity."[10] Elon explains that archaeology documented Israel's legitimate place in the land and provided an identity bulwark in the formative decades of the modern state (1950–1960s). Elon concludes, "Native Israelis—they are the large majority now—appear to have less need to search for roots; those who do turn rather to religion."[11]

Neither colloquial use of the Hebrew language nor archaeology *was or is* the same as study of the Bible, or guarantees the centrality of the Bible as a subject of study and veneration. Hebrew may traditionally be called *lashon ha-kodesh* (the holy language), but it can be applied for other purposes. There are Hebrew-language academic works, mystery novels, and pornography. Indeed, a slur of the ultraorthodox regarding the Israeli majority is that they are merely "gentiles who speak Hebrew" (*goyim sh'medabrim ivrit*). Similarly, archaeology today is the main academic discipline that has driven a minimalist view of the Bible's reliability as a historical source. We will have occasion to examine the views of these minimalists and their detractors. For now, it is worth reiterating that at midtwentieth century, archaeology and the Bible seemed more like a joyous wedding than an acrimonious divorce. The Hebrew-language revival and archaeology were linked to the Bible and thus linked to the Zionist project. But the master narrative linking modern Jews and the "Book of Books" was forged independently of the revival of Hebrew and the maturation of archaeology. The views of Ahad Haam and his detractors offer a good starting point for analyzing this linkage of present and past.

6

Early Zionism and the Bible
Ahad Haam and His Opponents

The Jewish national movement responded quickly to modern biblical criticism.[1] Historian Heinrich Graetz (1817–1891) adopted source critical methods in his commentaries on the Song of Songs (1871) and Psalms (1883). Like most nineteenth-century Jewish scholars, however, Graetz did not employ these methods on the Torah itself. His last project, incomplete at the time of his death, was a critical edition of the Hebrew Scriptures which included many emendations of the entire Bible.[2] Completed by his student Wilhelm Bacher, a pioneer of rabbinic literature, Graetz's posthumous *Emendations* appeared in 1892–1894; it did not have much impact on the scholarly world. But Graetz's Bible scholarship and visit to Israel yielded different fruit—namely, a vivid account of Israelite history in his *History of the Jews*. Graetz was the first nineteenth-century Jewish historian to write a nationalist history, narrated in grand style. Many scholars have documented the eye-opening impact that Graetz's history exerted on yeshiva students who, while they ostensibly studied their Talmud, furtively opened their folios instead to the flesh and blood stories of Samson, David, and the Prophets. Graetz began his *History of the Jews* with several paragraphs describing the land of Canaan, only then introducing Abraham by way of a flashback to Mesopotamia. For Graetz, the true birthplace of the nation was not Haran.

Bible criticism found a pair of advocates in Max Soloveitchik and Zalman (Rubaschov) Shazar, the latter Israel's third president.[3] Nevertheless, the overall attitude of Jewish nationalists toward "Germanic" Bible criticism remained negative. Given the secular, at times aggressively antitraditional orientation of much of the nascent Zionist movement, this resistance requires some explanation. While the eastern European

Zionists rebelled agains their parents' Judaism, they sought a modicum of continuity with the Jewish past, varying from figure to figure. In an illuminating article on Peretz Smolenskin (1842–1885), David Engel details the contours of Jewish nationalists' resistance to Bible criticism. Smolenskin, who redefined Jewish loyalty on a secular basis, considered both Christian and Jewish Bible scholars guilty of projecting their own values back onto literature of the distant past. This led, in Smolenskin's view, to all manner of unsupported assumptions about authorial intent and genre and far too much confidence about emending the redacted text. Smolenskin's judgment was aesthetic as well as editorial. The beauty of biblical Hebrew, a credo for Smolenskin as for most Zionists, could not be affirmed if one considered the biblical text corrupt throughout. His defense of biblical Hebrew had a national dimension: modern biblical criticism, in Smolenskin's view, supported a weak-kneed universalism that worked against the uniqueness of individual nations. Tellingly, Smolenskin savaged Mendelssohn's translation from Hebrew to German as abetting Mendelssohn's erroneous view that religious commandments alone bound Jewry together. This was a terribly unfair assessment of Mendelssohn's Bible project: Mendelssohn clearly affirmed the beauty of the Hebrew language and his commentary certainly elevated rather than denigrated the Bible.

The debate over the role of critical Bible studies at the elite level resurfaced dramatically in 1925.[4] When several distinguished Hebrew University supporters proposed filling the Bible position at the newly created Hebrew University of Jerusalem with Hirsch Peretz Chajes, the chief rabbis of England and France opposed Chajes's appointment on the grounds that he was an advocate of source critical methods. Chajes was rejected, to the dismay of many, including Ze'ev Jabotinsky: "Our apprehension about Bible commentary is, in my view, not well founded. I admit that this is not a simple question, but a faculty of Jewish philosophy in Jerusalem without Bible research would cry to the heavens. Has it been proven that the Mizrahi are threatening to use the same reasoning they used against the Gymnasium? After all, they themselves understand the difference."[5] Instead of Chajes, since Hebrew Bible could hardly be ignored in the Institute of Jewish Studies, Hebrew University turned to Moshe Hirsch Segal (1876–1968) and Umberto Cassuto (1883–1951), both severe critics of the source critical approach. In fact, although both men were masters of the Bible, neither were they primarily Bible scholars, Cassuto being a classicist and historian of the Jews of Italy and Segal being primarily a philologist specializing in the history of Mishnaic-era halachah. Not until after World War II would the Israeli academy embrace cutting-edge methods of biblical scholarship—wherever they might lead. Looking back from 1968, when he won a chair in Bible studies, Menahem Haran portrayed the previous fifty years of "biblical research in Hebrew" as a slow slog toward the critical method.[6] But we are getting ahead of ourselves and must return to the approbation of the Bible among the rank and file of the Zionist movement—a development that most scholars agree characterized the Second and Third Aliyah groups. Distance from the world of European Bible scholarship did not equal lack of passion about the Bible—quite the contrary. In fact, several major figures struggled to find a way to make the Bible central to the Jewish national movement. Despite many differences, a common purpose links the biblically inflected essays of Ahad Haam with the various promotional endeavors of David Ben-Gurion, and even the seemingly apolitical commentaries of Nehama Leibowitz.

AHAD HAAM, THE BIBLE, AND THE "NATIONAL JEW"

Understanding the development of modern Jewish culture without Ahad Haam (1865–1927) remains impossible, even though his accomplishments were eclipsed by others in virtually every arena. He was a major figure in the modernization of Hebrew through his editorship of *Ha-Shiloah*, but certainly less important than Eliezer Ben-Yehuda. He was a major figure in Zionism, its acknowledged moral voice in eastern Europe, yet certainly less pivotal than Herzl, who propelled the movement onto the world arena. Ahad Haam was less adventurous and radical as a secular ideologue than his contemporaries, Micha Yosef Berdichevsky (1865–1921) and Yosef Chaim Brenner (1881–1921). Socialist and Labor Zionists exerted more influence on the developing path of the Yishuv in the first two decades of the twentieth century. As Steven Zipperstein has demonstrated, Ahad Haam aspired and failed to be the leading figure of the Jewish renaissance. Nevertheless, his impact was enormous in all these arenas and some figures of arguably greater consequence, including Chaim Weizmann, Mordecai Kaplan, and Chaim Nachman Bialik, looked to Ahad Haam as their mentor.

Ahad Haam had much to say about the Hebrew Bible, but he had no interest in becoming an academic contributor to "Bibelwissenschaft." Even if Graetz and Smolenskin had not set a tone of resistance to pure Bibelwissenschaft on academic grounds, Ahad Haam would surely have seen that the agenda of Jewish national revival and the agenda of the academy could not have dovetailed. Ahad Haam shared the source critics' view that the Bible was a human rather than divine text, but while the latter pursued the various strands of authorship (J, E, P, and D), the former used the Bible as a guideline for contemporary Jewry. While Ahad Haam mentioned Julius Wellhausen's work, the differences between the two men were far more significant than their similarities, despite a scholarly attempt to portray them as kindred spirits.[7] Ahad Haam did not open the pages of *Hashiloah* to biblical criticism, and although he respected some of the biblical scholarship of his day, especially the Hebrew-language scholarly commentary initiated by Avraham Kahana, it would be a mistake to overestimate his overall interest in this discourse, which was less than that of Smolenskin, Graetz, Ben-Gurion, or Buber.[8]

What then was Ahad Haam's relation to the Bible? To begin with, he likely took his pen name from Rashi's understanding of the phrase in Genesis 26. Describing Avimelech, Rashi, following Onkelos, comments: "One of the people [*ahad haam*], the special one of the people, namely the King."[9] Biblical images, figures, phrases, and themes populate Ahad Haam's essays, even if his style, according to his early biographer, Leon Simon, owed more to Mishnaic than biblical Hebrew. Like many educated Jews of his generation, Ahad Haam could summon up biblical verses at will, though some of them do not really support his point terribly well.[10] He took pride in his biblical mastery and made a point of noting in his reminiscences and correspondence that he taught himself Tanakh, despite the traditional eastern European curriculum of Talmud and more Talmud. This was a familiar trope for Jewish Enlighteners and one which reinforces the consensus that he was a translational figure from the Haskalah to Zionism. Ahad Haam also began, though never completed, an essay on biblical style, and took notes on most of the Bible. Ahad Haam's readings of the Bible dealt mainly with their present-day lessons. This attitude contrasts not only with the Orthodox Nehama Leibowitz, who personified the ethic of Torah study for its own sake, but also with Buber, who strove to bolster his own religious reading with a deep attention to actual Bible scholarship. By contrast, Ahad Haam's declared lack of interest in biblical scholarship was a grand gesture, but also an excuse to ignore the field. The Bible functioned for Ahad Haam in two critical ways. First, Ahad Haam envisioned a national, organic, essentially Jewish past that began with the Bible and continued up until the present day. The classical Prophets marked a moral high point in our national history, but no part of that national history was dispensable. Second, Ahad Haam acknowledged the difference between "the Hebrew" and "the Jew," but to him they were close relatives, not distant strangers, as they were for many other Zionists. This position put him at odds with the other great combatant over the issue of what the Jewish past had to teach the nationalist movement—Micha Yosef Berdichevsky.

AHAD HAAM AND BERDICHEVSKY

Anita Shapira, the leading scholar of the Bible's use and misuse in modern Israel, explains the disagreement between Ahad Haam and Berdichevsky over the nature of Jewishness:

The fundamental dispute between Berdichevsky and Ahad Haam revolved around the national essence of the Jewish people. Ahad Haam selected certain elements from Jewish history and fashioned them into a vision of a monolithic Judaism, any deviations from which were mere aberrations unrepresentative of the generous and homogenous course of Jewish character. Berdichevsky disputed the existence of such an essential character. Judaism had, he contended, never been a single and unified system of values beliefs and opinions. Rather, it was a constantly altering complex of values whose source lay in changing external circumstances.[11]

And again:

It is not farfetched to contend that the Bible was the battlefield on which the struggle over the nature of the new national ethos was waged. Both camps were able to claim that they represented true Judaism as manifested in the most important work given the world by the Jewish people. . . . One of the most cherished and cultivated components of the new Jewish self-esteem was pride in the fact that it was the Jewish people that had created the Bible. Simultaneously, the Bible was also viewed as a source of written proof—evidence in support of the rights of Jews to their land. Neither camp was able to delegitimize the aspects of the bible unacceptable to them.[12]

Like any combatants close enough to disagree sharply, they shared a great deal. Both men were Hebraists, eastern European Jews contemptuous of Herzl's purely political Zionism, and each shared an idea that the Zionist movement needed to innovate a way for a modern Jewish culture. Both were secularists in the true sense of the word: raised as traditionally observant Jews, they knew exactly what they were rejecting. They were also national Jews, for whom abandonment or revision of religious suppositions did not invalidate, or even qualify, loyalty to the people of one's birth. They agreed too that the same could not be said of Western European Jews who had fallen from the faith—without a shared culture, language, and sense of peoplehood, Western Jewish identity was dubious. Both regarded Hebrew language and the Jewish past as critical: for Berdichevsky, most of this past required rejecting, while for Ahad Haam, most of it deserved reformulating or "revaluing," as his disciple Mordecai Kaplan might have said.

On specific historical judgments they also differed. As Shapira puts it elsewhere, for Berdichevsky, the military last stand at fortresses such as Betar and Masada represented the desirable point of historical reconnect for contemporaries, while for Ahad Haam the rabbinic leadership of Yohanan Ben Zakkai at Yavneh was the way forward from the disastrous revolt against Rome.[13] Regarding the biblical period, Berdichevsky was a "former prophets" champion, admiring the machismo of Joshua, David, and Solomon. Ahad Haam, by contrast, held the great moral prophets of the eight to fifth centuries BCE as the ultimate standard of Jewish value, which often centered and guided Jewish history.¹⁴ While these prophetic values did not characterize contemporary Jewry, Ahad Haam hoped that a new center in Zion might lead to rebirth of these values. That glimmer of hope, probably, was the most optimistic point in his generally pessimistic worldview.

To continue this dichotomy, both men were influenced by authentically Nietzschean strains: in Ahad Haam's case, the survival instinct of a people took top billing; while for Berdichevsky, the more radically individualistic idea of a "transvaluation of all values" offered the Nietzschean concept of greatest resonance. The more Ahad Haam tried to impose an ethical-elitist view of what was essentially Jewish, the more Berdichevsky, Brenner, and the younger Zionists rejected it in favor of a vitalist-existentialist view of Jewishness as an open-ended project.¹⁵ As "Jewish Nietzscheans," which is admittedly an odd-sounding formulation in the wake of the Nazis, the relationship of "Japhet" and "Shem" divided Ahad Haam and Berdichevsky. Ahad Haam, as editor of *Ha-Shiloach* (1896–1926), expressed a decided lack of interest in anything not pertaining directly to the Jewish condition or even that which could be described as merely belletristic. For Berdichevsky, Jewry existed in the larger world and should express itself in contemporary idioms and genres—anything of quality produced by a Jew was already Jewish enough to merit attention.¹⁶ The point of greatest divergence was over what part of the Jewish past could be deployed at present—a common dilemma in early Zionist thinking.¹⁷

Berdichevsky rejected Ahad Haam's romanticized view of biblical morality. For Berdichevsky, the Bible was full of violence, revenge, and double standards for God's chosen. Contrary to Ahad Haam's glamorization of the prophetic dictum from Zachariah: "not by power, but by spirit," Berdichevsky considered everything under the sun and found that the Bible often celebrated violence—as long as it followed divine command. This embrace of power would be championed, with qualification, by Ben-Gurion, and with even fewer qualms by Jabotinsky. Berdichevsky acknowledged that Ahad Haam's reading of Jewish values was the more usual one, but he thought this consensus was the unfortunate product of prolonged powerlessness. Berdichevsky wrote: "I cannot comprehend how a whole people can perceive itself to be a lamb and be content with that."¹⁸ In an early anticipation of the "Canaanite" ideology of the 1940s and 1950s, Berdichevsky celebrated the era of Israelite autonomy as one of strength, courage, and vitality. For Berdichevsky, unlike the Canaanites, it was not necessary to go behind and before the biblical era to discover a viable past. Nor did Berdichevsky celebrate aggression, unlike the Canaanites, who embraced militant nationalism. Berdichevsky was an explicit Nietzschean, with a concomitant rejection of national or racial exclusivism.

Ahad Haam's view that the Bible contained the moral essence of the nation and anchored its fundamental values invited disagreement. Yosef

Chaim Brenner criticized Ahad Haam's view that the Zionist settlers were compelled to set up a model society, consonant with their being descendants of those who had given the world the "Book of Books." For Brenner, as for many members of the Second Aliyah, the grim realities of survival made Ahad Haam's lofty calls not only highly unrealistic, but a typically diaspora ("galuti") attitude. For Berdichevsky and Brenner, the desire to create a complete national life was quite sufficient—they were more sanguine than Ahad Haam about the shape of that complete national life. The Zionist pioneers did not need to be a "Light to the Nation," a phrase often associated with religious reformers, but one which Ahad Haam fully endorsed. On the other hand, an acknowledgment of the ultimate validation provided by the Bible appears to not have been lost on even the most secular member of the Second Aliyah. For prominent Socialist and Labor Zionists such as Nachman Syrkin, A. D. Gordon, Berl Katznelson, A. S. Liberman, Yitzhak Tabenkin, and others, the Bible appeared as a precursor of socialist values, the giant gap between religiosity and secularism notwithstanding.[19] In Tabenkin's words:

> We cannot speak about the spiritual world of the members of the Second Aliyah in Palestine without mentioning the special influence of the Bible ... the Bible is the spiritual reflection of agricultural and military life, the image of a conquering people, a working people, a people of "this world." The Land of Israel lives in the memory of the Jews as a homeland and this memory was stored in the Bible. Throughout all the generations no other Bible was created, because the Jewish people had no other land. ... The influence of the Bible served as a link to and a hold on the entire land ... there was a copy of the Bible in nearly every worker's room.[20]

CONNECTING THE BIBLE TO THE JEWISH PAST

Ahad Haam and Berdichevsky differed over the nature of the Bible itself and over the relationship of the Bible to the rest of the Jewish past. In brief, Ahad Haam was no modern Karaite who dismissed postbiblical traditions. Unlike many early Zionists, he sought to demonstrate the lines of continuity from biblical past to nationalist present. Indeed, his most celebrated essays performed exactly this connect-the-dots function. In his early "Priest and Prophet" (1894), Ahad Haam lays out his basic position: the Prophet is the zealot, the idealist who also constitutes a primal force in religious and moral matters. The Priest, a necessary figure, applies and invariably compromises the prophetic spirit in the interest of forging institutions.[21] Ten years later in his essay "Flesh and Spirit" (1904), Ahad Haam traces the true living spirit of the nation from Prophetic to Pharisaic to spiritual Zionist attitudes. In each case and in each era, the most meritorious party avoided some excess of pure spiritualism or pure physicality. While his overall philosophy is sometimes called spiritual Zionism, this truly misleads the English readers. Ahad Haam used the word "spirit" (*ruaḥ*) precisely in the sense of integration of material and spiritual. Like many of his essays, "Flesh and Spirit" is schematic and self-serving politically, essentially reading his contemporary opponents as following dead ends similar to those their predecessors followed. The political Zionists appear as the heirs to the Sadducees and the Zealots; the Autonomists, like his friend Shimon Dubnov, as the heirs to the Essenes and other political quietists. Only the spiritual Zionists combine the spiritual and physical successfully.

Equally self-referential, Ahad Haam's "Moses" (1904) includes a reading of Moses as the greatest of Hebrew Prophets. In this characterization, Ahad Haam may or may not be correct in a critical scholarly sense; he certainly follows the reading of Moses by Maimonides, another hero of Ahad Haam's, who also exalts Moses's prophetic status above his other roles: lawgiver, military leader, and even judge (Exodus 18). This essay also includes his rejection of critical Bible scholars as the ultimate decisors of the Bible's importance for modern Jewish culture. As Ahad Haam stated with considerable sangfroid, he did not care if the archaeologists concluded that there was or was not a historical Moses, since the Moses who matters to Jewish culture, his lodestar, had been established by the veneration of generations. As Jacob Golomb argues, this attitude toward history relied on Nietzsche's distinction between "archeological truth" and "historical truth," and the strong preference of both men for the latter over the former. Golomb concludes that this preference for historical or "monumental" truth demonstrates that Ahad Haam internalized and transmitted Nietzsche as profoundly as did Berdichevsky. While all of these essays draw on the Bible, they cannot be considered biblical scholarship, or, for that matter, Midrashim.[22]

Finally, one might cite "Ancestor Worship" (1897), in which Ahad Haam explicitly considers the Bible, the Talmud, and even the much maligned *Shulchan Aruch* as reflecting the organic needs of the Jewish people in each of its three main eras. Although Ahad Haam affirmed the creativity of the Jewish people in every era, and rejected the more radical Zionists' deprecation of rabbinic Judaism, he confidently regarded certain works Jewish and others not. Ahad Haam's assumption of a Jewish canon infuriated Brenner:

> For me, the old Testament does not have the same value that it has for those who call it "Sacred Scriptures," the "Book of Books," the Eternal Book. I have long since been liberated from the hypnotic spell of the twenty-four books of the Bible. Many secular books from the last generations are dearer to me and strike me as greater and more profound. I consider the Hebrew Bible to be an important source of distant memories and the embodiment of our national spirit, and that of humanity in general, over the generations and ages. But I

also find and acknowledge this significance in the books of the New Testament. I am not addressing their literary power. The New Testament is also our book, an essential part of us.[23]

It would be hard to imagine a more provocative statement. Although Laurence Silberstein has documented Ahad Haam's unsavory attempt to stop this publication, Brenner's article was widely read and prompted a response by Ahad Haam. In "Torah from Sinai" (1911), Ahad Haam countered Brenner and other left-wing members of the socialist Zionist movement, who felt unbound by the Jewish past.[24] Ahad Haam, much like Smolenskin, rejected the desirability of freedom from the Jewish past. For without a connection to the biblical past, what was the rationale for settlement in Israel in particular? National Jews needed that connection to the distant past most of all, and only the Bible offered it. The New Testament and the Apocrypha were fine literary works and legitimate monuments of the Jewish past, too. But they lacked one thing that the Hebrew Bible had, namely, "Hypnose," the magic effect produced by generations of veneration and study in a Jewish context. If this seems like a curious concession to "feeling" for an archrationalist, one could put it a little differently: all the products of the Jewish past held value, but only the Hebrew Bible could be Scripture. In traditional Jewish theology, God, Israel, and Torah constituted the three legs of a stable stool. In modernity that stool became wobbly. Ahad Haam abandoned traditional belief in God and considered Israel's national spirit weaker than in times past. One could live in Israel and speak Hebrew and still not qualify as a "national Jew." Only the Bible was nonnegotiable: "Someone who says that he has no portion in the God of Israel, or in that historical force which has given our people life and influence that life, its sprit and its progress for thousands of years . . . can be a decent human being, but he is not a national Jew even if he lives in Eretz Israel and speaks Hebrew."[25]

AHAD HAAM AND THE BIBLE DEBATE AT THE HERZLIYA GYMNASIUM

Ultimately, the approach taken to the past by Ahad Haam was dialectic. He viewed modern Jewish nationalism as a revival of the classical past, but he did not embrace that heritage uncritically.[26] His "cultural Zionism," with its program of revaluing traditional Judaism in modern terms, offended the Orthodox far more than Herzl's indifference to religion. Likewise, he did not readily capitulate to European intellectual trends that he considered destructive to Jewish culture. Many of his polemics with Berdichevsky, Brenner, and others chide them for simply applying non-Jewish categories or adopting non-Jewish philosophies uncritically. Jewish nationalism depended on European models and the overall secularization of European culture—there is a good reason Zionism emerged in the late nineteenth century and not earlier.

The victory of Hebrew over Yiddish, French, and German took a good twenty years and culminated in the 1913 language debate at the Haifa Technion. Two years earlier, a "Bible War" broke out at the Herzliya Gymnasium in Tel Aviv/Jaffa. Despite German and English benefactors, the language of this fabled institution was already Hebrew. In 1911, the Herzliya Gymnasium was the Yishuv's premier academic high school; the school generated much pride among the members of the Yishuv, and also much scrutiny. The outspoken leader of the Herzliya Gymnasium, the principal Benzion Mossinson (1878–1925), embraced a blatantly secularist approach toward teaching the Hebrew Scriptures, and taught source criticism.[27] A gifted teacher, Mossinson's pedagogic goal as a Bible teacher seems to reflect an application of Berdichevsky's view. In Mossinson's words, "The Bible shall become their source of knowledge of the political, social and moral life of the ancient Hebrews in our land. That life must be made clearly visible to the new Hebrew, so that the Bible shall become for him an incessant fountain of feelings of national pride, feelings of reverence for the lucid past and of hope and confidence for a shining future."[28] Detractors of Mossinson considered this a horrendous way to teach sacred texts to children and pointedly "invited" those enamored of the Wellhausen method to go to Göttingen.

Enter Ahad Haam, who had much praise for the Gymnasium, but agreed with its critics regarding its approach to the Bible. He maintained that the Traditional Text deserved to be treated as sacrosanct. This paralleled, of course, his argument in "Moses" regarding the difference between archaeological truth and historical truth. This was, of course, a conservative way of affirming tradition without denying the human origination of the Bible—which the agnostic Ahad Haam could hardly do. The lower critical emendations used in Berne professor Karl Marti's Old Testament textbook, evidently the main source of Mossinson's lectures, particularly irked Ahad Haam. In two pages of tightly argued footnotes, he demonstrated that all the lower critical emendations proposed by the Christian scholarly world were either unnecessary or introduced other problems of comprehension into the prophetic text. (Ahad Haam used Jeremiah as his primary example—and it is a fine one. Not only do the Masoretic and Septuagint versions of Jeremiah differ greatly, the former being about a quarter longer than the latter, but the textual problems of this prophetic book are unending.) Ahad Haam also questioned the worthiness of teaching this sort of material to children, and I can only agree. He went out of his way to distance himself from source criticism:

> Behold, this is our national Tanach, just as if it was created from the first. And within the national perspective there is no desire at all to know the

original version as it came out of the Prophet's mouth. For this version was already changed in the generations close to the generation of the Prophet, and perhaps even in the Prophet's own day it had been written down in different versions, as was custom in those days, and in no way was this "original version" that which acted upon the national life then or since then, but rather only the version that is in our hands, with all its changes and additions.[29]

The biblical books, in Ahad Haam's view, should be read in their canonical order, and the threefold division of Tanakh ought to prevail over a fourfold division along genre lines, which was Mossinson's preferred method, coincidentally mirroring the fourfold division of the Christian Old Testament. Jewish law, found in the Torah alone, ought not to be neglected, and the later Jewish commentators should be given voice. This rejection of Mossinson's method should not be equated with Orthodoxy. As always, Ahad Haam sought a middle ground between traditional Judaism and surrendering Jewishness altogether:

It is true that the Bible is a part of Hebrew history. We know that everything that comes from a source changes and differs from the source. Neither you nor I have the same religion as our fathers did, but if we want our sons to have a religion, we have to tell them the truth, that the religion ruled over us; they need to know the source from which they will see the religion ruled over us; they need to know the source from which they will see the religious development. Research into the Bible has no place in the secondary school. They must become acquainted with the Torah and the Bible in its entirety; they must not be given fragments from one place and passages from another. Neither the religion nor common sense would suffer such a practice. It would be an imitation of the gentile scholars, but not knowledge of the Bible.[30]

CONCLUSION: BOTH JEWISH AND MODERN

Both the language debate at the Haifa Technion and the Bible debate at the Herzliya Gymnasium were decided in a distinctly modern Jewish direction. Affirming Hebrew as a language of instruction would certainly have been unimaginable at any time before the Haskalah, but affirming Hebrew rather than German was correctly seen as an ideological affirmation of Jewish culture, not as a purely practical matter. Likewise, actually studying the Bible head-on, especially the non-Pentateuchal parts largely ignored in traditional Jewish education, cannot be seen as anything but modern. Insisting that students had real textual knowledge of actual biblical books, and not just biographical knowledge of leading biblical figures as gleaned from textbooks or chrestomathies drawn from the Bible, can only be regarded as an intentionally Jewish move. Perhaps all traditional cultures insist that summary is no substitute for citation verbatim—traditional Judaism certainly does, and here Ahad Haam defends that form of cultural literacy, citing by rote large swatches of text. As he recounted it, the decisive turning point in his visit came when he realized that while a particular student could tell him about Jeremiah, that same student could not read a passage from Jeremiah comfortably.[31] But this affirmation of the Traditional Text and Ahad Haam's mockery of lower criticism illustrate a further point: the modernity of the critique. Traditionally, problems in the biblical text are not solved *either* by a canonical approach *or* by emendation: *they are solved by Midrash*.

In the end, Ahad Haam's visit to the Herzliya Gymnasium had a delayed effect. The school left intact the order of study established in 1892 by the members of the First Aliyah that began the study of the Bible with Joshua rather than Genesis (or Leviticus) and also left intact the procedure of beginning the Writings with Proverbs rather than Psalms. As a Dutch Christian, Jacobus Schoeneveld, demonstrated, the repeated reconsiderations of the Bible in Israeli education offer the best proof as to how important this subject seemed to both the early Zionists and the founders of the Israeli nation.[32] The 1923 curriculum dropped chrestomathies for actual Tanakh texts, the 1954 curriculum embraced Ben-Gurion's statism, and the recent attempts to permit use of a Bible lite, in easier-to-read modern Hebrew, have been met with outrage. To a non-Israeli looking in, the perennial debates over the role of the teaching of Tanakh as a mandatory subject in state schools remains powerful testimony to the triumph of the Bible in modern Israeli culture. That triumph, at least in part, was enabled by Ahad Haam.[33]

7

The Bible as National Linchpin
David Ben-Gurion and His Opponents

Born in Plonsk, Poland, David Gruen (1886–1973) became an avid Zionist by his teen years. He arrived in Turkish-controlled Palestine in 1906, threw himself into socialist Zionist activism, and adopted the name Ben-Gurion in 1910. He enrolled in law school, got deported to Egypt during World War I, came to the United States, married, and at the end of the war returned to Palestine, then under British rule. Ben-Gurion emerged as Zionism's leading labor organizer, and by the 1930s was Jewish Agency chair. Ben-Gurion led Israel during the War for Independence, and served on and off as Israel's first prime minister. Ben-Gurion provided critical leadership in Israel's struggle for statehood and transformed a socialist-labor movement into a modern state. His life and legacy remain controversial.

I intend merely to trace Ben-Gurion's promotion of the Bible as a key to modern Israeli identity through the eyes of other scholars, principally Michael Keren, Anita Shapira, and Yaacov Shavit. Despite Ben-Gurion's incessant references to Tanakh and his substantial publications in this area, it is easy to overestimate the role of the Bible in his identity or in the state that he helped create.[1] As biographer Shabtai Teveth noted, Ben-Gurion left a literary record which makes differentiating the oft-repeated and the essential difficult.[2] In response to the views of the "Canaanites," who denied any continuity between Hebrew and Jew, Ben-Gurion stressed the unbroken history of the people. Against attempts to rehabilitate rabbinic literature and to intimate that it belonged on the same par as the Bible, Ben-Gurion emphatically denied the creativity of the Jewish diaspora. Like any politician, Ben-Gurion spun his story differently depending on the context.

Ben-Gurion did not organize the Tanakh-heavy school curriculum of 1953–1954, which showed the impact of his "statism" doctrine, but also markedly departed from Ben-Gurion's preferences in that it increased the attention paid to the Pentateuch, and encouraged some recognition of the weekly order of Torah readings.³ Ben-Gurion never pretended to be a Bible scholar; he made a show of deferring to academics in scholarly matters, though he did not hesitate to disagree with them. Ben-Gurion described himself as "merely" a Bible enthusiast. Nevertheless, as a result of his unparalleled prestige, Ben-Gurion's stance regarding the Bible becomes more than a historical curiosity. Moreover, as a representative member of the Second Aliyah, for whom the first person plural was always the most natural voice, Ben-Gurion's relationship to the Bible tells us much about Israeli identity in the formative years of the nation. Michael Keren's *Ben-Gurion and the Intellectuals* summed it up:

> This was one area in which Ben-Gurion clearly dominated the "charismatic center." Not only did he play a personal role in the promotion of activities, such as the international bible contest, or bible study groups (one of which met in his home on a biweekly basis), he also determined, to a great extent, the subject matter to be discussed. A question such as what motivated the Hebrew to go to the land of the Canaan portrayed the return to Canaan as a major biblical event to be studied and debated. Military officers turned amateur archaeologists, and journalists engaged in the writing of long essays on questions such as how many kings Joshua actually overpowered. Prophetic statements were incorporated into the political language, often as a substitute for genuine public ethics. Ben-Gurion himself used biblical quotations in every speech. These quotations not only decorated his speeches but often served as sources of political insight.⁴

Keren was principally interested in the challenge to Ben-Gurion's status that began with the Lavon Affair. Shapira has meditated most of all on Ben-Gurion's adoption of the Bible after statehood and the unfortunate way that it monopolized his intellectual capital, previously drawn on a variety of sources, including the doctrines of socialism and the Hebrew literary renaissance. All of these lost their power, in Shapira's view, to Ben-Gurion's biblicism, which could not, on its own, nourish Israeli identity. In Shapira's chronology, the 1970s saw a natural decline in biblical influence as the rest of Jewish history, the Holocaust above all, returned as a subject of conscious reflection. With respect to the Bible's role in modern Israel, Shavit also tells a "rise and fall" tale, though he focuses on biblical scholarship, which Shapira does not. I will foreground Ben-Gurion's impact in four steps. First, I examine Ben-Gurion's hopelessly conflicted idea of secular biblical authority. Second, I highlight his radical view of the superiority of biblical over rabbinic Judaism, and his preference for

First Temple over Second Temple times. Third, I analyze Ben-Gurion's hostility toward source criticism and his concomitant championing of Yehezkel Kaufmann. Fourth, I reflect on his personal role in forwarding the Bible as linchpin of Israeli national identity. Finally, I briefly address figures in modern Israel who connected the dots of Bible and nation differently than did Ben-Gurion.

DILEMMAS OF BIBLICAL AUTHORITY

While Ben-Gurion's interest in the Bible as a basis for national identity emerged after 1948, its utility must have been latent in Ben-Gurion's mind much earlier.[5] Israel Tabenkin, another member of the Second Aliyah, contended that every pioneer had a copy of the Tanakh that he or she used as a field guide to the old-new land and as an inspirational text. In a similar vein, the writer Aharon Meged wrote, "The Bible was learned and read in the country not as a religious book, but as a literary work of genius, as a linguistic treasure filled with gems, as a historical source, as a geographic and archaeological guidebook, as a fount of wisdom, as a clarion call to idealism and social justice. From the first and in retrospect—the Bible was forging the bond between the people and their ancestral land the cradle of their civilization."[6] Even if Tabenkin and Meged exaggerate, the Second Aliyah clearly expended much energy integrating the Bible into their various ideologies. Ben-Gurion consistently named Harriet Beecher Stowe's *Uncle Tom's Cabin* and Abraham Mapu's biblical-historical novel *The Love of Zion* as the two books which made the greatest impression on him politically. The former taught him the value of freedom; the latter, an early biblically based Hebrew fiction, taught him love of homeland.[7] Ben-Gurion spoke for his generation when he claimed, "I am not religious, nor were the majority of the early builders of modern Israel believers. Yet their passion for this land stemmed from the Book of Books. That is why the socialists of the Bilu movement named themselves with reference to Ezra. And it is why, though I reject theology, the single most important book in my life is the Bible."[8]

A contrast can be made between Ben-Gurion's orientation and that of his perennial opponent, Vladimir Jabotinsky (1880–1940). Jabotinsky, a Russian cosmopolitan turned militant nationalist, had an interest in the Bible too, but when he addressed the British High Commission, better known as the Peel Commission, his argument rested solely on the relative benefit and relative suffering that both sides would experience.[9] The Arabs had a desire for another state, Jabotinsky conceded, but Jews had an existential need for one. By contrast, Ben-Gurion told the Peel Commission, "The Bible is our mandate," a clever play on the notion of the

Jewish people's initial right to the land of Israel, as well as a reminder of the religious motivations behind Britain's bestowal of the Balfour Declaration. Twelve years later, the Israeli Declaration of Independence echoed Ben-Gurion's version of Israel's right to a state as being, at least in part, biblically based. Dramatically delivered by Ben-Gurion from the Tel Aviv Museum at 4:00 p.m. on May 14, 1948, as the British mandate ended and as the civil war between Jews and Arabs escalated to a regional conflict, the declaration's opening sentences validated the specific Jewish stake to the land and the universal gift of the Jews: "The Land of Israel was the birth place of the Jewish people. Here their spiritual, religious and political identity was shaped. Here they first attained to statehood, created cultural values of national and universal significance and gave to the world the eternal Book of Books." This brings us to the first set of contradictions in Ben-Gurion's Bible.

When Ben-Gurion told the British that "the Bible is our mandate," it is easy to dismiss this claim as a mere rhetoric, for Ben-Gurion was ultimately a political animal. He regarded himself as a pantheist like Spinoza, and rejected a personal God or the divine authorship of Scripture. Had Ben-Gurion been a pious Jew, this statement to the British would be self-explanatory. If God promised the Jewish people the land of Israel, then took it away for bad behavior, God could give it back when it suited Him, just as Rashi had commented on Genesis 1:1. Ben-Gurion often expressed messianic aspirations for the new state, and he had his own ideas about redemption. He was no Rashi, however, and his idea of redemption was far removed from either that of Rashi or that of today's settlers. If Ben-Gurion was closer to Spinoza than Rashi in theology, how then could the Bible be his "mandate" for the Zionist movement or for a claim to rightful possession of any part of the land of Israel? This is a paradox in Ben-Gurion's relationship to the Bible. For Ben-Gurion, Jewish longevity, influence, and national self-consciousness were inextricable from the Bible's legacy. The Bible stamped Jewish character, yet was itself a creation of the Jewish people. Since the Bible remains in the realm of the human, however, it is necessarily temporal, not eternal. How can any ancient classic (Homer's *Iliad* or Virgil's *Aeneid*) bestow political rights in a contemporary context? Ben-Gurion spoke frank words on the Bible's origins:

> The Bible, in my humble opinion, is the creation of the Jewish people, and did not come to it from outside. I also do not accept the explanation that Job was translated from another language. Without a doubt the Bible was one of the chief factors in the molding of the image of our people; but this factor came from within, from within the people. The greatness of the Bible is the greatness of the spirit of the Jewish people; it is the fruit of its spirit, the fruit of the great men of our people.[10]

And again:

> And truly in chapter 24 of the Book of Joshua we hear that Israel chose God, and not the other way around. It is inconceivable that this chapter was inserted later, because no one would dare to contradict the accepted tradition that God chose the Israelites, and to fabricate a story that the people chose God. But it is understood that the people did choose God—was captivated by a faith in one God—it became a chosen people by virtue of having been the one and only nation which for many hundreds of years believed in one God.[11]

But what created the Jewish people and how to account for their genius in creating the Bible? To this objection, Ben-Gurion offers the stock nineteenth-century answer: the Jews possessed a spirit of genius in the ethical arena, just as the Greeks possessed a genius for literature, or the Romans for laws and mechanics. The claim that the Jewish people possessed a more refined ethical or spiritual sense, a peculiar "genius," was made explicitly by Abraham Geiger, who agreed that the biblical era represented a high point in Jewish creativity and humanism. As we have seen, Ahad Haam also inclined to this view of high ethical standards as a national characteristic. Centuries of relative Jewish powerlessness combined with a nineteenth-century nationalist impulse fuel this line of argument. To phrase Jewish national excellence as embodying "religious piety" would not have appealed to our secular figures; to phrase it as "commercial enterprise" would not have appealed to anyone. In retrospect, it is much easier to maintain purity of aims when one is not engaged in an existential struggle, as Zionism was and as the State of Israel is. This leads to another source of ambivalence for Ben-Gurion, biblical humanism versus militant nationalism.

Among the many contrasting views of Ahad Haam and Micha Berdichevsky on the Bible, one difference can be isolated as the former's preference for the Latter Prophets with their soaring ethical dicta, and the latter's preference for the Former Prophets with their essentially political-historical narrative. Ben-Gurion seemed stuck between the two. On the one hand, Ben-Gurion never tired of praising the humanistic values of the Bible. One member of his famed Bible study group at his kibbutz home of Sde Boker in the 1960s recalls the biblical quotes that were inscribed on Ben-Gurion's coffee table: "Nation Shall Not Lift Sword Against Nation," "Love Thy brother as Thyself," and so on. He cited the high-minded ethics of the Latter Prophets in numerous addresses and clearly considered the synthesis of spirituality and physicality desirable, as Ahad Haam had argued in "Flesh and Spirit." Ben-Gurion also followed Ahad Haam in his unquestioning belief in an eternal Jewish essence; both men were drawn to vague, organistic metaphors of the Jewish people's survival through history: "national uniqueness" or "vital inner strength."[12] Ben-Gurion sided with Ahad Haam in his unwillingness to accept that the secularization of the Jewish people necessarily entailed a de-Judaizing of that people, a prospect that did not fill Berdichevsky and Brenner with dread, and one which the Canaanites embraced. For Ben-Gurion and Ahad Haam, Israelite and Jewish history displayed consistency, though as Jewish nationalists, both considered the diaspora setting of most of that history inferior. Ben-Gurion differed from Ahad Haam on the issue of biblical historicity. As we have seen, to Ahad Haam, the reality of even so central a figure as Moses was a peripheral concern. Not so to Ben-Gurion, for whom the basic historicity of the Bible was required as a basis of national guidance. Ben-Gurion thus adopted aspects of Ahad Haam's reading of Moses, but rejected Ahad Haam's "postmodern" concession.[13] Ben-Gurion's historicism prevailed. Writing in 1982, Benjamin Beit Hallahmi (Haifa University) complained, "Most Israelis today, as a result of Israeli education, regard the Bible as a source of reliable historical information of a secular, political kind. The Zionist version of Jewish history accepts most biblical legends about the beginnings of Jewish history, minus divine intervention. Abraham, Isaac and Jacob are treated as historical figures. The descent into Egypt and the Exodus are phases in the secular history of a developing people, as is the conquest by Joshua. The Biblical order of events is accepted, but this interpretation is nationalist and secular."[14]

In the 1950s to 1960s Ben-Gurion engaged in a moralistic rhetoric of "mission" that Ahad Haam employed in very different circumstances. Ahad Haam had a parochial streak; his rejection of non-Jewish subjects, as editor of *Ha-Shiloach*, had provoked Berdichevsky's break. Ben-Gurion, on the other hand, constantly applied the Bible to non-Jewish issues. He believed that the Bible had captured the essence of the human condition: self-conscious creativity. Of course, Ben-Gurion gave this humanism a Jewish spin:

> In this respect, the Book of Genesis is most revealing. Christian Gospel begins with the birth of Jesus; the Koran with Mohammed. Torah, however, doesn't start either with Moses or even Abraham, the original Jew, the man who traveled from Chaldea into unknown territory beyond the Euphrates River thereby becoming a pioneer and the first "Hebrew" or "man who crossed over" the river. Torah begins with creation and we are told that six days after conceiving the light, the grass, and all the animals, on the final day of genesis a man and a woman were made and they were in the image of God. Of course speaking personally as one who is non-religious, I believe that theology reverses the true sequence of events. To me it is clear that God was created in the image of man as the latter's explanation to himself of the mystery of his own earthly presence.[15]

Ben-Gurion cited the Bible as a text of conflict resolution, a use that would be dismissed by both Palestinian Arabs and his right-wing critics, albeit for entirely different reasons. As the principal formulator of statism, Ben-Gurion also deployed the Bible as a text that could solve class conflict, or at least ease the tensions between worker and owner, an important element in the transition of Zionism from class movement to nation.[16] The utility of the Bible for current-day problems, manifested in Ahad Haam's essays, may be found in Ben-Gurion too in an obsessively "presentist" manner, as if the Bible obviously applied to the 1950s.

Despite these Ahad Haamist elements, Shapira argues that Berdichevsky's influence on Ben-Gurion predominates. Ben-Gurion's literary icons, such as the poet Saul Tchernichovsky, clearly drew from the vitalist tradition. As Shapira puts it, "though he employed concepts that might hint at a link with the elitist-ethical thought of Ahad Haam, a closer enquiry reveals that this element was less vital and binding, and more given to the opacity of the future. Ben-Gurion remained the faithful disciple of Berdichevsky, seeing Israel's existential and material health as a precondition for moral and spiritual pre-eminence."[17] The bottom line for Ben-Gurion, as Shapira rightly notes, was not coherent philosophy, but the political needs of the moment. Ben-Gurion knew the Bible contained both humanistic and nationalist teachings. The latter predominated in Ben-Gurion's Bible, though not to the exclusion of the former. For some readers, this will seem obvious. From a Palestinian perspective, the Bible served the Zionists and their Christian supporters as a warrant for colonization, expropriation, and the "politicide" of Palestinian Arab aspirations. While this point of view has some validity, it overlooks the reality that Zionism's quest for a usable past germinated from dilemmas of Jewish modernity predating the Arab-Jewish conflict in British-controlled Palestine. Jewish culture since the Enlightenment was bound to wrestle with the biblical legacy. This is not to deny Zionism's "resort to force," as Shapira puts it. But the horse and the cart should be placed in the right order. The pioneers of the Second Aliyah did not read their Bibles and then decide to war against the Palestinians. Rather, as tensions with Palestinians rose, and after the Israeli state, like most states, was established through violence, certain parts of the ancient text seemed more relevant than others. The parable of national struggle in the Bible loomed larger and larger.

Joshua, the biblical character with whom Ben-Gurion most closely identified, conquered the land of Canaan in the traditional account. With the possible exception of the book that comes right after it (Judges), there is no more martial and violent book in the Hebrew Bible. Ben-Gurion went so far as to say that he considered Joshua greater than Moses, who, after all, prepared the nation for the Promised Land, but did not lead them into it. Yet Ben-Gurion's evaluation of Joshua's accomplishment is noteworthy precisely because it would certainly have been possible to read the story of Joshua, and the Bible overall, as praising brute force, "a wall of iron," in Jabotinsky's phrase. Ben-Gurion does not do that. As a matter of fact, the heart of Joshua's accomplishment, in his eyes, is to be found in the book's final chapter, where Joshua established the basis for a unified Hebrew nation on the basis of mutual agreement:

> Chapter 24 in Joshua, with the possible exception of several verses which were added later, is one of the principal and most important documents—if not the most important, in the history of the life of our people.... This chapter bears the stamp of historical truth and isn't adorned with miracles and supernatural feats. This is a lofty dialogue between the nation's leader—its political and spiritual leader—and the nation's most prominent people from every stratum of society.[18]

Ben-Gurion's democratic tendencies checked his admiration for conquest and the pure realpolitik of the political right. His secularism checked any impulse to celebrate Israel's victory as God-given. The relative absence of God as an actor in Joshua 24, where God is invoked by the Israelites, but as standard of national fealty, probably attracted Ben-Gurion, and the consensual nature of the social compact in Joshua 24 is far removed from the dynamics of the covenant at Sinai. Unlike the miraculous events at Sinai, which had limited utility for the modern nation, the covenant renewal at Schechem had plenty of relevance. Thus, what drew Ben-Gurion to this chapter above all is pretty clear: the nation was created by consent of the covenanted and from the bottom up, not the top down. Jews are not the chosen people; they are, however, the choosing people.[19]

At least in theory, Ben-Gurion believed that right, not might, should guide Arab-Jewish relations. In practice, his record is much cloudier, and one suspects that Ben-Gurion projected an ideal situation on a past to compensate for the murkier present. Ben-Gurion professed wildly inflated views of the Bible's current applicability and moral clarity: "Anyone carefully perusing the Bible will find a solution to the two crucial problems of humankind in our time: the problem of capital and labor in society and the problem of war and peace among the nations."[20] Modern readers of the Bible have accomplished a great deal in regard to creating a meaningful text. But the Bible in our time has not stopped economic privation or ended bloodshed in the Middle East or anywhere else.

THE BIBLE AS CREATIVE HIGH POINT IN JEWISH HISTORY

Like most Zionists, Ben-Gurion believed that the Bible represented a high point in Jewish creativity. In a response to an issue of *Davar*, Ben-Gurion took umbrage at the suggestion that the Midrash, a running rabbinic commentary to the Bible, could actually surpass the original text itself in creativity or literary quality. In an essay, "The Bible Is Illumined by Its Own Light," Ben-Gurion revealingly commented that, "Large segments of orthodox Judaism relate negatively to the Bible and see it as an almost heretical book. In any case, the Talmud, the Responsa and the Midrashim are closer to their hearts."[21] While "rabbinic" literature did occupy most of the advanced school years in a traditional yeshiva, by dint of both its size and technical difficulty, it would be perverse to present the Orthodox view of the Bible as a view of it as a heretical book—unless, of course, one meant that the Orthodox viewed the academic, secular study of the Bible as heretical, which is an entirely different charge. When Ben-Gurion goes on to attack Rashi and traditional commentary as abstract (*mufshat*) and detached from the realia of the Bible, Ben-Gurion is simply drawing up lines of battle: On the one side, Zionist, Israelocentric, biblical; on the other, Orthodox, diasporic, and rabbinic. Nobody familiar with Rashi, as Ben-Gurion, a product of a *ḥeder* education, surely was, could characterize him as "abstract." Rashi used illustrations, contemporary French synonyms, simple math, and a slew of other explanatory devices to render what he took to be the teachings of Torah. But Ben-Gurion believed that traditional Judaism lacked the one critical element to unpacking the biblical text properly, a national orientation:

> Without a familiarity with the environment, there can be no understanding of the Bible.... During the exile the image of our people was distorted, and the image of the Bible twisted. Christian Bible scholars, with Christian and anti-Semitic motives, turned the Bible toward Christianity. Even Jewish commentators were uprooted from the environment of the Bible—from its spiritual and physical climate—have not yet been able to understand the book of Books properly. Only now that we have again become a free nation on its own soil, and can again breathe in the air which surrounded the Bible at its creation, has the time come, it appears to me, to deal with the essence of the truth of the Bible historically and geographically, as well as religiously and culturally.[22]

And again, from the same essay:

> The rebirth of Israel and the War of Independence placed the Bible before me in a new light. After I delved into it, considering the facts of the War of Independence and the settlement of Israel in our day, questions were raised within me to which biblical commentators in Israel throughout the generations had not paid sufficient attention, because to them the concepts nation, tribes, conquest war, geography, Israel, settlement, and mother tongue were abstract concepts.[23]

We will return to the pointed attack on Christian interpreters in the first citation. For now, let us fully register this deprecation of Jewish exegetical tradition. I would stress both the pragmatic elements of this formulation, namely, the appearance of a free nation under its own governance, and the more mystical ones, namely, the connection between a people and its native soil as the sole factor enabling creativity. One could parse these two components as the Ahad Haamist and the Berdichevskian strains. For Ahad Haam, Palestine-Israel was to be preferred to the diaspora because only there could modern Jews develop a cultural center organically, with some degree of independence, not looking over their shoulders all the time to see what the non-Jews were saying. That practical focus on the importance of context separated Ahad Haam from Autonomists such as his friend Shimon Dubnov. Dubnov held that Jewish autonomy could be achieved under a reformed czarist regime; Ahad Haam considered that position tantamount to settling for half a loaf. But the archrationalist Ahad Haam did not think merely transporting Jews to Israel would achieve some kind of magic effect—as anyone reading his gimlet-eyed essays on conditions in the early Yishuv would realize. It was the camp of Berdichevsky and Brenner, among secular Zionists, who were swayed by Nietzsche and the currents of vitalism to believe that removal to Israel and adoption of Hebrew would magically ensure a creative Jewish culture. Ahad Haam became increasingly conservative and increasingly wedded to a search for a national essence—an anxiety much less pronounced in his early writings. He did not believe that any mystical power existed.

Ben-Gurion's laudation of the Bible over the rabbinic literature was standard Zionist fare, but the lengths to which Ben-Gurion took this dichotomy invited rebuttal. An article in *Davar* praising Midrash infuriated Ben-Gurion and prompted his dismissive comments about rabbinic literature, but Ben-Gurion discovered other secular intellectuals who disagreed with his viewpoint. Avraham Kariv, author of *Seven Pillars of Biblical Wisdom*, could hardly be accused of lacking enthusiasm for the Bible, but he too found Ben-Gurion's assessment of rabbinic literature lacking. Ben-Gurion's subsequent debate with the author Hayim Hazaz (1962) revealed even more clearly the weakness of Ben-Gurion's elevation of the Bible.[24] Hazaz argued, on historical grounds, that rabbinic literature provided the real link between generations of Jews; whatever the Zionist movement did to reinvigorate the biblical past, the link to that past had been the rabbinic traditions, not longing for Zion. Additionally, Hazaz rejected the idea that the Bible exhausted the spiritual resources of Judaism. Ben-Gurion recognized in these words, uttered by Hazaz, a fellow secularist, echoes of the philosopher Yeshayahu Leibowitz's charge of bibliolatry. Ben-Gurion rejected the idea that love of Tanakh was some kind of idolatry by another name, but he also backpedaled somewhat, agreeing with Hazaz that without the Mishnah one could not know Hebrew.[25] That concession could have been a major one: the Mishnah was written in Hebrew, in the land of Israel, but after the destruction of Jewish sovereignty. In other words, the Mishnah straddled the border between biblical and rabbinic and challenged Ben-Gurion's dichotomy of Jewish history. Ben-Gurion was a politician, not a logician; he did not pursue the example.

Ahad Haam and Berdichevsky differed on the nature of the ending of the biblical period, but not its basic chronology. On occasion, Ben-Gurion also dated "Zionism" from the destruction of the Second Temple: "From when can one date the Jewish return to Israel? One can say, therefore, without being accused of mysticism that the Jewish return to autonomy in Israel really dates from the fall of Jerusalem and Masada in the eighth decade of the Common Era."[26] But elsewhere, he strikes a more radical note. For Ben-Gurion, the Maccabean dynasty was short-lived and impressive mainly as a national refusal to assimilate; Masada and Bar Kochba were defeats. Ben-Gurion found the Second Commonwealth on a far lower level than the first. Abraham, Moses, David, and, above all, Joshua were Ben-Gurion's heroes. Although Ben-Gurion lavished praise on the Persian-era King Cyrus for allowing the restoration of Jewish sovereignty, and conceded that the religious consolidation of Israel took place in the Persian period, his main interest was in Nehemiah's account of the combination of labor and defense needed to rebuild the walls of Jerusalem. Granted, this speech was given to the Israel Defense Forces on the theme of the army's role in educating the nation, but Ben-Gurion's preference for early events in Israel's history is consistent. Rather radically, Ben-Gurion imagined a nation interruptus, in which the entire Jewish people treaded water from 586 BCE all the way to the beginning of Zionism. It might be mentioned that this explicit preference for First Temple over Second Temple is found in both Spinoza and Mendelssohn. Ben-Gurion's admiration for Spinoza was boundless, though his attempts to rescind Spinoza's excommunication were unsuccessful.

BEN-GURION, YEHEZKEL KAUFMANN, AND ISRAELITE AUTOCHTHONY

We have examined Ben-Gurion's extreme elevation of the remote biblical past, which Yeshayahu Leibowitz termed bibliolatry. But there are other, pugnaciously Jewish, elements in Ben-Gurion's orientation to the Bible, beyond his boundless admiration. "The Bible Is Illumined by Its Own Light," cited above, illustrates not only his disdain for rabbinic Judaism, but also his animosity toward Protestant Bible scholarship and, arguably, toward "Christianity," at least in its millennial treatment of the Jew. Today, scholars unanimously agree that Julius Wellhausen and the German Protestant source critics possessed a very negative view of Judaism, which they regarded as degeneration of the Bible—and which they derogatorily called "Spätjudentum," "late Judaism." The Jewish response to this attack on the Mosaic nature of the Torah and the so-called degeneration of Second Temple Judaism was transcontinental; in Israel, it included Cassuto, Segal, Kaufmann, and that pioneering archaeologist Eliezer Sukenik, who called for a "Jewish archaeology." All of these rejected the academic characterization of Judaism in the centuries before Jesus as "spent."

Although Segal and Cassuto wrote books confuting source criticism, the Israeli rejection of its findings was epitomized by Yehezkel Kaufmann (1889–1963).[27] Kaufmann made extreme claims for the antiquity of Israel's presence in the land and for the autochthonous nature of Israel's faith. Kaufmann poured his monumental learning into his multivolume *History of the Israelite Faith* and his meditation on the origins of the diaspora, *Exile and Estrangement*. His influence on Israeli Bible scholarship in Ben-Gurion's era was predominant, and he was the guiding spirit at New York's Jewish Theological Seminary in the immediate post–World War II years as well. Stephen Geller has highlighted Kaufmann's dialectical relationship with the synthesizer of source criticism, Julius Wellhausen. On almost every point, whether dating individual documents, assessing the nature of Israelite faith, judging Israel's dependence on external cultures, or visualizing the final redaction of the Bible and its implications for subsequent Judaism, Kaufmann dissented vigorously from Wellhausen. Indeed, this polemical spirit so animated Kaufmann that by the end of his career he was still battling Wellhausen, largely oblivious to the ascent of very different methods in the field of Bible, including form criticism and the study of oral traditions. On the other hand, it might be noted that most Christian scholars did not read Kaufmann at all, presumably because he wrote in modern Hebrew. In 1960, Moshe Greenberg translated and condensed Kaufmann's biblical magnum opus into *History of Israelite Religion*, giving it a second lease on life for English-only readers, and Leo Schwartz's successful anthology *Great Ages and Ideas of the Jewish People* (1956) assigned the essay on the biblical period to Kaufmann, whose views were even more out of the scholarly mainstream by then than when he originally published them. Kaufmann's conceptions have received a great deal of scholarly treatment, much of it beyond the interest of the general reader. But a few highlights of Kaufmann's approach are worth noting. As Nahum Sarna wrote:

> Most important for Kaufmann's thesis is his conclusion that the "Torah book" was fixed before the organization of the prophetic literature had worked its decisive influence upon the people. For Kaufmann, the implications of all this for the history of the religion of Israel are clear. The Torah becomes, once again, the starting point for historical inquiry. The sources do furnish us with genuine traditions about the times with which they purport to deal. Monotheism appears as a popular national phenomenon pervading the earliest traditions and molding the earliest institutions of Israel. This,

indeed, is the very core of Kaufmann's thesis, the elaboration of which takes up the more than 2,500 pages of the as yet unfinished Hebrew original.[28]

Regarding monotheism, Kaufmann wrote, "Biblical tradition represents the fathers of the race and the patriarchs of Israel as monotheists. Adam, Noah, Abraham and his descendants all knew God and received his commandments. Idolatry arose as a later degeneration. This view prevails in Judaism, Christianity and Islam and was dominant in western thought until modern times."[29] If only the word "biblical" were replaced by "Judeo-Christian-Islamic," the trio of monotheistic religions the Bible spawned. In the opinion of most Bible scholars, the ancient Israelites generally, and the figures in Genesis all the more so, were monolaters or henotheists, who affirmed their allegiance to one God (YHVH), but acknowledged the presence of other gods for other nations. Not until a much later period, usually associated with the classical Prophets of the eighth to seventh centuries BCE, did Israel accept that God was one and omnipresent. Popular internalization of this concept took even longer. The prophetic denunciations of Israelite idolatry, regarded by Kaufmann as zealous overreaction, have been read by most scholars as entirely warranted. Archaeologists have turned up numerous statuettes of YHVH's divine consort Asherah centuries after the prophet Amos had proclaimed God's universal sovereignty. Synagogue services feature the verse from Exodus 15, "Who is like you among the gods, YHVH?" a question that makes more rhetorical sense if there are other gods, albeit false ones, with whom to compare the God of Israel. As Jon D. Levenson argued, Kaufmann did not take into account more sophisticated understandings of myth, and made little distinction between "myth" and "fable."[30]

Equally dubious, in retrospect, was Kaufmann's view that ancient Israel viewed the surrounding religions with incomprehension, as mere idolatrous fetishism. For Kaufmann, the inability to compile an accurate picture of Canaanite practices was only further proof of the theological distance between Israel and her neighbors. But practically every genre of biblical literature has ancient Near Eastern analogues. The royal and priestly architecture of Israel, however early or late one dates it, clearly adopted ancient Near Eastern models. Beginning with Sarna, if not earlier, it has seemed plausible that much of the canonically earliest material in the Bible engaged in a studied polemic against the views propounded by ancient Near Eastern models. This is not indifference or incomprehension, as per Kaufmann—it is conscious animus.

The preeminence of the Torah over the Prophets, for Kaufmann, was more a chronological claim than a qualitative one. He conceded the superior theology of the Prophets, but relished the folk nature of the Torah literature: "The faith of the Torah has a naive, popular character quite different from that of prophecy."[31] Kaufmann maintained that Torah literature contained a fundamentally historical account, correcting for the Bible's very different views of historiography, and was all produced before the Prophets and before the Babylonian Exile of 587/586 BCE. The Torah preceded the Prophets. While Kaufmann argues this at length, the gist is that the Torah appears to know nothing of the prophetic standards of socioeconomic fairness, and nothing of prophetic monotheism, as explained above. Contrariwise, the Prophets take the composite teaching of J, E, P, and D for granted. (Kaufmann acknowledged the likelihood of these authorial strands.) This dating of the Torah to before the exile provided the natural line of defense for Kaufmann and an entire generation of Israeli scholars. The Bible—the Torah—might not be from God, it might not even be from Moses, but it was produced by the Jewish people on their own land and in their own nation. True, the Torah as canon, as a binding unified work, did not exist until after the exile. But, for Kaufmann, that process was one of assembly; all the component parts were domestic product (*tozeret ha-aretz*). No issue shows Kaufmann's dogmatism on the indigenous nature of the entire Torah better than the seemingly arcane one of who came first, P or D.

Poor P, maligned as priestly, post-exilic, stultifying. Inserter of all those genealogical lists, apologist for the erring Aaron, formulaic and lacking in the spontaneity of J and E. Worst of all, P was suspected of being Ezra or a member of his school. In addition to lowering the overall quality of the Old Testament, P provided the animating spirit of Pharisaic Judaism, and for most non-Jewish scholars in Kaufmann's day that was damning. Kaufmann argued at length for the chronological priority of Torah over Prophets; he argued endlessly for the early dating of P to Hezekiah, if not earlier. Kaufmann, revealingly, was less vexed by the issue of whether Josiah's courtiers discovered D or just composed it to justify the Josian reforms carried out in II Kings 22–24, a "pious fraud" in Wilhelm De Wette's phrase. Kaufmann himself believed D contained demonstrably older materials, but that was a trivial matter beside his key point—nothing in D suggested postexilic dating.

Did the Deuteronomic code influence the Priestly code, or vice versa? Kaufmann considered this the central either/or question in Pentateuch studies. Unlike the narrative material, which had been well integrated and was not so easily identified as J, E, P, and D, the legal material of the Torah, in Kaufmann's view, existed in three clearly defined legal corpora. Thus, simple comparison among these corpora was possible. For Kaufmann the findings were obvious: P knew nothing of D's emphasis on the centrality of the cult in Jerusalem. (Kaufmann regarded the idea that P fabricated a Tabernacle narrative to validate the Solomonic Temple as a scholarly fantasy.) The firstling sacrifice of P was older than that of D; so was P's version of the Levitical tithe; so was P's version of sacred meals, including the home Pesach (Passover). P before D. That is Kaufmann's claim, no exceptions allowed. The net effect, in addition to the dating of *all* the Torah components before the exile, was granting Deuteronomy, with its strong legal, corporate, rational, egalitarian, and nationalist ideology, the final word in the Torah. Not coincidentally, this mirrors the important place of Deuteronomy as the swing door from the Torah to the Prophets, as well as the central place of Deuteronomy in Judaism.

Ben-Gurion identified himself as a Kaufmann disciple, and on numerous occasions stated his view that Kaufmann's scholarly work was the most important book in the field.[32] Nevertheless, their disputes over the Bible were numerous. When it came to highlighting the connection of the people Israel and the land of Israel, Ben-Gurion went even further than his mentor. Ben-Gurion held radical views of both Abraham and Exodus: "My first assumption is that the Jewish people or the Hebrew people was born in Israel and grew up in Israel even before the days of Abraham, as one of the nations of Canaan, and, at that time was scattered in the south, central sector, and the north with its spiritual and political capital in Shechem. But, in my opinion, only a few families, among the most highly ranked, descended into Egypt. The remaining masses of the children of Israel remained among the peoples of Canaan."[33]

Even Kaufmann never claimed that there were Hebrews in the land before Abraham, or that most Israelites never went down to Egypt, but rather remained in Canaan. But any approach to the Bible that did not consistently reaffirm its status as a Zionist mandate ultimately had no appeal to Ben-Gurion; at the end of the day, his reading of the Bible was tendentiously political. This particular reading of the early history of the nation ignited a firestorm. On May 12, 1960, Ben-Gurion called a press conference to report these speculations on ancient Israel, and after *The Jerusalem Post* dutifully reported these remarks, the National Religious Party moved a motion of nonconfidence, accusing Ben-Gurion of lending support to the Canaanites. Ben-Gurion tried to prove an Exodus of about six hundred people through biblical arithmetic, genealogical analysis, and at least one proposed emendation: that the Hebrew word *elef* be rendered as "family" rather than "thousand," an interpretation he supported by many instances where the word could mean the former.[34] Ben-Gurion's eagerness to enter into the nitty-gritty of Bible scholarship was typical. Ben-Gurion, insatiable bibliophile and late night reader, liked to be thought of as an *intellectual*. Why a brilliant politician would crave this title eludes me, but his interests were ultimately practical, not academic. How did Israel sustain itself in its formative years? How could a small state sustain itself economically and forge diplomatic alliances? How did the Jewish people survive indefinite conflict? These questions, asked repeatedly by Ben-Gurion of the Bible, were blatantly driven by the imperatives of the present—there is little sense of an unfolding academic discourse.

Ben-Gurion's cannot be called "Bible scholarship" any more than Ahad Haam's can. Nevertheless, Ben-Gurion's personal role in forwarding the centrality of the Bible should not be underestimated. The Bible study group at Ben-Gurion's kibbutz Sde Boker home was a serious and sincere meeting of professors, amateur Bible enthusiasts, and family favorites, including Paula Ben-Gurion's doctor. As recalled by Haim Gevaryahu, the group met every fortnight for a couple of hours, usually until Paula protectively entered and announced that her husband needed his rest. The symbolism of the nation's founding father spending his time surrounded by fellow intellectuals studying the Jewish mandate corresponds to that of the founding generals (e.g., Yigael Yadin, Moshe Dayan) excavating the Jewish patrimony. One struggles to imagine a modern parallel. Thomas Jefferson assembling his fellow Virginia planters at Monticello to pore over the words of John Locke seems plausible; Jefferson did, after all, author a New Testament with the offensive sections removed. But imagining Bismarck at Berlin, studying Luther with a cohort of Prussian Junkers? This fictional scene boggles the imagination. Consider again the no-confidence vote prompted by Ben-Gurion's claims of a limited Exodus. If Angela Merkel declared Otto the Great overrated, or Nicolas Sarkozy called the Merovingians uncivilized, who would care? What other nation would be so *bookish* about its identity? Ben-Gurion neither advanced biblical scholarship nor managed the Israeli Bible curriculum, but for better or worse, Ben-Gurion shaped the modern Jewish Bible.

REJECTING BEN-GURION: BIBLICAL HUMANISM

Even within the Zionist mainstream, as we have seen, figures like Hazaz and Rotenstreich and Kariv took issue with Ben-Gurion's view of the Bible. I have portrayed Ben-Gurion's biblical views as oscillating between the poles of idealism and force, but detractors from the left did not see it that way. The calls for "biblical humanism" expressed by Martin Buber and others involved in the Brit Shalom and Ichud movements had very different political goals. For these figures, advocates of a single, binational state with complete cultural autonomy for Jews, Christians, and Muslims, the matter of statehood should never have been settled through violence. Buber, who applied his "dialogical philosophy" to biblical texts so fruitfully in the 1920s, considered Israeli dealings with the Arabs incompatible with dialogical values or biblical ones.[35]

REJECTING BEN-GURION: EXTREME SECULARISM

Ben-Gurion's biblicism faced equal disdain from the political right. By the 1920s Jabotinsky became the principal exponent of a maximalist view regarding the borders of the state, and the inevitability of armed conflict. Even more utilitarian in his Bible-reading than Ben-Gurion, Jabotinsky found a different message. His biblical novel *Samson* (Russian 1926/Hebrew 1930) offers a thoroughly secularized view of the period of Judges, complete with the admission that there was much to admire in Philistine culture. Jabotinsky's Samson applauds the Philistines' use of steel and the importance of boundary stones. Jabotinsky reiterates these themes at the end of the book and adds another: Samson counsels his fellow nationals to find themselves a king. *Samson* serves as a cautionary tale about lagging military technology, failure to make forceful territorial claims, and the resulting chaos, "when there is no king in Israel." Strikingly absent from the novel is any value that could be identified as Jewish, or even humanistic.[36]

REJECTING BEN-GURION: THE CANAANITES

Even more convinced than Jabotinsky that the Bible was "too Jewish," Jonathon Ratosh (1909–1981) advocated a return to the primitivism and animism of the early Canaanites who flourished briefly in the 1940s and 1950s. Calling themselves "Hebrews," they rejected any connection between the settlement of Israel and the Jewish tradition. They never captured a significant part of prestate secular Zionists, but, as Baruch Kurzweil suggested, and James S. Diamond proved, the Canaanites represented a logical extension of a secularist rejection of Judaism that began with Berdichevsky and Brenner. Diamond concludes, "Armed with the approach and findings of higher biblical criticism and archaeology, Ratosh is able to construct a new historiography, one that relativizes the absolutes of the biblical understanding of Jews." Ratosh's anti-biblical value system comes through clearly enough in his funeral hymn, "The Soul," which evokes the very Canaanite pantheon which the Prophets fulminate against. Although Ratosh is extreme, his case dramatizes an irony: the Bible remained a touchstone to even the most secular Zionists—albeit a negative one.[37]

ORTHODOX REJECTIONS OF BEN-GURION'S BIBLICISM

The founding of a religious Zionist party in 1902 met with vocal opposition on the part of traditional authorities in eastern Europe. Without entering into Ehud Luz's exquisitely told tale, this traditionalist leadership sensed that Zionism's desire to return to the land could revive messianic sentiment that had lain dormant for centuries.[38] Religious Zionists countered their traditionalist opponents with biblical passages that placed great emphasis on the land and its special properties. Nobody shaped religious Zionism's views of the Bible more than Abraham Isaac ha-Kohen Kook, the first Ashkenazic chief rabbi of the Yishuv. Rav Kook was a messianic thinker who used biblical metaphors constantly. He believed that the secular Jewish settlers were unwittingly doing God's work and that the establishment of Israel would be a boon to all humanity, Palestinian Arabs included.[39] His son, Rabbi Zvi Yehuda Kook, displayed a different combination of messianism and nationalism. In the wake of the 1967 war, Zvi Yehuda Kook encouraged a militant stance regarding territorial integrity of the land and the absolute right of Jews to settle in it on religious grounds. The Kookist view lies at the heart of Israeli religious nationalism, although their synthesis of messianism and the Bible has had many critics within Orthodoxy. These developments were largely post-1967 ones, and beyond the scope of this chapter. Already under way in Ben-Gurion's day was a transformation in Torah studies wrought by Nehama Leibowitz, the most influential Bible teacher of the twentieth century, and the subject of our next chapter.

8

Nehama Leibowitz's Bible
Returning Tradition to the Text

Nehama Leibowitz (1905–1997) was the most influential teacher of Torah in the twentieth century. She taught hundreds of students in classrooms throughout Israel and in her modest Jerusalem apartment. She influenced thousands more, most of all through her weekly "pages" (*gilyonot*) beginning in 1941[1] and her *Studies in Genesis–Deuteronomy* (seven volumes), written initially in Hebrew and subsequently translated into many languages.[2] Justly celebrated as a master educator, she has already generated five book-length treatments, including two full-length biographies, as well as numerous articles, mainly focused on her pedagogical approach.[3] A supremely modest woman, Leibowitz's gravestone contains just one word besides her name and birth and death dates: Teacher. Even as her students' students continue to apply her pedagogical methods, the historical context of her achievement seems to be slipping from view. Moreover, her own students have taken her modest self-appraisal as being merely a conduit of masters past too much to heart, obscuring her originality as an exegete and as a contributor to the making of the modern Jewish Bible. This project comprises several elements: a desire to place the Bible and its commentaries at the center of Jewish intellectual life; a desire to make the Bible accessible and relevant through translation and production of children's Bibles, commentaries, and Bible guides; and an insistence on affirming the Jewishness of the Bible, often in polemical response to early source critical works.

Whether construed religiously as Torah, or culturally as "the book of books," an important chapter of this Bible story was written in the land of Israel in the years following the formation of the state. For Zionists, the need for suitable translation, critical for diaspora Jewries, played no significant role. But enough of this program remains to encompass Zionists as different as Ben-Gurion, Yigael Yadin, and Leibowitz, all proponents of the Bible's centrality. My discussion attempts to highlight Leibowitz's unique role: (1) I will provide some historical context for Leibowitz for the vast majority of those students and teachers who encounter her only via her published writings, (2) I will revisit the often overlooked presuppositions of her Bible studies as reflected in the *Studies* and *gilyonot*, and (3) I will detail her specific debt to modern German-Jewish commentators, some of whom she knew personally, and most of whom she incorporated into her thinking, their heterodoxy notwithstanding.

NEHAMA LEIBOWITZ: NECESSARY BACKGROUND

Leibowitz came from a merchant family in Riga, Latvia, the younger sister of the philosopher Yeshayahu Leibowitz. She and her brother both received home tutoring, not unusual for middle-class Jewish families. While the common tongue of Jews in the Baltic states was Yiddish, the Leibowitz household used Hebrew, and her mother was a fervent admirer of German literature as well. The Leibowitz family moved to Berlin in 1919 where she received her higher education, both academic high school and university, in German public institutions from 1920 to 1928, overlapping the best years of the Weimar Republic, dubbed by Michael Brenner the "renaissance" of German Jewry. A denizen of Berlin, a student at the liberal Berlin Hochschüle, and a member of the Blau-Weiss, a German-Jewish student group, Leibowitz experienced this phenomenon intimately. While her biographers pass over this quickly, the impact of this German and German-Jewish intellectual milieu seems pronounced. Like many eastern European luminaries on the way to either Israel or the United States of America (e.g., Abraham Joshua Heschel, Salo W. Baron, Harry A. Wolfsohn, Jacob Katz, Yehiel Y. Weinberg, and Joseph Soloveitchik), she earned her doctorate in Germany, in her case from the Philipps University in Marburg, a bastion of liberalism compared to the older Prussian universities. Marburg University enjoyed the presence of extraordinary intellectual talents in this era, including the German- Jewish philosopher Hermann Cohen and the philosopher Leo Strauss, a fellow member of the Blau-Weiss fraternity and student at the liberal Hochschüle.[4] Leibowitz's doctoral inaugural address from Marburg, *Techniques in the Translations of German-Jewish Bible in the 15th and 16th Centuries*, was a model of clarity and erudition. Her thesis was straightforward: German-Jewish Bibles in Yiddish, in particular Psalms, owed something to the German background, but more to the indigenous tradition of Jewish commentary.

The Leibowitz family was religious-Zionist and Nehama and Yeshayahu made aliyah in 1930 and 1935, respectively. Although she arrived as a credentialed teacher, she took some time securing a place in the academy; this, too, was typical for scholars who did not fit the prestate mold. The historian Jacob Katz, deeply influenced by sociology and social history, had a hard time with the more intellectual history– and religious history–focused scholars of the Jerusalem school. It took some time for Katz, now generally acknowledged as one of the most important Jewish historians of the twentieth century, to get the position he deserved.[5] Leibowitz suffered similar bias, and no doubt her gender played some role in this retarded acknowledgment of her unique qualities. Leibowitz spent some time at the Teacher's Institute, offered adult education classes for years, began lecturing at Tel Aviv University in 1957, and became a full professor in 1968. I would term this series of intellectual encounters "the triple immersion," a phenomenon that deeply fructified Jewish intellectual life in the middle decades of the twentieth century. This triple immersion (eastern Europe–Germany–Israel/America) deserves more attention than it has received, despite a very readable book by Hillel Goldberg, and despite the fact that several of the beneficiaries of this triple immersion have dwelled at length on this phenomenon in their autobiographies.[6]

To define this phenomenon: This generation stemmed from a deeply traditional eastern European background, including intimate knowledge of Jewish halachah, custom, and liturgy. They all had diglossic competence—that is, they all knew at least Yiddish and Hebrew from an early age. In most cases, including Leibowitz's, they leveraged their linguistic virtuosity for their doctoral work. They then encountered the world of German academia in its Weimar-period heyday, in many cases studying with the undisputed pioneers in a variety of social sciences, including sociology, anthropology, psychology, economics, and linguistics. Katz, for instance, came from a deeply Orthodox Hungarian background, and studied with Karl Mannheim before making aliyah. Joseph Soloveitchik came from a Lithuanian rabbinic dynasty and mastered neo-Kantian philosophy at Berlin before coming to America. Finally, all of these figures needed to deal with a new reality, immigrant life, whether in Israel or the United States. From a Zionist perspective, principled aliyah to Israel (the Leibowitzes, Katz, etc.) might seem very different from migration to the United States, whether professionally motivated (e.g., Baron, Wolfson) or in flight from persecution (e.g., Strauss, Schneersohn, and Heschel). But all these figures needed to confront yet a third cultural-sociological-intellectual milieu, distinctly different from what they had experienced either as children or as formative intellectuals. Although this third stage generally involved considerable hardships professionally, the overall impact was positive and lasting.

What difference did this eastern European Orthodox background exert in Leibowitz's case? One may observe that at neither Hebrew nor Tel Aviv universities did the Bible departments appreciate her scholarly importance or her rehabilitation of midrashic methods—as well as her critical perception of the correlations between *parshanut* and New Criticism. Leibowitz taught exclusively in the education department and the overseas programs. She received no mention in Menahem Haran's overview of Bible scholarship at Israeli universities; nor in Shavit and Eran's more recent *The Hebrew Bible Reborn*. Anita Shapira, doyenne of historical studies on the Bible and Israeli identity, mentions Leibowitz in the context of explaining the declining hold of the Bible!⁷ Leibowitz developed her method early and did not accommodate academic expectations. Undeterred by the preference of university mandarins for footnotes over parentheses, she wrote, taught, and published until the end of her long and productive life, never leaving Israel. She won many major awards, but remained a marginal figure in the Israeli academy—needless to say, as a woman, she would have fared no better in the yeshiva world.

NEHAMA LEIBOWITZ: FOUR ACCOMPLISHMENTS

Almost single-handedly, Leibowitz restored the Jewish tradition of *parshanut ha-mikra* to a central place among Israeli Bible scholars. For David Ben-Gurion and other secular Zionists, traditional commentators lacked the insight that living in the land of Israel and participating in a state afforded. Many of Ben-Gurion's secular contemporaries, shared his lukewarm attitude toward rabbinic commentary as a guide to the Bible. Although a grudging acknowledgment might have been awarded to the medieval *pashtanim* as scholarly precursors, Leibowitz treated the early midrashim/aggadot with equal respect. First and foremost, Leibowitz made it impossible to ignore this indigenously Jewish exegetical tradition. Elevating rabbinic commentary to a central place in Bible studies would be an accomplishment sufficient for a lifetime, but I believe at least three more achievements must be credited to Leibowitz.

First, Leibowitz fiercely advocated Tanakh as an intellectual meeting ground for modern Jewry. As Aryeh Newman lovingly recounts it, Leibowitz read and corrected submissions from soldiers fighting on the front lines of battle in Israel's wars, from still-persecuted Jewish communities in the Soviet Union and South America, and from the deeply observant and the secular. Moreover, Leibowitz attracted secular Jews to engage in her minute analysis of the Torah, which often got less attention from secular Zionists than the more overtly political-military material contained in Former Prophets (I Samuel–II Kings). Ben-Gurion was certainly attuned to the Bible as a national linchpin that could anchor "Sephardim" and Holocaust survivors in a way that socialism-Zionism could not. But Ben-Gurion and his generation assumed that the straightforward national narrative of ancient Israel in its (ostensible) historical reality ought to suffice. Ben-Gurion's advocacy of the Bible, while sincere, often had an instrumentalist flavor. Leibowitz, more reflective of a traditional Jewish attitude, treated the Torah as a text with infinite depth and subtlety. Although she employed a distinctly traditional idiom, Leibowitz spoke to contemporary Israeli realities. Indeed, if one wanted to study with "Nehama," as she insisted on being called, one had to go to Israel, since she refused all offers to leave the land of Israel to teach from her aliyah (1930) until her death (1997). Leibowitz took the return of students to the diaspora very much to heart, and expressed bewilderment at Jews less committed to building the homeland.[8]

Second, Leibowitz identified affinities between the "New Critics" and the literary mode of reading Scripture favored by the "maximalists" within the Jewish tradition.[9] Much of the Israeli academy struggled to establish a scientific approach to the Bible without capitulating to the source critics wholesale. Although Moshe Segal and Umberto Cassuto were great scholars, and the latter in particular made many innovative comparisons between the Bible and other ancient literatures, both men were often shadowboxing with the ghost of Wellhausen, as was Kaufmann. But Leibowitz identified a disciplinary trend outside the guild of Bible scholars as applicable to Scripture. The New Critics insisted on treating literary works as self-contained autonomous entities. Texts could not be fully grasped either as historical artifacts or as purely subjective experiences—neither authorial intent nor effective intent could be relied upon. Rather, the New Critics championed a "close reading" that paid primary attention to the interconnectedness and integrity of a given work and its genre.[10] Before Erich Auerbach and Robert Alter, Leibowitz was paying attention to the very things that these and many "new literary critics" would take up.

Third, it is difficult to imagine the current crop of leading Israeli Bible scholars who are women, the proliferation of female-only yeshivot, or the presence of superstar Orthodox women Torah teachers without Leibowitz's unparalleled role. Only radical changes in European and Jewish society allowed Leibowitz to take on this role. In traditional Judaic culture, women had more latitude studying the Hebrew Bible than the Talmud. While *The Women's Bible* (Tsenah u'Renah) went through multiple editions, no analogous example of rabbinic work exists. Nineteenth-century openness to female education made a phenomenon like Leibowitz possible. Hirsch, we saw, directed his law code *Horeb* to men and women alike. In eastern Europe, the Bais Yakov movement made Jewish and general education available to women in a traditional context; the ability of "Bais Yakov girls" to navigate traditional Bible commentary was legendary. In Leibowitz's case, her parents were among the Orthodox Enlightened who believed in education for both boys and girls. Leibowitz's formal education at several German universities must also be mentioned: women did not attend university until modern times, and the enrollment of Jewish women naturally lagged behind that of men. Leibowitz's gender, in my opinion, is therefore an important part of her story as a teacher-scholar, even though she was hostile to feminism when it overstepped the bounds of traditional halachah, and never demonstrated special interest in female biblical characters or incidents. The furthest Leibowitz went in this direction seems to be her reading of Genesis 30:1, where Jacob reproaches Rachel for her exclamation, "Give me children or I will die." But even here the conclusion is quite ambiguous: Leibowitz focused on Jacob, not Rachel, and sided with those commentators who defended Jacob's retort on the grounds that a woman's existence transcended procreation. Whether Jacob's reproach to Rachel can be considered biblical protofeminism or not, Leibowitz clearly believed that Rachel misunderstood the Torah's view of ontological equality between the sexes.[11] This tension between establishing a new model for female activity and affirming traditional Jewish values may be found is several pivotal figures: Bertha Pappenheim, Henrietta Szold, Sarah Scheinerer, Ray Frank, and Julia Richman. Still, Torah scholarship remains a special domain, and the first to shatter the glass ceiling, as Leibowitz did, deserves praise.[12]

NEHAMA LEIBOWITZ:
SEVEN PRESUPPOSITIONS OF HER BIBLE EXEGESIS

Leibowitz contributed to the project of making the modern Bible a centerpiece of Israeli and Jewish identity, with a determination comparable to that of Ben-Gurion. The first step in this recognition is to deny her self-description: "I have no *derech* . . . I only teach what the commentaries say. Nothing is my own." Leibowitz's personal modesty notwithstanding, the idea that "the Bible can be illumined by its own light" (Ben-Gurion) or "be interpreted by itself" (Hirsch) is never accurate.[13] Ironically, her devoted students have abetted the underestimation of her importance to Bible study by presenting her as a transmitter of genius whose teaching method can be successfully replicated. When it came to Bible, Leibowitz asked questions about specific word choices, about minute differences in "seeming" biblical repetitions, about the epithets used to describe characters, about the context of a particular verse, about seemingly extraneous words and seeming gaps. She paid attention to repeating words (*Leitwörter*), to unusually used words, and to any oddity in the biblical text. She had students read aloud and dramatize the scene in question, and forbade students from writing. She eschewed frontal lectures and taught technique, not material; active learning as she saw it. As Marla Frankel noted, when dealing with the short, religiously intense story such as the Binding of Isaac, she focused on the universal; when dealing with the seemingly universal secular Joseph narrative, she highlighted religious elements.[14] No other teacher had the ability to impart a pedagogical method which could be replicated to the same degree, yet Leibowitz also reveals a distinct, historically specific Bible exegesis. The following seven presuppositions may be obvious, but they deserve acknowledgment:

1. Leibowitz was an unapologetic Orthodox modernist, deeply influenced by the Maimonidean-Haskalah tradition that one should accept truth from whatever source. Leibowitz included every stratum of Jewish creativity: early midrash, medieval commentators, and moderns. Unlike a certain stream of contemporary American Orthodoxy which takes the assumption of "a decline in generations" very seriously, and privileges early rabbinic and medieval insights, Leibowitz comes much closer to Rav Joseph Soloveitchik's affirmation of the dignity of modern man, expressed in the opening pages of his landmark essay "The Lonely Man of Faith." Leibowitz frequently cited Maimonides and Nachmanides, and she frequently cited such eighteenth- to twentieth-century commentators as Mendelssohn, Mecklenburg, Malbim, Hirsch, Hoffmann, and Naphtali Zvi Yehuda Berlin (the Netziv) as well. While Leibowitz did not engage archaeology or ancient philology herself, she appreciated Cassuto, who did. Here is her comparison of a medieval and a modern expositor who come to similar conclusions regarding the Tabernacle:

   Only in the last 150 years with the development of the literary historical approach do we find this type of explanation being advanced. Cassuto, for instance, explains the recapitulation in terms of the narrative conventions of the ancient east. It is usual for an account of the execution of a certain series of acts previously outlined to repeat verbatim the acts that were executed and not to report merely that they were repeated. The difference between Ralbag and modern scholars is that the latter based their findings on actual records discovered in their days. Ralbag on the other hand, merely suggested this might be so without having any independent data on which to base it.[15]

2. Leibowitz was an unapologetic Jewish pluralist, a rationalist Litvak who cited the Zohar liberally. She inclined toward maximalists, but sided with minimalists such as Ibn Ezra or Rashbam when she thought it warranted. She cited Philo and Josephus from the exegetically unruly world called Second Temple Judaism. Finally, her affirmation of modern exegesis included consideration of figures who were great Bible scholars, but non-Orthodox Jews. Leibowitz did not spare liberal Jewish Bible scholars such as Martin Buber or Benno Jacob from criticism, either as transgressors of the commandments or as misrepresenters of the Jewish tradition. But she cited them frequently and often agreed with their views.

3. Leibowitz relished dissent within tradition. Unlike some contemporary Orthodox works, which report the opinions of traditional commentators more as complements than as conflicts, Leibowitz generates her discussions by highlighting these differences of opinion, showing their strengths and weaknesses, drawing out their philosophical implications, and, sometimes, taking a stand when she thinks one solution is preferred. Leibowitz is unafraid of the diversity within the Jewish tradition; it turns out to be the generative, creative motor of that tradition. To contrast her method with that of the ArtScroll/Stone Chumash: Maimonides and Nachmanides often said complementary things, but just as often, conflicting things, about the meaning of Torah.
4. Leibowitz favored maximalists over minimalists. She considered the Torah text infinitely deep, subject to endless interpretation. This inclines her away from the *p'shat* approach, and inclines her in the direction of probing psychological treatments of commentators such as Nachmanides, Abravanel, and Hirsch. In Leibowitz's case, the maximalists usually win the argument, and she relished showing the implausibility of a minimalist approach. Her comment on the Tree of Knowledge manages to reproach the rationalist Ibn Ezra and skewer traditional Christianity interpreters:

> Some of our commentators and authorities reject the allegorizing of the biblical narrative as dangerous, others enthusiastically embrace this approach and there are those who take the middle way. But even those who tend to reject it or reduce their employment of it to the minimum (like Ibn Ezra who devotes a large part of his introduction to his Torah commentary to attacking the allegorists—chiefly aimed at Christian controversialists who wished thereby to justify their repudiation of the law in favor of faith in the articles of their creed) admit that it is the allegorical, hidden meaning of the story of the garden of Eden and the tree of knowledge that we must seek.[16]

5. Leibowitz was a Jewish nationalist. Leibowitz missed few opportunities to talk about the differences between Eretz Yisrael and exile, and often badgered her students in the diaspora into considering aliyah. The centrality of Israel and the reality of Jewish nationhood served as a major theme in her works. She found in Nachmanides and Abravanel, prominent as statesmen and Jewish advocates as well as Bible commentators, distant echoes of proto-Zionist sentiment, and applauded them accordingly. Where she disagreed with Hirsch, with whom she generally saw eye to eye, Hirsch's lack of a strong sense of Jewish nationhood or excessive universalism seems to underlie those dissents. One gets the impression that Leibowitz liked to bring sources relevant to building the Jewish nation. Regarding the Tabernacle, Leibowitz opined, "The Torah did not therefore content itself with recording the

instructions to build the Tabernacle, but repeated each detail of their execution. This was done in order to stress the symbolic significance of each detail, the dedication of each labour to God in preparation for life in the Promised Land."[17] Leibowitz based this comment on Mendelssohn, who, surely, was no proto-Zionist. However, the Haskalah, with its emphasis on Jewish economic normalization, did prepare the way for Jewish nationalism in the view of most historians. In "Ki Tavo," with its bloodcurdling curses, Leibowitz approvingly cited Isaac Abravanel's reading that the verse "And there thou shalt serve other gods" (Deuteronomy 28:64–65) indicates that the punishment of exile is tied to that of forced conversion and hence forced apostasy. Leibowitz summarized Abravanel's point as follows: "Jews would thus be forced to serve idols not out of conviction but against their will knowing it to be false and foolish."[18] Leibowitz continued this line of thought in "Nizzavim," again citing the last great representative of medieval Spanish Jewry: "Abravanel wrote these words at the time of the Inquisition during the persecution of the Marranos when events proved that the covenant of Sinai could not be so easily shaken and that all their efforts to assimilate would be of no avail. Abravanel thus drew from the sacred text a message for his generation. May we not learn from him to find in the words of the Torah a similar message for our time and own generation?"[19] In "Ha'azinu," also known as "The Song of Moses," Leibowitz began with a long quote from Nachmanides regarding the hatred of the nations for Israel and Israel's close relationship with God in the wilderness. Her reading of these concluding parashot of the Torah constitutes a paean to the relationship of the Jews and the land of Israel and a believer's take on the Zionist principle of "autoemancipation."

6. Leibowitz loved the entire Torah and one may regard her efforts as a specific rehabilitation of Chumash or *parashat ha-shavuah* and not just Bible in general. Yet Leibowitz had an equally deep interest in the halachic and narrative material. Her studies in those weekly portions rich in legal material are as brilliant as her long-acclaimed studies on the narrative portions of Genesis. Observance of the commandments was one of her stated goals in Torah teaching, and this is amply reflected in her discussion of portions rich in legal and ritually symbolic significance. With the exception of Rav Hirsch, most modern commentators from western Europe had little to say about such issues as the construction of the Tabernacle or the Tabernacle Menorah, neither of which have contemporary halachic significance (unlike mitzvoth regarding criminal law, property law, and ritual items still in use, such as tzitzit, tallitot, etc.) At the end of the day, most modern commentators lean toward either the narrative or the legal. Hirsch, Mecklenburg, and Malbim, no doubt conditioned by

their defense of Oral Law, expended their greatest energies on legal matters. Contemporary Jewish academics focus on narrative, I suspect, because it is perceived as the more inclusive part of Torah. Not so Leibowitz: she subjected all of Torah equally to her minute form of analysis, even though she eschewed a linear commentary in Rashi style, and arguably avoided texts lacking in religious edification.[20]

7. She despised German Protestant higher criticism. As the distinguished Bible scholar Yaira Amit noted, Leibowitz cited Christian writers, and this got Leibowitz involved in controversy with those holding more right-wing approaches. But her apparent openness is somewhat deceptive: much like Joseph Hertz, Leibowitz cited Christian scholars mainly when they were offering praise of the Bible's stellar qualities, or making an interpretive move in a direction anticipated by classical Jewish commentary. In other words, she cited Christian interpreters approvingly when they offered support to a Jewish position. When a particular Protestant scholar missed the point of a narrative, or failed to read the text carefully, she could be brutally dismissive.[21] Every bit as aware of the documentary hypothesis as Schechter, Cassuto, or Kaufmann, she considered the majority of source critics ham-handed interpreters who violated the prime rule of interpretation: "to respond to the spirit, tone, and intention of the narrative."[22] This revealing quote illumines the bottom line of Leibowitz's approach: at the end of the day she is a gifted close reader of the text, more concerned with literary qualities than either historical matters or even philological ones.[23] Leibowitz presumes the fundamentally sacred nature of the biblical text. Source critics questioned whether the text itself was trustworthy—and this placed them beyond the pale.[24]

NEHAMA LEIBOWITZ'S DEBT TO THE MODERN GERMAN-JEWISH TRADITION

While Leibowitz took Rashi as her fundamental guide, she has earned plaudits for the recovery of classical rabbinic midrash as rigorously exegetical, and for rescuing from oblivion some of the early-modern (Abravanel, Caspi, and Arama) and modern (Mecklenburg, Malbim, and the Netziv) commentators who do not appear in standard editions of the rabbinic Bible (*Mikraot Gedolot*). Nevertheless, in the most comprehensive study of her opus, *Pirkei Nehama*, only Rivka Horwitz's illuminating essay deals with her debt to modern German-Jewish commentators, while there are several essays on her use of Rashi and Ramban, one on Ibn Ezra, and even one on the Targum. However, if one is willing to overlook denominational differences (as Leibowitz was) and thumb through her pages, one will quickly see that Wessely, Mendelssohn, Hoffmann, Hirsch,

Jacob, and Buber-Rosenzweig appear quite frequently. Focusing on the last three only, I would like to draw out some affinities that, given the bibliocentric view of both German Jewry and Israeli Jewry in the modern era, turn out to be unsurprising.

LEIBOWITZ AND HIRSCH[25]

Leibowitz often refused to take sides in battles between commentators, and there are many discussions which leave the reader wondering what her own opinion was. Other times, she gave one side of an argument the last word, and one can infer her support. Once in a while, however, she pulled no punches, and clearly declared one view right and one wrong. Such is the case in her contrast of the attitude toward vows found in Hirsch's comment to Genesis 28:20, discussed by Leibowitz in her commentary to portion "Ki Teze" in Deuteronomy, and that of Mahatma Gandhi, the father of modern India.[26] For Gandhi, the vow was a way of drawing a line in the sand for oneself, of going beyond the norm, whether it is a vow of vegetarianism or sexual chastity. While one could imagine a positive attitude toward exceeding the behavioral norms on Jewish grounds ("going beyond the letter of the law"), Leibowitz considers this attitude self-congratulatory and holds, "Our Torah wished man to remain free in those matters not covered by its commands and prohibitions."[27] She much preferred Hirsch's view, which was present-focused: "Man should rest content with directing his actions every moment of his present existence, living it as it should be lived."[28] In terms that do seem Kantian (I tend to think the oft-mentioned influence of Kant and Hegel on Hirsch is overrated when it comes to his Torah commentary), Hirsch contends that either an act is a duty (*Pflicht*) and is therefore nonnegotiable, or it is trivial and therefore cheapens the invoking of God's name, especially as all things in the future depend on God's Providence.[29]

In a similar vein, Leibowitz endorsed Hirsch's understanding of the commandment to leave the edges of the field for the disempowered in Israel, often grouped as the threesome sojourner (*ger*), widow, and orphan. Gleanings (*leket*) and Corner (*pe'ah*) are mentioned in several places in the Torah. The simple sense of this commandment is that it constitutes a form of welfare, but Leibowitz, following the lead of several classical sources, notes that this welfare would be inadequate. *Sefer ha-Chinuch* had stressed the character formation aspect of this commandment, but Hirsch, who dealt at length with this commandment in two weekly portions ("Kedoshim" and "Ki Teze") had, in Leibowitz's view, finally penetrated to the core teaching:

> The gifts to the poor constitute a contrast, a protest against the concept of "Mine." The Corner and the Gleanings remind you of your duty not to regard your field and vineyard as your own and not to monopolize all that

nature with God's blessing has grown for you. Peret and leket remind you that you are not to exploit the labour of your hands exclusively for your own benefit till the very last straw. . . . The Torah adds the precept of the Forgotten Sheaf to teach you that even the thoughts of yours connected with the labour you expend on your possessions must not be exclusively directed for your selfish good, and that includes that which is overlooked by your thoughts during the harvesting.

Leibowitz ought to have liked Hirsch. They were both Orthodox in a decidedly secular environment, they were both maximalists who inclined toward making the most of the Torah text, and they were both Jewish partisans, who worked mainly within the Jewish exegetical tradition and had no (Hirsch) or limited (Leibowitz) interest in integrating contemporary scholarship. Nor do I find that Hirsch's extreme originality was off-putting to her; as with *pe'ah*, if she felt he had the better argument, she endorsed it. Certainly, Hirsch has been judged far-fetched by many scholars, and Leibowitz also detected this in some of her analyses of Hirsch. On Exodus 21:37, for instance, Leibowitz finds Hirsch's explanation of a different restitution for theft of an ox and a sheep unlikely. Hirsch's view is that the twofold restitution is warranted by the commission of two offenses: one, against the individual, and two, against the general public order, or the community. But Leibowitz, in a typical instance of close reading, rejects this. If this was the case, she reasons, the criminal would pay restitution to both the individual and community, whereas the double restitution goes to the owner only.

For all his virtues, however, Hirsch was no Jewish nationalist; living in the optimistic nineteenth century, Hirsch consistently took passages in a universalist direction. In my chapter on Hirsch, I mentioned his psychologically acute understanding that Isaac and Rebecca bore some of the blame for the brothers' enmity on account of their bad parenting, and his view that Esau's forgiveness of Jacob was wholly sincere. In an exchange with Professor Shmuel Hugo Bergman, a member of the left-wing Brit Shalom, Leibowitz dissented from Hirsch's understanding of Esau's embrace of Jacob in Genesis 33:4. Leibowitz, perhaps conditioned by the rejection of Esau's sincerity by both Rashi and Nachmanides (her two favorite guides), dismissed Hirsch with these words: "We shall not quarrel with Hirsch who didn't know what we know today about the 'sword' turning into holocaust and not love."[30] Bergman had heard the original discussion of this passage on Israeli radio; he understood that Leibowitz favored the harsher verdict of Rashi, Nachmanides, and Benno Jacob. He wrote her, testily accusing Leibowitz of creating an attitude that would foment anti-Arab violence. But Leibowitz responded sharply to Bergman, "I did not understand why we're forbidden to analyze Esau's position vis-à-vis Jacob throughout the generations. This would not necessarily lead to hatred and a desire for revenge, but rather to hope for the end of days when we would truly be able to say (as in the Aleynu prayer) 'that all the world's people will recognize and that every knee should bend to you.'"[31] Sometimes, as Rashi wrote, Esau did hate Jacob, and it was Jewish self-censorship, in Leibowitz's view, to paper over that reality.

LEIBOWITZ AND JACOB

Leibowitz's comment on Reform Rabbi Benno Jacob's wonderful book on Genesis, cited above, was worth undertaking this entire project: "I learned more from him than from the books of good Jews." In fact, Benno Jacob was well suited to help Leibowitz in her task: he was a savage critic of higher critics, he was extremely combative vis-à-vis antisemitism, and he had no ambivalence about working inside the tradition of *parshanut hamikra* and in the same spirit as Leibowitz herself—critical and hard-nosed. And again, while Jacob did write some books that contained extended arguments, including *An Eye for an Eye: Source Criticism and Researches in the Hebrew Bible*, Jacob's two greatest works were clearly exegetical: his commentaries on Genesis and Exodus. Interestingly, Rosenzweig would tell anyone who would listen that Benno Jacob could read Tanakh like nobody else and should be the Rashi of his generation—a view that Leibowitz probably shared. But, like Leibowitz, Jacob did not want to be a twentieth-century Rashi. He lacked Rashi's restraint, as evidenced by his Genesis commentary, which runs over eight hundred closely argued pages. Leibowitz's reticence is a little less obvious—given her view of active Torah learning, I suspect that she had no desire to become a text mechanically regurgitated by students, as Rashi sometimes was in traditional eastern European quarters. Jacob appeared frequently in Leibowitz's footnotes, but sometimes in the main body of her text as well. We will take a look at a few examples of the latter.

In her evaluation of Noah, Leibowitz tended to side with those who took the last word in the following verse as qualification: "Noah was a whole-hearted man, righteous *in his generation*" (Genesis 6:9), only relatively righteous, not absolutely righteous. Nevertheless, she cited Jacob's observation that Noah elevated God's spoken word into the status of a commandment, "according to all which the Lord commanded him, so he did," a locution found often in the building of the Tabernacle. This, Jacob observed, and Leibowitz agreed, placed Noah spiritually above Adam, though below Abraham.[32] Similarly, while she may not have agreed with Jacob in his interpretation of the mysterious revelatory-covenantal scene enacted in Genesis 15, she admitted that Jacob had observed something his predecessors did not. Rashi and Radak saw this text as an allusion to Israel's covenantal loyalty; Nachmanides, however, took the four terms in Genesis 15 as foreshadowing the downfall of four great kingdoms. But Leibowitz did not find these medieval answers any more persuasive than Jacob's: "But can we say that this interpretation [that of Nachmanides] exhausts all the possibilities of the text? Benno Jacob, a modern German-Jewish commentator in his book on Genesis avers that no reference to sacrifices is to be found in our text, since no utensil or act relating to the sacrificial ritual is remotely alluded to. There is no altar or reference to slaughter in the whole vision. . . . According to Jacob it was not the animals that were suitable for sacrifice which were taken but those nearest to man and under his control."[33] Some questions in Torah are not liable to resolution, and this is one of them. As Leibowitz sums up the matter, "We do not wish to force any particular interpretation on the student."[34]

By her own admission, Leibowitz relied heavily on Jacob's *Source Division and Exegesis*, an attack on source criticism based mainly on the Joseph narrative (Genesis 37–50).[35] Leibowitz credited Jacob with solving one of the more intractable problems in the Joseph cycle—who bought and who sold Joseph at the end of Genesis 37 and the beginning of Genesis 39. The biblical text truly invites scrutiny: the Midianites sold him in 37:36, but it is the Ishmaelites who sell him to Potiphar in 39:1. Various medieval commentators had taken a crack at this, and so had Moses Mendelssohn, who tried to solve the problem by reading "Midianites" as a general term for "merchants." Writing rather more recently, Ed Greenstein, of Tel Aviv University, argued that the author had left the matter—wittingly or unwittingly—ambiguous. Applying a postmodern approach, Greenstein thinks the lack of clarity of the narrative mirrors Joseph's disorientation and the murky chain of events that are recollected quite differently by Joseph and his brothers. But Jacob and Leibowitz shared a modernist, positivist approach: they may have conceded certain biblical questions could not be resolved, but that reflected as much on the ingenuity of competing commentators as on the biblical text. In principle, both wanted firm answers, and were not satisfied with ambiguities. Joseph's campaign to bring the God Israel into Pharaoh's consciousness serves as a linchpin for Leibowitz's reading of Genesis 39–41, the chapters that chart Joseph's rise to prominence. Attending to the repetition of the divine name in Joseph's speech to Pharaoh (Genesis 40:8, 41:15–16, 41:25–33, 41:38–39), Leibowitz wrote, "It is obvious that this emphasis is deliberate to show the king of Egypt, his wise men and princes, his people and the whole heathen world who is the Doer, the Declarer, the Shower, and the Bringer to Pass."[36] And in her notes, she generously credited Jacob as "the first to detect this underlying meaning in Joseph's speech."[37] Both Leibowitz and Jacob, to conclude the matter, were extreme opponents of a racial reading of biblical texts, hardly a surprise, but hardly trivial either in light of the path of German "scholarship" in the 1930 to 1940s.[38]

LEIBOWITZ AND BUBER-ROSENZWEIG

Overall, the fidelity of Buber and Rosenzweig to the Hebrew Bible, their insistence on the ultimately religious content of Scripture, and their role in the German-Jewish renaissance were bound to find a sympathetic hearing from Leibowitz. Moreover, if she was willing to compartmentalize the ideological heterodoxy from the Torah insights of Benno Jacob, who held Sabbath services on Sundays and whom she described as a radical reformer, she surely ought to have been able to do the same for Rosenzweig (a *ba'al teshuva* whose path toward halachic conformity only ended with his incapacity and death) and for Buber, whose Jewish "background" and Jewish activism were unimpeachable. Leibowitz's appreciation of the Buber-Rosenzweig Bible and their literary-theological insights has been grossly underestimated. Leibowitz cited their works in her two Exodus volumes alone no fewer than ten times, most of these, by Leibowitz's terse standards, extended discussions. She understood and appreciated their literary sensitivity to repeating words, root-oriented wordplays, and elevated language within Tanakh; and their theological understanding of prophecy, message, freedom, and taking the Lord's name in vain. Leibowitz knew their biblical essays and was a very careful student of their translation, often noting the differences in various editions, and often differentiating Rosenzweig from Buber.[39]

While these differences between Buber and Rosenzweig are too technical to be of general interest, I would like to give a couple of examples as indicators of Leibowitz's close attention to their work. Analyzing their renderings of two conceptual words, *tevunah* and *da'at*, Leibowitz compared three different editions of Buber-Rosenzweig, noting the tension between Rosenzweig's strict adherence to Hebrew and Buber's tendency toward everyday idiom. Only *Hokhmah*, usually translated "wisdom," had a constant rendering in Buber-Rosenzweig: *Weisheit*.[40] Addressing their translation of *l'shav* in their treatment of the third Commandment in the Decalogue, rendered in the Old JPS as, "Thou shalt not take the name of the Lord thy God *in vain*" (Exodus 20:7), Leibowitz noted Buber's theological problem with Rosenzweig's proposed rendering of *l'shav* as *Nichtigkeit*. For Buber, this proposal accorded too much substantive reality to this transgression. Leibowitz acknowledged that Rashi and Hirsch were the principal influences in her understanding of the dramatic warning in Exodus 22:22, in which God threatens vengeance on those who abuse the widow and orphan. As Leibowitz explained, Rashi and Hirsch read the first part of the verse as a full sentence, with the maddeningly flexible *ki* beginning a second sentence.[41] After Rosenzweig's passing, Buber retreated to a translation "more in line with German idiomatic usage," clearly to Leibowitz's displeasure.[42] This lexical loyalty equals maximalism of Rosenzweig's is praised by

Leibowitz once again in Exodus, portion Terumah, where Leibowitz endorses Rosenzweig's criticism of Kautsch for trying to "improve" the Bible by altering his renderings of the verb to make/to do (*asah*) rather than simply reproducing them. In this portion, Leibowitz made her debt to Buber-Rosenzweig explicit: "This last section of study on the sidra is based on the article of M. Buber: 'Der Mensch von heute und die jüdische Bibel.'"[43] What needs highlighting is that Leibowitz, by no means a casual student of their efforts, (1) saw Buber-Rosenzweig as standing in the tradition of *parshanut ha-mikra*, specifically influenced by Rashi and Hirsch; (2) understood that Rosenzweig and Buber disagreed over what must be called an internal issue of Jewish *parshanut*, mirroring the disagreements of sages past; and (3) had a pronounced preference for Rosenzweig's lexical allegiance to Hebrew, which inclined him in the direction of maximalism—reproducing seeming repetitions in Torah.

At times, Leibowitz went out of her way to bring Buber's insights to her reading audience. In Leviticus, in parashat Behar, Leibowitz opened her minute differentiation of two closely related words for freedom/liberty (*dror* and *hofesh*), with a citation from Buber's most important Hebrew work on the Bible, *The Way of Scripture*. "The term *dror* in the sense of liberty appears only this once in the Torah. M. Buber calls it the rare and dear word, and draws an analogy with other meaning in Exodus 30:23, 'Take thou also to these the best spices of flowing myrrh—the myrrh that flows freely from the shrub without piercing the peel.'"[44] Ultimately, Leibowitz endorsed the view that *dror* suggests the positive gift of freedom while *hofesh* signifies release from a yoke, hence, a negative idea. But, having understood *dror*, what was the ultimate teaching of Leviticus 25:20, inscribed on America's Liberty Bell, "And proclaim liberty throughout the land and to all the inhabitants thereof"? Leibowitz gave Buber the final word, "God allows fateful misfortune free rein to strike at those who yearn for freedom but do not grant it to their fellow." To take another instance, in Numbers, parashat Shelach, which deals with the report of the spies, she cited Buber's *Teaching of the Prophets* to argue that true fidelity to the divine demand turns on the historical reality—neither a message of salvation or calamity ensures the correctness of the messenger. Anyone familiar with Buber, as Leibowitz surely was, will automatically connect her citation to a key Buberian word, "message" (*Botschaft*), and to one of his more celebrated discussions, "False Prophets," a thoughtful reading of the confrontation of Jeremiah and Hananiah in Jeremiah 29. Finally, in her very powerful reading of David's Lament (2 Samuel 22) as the appropriate prophetic reading for Moses's Song in the penultimate reading of Deuteronomy,[45] she turns to Buber's nuanced understanding of the I-It and I-Thou duality of the world. So Leibowitz: "The borderline between the individual 'I' and the national 'I' is here blurred." Regarding this merging of personal and suprapersonal national experience of the whole generation, Buber writes in his book on Job: "More than you sense in this passage the echo of the individual's suffering you hear it in the groan of pain of the exiles . . . behind this 'I' stands the 'I' of Israel."[46]

CONCLUSION: LEIBOWITZ'S DOUBLE VALIDATION OF THE BIBLE

My point, in case some readers should think otherwise, is not to offer Leibowitz condescending praise for being an open-minded Orthodox scholar. Rather, I wish to note that Leibowitz served as one critical link between the German-Jewish tradition and the study of the Bible in Israel. She treated the German-Jewish commentators, from Mendelssohn to Buber-Rosenzweig, by the same standard as all prior commentators: How could they shed light on the Torah? Her dissents from Hirsch, Jacob, and Buber-Rosenzweig were no different from her dissents from Rashi or Nachmanides. Bible translation and commentary always reveal a great deal about the general environment in which they were produced. Leibowitz's works bristle with the issues facing the newly created State of Israel: relations with the outside world, establishing Jewish social and economic values, understanding the message of God in a secular context. Leibowitz found Torah sufficient to answer these questions: like Ben-Gurion, she probably glamorized "the Bible" unduly, as did the German-Jewish commentators who shared a view of Tanakh as an indispensable guide for modern Jewry. Unlike Ben-Gurion, of course, Leibowitz held that the Bible spoke most precisely through the Jewish exegetical tradition. Leibowitz remembered, as Ben-Gurion in the 1950s and 1960s forgot, the preeminence of commentary in all Jewish thought:

> The teacher of Tanach in a Jewish school is not teaching a book of ancient Near eastern literature, but rather the sacred text from which generations have drawn and continue to draw nourishment, and upon which all of Jewish literature through the ages—Halachah and Aggadah, prayer and liturgy, lament and selichah, Kabbalah and scientific research, books of Musar and Hasidism—are nothing but expositions. They are all offshoots of the Torah in their ideas, idioms, allusions and concepts.[47]

Her many students have become teachers in American rabbinical seminaries, day schools and supplemental schools, and adult education classes. An investigation of her influence on Jewish Bible study in America, as in Israel, would be worthwhile. By treating the Jewish exegetical tradition as rigorous and textually acute rather than merely homiletical or merely speculative, Leibowitz elevated Midrash, medieval commentary, and more recent commentators to the level of scholarship in general, and the New Criticism in particular. As Israeli Bible scholar Yaira Amit notes,

"The real significance of her method lies in the creation of a meeting point between traditional Jewish exegesis and the school of historical-philological research developed by Protestant scholars beginning in the late eighteenth century. Presenting both schools side-by-side, Leibowitz shows that such problems as duplications, or even contradictions, which served as the starting points for historical criticism, are nothing new."[48] Leibowitz made it mandatory, for Jewish writers at least, to take their indigenous tradition seriously. In her own person, as well as in her work, she demonstrated the "chain of tradition" at work.

Just as significant, Leibowitz validated the Bible as an object of serious study. As obvious as it may seem, Gavriel Cohen hit upon something very important when he wrote: "In practice, what Nehama did was to adapt the Yeshiva method of studying Talmud [to the Bible]. Just as in the Gemara, Tennaim, Amoraim, Saboraim, Rishonim and Achronim deliberated upon the *sugiah*, so too in Torah study commentators from different generations participate in an intensive and continuous symposium."[49] The idea that the Hebrew Bible, the Written Torah, could be approached with the same seriousness as the Oral Torah, Leibowitz demonstrated in her teaching. This reference point, in contrast to the aforementioned dichotomy of "Jewish *parshanut ha-mikra*" and "secular-contemporary Bible scholarship," is both indigenous and diachronic. While she and her brother were both pious, observant Jews, the following polemic by Yeshayahu Leibowitz, aimed at secular Zionists, cannot be reconciled with Nehama Leibowitz's orientation either:

> Current attempts to identify Judaism with the Hebrew Bible, which is presented as proclaiming values, ideals and a vision that "shine with their own light" are unrelated to the Halakhah and are independent of it. This kind of bibliolatry is Lutheran, not Jewish. Historically, Israel never lived or intended to live by Scripture, nor was it ever intended to live so religiously. Israel conducted its life in accordance with the Halakhah as propounded in the oral law. From the viewpoint of human values the above identification overrates the importance of the Bible. As instruments of moral education, Sophocles' *Antigone* or Kant's *Grundlegung* are possibly superior. As philosophy, the Bible's importance cannot compare to that of Plato, or, again, Kant. Regarded as poetry, Sophocles or Shakespeare may surpass it. As history, Thucydides is certainly more interesting and profound. Only as the words of the living God is the Bible incommensurable with Sophocles and Shakespeare, Plato and Kant, Thucydides or any other work of man. But what way have I of knowing that these twenty-four books are Holy Scripture other than through the Halakhah which canonized them?[50]

Yeshayahu Leibowitz's final question may be very simply countered: "bibliocentrism" need not be "bibliolatry," need not be Lutheran, and need not come at the expense of halachic fidelity. No better proof can be offered than Nehama herself.

Part III

THE FLOWERING OF JEWISH BIBLE STUDIES IN NORTH AMERICA

INTRODUCTION: AMERICA AND THE JEWISH BIBLE

Beginning this section in the mid-1960s could suggest that no American Jewish Bible scholarship (books, essays, translations, children's Bibles, etc.) before this merits discussion. This is surely untrue. From the beginning of the American experience, Christians regarded Jews as special conduits to the Old Testament, especially as philologists and grammarians. Judah Monis needed to convert to Christianity to become Harvard's first instructor in Hebrew, but by the middle of the nineteenth century Jews taught Hebrew in Oberlin, Ohio, Hanover, New Hampshire, and elsewhere. Naturally, "Hebrew" meant *biblical* Hebrew—rabbinic Hebrew interested American Protestants less and modern Hebrew had not yet been invented. When Isaac Mayer Wise, Sabato Morais, and Bernard Revel founded the Reform, Conservative, and Orthodox seminaries, respectively, they were not the first to offer Jews employment at the college level. By the 1880s, when the mass immigration of eastern Europeans thoroughly altered the nature of American Jewry, full-time professors of Judaica, often called Semiticists, were to be found in several universities.[1]

One reality looms above all others: America has been the quintessential Bible land of the modern era.[2] For all of the importance of the Bible in modern Britain and Germany, well documented by Jonathan Sheehan's *The Enlightenment Bible*, that importance has faded dramatically in the twentieth century, while American biblicism, often including fascination with the Hebrew language and with the Jewish people, has remained strong into the twenty-first century.[3] "Calculating how many Bibles sold in the United States is a virtually impossible task, but a conservative estimate is that in 2005 Americans purchased some twenty-five million Bibles—twice as many as the most recent Harry Potter book. The amount spent annually on Bibles has been put at more than half a billion dollars."[4] In America, the Bible makes the best seller list every year, a fact not lost on publishers, who continue to increase their Bible lists, or on bookstore chains, which house a Bible section in even the bluest states. Even before the nation's founding, the First Great Awakening involved an intensive encounter with the Old and New Testaments. The Founding Fathers, however deistic, had a deep interest in the Bible, exemplified by Thomas Jefferson's famous New Testament version, with all offensive parts deleted. The American Bible Society distributed *millions* of Bibles, and the Gideons, long before pay-per-view, made sure that no one would be without reading material in whatever lodging they found. Throughout the nineteenth century, the Bible continued to be the reference point for social debates. The Second Great Awakening, which reignited interest in the Bible, profoundly affected Jewry too. The conflict between liberal and conservative Protestant understandings of the Bible at the end of the nineteenth century also found an echo in Jewish circles, as Reform Jews struggled with the twin challenges to biblical authority of Darwin and source criticism. American Jewish engagement with the Bible is partly explicable as a subset of the American experience in general. The rise of the interfaith movement, the maturation of classical Reform Judaism, and even American Zionism all enhanced the prestige of Bible studies at the expense of traditional rabbinic learning.[5] The strong inclination toward intellectual history in European Wissenschaft des Judentums made the absence of seminaries, brilliant intellectuals, or worldwide leading rabbis a black mark against American Jews, as did the dicta of the Russian Jewish leaders who inveighed against Jews fleeing to that "impure land" in search of refuge from poverty and pogroms. The impact of this scholarly bias, which overlooked the economic, organizational, and political creativity that characterized American Jewry, also led to deprecating what American Jewry had achieved.

Early on, American Jews expended great energy creating a Bible of their own. Newman, De Sola, Bagster, and Benisch tried their hands, even if only the Leeser and Old JPS Bibles became commercial successes. The Old JPS printed one million copies, many used in synagogues and many given as bar mitzvah presents—I still have mine, kept safe over the decades in its cardboard house. These introductions to these works show the sort of ethnic ownership that marks the American chapter of the making of the modern Jewish Bible:

> The Jew cannot afford to have his own Bible translation prepared for him by others. He cannot have it as a gift, even as he cannot borrow his soul from others.[6]

And Isaac Leeser:

> The Book commonly known as the Authorized or King James version, has been so long looked upon with a deep veneration almost bordering on superstitious dread, that to most persons the very thought of furnishing an improved translation of the Divine records will be viewed as an impious assumption and a contempt of the wisdom of former ages. But even if no colouring had been given to the English words not warranted by the Hebrew, it would be a species of mental slavery to rely for ever upon the arbitrary decree of a deceased King of England who was surely no prophet, for the correct understanding of the Scriptures, upon which our life in this world and the next depends.[7]

Leeser's points may be quickly summarized: (1) King James was not a prophet, (2) the Hebrew Bible contains all that is needed for Jewish life, (3) Christians cannot be counted on for accurately translating Hebrew, and (4) American Jews must show their independence through producing a Bible of their own. As cantor of Philadelphia's Mikveh Israel, Leeser preached on the Bible regularly in hourlong increments, giving him deep familiarity with its contents. Leeser provided Jews with home Bibles that contained the books of the Jewish canon only, and in their traditional order; that followed the division of the Pentateuch into weekly portions; that hewed closely to the Masoretic text; that avoided christological renderings of key passages and contained a few blank pages to record family births, circumcisions, marriages, and deaths.[8]

Leeser's Bible lacked the consistency of its German counterparts. He chided Isaac Mayer Wise for casting doubt on the historicity of biblical miracles, yet conceded that Moses compiled Genesis rather than scribed it at the dictation of God—hardly a minor concession, nor one that either Mendelssohn or Hirsch would have made.[9] Wise's major work on the Bible, *Pronaos*, similarly inconsistent, rejected a strict historical reading, yet insisted on Mosaic authorship of Genesis—putting him to the "right" of Leeser on this issue. Similarly, Leeser insisted that he followed the literal wording of the Traditional Text, but Sussman and Sarna have shown numerous instances where antichristological motives or pieties suggested by rabbinic readings led Leeser to violate this self-imposed standard egregiously. Stylistically, Leeser did not achieve as much independence from the sonorous King James as he thought, and neither did the Old JPS. Still, creating a Jewish Bible on American soil was a tremendous feat. When Sussman praises Leeser for bringing "the Protestantization of American Judaism to completion," he also means that Leeser made the Bible central to American Jewry.[10]

By the end of the nineteenth century, Leeser's scholarly deficiencies had become apparent. The newly founded Jewish Publication Society (JPS) commenced work on a translation, encouraged by the new head of the Jewish Theological Seminary, Solomon Schechter (1850–1915). By the time this Bible appeared, Schechter had passed away, but his hostile attitude toward Protestant Bible scholarship remained. At the Jewish Theological Seminary, this impeded an open-ended approach to the world of biblical scholarship, with special animus directed toward source criticism. As Sabato Morais announced, several years before Schechter's arrival, "I do not presume too much when I declare in the name of its founders, that the icy cold criticism of the German and Dutch schools of modern times shall not be permitted to blight the growth of religious enthusiasm in the hearts of our people."[11] The practical necessity of bringing American rabbinical candidates up to speed made the curriculum at the fledgling Jewish Theological Seminary not that different from its Reform counterpart, the Hebrew Union College—both stressed mastery of the Hebrew Bible and its commentators far more than eastern European yeshivot. At both institutions, tensions existed between what individual faculty thought of source criticism and what they thought American rabbis needed to know and teach in practice.

Schorsch refers to Schechter's "baneful influence" on Bible studies, but I think this judgment is too harsh. David Fine demonstrates that Schechter understood source criticism, but the latter was unimpressed with the Protestant scholars' mastery of Hebrew, law, close reading skills, or awareness of their own biases.[12] Schechter, like Graetz and Zunz, drew a line between the Torah and the Prophets and Writings when it came to applying critical methods. In fact, Schechter was eager to show creativity and development in the later biblical books because it showed a Persian-period Judaism far from the ossified stereotype of Wellhausen. Schechter displayed a healthy anticolonialist attitude toward mainstream Bible scholarship; complete capitulation to all its claims would have been terribly mistaken, and it is not clear that the source critical method was/is a useful way to train rabbis to read Torah. I am not defending Schechter's judgment "Higher Criticism—Higher Antisemitism," but there was more to his position than that pithy statement, and more to the ways his successors negotiated the challenge of source criticism, even beyond the obvious example of H. L. Ginsberg, an enthusiastic emender of biblical texts.

The best evidence that Schechter's influence was not altogether "baneful" may come from his admirer Rabbi Joseph Hertz (1872–1946). Hertz graduated from the Jewish Theological Seminary before Schechter's arrival, served as a rabbi in South Africa, and became, with Schechter's endorsement, chief rabbi of Great Britain. Hertz also wrote the longest-lived Chumash in the English language to this date. First appearing in 1929 as a two-volume work, the "Hertz Chumash" has been reissued often and helped inspire a companion "rabbinic Bible" (*The Soncino Chumash*, 1947). For two generations, until the appearance of denominational Chumashim in America, the Hertz Chumash was the synagogue Bible of choice for Anglo-American readers. Hertz may have nearly succeeded in "placing a Chumesh [sic] in every English-speaking home," as he wrote in the preface to the one-volume Soncino edition. Hertz and his team, writing in the 1920s, needed to address ancient Near Eastern analogues and composite authorship issues more than their predecessors, but the result was exactly what Harvey Meirovich's book title suggests: *A Vindication of Judaism*.[13] While many of Hertz's assertions are unsupportable today, he introduced Jewish readers, many relatively unlearned, to the issues of modern Bible scholarship. Hertz's pungent defenses of biblical originality, of the wholesomeness of Jewish values, and of Hebrew humanism found an enthusiastic response. Hertz took a radical stance against source criticism: "My conviction that the criticism of the Pentateuch associated with the name of Wellhausen is a perversion of history and a desecration of religion is unshaken."[14]

Hertz wrote this in 1936. Hitler had already come to power in Germany; the Jewish Agency was shortly to be presented by the Peel Commission with a disappointing Partition Plan for Palestine; American Jewry was facing the worst decade of antisemitism since its arrival in the New World. For world Jewry, the 1930s were a terrible decade, and the first half of the 1940s would be far worse. Not until American Jewry recovered from this trauma would scholars find new idioms for a modern Jewish Bible. The Anglo-American tradition of Jewish Bible scholarship before the 1960s was real, but only with the maturation of a generation of native English speakers did Jewish Bible scholars begin to speak with a more distinctive voice.

9

Finding a Jewish Voice
Nahum Sarna and Robert Alter

Given the unbroken history of American Jewish Bible scholarship, an attempt to identify a turning point will be somewhat arbitrary. Still, I claim that 1966, when Nahum Sarna published his seminal *Understanding Genesis*, marks a turn in our story. Simon Greenberg, then vice-chancellor of the Jewish Theological Seminary, introduced Sarna's book on this modest note: "Though this book was written primarily with the traditional Jewish religious school in mind, we believe that it can have great meaning for adults who want to understand what it is that the Book of Genesis seeks to tell us."¹ Writing thirty-four years later, Bible scholar Jeffrey Tigay, one of Sarna's numerous students, introduced a series of essays by Sarna as follows, "No scholar has done as much as Sarna to educate English-speaking Jewry about the Bible."² My discussion offers a lengthy footnote to Tigay's comment. Born in London, Sarna (1923–2005) settled in the United States and received his doctorate under Assyriologist-Semiticist Cyrus Gordon at Philadelphia's Dropsie College in 1955. Sarna served as librarian and professor at the Jewish Theological Seminary, and spent most of his career at Brandeis University. *Understanding Genesis* was followed by *Exploring Exodus*, the JPS Torah commentaries on these two books, and a slew of specialized studies that run several pages in the JPS Scholars of Distinction series, which has featured three Biblicists.³

Sarna's allocation of scholarly energies requires comment. Genesis and Exodus were *not* the two Torah books most dominant in traditional Jewish education. Jewish males began their early education with Leviticus, a book of purities, and the straightest line between ancient Israelite religion and subsequent Jewish practice will be found in Deuteronomy.⁴ Nevertheless, Genesis and Exodus are certainly the two Torah books most taught in elementary Jewish education and in adult Jewish education, and most discussed from the pulpit. Sarna deserves credit, then, as an important guide to the most important works that inform committed Jews today. The other book that Sarna addressed comprehensively also reflected this bibliocentrism. His *Songs of the Heart: An Introduction to the Book of Psalms* (1993) provided a guide to the longest book in the Bible, the one most represented in the Jewish prayer book (*Siddur*), but also a book much harder to digest than narrative works. Sarna's many scholarly essays, along with his books, advanced the field of Bible studies, but they did something more—they provided English speakers with a distinctively critical and Jewish voice. No sleuth is required to locate Sarna's fingerprints on the making of the modern Jewish Bible. Directly and through his many students, they are ubiquitous. Nevertheless, I would like to draw attention to the following features: Sarna's combination of history and theology, his alignment of modern Jewish Bible scholarship with tradition, his updating the polemic against the source critics, and most delicately, his invitation to an ethnic reappropriation of the Hebrew Bible.

FINDING A JEWISH VOICE IN BIBLE STUDIES

As noted, Sarna was hardly the first contributor to a modern Jewish Bible in America. Sarna cannot even claim to be the first to utilize rabbinic insights in the scholarly interpretation of Bible, as seminary professors at Hebrew Union College, Jewish Theological Seminary, and Yeshiva University had been doing this for decades. Even in the secular academy, American Jews had not needed to hide their identity, though the early membership of the Society of Biblical Literature had few Jewish members. Samuel Sandmel, the president of the Society of Biblical Literature in 1961, offered a touchstone for later attempts to study the process of the Bible interpreting itself. Sandmel's "The Haggadah Within Scripture" presciently described a phenomenon that proved to be a useful method of charting the development of later biblical texts, and also a means of showing affinity of biblical and rabbinic interpretative methods. Not so incidentally, Sandmel commented in this article that this approach might furnish "another nail in the coffin of the Graf-Wellhausen approach, although that was not its main purpose." Sandmel's wry comment about the Graf-Wellhausen approach notwithstanding, he followed its chronology in his *Introduction to the Hebrew Scriptures* by assuming that the prophetic material preceded the Torah, an approach thoroughly antithetical to the views of Jewish scholars such as Jacob, Kaufmann, Cassuto, and Segal.[5]

Sandmel argued that the rabbinic methods of biblical exegesis were indigenous to the Bible. But Nahum Sarna was the first, to my knowledge, to name this important phenomenon, in his 1963 essay "Psalm 89: A Study in Inner Biblical Exegesis." Regarding this phenomenon, Sarna wrote, "I wish to advance the thesis that the traditional Jewish approach to the text as a living organism that perpetually rejuvenates and transforms itself was not a rabbinic innovation but a continuation of an established process that was contemporaneous with the formation of biblical literature itself."[6] Sarna's students, foremost among them Michael Fishbane, in *Biblical Interpretation in Ancient Israel*, would develop what Sarna termed inner-biblical interpretation, which has tended to demonstrate the exegetical links between biblical and rabbinic Judaism. Like most developments in Jewish Bible scholarship, this one was paralleled in the larger academic field. The appreciation of scripture unfolding in the context of a worshipping community, rather than in a set of discrete authorial enterprises, has been called canonical criticism and associated with the names of James Sanders and Brevard Childs—Christians with a neotraditionalist orientation. Inner-biblical exegesis may be seen as a sort of Jewish counterpart to this development, grounded in a deep knowledge of both biblical and rabbinic literature.[7]

Bernard Bamberger, another contemporary of Sarna's, thoroughly embraced the source criticism but sought to convince that the anti-Judaic biases of Wellhausen and his ilk were separable from the legitimacy of the methodology.[8] Bamberger's booklet *The Bible: A Modern Jewish Approach* assured readers that understanding the ancient background of the Bible could be beneficial, not destructive. Nevertheless, Bamberger's work begged the question as to whether the source critical approach was the most fruitful way to approach the Bible. As Jon D. Levenson (no relation) has argued in a slew of sophisticated works beginning in the mid-1980s, the fascination with recovering the "original Bible" is itself an inherently Protestant endeavor, paralleling the quest for the historical Jesus, his exact words, and the life of the early Church. In Roman Catholicism, as in Judaism, however, Scripture has always seemed most compelling in the context of tradition—an unbroken chain of practices and commentaries. Once again, Sarna pointed the way to this dissent from source criticism, "For this reason, the disentanglement of literary strands does not constitute the apotheosis of scholarship."[9] Bamberger's defense of a modern approach to the Bible receded to the background in his Leviticus commentary for Reform Judaism's *The Torah: A Modern Commentary* (1981). While Bamberger's Leviticus commentary was certainly scholarly-critical and historical, it confined its discussion of sources (P and H) to the introduction and leaned heavily on traditional Jewish sources, and also on the modern Jewish scholars who treated the source critics so harshly. While defending a modern approach to the Bible, Bamberger's Leviticus avoided those features of source criticism Jews found particularly obnoxious. Typical of American Jewish Bible scholarship, Bamberger respectfully treated time-honored traditions of Jewish life, regardless of his own theology. Thus, Bamberger's treatment of kashrut as a mode of eating seriously from a religious point of view may seem prescient to a twenty-first-century reader: "Moreover the problem of food supply has become urgent and critical everywhere. Millions are always hungry, while others eat too much for their own good. Even in the affluent United States, large numbers are malnourished while others oscillate between gourmet cookery and reducing diets."[10]

Sandmel and Bamberger were not alone as Jews who embraced the source critical approach without censoring their Jewish upbringing and training.[11] No more devoted student of source criticism can be imagined than Ephraim Avigdor Speiser (1902–1965), whose *Anchor Bible Genesis* got rough treatment by literature professor Robert Alter, the focus of the second half of this chapter. Speiser's works display an exceptional philological excellence, grounded in the cognate languages of the ancient Near East. Speiser promoted the significance of biblical archaeology and applied it consistently to the biblical text. Speiser's defense of translating Genesis 1:1 as "At the beginning" (versus the King James Bible's "In the beginning") relies on grammar, context, and the ancient Near Eastern creation myths. As the author of *Anchor Bible Genesis*, which included a remarkable, though now dated, summary of the documentary hypothesis, Speiser initiated the tradition of the Anchor Bible editors' assignation of the Pentateuch to Jewish scholars, a notable acknowledgment of Jewish talent in Bible studies on American soil. In his belief in the great antiquity of Genesis traditions, Speiser followed Albright and other proponents of the view that the patriarchal tales showed analogous legal-social-economic patterns consonant with other eighteenth-century-BCE Mesopotamian societies. The lives of the patriarchs and matriarchs, following this line of thought, were demonstrably pre-Mosaic and fundamentally historical. This represented a retreat from traditional Jewish views of Mosaic authorship, but otherwise forwarded what would today be considered a maximalist view of the historicity of Genesis.

Sarna would retreat a bit from such maximalism in his *JPS Torah Commentary* (1989), but still affirmed a slew of particulars (e.g., divine names, stone pillars, familial marriages, angelology, personal names, place names, and ethnographic data) that testified to the "singularity" and "antiquity" of the Genesis traditions. Any attentive reader of Sandmel's, Bamberger's, or Speiser's academic works would have realized that their authors were Jewish. What these lacked was Sarna's distinctively Jewish voice, sought after by post–World War II American Jews.

THE MAKING OF A BIBLICAL-HISTORICAL THEOLOGIAN

Competent biblical scholars have provided assessments of Sarna's scholarly opus. I suggest that whatever his academic contributions, he successfully articulated a mode of Bible studies with a Jewish voice, a communal-cultural contribution as much as an intellectual one. One example is his treatment of the nexus of the Bible and rabbinic commentary. In his *Understanding Genesis* (1966), Sarna embedded rabbinic insights in his discussions, but the rabbis do not appear by name in the book's body or endnotes, a striking contrast with Sarna's JPS Genesis and Exodus commentaries, where he openly displayed his astonishing mastery of rabbinic literature in all eras—midrashic, medieval, and modern—or even *Exploring Exodus* (1986), where rabbinic literature re-emerges, albeit in the endnotes. One could argue that the *JPS Torah Commentary* invited the explicit citation and discussion of rabbinic sources in a way that *Understanding Genesis* or *Exploring Exodus* did not. The former were Bible commentaries; the latter were teachers' guides. But *Understanding Genesis* was published under the Jewish auspices of the Melton Center, so that explanation may not suffice. Just as likely, Sarna wrote *Understanding Genesis* (1966) at a time when Jewish readers needed to feel they were receiving an "objective" and "universally valid" reading and not just a parochially Jewish one. As Adele Berlin explained, for a long period rabbinic insights were suspect on the grounds that they were not truly scholarly, and thus appear in Jewish Bible scholars' works either not at all, or in suppressed fashion. With the emergence of postmodernism in Bible studies and the increased appreciation of the Bible as literature, Jewish scholars began to apply Midrash and medieval *pashtanim* to Bible studies, even in a secular environment. In short, the gradual emergence of the rabbinic presence in Sarna's biblical works partly paralleled, and partly fueled, this development.

Sarna remained a positivist in his approach to uncovering biblical truths. Nevertheless, like other recent Jewish Bible scholars, Sarna frequently threw in his lot with Jewish tradition over or against nineteenth-century scholarship. In a discussion of Abraham's endangering the chastity of Sarah (Genesis 12, 20), Sarna first cited some famous—and hostile—liberal Protestant interpreters of Genesis 12:11–20. These commentators cast Abraham in an unchivalric, un-Christian light. Sarna did not shy away from acknowledging Jewish criticism of Abraham, or any other biblical character, but credited the medieval *pashtanim* with a far deeper appreciation of Abraham's real-life dilemma. Sarna wrote: "Unlike the above-mentioned moderns, he [Rabbi David Kimchi] does not confuse chivalry with morality. What is of significance is that both Nahmanides and Kimchi are sensitive to a problem of biblical morality."[12] As exegetical guides, Sarna held, the medieval *pashtanim* were reliable, and, ironically, less prone to hasty moral judgments than twentieth-century scholars. Regarding Bible exegesis, Sarna rejected an approach that presumed the more atomistic, the more scientific; he also rejected the presumption that the more recent, the better. To put it baldly, Sarna thought Nachmanides read Scripture with as much insight as contemporaries, and maybe more.

Sarna did not present himself as a theologian in *Understanding Genesis*. Ostensibly proceeding as a mere historian, Sarna showed the narratives of Genesis against their ancient Near Eastern environment. Indeed, the opening pages took a highly critical view toward both "literalism," there defined as a fundamentalist assumption that the historical environment and ancient analogues can be neglected, and also "scientism," an insistence that the teachings of Genesis must be squared with developments in paleontology or astrophysics or be abandoned. Sarna devoted several pages to demonstrating the fallaciousness of these views, stressing that a person of faith should never be afraid of facts, a position that Maimonides also articulated in the twelfth century. But Sarna added a modern argument that any medieval would have found incomprehensible: namely, that religion had the same right of development as any other human endeavor. Carving out this middle ground between fundamentalism and dismissive scientism was, of course, a thoroughly ideological move, and one that has sat well with the vast majority of American Jews who are not fundamentalists and are quite capable of compartmentalizing their understanding of what Torah teaches from their understanding of the Tuesday "Science" section of the *New York Times*. What Sarna rejected is manifest: literalism and dismissiveness. What his positive contributions are is harder to articulate, but worth a foray beyond the newspaper obituaries and Wikipedia.

UPDATING THE TRADITION: FROM MEDIEVAL *PASHTANIM* TO MODERN BIBLE SCHOLARS

Sarna consistently placed his work, a modern, scholarly approach to the Bible, squarely in line with Jewish tradition, most specifically the medieval rationalists (*pashtanim*). As Sarna wrote, "The medieval scholars made use of all the limited tools at their disposal." This was no offhand comment, as other essays and lectures of Sarna demonstrated. By arguing that medieval Jewish scholars were willing to use whatever linguistic tools were at their disposal, even coming to conclusions about the "simple sense" of Scripture that ran counter to accepted halachah, Sarna implied that had the twelfth-century-CE commentator Rashbam had the fruits of archaeological tools at his disposal, he would have employed them. To be more concrete, Sarna showed that medieval scholars used linguistic parallels among three cognate languages, Arabic, Aramaic, and Hebrew, to "solve" problems in Hebrew Scriptures. Had Rashbam lived in the twentieth century, he would presumably have done the same with such languages as Akkadian and Ugaritic. Rashbam, moreover, came to the conclusion that repetition of the famous formula of Genesis 1, "it was evening, it was morning, day one," did not suggest that the day actually begins the nightfall before. The legal implication of Rashbam's insight is that Jewish holiday observances properly ought to begin in the morning, not the evening before—which, of course, they do not. Sarna's presentation of the boldness of the medieval exegetes implicitly defined his own scholarship as consonant with Jewish tradition—and more fundamentalist approaches as opposed to it. This, surely, is an exegetical-theological point of view, as well as a purely historical one.[13]

Sarna's technical studies in the preservation and ordering of biblical manuscripts gave a fillip to a nonfundamentalist viewpoint and to a nonfundamentalist reading of the Jewish interpretive tradition. Writing on the biblical canon for *Encyclopedia Judaica*, Sarna opined, "the quantitative disproportion between the literary productions of the literary remains of ancient Israel is extreme."[14] The external books of ancient Israel, some thirty-six named by Scripture itself, and surely these are not all the literature produced by ancient Israel, have not been preserved. Why? One might forward chance as a factor, but this, in Sarna's view, was highly unlikely. Rather, these named and unnamed books were lost because they were not considered as "inspired" as the preserved canon. Sarna affirmed the centuries-long process of canon formation in the order of Torah-Neviim-Ketuvim, a nonfundamentalist view, but one which preserved pride of place for Torah, attributed to Moses with increasing certainty over the course of biblical history. The "Torah of Moses," noted Sarna, was a post-Pentateuchal term. Sarna further observed that the combination of the twelve minor prophets on a single scroll—which created the *Jewish* biblical unit *trei asar*—the twelve—was probably a practical scribal device to prevent these small books from being lost, although the internal ordering of these twelve scrolls was loosely chronological.[15] In all, Sarna affirmed that while the canonical process was neither divine nor uniform, it was not arbitrary either, but rather represented the final product of a sustained encounter of Israel with texts increasingly regarded as binding on the community.

Martin Buber's claim that the Bible is "one book" notwithstanding, the creation of a single Bible probably meant more to Christians than to Jews in Late Antiquity. As Sarna noted, many of ancient terms used for biblical materials—"Scrolls" (*megillot*), "Books" (*sefarim*), "Holy Books" (*sifre ha-kodesh*), "Sacred Writings" (*kitvei ha-kodesh*)—reflect comfort with a plural conception. Certainly, in Sarna's view, "The Bible does not constitute an ideological monolith."[16] This leads to a relaxed, inherently antifundamentalist posture on Sarna's part regarding the transmission of texts. Although Sarna was committed to arguing a coherent scriptural message, the parts also have integrity. Regarding relations between Genesis and Exodus, Sarna wrote, "While the book [Exodus] is more or less a self-contained literary unit, it is incomprehensible except as a sequel to the Book of Genesis."[17] Practically speaking, the Redactor becomes the departure point for his commentary, rather than the Masoretes. Sarna was far less inclined to rest his commentary on cantillation and vocalization than either Hirsch or Mendelssohn. The orality of the Hebrew Bible, so important to Mendelssohn and Hirsch, played a negligible role in Sarna's works. Sarna confided in the superiority of the received Hebrew text, but he accepted the view that this text remained in a fluid state before canonization.[18]

THE DOCUMENTARY HYPOTHESIS AND MODERN JEWISH BIBLE SCHOLARS

Wikipedia notes that Sarna "accepts the basic premise of the Documentary Hypothesis," but emphasizes the negative in this position. Robert Alter captured Sarna's position with more precision: "He [Sarna] then proceeds to write a commentary [JPS Genesis] that makes an occasional discreet reference to an evident discontinuity in the text, but prefers to invoke a unifying agency called the "Narrator" and—this surely constitutes a landmark in modern biblical scholarship—manages to dispense entirely with the source designations E, J, and P without seeming apologetic."[19] Especially in his early works, polemical-apologetic elements animate Sarna's work. As he wrote in *Understanding Genesis*, "But is it not to circumscribe the power of God in the most extraordinary manner to assume the Divine can only work effectively through the medium of a single source, but not through four?"[20] Sarna also adumbrated a way forward that became common for Jewish Bible scholarship in America, that is, focus on the composite lessons of Genesis, Exodus, and Psalms. Whatever the origins of biblical sources (J, E, P, and D), none of them have been preserved as actual texts; they are only hypothetical, while the canon has come down to us through the ages. Sarna's overview of the "Canon, Text and Editions" in *Encyclopedia Judaica* does not mention source criticism; canonical development ostensibly answers the question "how did the Bible come to be?" and nobody can contest the claim that only the canonical whole influenced subsequent literature, sacred and secular. As we shall see below, Erich Auerbach's discussion of the Binding of Isaac had enormous influence on a purely literary appreciation of the Bible. But Sarna made this point about sacred literature as well. In his *JPS Torah Commentary* on Genesis: "The present Commentary is primarily concerned with the completed edifice and only to a minor extent with the building blocks. It is not based on the coroner's approach, that is, on dissecting a literary corpse." For Sarna, then, source criticism, however correct, can only be an exercise, "of limited value."[21]

Sarna, without invoking divine inspiration, could nevertheless insist on a coherent voice that animated the Bible. Sarna was fond of the word "kerygma," originally a Christian term referring to "herald or proclamation." While the details of biblical history may remain obscure, in his view, the basic message is rarely in doubt. "The Torah is not a book of history, but one that makes use of historical data for didactic purposes."[22] Thus we have the Exodus, whatever its historicity. Sarna stridently defended this basic historicity in *Exploring Exodus*, the JPS Exodus commentary, and in his contribution to Hershel Shanks, editor, *A Short History of Ancient Israel*. The Exodus narrative is indisputably the centerpiece of the Torah and the perpetual point of reference for later books of the Tanakh—this alone lends it considerable credence. Sarna cites no fewer than seven thematic uses to which later biblical authors put the Exodus narrative. As Sarna put it in his elegant way, historiosophy, not historiography, was the Torah's preferred mode of discourse.[23]

RECLAIMING A MODERN JEWISH BIBLE SCHOLARLY TRADITION

Sarna's biblical scholarship, modern, critical, nonfundamentalist, and nonscientist, describes most non-Jewish scholars as well. Yet Jewishness remains an intriguing aspect of his work. I have noted the ideologically charged way in which Sarna makes his brand of Bible study part of an ongoing Jewish tradition by implying that had the medieval rationalists (*pashtanim*) been alive, they would have taken up the cudgels of the modern method. I would add that while Sarna does not explicitly discuss midrash or other commentators in either *Understanding Genesis* or *Exploring Exodus*, he does cite, very frequently, his modern Jewish predecessors. Cyrus Gordon, Cassuto, Jacob, and, above all, Kaufmann appear prominently in his notes. Kaufmann's influence on American Jewish Bible scholars nearly approached his influence on fellow Israelis, detailed in the previous chapter. Even Geiger, it seems to me, influenced Sarna greatly in his invocation of a "national genius" as a nontraditionalist way of affirming the miraculous breakthrough to monotheism and prophetic ethics, what Geiger called the period of revelation. Actually, both the antinationalist Geiger and the intensely nationalist Kaufmann voiced this idea of national genius—and Sarna knew both their works intimately. One figure who surely did not believe in Jewish genius was the heretic Spinoza. Yet Sarna credits him as providing the "missing link between medieval and moderns . . . the true founder of the modern scientific approach to the Bible."[24]

Sarna also continues a particular tradition regarding non-Jewish authors. Moses Mendelssohn, at the end of the eighteenth century, showed great reluctance in citing Christians when it came to his commentary—though not, of course, when it came to his general philosophical works. Samson Raphael Hirsch adopted the same basic stance, acknowledging Christian writers with enthusiasm in his many writings and sermons, but not in his

Torah commentary. By the late nineteenth century, this sequestering of Jewish and Christian had proven untenable for Jews interested in engaging with modern critical Bible scholarship. As with Benno Jacob and Joseph Hertz, the Christian authors cited by Sarna are highly unrepresentative of the field of biblical studies; almost all are historical maximalists like the biblical archaeologist Albright, source criticism skeptics, and overall textual conservatives. If the terms philosemitic or philozionist are appropriate here, and in Albright's case they are, this turns out to be an unstated criterion for inclusion in Sarna's works, as it was for his Jewish predecessors in Israel and Germany. Obviously, this does not apply to those Protestant Bible scholars cited for polemical purposes. Indeed, Sarna and his Israeli and German-Jewish predecessors often set up "Protestant Bible scholarship" as uniform and equivalent to the Wellhausen school, then display its anti-Jewish animus, and then discredit it with a flourish. This rhetorical mode often skirted the underlying validity of the source critical method and the unquestionable reality that conservative Christians—Protestant and Catholic—found this approach equally problematic.

THE POWER OF POLEMIC

The term *polemic* has a negative connotation in religious studies, but it can serve a constructive purpose. A good example of this may be found in Sarna's treatment of the Bible's treatment of ancient Near Eastern literature. For it is central to Sarna's understanding of Genesis that much of it is shaped by a polemic against the verities of ancient Mesopotamia. Delitzsch's *Babel and Bible* can hardly be called either objective or lacking an agenda. His clear goal was to diminish the prestige of the Bible—naturally, this option did not appeal to Jewish scholars. It is important here to distinguish Sarna from Solomon Schechter, Joseph Hertz, Yehezkel Kaufmann, or Moshe Segal. By roughly 1900, the existence of ancient Near Eastern parallels could not be denied. A variety of "options" emerged with respect to dealing with this material. One option, practiced by Orthodox Jewry mainly, was to simply ignore this reality. (Not accidentally, Orthodox scholars in Israel, where the relevant archaeology takes place, have gone farther than diaspora Orthodoxy in integrating this evidence.) Another option, favored by Joseph Hertz, was to discuss ancient Near Eastern parallels by way of acknowledging that he knew of their existence, but to resolutely exclude them from casting light on the sacred Scriptures. Sarna evidenced a third option: to insist on the ability of the ancient parallels to shed light on the Hebrew Bible, but to also insist on the religious and moral superiority of the biblical version. In fact, unlike earlier generations of Jewish Bible scholars who knew of this Mesopotamian and Egyptian material, Sarna deployed it constantly to illuminate the Bible. This represented a giant step beyond Kaufmann, who acknowledged that the Bible polemicized against the mythological, pagan background, but contended that the Bible did so dismissively, that the Bible did not truly grasp the nature of polytheism, and that one could not construct a plausible picture of ancient religion from biblical material. Sarna demurred, arguing that the Bible knew ancient creation and flood myths intimately and that biblical verses were daggers aimed at the heart of these myths' underlying ethos. (A fourth option, to use all ancient materials equally to build a composite, nonjudgmental picture of the ancient Near East, is now the scholarly norm. In my nonexpert view, however, that methodological step has been taken only fairly recently.)

Before we turn to Sarna's chapters on "Creation" and "Flood," a couple of examples from Umberto Cassuto (Genesis 38) and Moshe Greenberg (Exodus 21) will show that Sarna was not alone in this approach. Cassuto (1883–1951) received a doctorate at the University of Florence and rabbinic ordination in Italy. Trained as a classicist and historian of Italian Jewry, Cassuto moved to Israel in 1939 as result of the Italian adoption of Nazi racial laws, and became a professor of Bible at Hebrew University. In Israel, Cassuto exerted enormous influence through his impressive Genesis and Exodus commentaries, published in 1944 and 1951, respectively. Cassuto's approach, extended to the whole Pentateuch in simplified language by Rabbi Elia Samuele Artom (1887–1965), became the single most popular Bible commentary in Israeli classrooms for decades. Although a generation older than Sarna and Greenberg, Cassuto anticipated many of their positions, and may even be seen as a forerunner of a more purely literary approach.[25] Cassuto rejected a slicing up of Genesis, connecting the tale of Jacob and Tamar to what comes before it. Like Benno Jacob, Cassuto perceived Tamar as one of a long line of righteous gentiles, and devoted a paragraph to explaining why "Ruth is the worthy successor of Tamar." Perhaps this connection is obvious: both are foreigners who take the sexual initiative for a holy purpose, and both forward the messianic line of Judah-David. But Cassuto argued that modern source critics did not understand ancient literature well enough to perceive the biblical methods. Cassuto found similar-sounding words or repeated key words or even partial phrases as making sense of editorial processes that source critics tended to regard as simply sloppy. Like many modern Jewish commentators, Cassuto believed that the so-and-so begat so-and-so lists (*v'eleh toldot*), generally comical to nonreligious contemporaries, played a critical editorial function. As to the variation of divine names, so essential to the source critical approach, Cassuto followed Jewish tradition, amplified by his knowledge of ancient Near Eastern usage, in linking a particular divine name to a particular divine function. While Cassuto had no trouble accepting the post-Mosaic authorship of much of Torah, he found the documentary hypothesis artificial, and in a book of that same name devoted five succinct chapters to undercutting each of its regnant assumptions.

Moshe Greenberg (1928–2010) received his doctorate at the University of Pennsylvania from Ephraim Avigdor Speiser and his rabbinic ordination from the Jewish Theological Seminary. Greenberg was part of a "Philadelphia circle" of well-trained Semiticists that included Gordon, Speiser, Berlin, and others. Like Cassuto, Greenberg also immigrated to Israel, though out of Zionist conviction rather than because of persecution. At Hebrew University, he too produced a distinguished body of biblical scholarship in a Jewish cadence, significantly influencing both Israeli and American Bible scholars. Greenberg polemicized against an excessively emendatory-excavative approach and in favor of a reading that paid attention to the literary and theological integrity of works—even difficult ones such as Ezekiel, for which he supplied the Anchor Bible commentary. But Greenberg's most lasting impact on the modern Jewish Bible, like Cassuto's, was arguably secondhand, for Greenberg translated and condensed Kaufmann's seven-volume Hebrew text *History of Israelite Faith* into a one-volume English translation, *History of Israel* (1960), as well as Kaufmann's entry for the Modern Library's widely distributed *Great Ages and Ideas of the Jewish People* (1956). By making Kaufmann available in English, Greenberg effectively broadened his reach to a Jewish lay audience as well as to Christian scholars unable to read modern Hebrew. (Capably parsing the grammar of biblical verses does not guarantee that someone can read a book in modern Hebrew.)

In a celebrated discussion of "an eye for an eye" (Exodus 21:22–25), Moshe Greenberg offered a point-by-point comparison of Israelite and Mesopotamian criminal law, specifically, the famous codes of Eshnunna and Hammurabi. Greenberg's argument was that the Bible's insistence on corporal punishment marked a strong egalitarian push against an earlier system where the social status of the perpetrator and victim determined the penalty. In the history of law, then, Exodus 21:22–25 marked a giant step forward from its Mesopotamian predecessors. Moreover, the relative harshness of Israelite law regarding offenses that involved bodily injury and loss of life, and the relative mildness regarding monetary transgressions, proved to Greenberg the abiding commitment of the Hebrew Bible to what is arguably the formative dictum of Genesis, that humans are made in God's image. That Greenberg, an ordained Conservative rabbi, was willing to forward this argument despite the fact that it runs counter to the traditional rabbinic understanding of this verse seems to me a comment not only on Greenberg's scholarly integrity, but also on the confidence he placed in letting the biblical teaching speak in its historical context. Greenberg did not mention another polemical motive at play, the role that this very passage has had in Christian derogations of Judaism as the religion of the Old Testament God of vengeance as opposed to the New Testament God of love. By mentioning the laxity of the Hebrew Bible regarding monetary offenses, I suspect that Greenberg was also taking aim at another antisemitic canard, that of Jewish stinginess, but that may be my eisigesis, not Greenberg's exegesis. Greenberg, well versed in rabbinic literature and insistent on a holistic reading of the biblical text, may be grouped with Cassuto and Sarna as exemplars of a "Jewish school" of Bible studies. Collectively, these three and others paved the way for an integration of rabbinic materials, of ancient Near Eastern texts, and of literary sensitivity. What Ellen Frankel, the learned editor in chief of the Jewish Publication Society, said of Sarna after his passing could have been said of Cassuto or Greenberg as well: "Nahum Sarna was one of the first Jewish scholars to bridge traditional Jewish approaches to Bible interpretation with modern scholarship."[26] Much more could be said about both Cassuto and Greenberg; my main purpose is to underscore that the figures I have focused on do not exhaust the story. Sarna was working on a path paralleled by others.

NAHUM SARNA ON THE GENESIS CREATION AND FLOOD NARRATIVES

> The foregoing study of the biblical deluge story leaves no room for doubting the direct connection between it and the Mesopotamian tradition. Yet a closer look at the two and a careful understanding of the purposes of the Bible leave us with quite a different impression. The Hebrew version is an expression of the biblical polemic against paganism. This assault is carried on not on the level of dialectics, but indirectly and inferentially. Through an inspired process of selection, revision, and addition, whether deliberate or intuitive, the original material has been so thoroughly reshaped as to become an entirely new and original creation purged of its polytheistic dross. What in the Mesopotamian tradition was apparently of local importance became in the Bible a major event of cosmic significance. What there is largely casual and contingent has become here causal and determinative. Like the creation narrative, that of Noah and the flood has been made into a vehicle for expression of some of the most profound biblical teachings, an instrument for the communication of universal moral truths, the medium through which God makes known what He demands of man.[27]

Sarna freely acknowledged two items that troubled many earlier Jewish interpreters. First, there is no doubt in Sarna's mind that the Genesis account knew of the Mesopotamian story, although Sarna considered the process of transformation so thoroughgoing as to obscure which precise cuneiform version was available. Second, Sarna accepted that the flood narrative of Genesis was a "fusion of traditions."[28] In other words, although he did not name them as such, Sarna was not troubled by the thought that J and P both had a hand in the final creation and flood narratives. However, unlike Speiser and Friedman, and many non-Jewish Bible scholars, too, Sarna's emphasis was not on a demonstration (or refutation) of that documentary claim, nor on which particular sources contributed which particular verses. The point of reference becomes the composite narrative, the Redacted text, and its dissent from the ancient Near Eastern record. The adjective "inspired" in this passage is ambiguous, no doubt intentionally so. Did Sarna mean "inspired" in the secular sense—artfully woven together by R, as he implied in "the inspired genius at work"? Or inspired in a religious sense, guided by divine revelation in one way or another?[29] Sarna's agnosticism on this point strikes me as edifyingly representative: the vast majority of Jewish readers will find themselves unsure before these two options, but thoroughly convinced that Genesis stands above its closest analogues—those of the ancient Near East.

Sarna devoted the end of his Genesis introduction to an explicit statement of analogy and difference. Sarna again took a cue from Sandmel's devastating critique of Protestant treatments of the many parallels between rabbinic teachings and the sayings of Jesus. From Sandmel's point of view, the acknowledgment of Jesus's Jewishness had led to a second line of Christian denialism, exemplified in the Strack-Billerbeck compendium of rabbinic sources and their Christian parallels. In Sandmel's view, the main thrust of their work was to demonstrate that whatever the rabbis had said, Jesus had said better, or more concisely. For Sandmel, this motive drove this scholarly enterprise to ignore the comparison of two entire religious systems, and to wrench rabbinic statements out of their proper context. Nevertheless, when Sarna wrote in *Exploring Exodus*, "I am not addicted to parallelomania," he meant something a bit different from Sandmel.[30] For Sarna, the fault of Bible scholars was not principally their piling up of Israelite and Mesopotamian parallels to show the superiority of the latter, though this indeed was Delitzsch's inclination. Rather, it was a different methodological error that Sarna attacked: the tendency to think that parallels diminished difference, whereas for Sarna the opposite was true. Precisely the differences in the biblical account distinguished the biblical text. "Accordingly, we have constantly emphasized in this book the importance of difference, and have been at pains to delineate those areas in which Israel parted company with its neighbors."[31]

Israel's dissent from the ancient Near East comes across just as powerfully in Sarna's writings on Exodus. His essay "The Decalogue" compared Exodus 20 with the legal material of Hammurabi, the best preserved from this era. "A further crucial distinction between the Decalogue and ancient Near eastern Codes lies in the source and sanction of law. No biblical law is ever attributed to Moses himself or to any prophet personally. The narratives know nothing of a law-giver sage or lawgiver-king. The great empire builder . . . makes no claim to innovation. The only name exclusively connected with law is that of Moses and he is a prophet who mediates the divine communication to Israel. This picture is in striking contrast to the situation in the ancient world."[32] For Sarna, then, the axioms of Israelite law, its eternal validity and transnational relevance, were part of Israelite consciousness from the beginning.

SARNA'S BIBLE: A SUMMARY

1. *Sarna's Bible is decidedly modern.* Sarna used modern methods, principally archaeology, Semitic philology, and, to some extent, comparative religion. Sarna was historical in his treatment of the Bible as a humanly produced document, which consistently and constantly reflected the times in which it was composed, if often in the spirit of antipagan opposition. Sarna is sincere in terming Spinoza the father of modern Bible science, even if the intent of their respective inquiries could not be farther apart.
2. *Sarna's Bible is decidedly noncommittal on the delicate issue of authorship.* Was the Redactor indeed the author, as Benno Jacob contended? Was the Bible "inspired" in some traditionalist way, or "inspired" in the sense that Shakespeare was inspired—great literature with ethical and spiritual dimensions, but in no way God-driven? Sarna relies on a nebulous construct, ancient Israel's "national genius" that makes "Israel" the default author of Torah, and necessarily lightens the load for the third leg of the stool of traditional Jewish theology—God.
3. *Sarna followed a theme that Judaism paralleled but transcended its ancient Near Eastern counterparts.* The ancient Near East and Israel were both similar and different, but to Sarna the differences count for more than the similarities: this is a fundamental principle of his that has no logical justification, but which he asserted repeatedly. Sarna's Bible is Jewish in some obvious ways too: reliance on Jewish exegetical traditions, awareness of modern Jewish commentators including Israelis, and reference to contemporary Jewish practices.
4. *Sarna's Bible is non-Orthodox.* Orthodoxy's hesitancy to enter into a sustained comparison with the ancient Near East during his lifetime, especially in the diaspora, deprived Judaism of a valuable weapon in showing the superiority of the Bible, exactly Sarna's endgame. If you will not engage in comparison, you cannot claim relative greatness, only absolute perfection.
5. *Sarna's Bible is decidedly compatible with Jewish ethnic pride/ethnic ownership of the Bible.* Sarna himself was "personally loyal to observant Judaism," as Simon Greenberg put it (not irrelevantly) in his preface to *Understanding Genesis*. His reading of ancient history Israel held

that Israel differentiated itself from its environment and never capitulated to it. Even when local circumstances forced accommodation, such as the embalming of Jacob and Joseph in Egypt, this was not tantamount to abandoning the essentially Jewish: "the embalming of Jacob and Joseph has no religious setting, but seems to have been purely a practical measure."[33] The greatness of the Bible that emerges from *Understanding Genesis, Exploring Exodus,* and *On the Book of Psalms* is historical, but does not turn on complete historical veracity; is literary, but does not turn only on artistry; is theological, but does not turn on an assertion of divine revelation. Sarna's Bible may not be Herodotus, Homer, or the Truth. It is, however, ours.

ROBERT ALTER: RECLAIMING THE JEWISH BIBLE AS LITERATURE

Robert Alter (1935–present) has produced elegant translations of the Torah and I and II Samuel; written a trio of well-read and highly influential books on the Bible, *The Art of Biblical Narrative* (1981), *The Art of Biblical Poetry* (1985), and *The World of Biblical Literature* (1992); and coedited, with Frank Kermode, *The Literary Guide to the Bible,* a landmark in the contemporary reappropriation of the Bible as literature. *The Art of Biblical Narrative,* hereafter *ABN,* which won a National Jewish Book Award for Jewish thought, has sold over seventy thousand copies, and received the singular honor of meriting a special issue of *Prooftexts,* a premier Jewish literary journal. Nevertheless, there have been several dubious responses to Alter's biblical-literary approach. S. David Sperling regrets that the new literary school does not pay sufficient attention to the ancient Near East genres and literary legacy. Since Cassuto and Sarna have both made these comparisons without compromising the literary unity of the Bible, one can understand this complaint—Alter adduces examples from the European novel in his biblical works freely, but without taking a stand as to how far these comparisons can be taken.[34] James Kugel doubts that the genres of modern literature can be superimposed on the biblical materials, and even dismisses the idea that the overall literary quality of the Bible really can be compared with Homer or Virgil. More sharply still, Kugel doubts that the literary devices so magnificently elaborated by Alter to show connections, allusions, and careful editing actually exist. For Kugel, the repetition of a common verb such as "to recognize" in several conjugations does not prove very much given the limited vocabulary available to the biblical author. Putting it more charitably, Kugel is often more impressed with Alter's genius as a reader than with the Bible's literary merit. David Berger, a renowned medievalist, responded to the initial appearance of *ABN* by criticizing Alter's opening chapter for contributing nothing substantial beyond the midrashic tradition on Genesis 38, a tradition which Alter deliberately invoked. As Mara Benjamin astutely notes, Alter made a point of praising the literary sensitivity of midrash over and against nineteenth-century source criticism, forging an alliance with modern readers who may not share the operating assumptions of Midrash, including the Torah's divine origins. Where Alter goes beyond midrash, in his own estimation, if not Berger's, is his commitment to offering sustained readings of narratives and character. Additionally, Alter eschews the didactic nature of midrash. As we shall see, Alter believes the meaning often emerges from the Bible's ambiguity, which midrash tends to eliminate.

Another set of critics has attacked Alter's *ABN* from a more political view: Mieke Bal accused Alter of validating the socially constructed gender assumptions of the Bible by failing to critique them, and Burke Long believed Alter avoided problems of authorial intent and of assuming textual coherence without any real evidence—in other words, that Alter was not a deconstructionist reader of the Bible. Regarding this last type of criticism, which has gained adherents since the 1980s, I have little to say. I think that there is an unbridgeable divide between those who believe that we have something to say to the Bible and also that the Bible has something to say to us, and those who *believe only the former*. Alter may be agnostic about many things, but he clearly belongs to the camp that thinks the Bible ought to be interpreted and not only critiqued. That Alter was not a Bible scholar by dint of academic training may make him more vulnerable to criticism, but I will certainly vote with his seventy-thousand-plus readers. My purpose in the following discussion is to extend the appreciation of his contributions beyond *ABN* to his other Bible books, to place Alter in a broader context, and to argue that Alter's literary approach to the Bible parallels Sarna's historical approach in validating a Jewish perspective.[35]

Robert Alter, a native New Yorker, received his BA from Columbia and his MA and PhD in literature from Harvard. Susanne Klingenstein's *Enlarging America* focuses on Alter's many contributions to the modern novel, the popularization of Israeli literature, and his forceful arguments in favor of literacy in some Jewish language and in some Jewish literary tradition. Along those lines, Alter argued in the 1960s for the genius of Shmuel Yosef Agnon, and against the exaggerated status of Saul Bellow–Philip Roth–Bernard Malamud as Jewish authors.[36] Klingenstein's analysis, though entirely justified, tends to sequester modern Jewish Bible studies from Jewish thought, or in Alter's case, Jewish literature. *ABN* enjoyed unprecedented success and Alter has arguably done more than any other figure in the American academy to revive "the Bible as literature," although what that means for Alter and those he has influenced requires elucidation.

"MERE" VERSUS "EXALTED" LITERATURE: FROM AUERBACH TO ALTER

The story of Bible instruction in American universities would make a fascinating study. My cursory glance at courses on the Bible at mid-twentieth century suggests that courses divided into two main groups. The first set of courses were hard-core historical-technical inquiries of the Bible against its ancient Near Eastern background, involving mastery of Semitics, or at least that scholarship as translated for undergraduates, what Gordon called the "Pennsylvania tradition" of Bible studies. Alternately, American colleges offered courses that taught the Bible as a foundation stone of the Western literary tradition, as elevating literature like Virgil, Dante, and Milton. Anyone reading the works of Mark Van Doren or similar critics would acknowledge the power of this approach, undertaken by great readers without a smattering of the original language. Both developments took place on the margins of the field of Bible studies and both approaches—the "Semiticist" and the "Bible as literature"—tended to bracket out the broader issues of politics, culture, and religious belief. Within the mainstream of Bible scholarship, the birth of a more rigorous literary approach is often associated with James Muilenberg and his many students, including Phyllis Trible, the first female president of the Society of Biblical Literature. Alter, however, comes from the margins of the field of Bible, as does an important precursor, Erich Auerbach (1892–1957).

Auerbach did not emerge from the world of Bible studies, and unlike Alter, never mastered Hebrew, though he read an impressive number of European languages as well as Greek and Latin. "Odysseus's Scar," the introductory chapter of *Mimesis: The Representation of Reality in Western Literature*, has had enormous influence on a literary appreciation of the Bible and is taught widely in Jewish adult education programs such as the Wexner Fellows or Meah. Auerbach contrasted the narrative styles of Homer and the Bible, arguing that the laconic style, rich characterization, and religious intent of the latter made the Bible, ultimately, a deeper work. This depth, epitomized in Auerbach's most repeated phrase, "fraught with background," demanded interpretation in a way that Homer precluded. "Homer can be analyzed . . . but he cannot be interpreted."[37] Auerbach's claims would be apparent to any careful reader, but I doubt that the backstory and political intent of this book have been sufficiently emphasized. Auerbach, an acculturated German Jew, was dismissed from the University of Marburg by the Nazis in 1935 and wrote *Mimesis* at Istanbul State University during World War II, without a major library at his disposal. Auerbach's revival of the nineteenth-century Hebraic versus Hellenic dichotomy was clearly colored by his own experiences with Nazi neopaganism—briefly noted in "Odysseus's Scar." In this essay, as in his equally seminal "Figura," Auerbach deliberately offered a Judeo-Christian tradition, which, in his view, defined the literary canon of Western civilization as much as the Greco-Roman tradition. Auerbach assumed the fundamental historicity and social realities of the Hebrew Bible, and the coherence and ideological sincerity of the biblical author(s), but those claims were secondary to the real reason that the Bible should be treated as a coherent whole, and why the Redacted text was the only relevant point of departure. As he wrote in the concluding paragraph:

> Since we are using the two styles, the Homeric and the Old Testament, as starting points, we have taken them as finished products, as they appear in the texts; we have disregarded everything that pertains to their origins, and thus we have left untouched the question whether their peculiarities were theirs from the beginning or are to be referred wholly or in part to foreign influences. Within the limits of our purpose, a consideration of this question is not necessary; for it is in their full development, which they reached in early times, that the two styles exercised their determining influence upon the representation of reality in European literature.[38]

I do not think it is much of an exaggeration to claim that Alter picks up where Auerbach left off. Although Alter cites many influences on his work, none expressed the connection between the Bible's literary greatness and its role as a cultural canon as clearly as Auerbach. Indeed, Alter terms the phenomenon both men were describing as a "secondary canonicity," in contradistinction to a "primary canonicity," which would accept the inspired nature of the canonical books at face value. What Alter has done, as Benjamin rightly notes, has been to offer the substitution of literary greatness for religious belief, or at least to accommodate those inclined to make this substitution. Benjamin writes: "Alter enjoins the reader to view the textual contradictions as fruitful; he offers himself not only as a commentator of literary training but as a reader of existential proclivities. His assessment of the Genesis narrative(s) does not require any particular religious belief, but, as David Norton has pointed out, it certainly accommodates belief. This balance is surely key to the book's tremendous appeal. But beyond a carefully maintained agnosticism lies something yet more appealing: Alter's glosses on the significance of the literary structure of the Bible offer readers a *substitute* for belief."[39]

Whatever Alter's intent, a sense of the ambitiousness of his agenda must have been there early on for Alter to have devoted more than a quarter century to his Bible project. Klingenstein identifies a series of seminars taught at Berkeley in the 1970s as Alter's point of departure for his biblical works; by 1981 he had published *ABN*; by 1996, *Genesis*; and by 2004, *The Five Books of Moses*. Alter rejects, on numerous occasions, a dichotomy between the literary and the divine. For Alter, the famous rabbinic dictum "the Torah speaks in a human tongue" hits the nail on the head. With what vehicle would God or God-inspired humans communicate aside from literature?

Alter's translation reflects a conscious decision to render into English what had always been intended as the Bible's elevated speech. For Alter the consensus that the Bible was heard in the ancient world (and not just read) does not militate against the idea the authors meant their readers to hear something elevating—Alter mocks the notion that ancient readers and translators possessed nothing loftier than the ancient equivalent of *Time* magazine and that that should guide the level of language employed.[40]

Alter's interpretive crux, surely, is his rejection of the source critical school conception of how and why the Bible should be read. This dismissal parallels Sarna's, on literary rather than historical grounds, of the source critics' procedure as analogous to dissecting a corpse. Alter likewise rejects the "excavative approach," and while he is properly thankful for the light shone on the Hebrew Bible by ancient Near Eastern cognate languages and genres, he does not feel bound to resort to them, as does the more historically oriented Sarna. In numerous polemics against E. A. Speiser, Alter's favorite example of the limitations of even the best of the source critics, he attacks Speiser's fixation on finding the particular source as the focus of his exegetical energies. Speiser, in Alter's view, got snared by a conception of the Bible's cruxes as a series of problems to be solved, analogous to contemporary religious studies' critiques of Rudolph Otto's seminal *The Idea of the Holy*, and Speiser's overall low regard for the composite text, that of the Redactor. Here is a typical example of Alter's critique: "For the documentary critic, however, the real concern is not the imaginative coherence of the narrative invention—Frei's 'realism'—but the historical mediation of the text. Thus, in Speiser's [Anchor Bible Genesis] commentary it is not Jacob and Esau but E, J, and P who become the subject of investigation. In this way the text is held at a distance for inspection, and any voice that might speak from its imagined situation to our actual one is in effect suppressed."[41]

Alter's animus goes beyond source criticism narrowly defined to almost any exercise of historical criticism whose final effort is to get behind the text rather than deal with the text itself. In a reproach to Harold Bloom, like Alter a scholar of literature who also turned to the Bible after establishing his credentials in modern literature, Alter is untroubled by Bloom's suggestion that the first biblical author J was a woman, and untroubled that Bloom regarded J as essentially a secular author, an idea I find implausible. But Alter considers the *Book of J* flawed not only by its translation of the ostensible J texts, but by Bloom's growing fixation with the historical reality of a female J, which Bloom admitted as little more than an enjoyable speculation at the beginning of his book. Alter: "Not surprisingly, however, as Bloom continues to expatiate on J 'she' more and more becomes a definite historical figure, not an arbitrary fiction, assigned a definite location in time, place and social standing, which in turn is used to explain the intentions of her writing."[42] While there is much that one might object to in the *Book of J*, Alter's complaint is that Bloom, of all people, abandoned the literary enterprise of *interpreting* the text in favor of the historical enterprise of *explaining* the text.

"Explaining the text," as Alter comments in the introduction to *The Five Books of Moses*, constitutes the heresy par excellence when it comes to translation.[43] The temptation to use translation to explain is understandable: the nature of the text cries out for understanding, yet the biblical Hebrew is difficult and resistant to easy conversion into English that is both straightforward yet elevated. Significantly, Alter finds Everett Fox's translation the one sterling exception to this offense: it achieved what Scholem said about the Buber-Rosenzweig translation, the very one that inspired Fox.[44] The Buber-Rosenzweig translation kept the difficult and the strange intact, principally through their "Hebraizing" techniques. But Fox, in Alter's view, paid his dues to the Hebrew at the expense of his debt to English. The same reproach was raised against Buber-Rosenzweig in the 1930s, as Alter was no doubt aware. Alter appreciates Fox's contribution, yet argues that a translator must have a love affair with both languages, not only the source language.

Bloom's slide into historicism commits another common offense in Alter's estimation, namely denuding the biblical text of its indeterminacy and multivalence and, one might even say, its "mystery." Not everything in the Hebrew Bible can be nailed down. Michal, David's wife/Saul's daughter, remained childless to the end of her life, but we cannot be sure whether the biblical narrator is chastising her reaction to David's triumphant movement of the ark to Jerusalem (in her eyes unfitting), or whether the narrator is expressing sympathy with a woman who grew up a king's daughter but has seen her father and brother killed while her love for David has been used as a political football, or both. Do the narrator's sympathies lie with the anguished Esau, deprived of both blessing and birthright, or is his earthy appetitive nature a clear sign that the blessing must be carried forward by the younger twin, or both? Alter finds that most historically oriented Bible scholarship is tone-deaf to this note of the unresolved in the text, and that when the particular commentator catches it, he or she cannot resist pushing to one pole or another.

WHAT IS JEWISH?

Alter himself, as Mara Benjamin insightfully argues, picks up and continues the polemic of Buber and Rosenzweig against dichotomizing the "Jewish" and the "human." Martin Buber, who wrote in a distinctly religious vein, portrayed the more spiritual impulse as the more primal, mythic, and human. Thus the most authentic Jewish religiosity was also the most human. Benjamin pegs the cultural significance of Alter's recourse to the Jewish tradition as deriving from a metaexegetical motive:

> Alter's use of midrash in *ABN* is better understood, however, as revealing both a hope for and the expression of the success of Jewish intellectuals in late twentieth-century America. Nearly twenty-five years after his classic work on biblical narrative appeared, Alter's own acclaimed translation of the Pentateuch has become widely recognized as a scholarly yet accessible guide for anyone interested in the Hebrew Bible: Jewish, Christian, or secular; believing or critical.
>
> That Alter's work could attain such success as it interwove the archaic and the Aramaic into a text for lay readers, students, and scholars beyond the Jewish world testifies to a historical *novum*. The "Jewish," long maligned as merely "particular," now might hold the promise of representing the "universal."[45]

I have no desire to undo the argument that the Jewish might also "hold the promise" of representing the "universal." But even if the "essentially" Jewish is a chimera, the "self-constructed" Jewish is a collective necessity in a contemporary, integrated environment, nowhere more so than in a country where the biblical legacy exerts such a heavy hand. It may be illuminating, without being conclusive, therefore, to tease out the "Jewish" in Alter in light of what I see as a two-hundred-year tradition of modern Jews in the field of Bible doing exactly that. To begin with, and following the lead of Spinoza, Alter leaves the New Testament alone. "New Testament" does not even appear in the index of *ABN* or *Art of Biblical Poetry*, though "New Critics" does, and in *The World of Biblical Literature*, both times it appears are by way of contrasting the New Testament with the Old.[46] For some of our subjects this would require no comment: as self-identifying Jewish expositors, rabbis even, the Hebrew Bible naturally stands on its own. But as a scholar of literature, it would certainly have been legitimate for Alter to extend his inquiry to the New Testament, as did Erich Auerbach, Hans Frei, and Northrop Frye, to mention a trio of heavyweights who also advanced a literary approach to the Bible. Especially given the boldness of Alter's three book titles, a Christian reader might legitimately ask, where is the place of the Sermon on the Mount, if not in *The World of Biblical Literature*? Although some judicious comments about the differences between the Jewish and Christian canons may be found in the joint introduction of Alter and Kermode to *The Literary Guide of the Bible*,[47] the most revealing comment comes in Alter's approbation of Harold Bloom's reference to "the Christian triumph over the Hebrew Bible, a triumph which produced that captive work, the Old Testament."[48] Alter suggests that the Greek Scriptures simply lack the literary features—background versus foreground, vertical composition over centuries—that he finds of greatest interest. It could also be argued that Alter finds it dubious to engage in Greek Scriptures when one does not know Greek, since the Hebrewness of the text has been a cardinal tenet of modern Jewish Bible scholarship. (I am sure some Hebrew Scripture doyens have grumbled about Alter's mastery of Akkadian or Ugaritic.) But I also catch a "whiff of polemic," however gentle. Perhaps Alter seeks to legitimate a core facet that Buber identified—a "Jewish Bible" unfolded in dialogue between God and Israel, in other words, a Bible unfolded in the middle of a life of the people?[49] In *Pen of Iron: American Prose and the King James Bible* (2010), Alter suggests that this argument explains colonial America's apparently greater identification with the Old rather than the New Testament. Perhaps not, but if Alter's Bible is not Jewish, it is certainly not Christian. This may seem like a negative starting point for a positive appropriation, but it has been a common, and maybe necessary, starting point for Jewish scholars given the Protestant flavor of the field.[50]

Robert Alter's canon of great literature is a large one. In biblical studies, it includes some great non-Jewish readers of the Bible and students of Hebrew, but a healthy representation of members of the tribe. Although Alter employs Jacob and Cassuto in his commentary, the key figures are Erich Auerbach, Benjamin Harshav, Menachem Perry, and Meir Sternberg—secular Jewish authors, but all authors who reach beyond a "merely" literary approach to make a statement of transcendent meaning. The beginning of every book of Alter's is largely a discussion of Jewish authors, many of them in Hebrew. Some of this is part of Alter's lifelong project to integrate Hebrew and Israeli culture into diaspora Jewish life and into academic fields inclined to ignore such "Jewish" contributions. The citation of other Jewish authors serves another function too: it indicates to Jewish and non-Jewish readers a message about the belatedness of Jewish studies and Jewish studies in Bible especially. Jews, mainly, have been sitting on the sidelines with respect to the Bible since Zunz first defined the parameters of Jewish Wissenschaft, but we have been sitting on our hands, ready to speak when we found the right words.

One final comment of Alter's on the Hebrewness of the biblical text, from his *Art of Biblical Poetry*: "One of the chief ways in which ancient Hebrew poetry has continued to live is in the poems later writers have fashioned out of it. This is most strikingly true of post-biblical Hebrew poetry, which forms a remarkable continuous tradition over nearly two thousand years that again and again recurs to biblical language and biblical images, down to the latest Israeli contemporaries."[51] One thing that Hebrew Bible has been for Jewish culture, and here a note of exclusivity is warranted, is the point of origin of Jewish literature, that theme of "double canonicity" described above. What kind of status is Alter suggesting? Consider this comment about the likelihood of the existence of a colloquial Hebrew in ancient Israel, different from the elevated language of the Hebrew Bible.

> There is evidence, moreover, that people in everyday life may have had different words for many of the basic concepts and entities that are mentioned in the Bible. The argument was persuasively made by the Israeli linguist Abba ben David in his still indispensable 1967 study, available only in Hebrew, *The Language of the Bible and the Language of the Sages*. Ben David offers a fascinating explanation for one of the great mysteries of the Hebrew language—the emergence, toward the end of the pre-Christian era, of a new kind of Hebrew, which became the language of the early rabbis. . . . Where did these words come from?[52]

Alter's amphibolous use of "mysteries" and his dating of this development before the advent of Christianity seem pointed. Just as inner-biblical interpretation, as we have seen in our discussion of Sarna, constitutes an argument for an indigenously developed exegesis, Alter's reading of the relationship of biblical Hebrew and colloquial Hebrew buttresses a case for indigenous philology; for a chain of tradition, as the rabbis put it. Sometimes you can judge how badly an author wants an argument to be true by the paucity of evidence. Alter adduces exactly one half-verse, Esau's plaint, "Let me gulp down some of this red, red stuff, for I am famished." To be clear: any claim about the Bible that can be argued with only one of its verses is speculation.[53] Calev Ben David and Avi Hurwitz provide important data about the linguistic developments of biblical Hebrew that evidence importations of Aramaic, continuities with later Mishnaic-era Hebrew, and findings incompatible with the claim of biblical minimalists that the entire Bible comes from one very late period. But they fall short of evidencing a two-layered Hebrew, one colloquial and one literary.

Whether in a primary sense or a secondary sense, the Bible remains a canonical text for American Jews, creating a transhistorical textual community. The works of Alter and Sarna, naturally, lack this canonical status, nor do they aspire to it. Their works do, however, deserve to be considered key texts, which "give us entry into cultural universes that are intricately connected to specific social, economic and political moments, while at the same time being collective or social."[54] The next chapter attempts to probe the "cultural universe" of contemporary American Jewry by examining its deployment of the Bible, its canonical text.

10

Seeking an American Jewish Bible

My inquiry in this overambitious chapter starts with a simplistic, counterintuitive observation: the Chumash, as American Jews know it, is a modern book. Chumash refers to the Five Books of Moses. Sometimes, this appears as *chamishei chumshei ha-torah*, the five-fifths of Torah, that is, the whole thing. Jews in synagogues are content with the Five Books of Moses alone; for Christians, this would be inconceivable. For several decades, American Reform Jews found the Old JPS Bible translations (English-only) in their pews, but since the publication of Plaut's *The Torah: A Modern Commentary* (1981/2005), this has become the exception. Like *Bible*, *Chumash* can have more than one meaning. In the "Old World," the "Chumash on braeshis" meant the book of Genesis surrounded by traditional commentary. This Chumash, really a sliver of the entire "Rabbinic Bible," turns out to be an illuminating negative touchstone. This Old World Chumash is *not* what most American Jews would call a Chumash, for the following reasons.

THE MODERN AMERICAN CHUMASH: THE PRESENCE OF HEBREW

Most American Jews cannot read biblical Hebrew without an English translation, but they would not be happy without that Hebrew text, whether as a symbolic link to the past, a symbol of Jewish affirmation, or a partial reverse pony to the English. Even if most American Jews could not read and translate the Torah line for line or explain its grammar, many can identify individual Hebrew words with pleasure, or even prefer to follow the Hebrew with partial comprehension than read the English with full understanding. I cannot pursue the psychodynamics of this; any Chumash that calls itself such must have Hebrew and a vernacular, laid out in a traditional fashion, with English, in the following examples, occupying the place that the Aramaic translation of Onkelos once did. American Jews, when they go to synagogue, want both English and Hebrew at hand. Naturally, all Chumashim and Jewish study Bibles use a translation produced by Jews.

THE PRESENCE OF RELEVANT COMMENTARY

American Jews would not find Old World Chumashim responsive to their own lives and times. The three *denominational* Chumashim are more than a pastiche of traditional sources; they are written with the standard of contemporary relevance in mind. This reflects an admission that the Bible will not speak to contemporary Jews in an unmediated fashion. Protestants, beginning with Luther, considered a return to the original Bible a high priority, and saw commentary as antagonistic to that goal. Jews find commentary indispensable, and do not understand Luther's soteriological impulse. To put it in English, Jews expect to be illuminated by the Bible, not "saved" by it. Were one to start speaking in tongues during the prophetic reading, someone would likely call a psychiatrist—Jews are not Lutherans or Pentecostals.

THE PRESENCE OF RASHI

Most American Jews cannot read the Rashi without a translation or paraphrase. The Stone/ArtScroll Chumash reproduces Rashi in late medieval Rashi-print, which is surely incomprehensible to most American Jews without a day school or yeshiva upbringing; for most American Jews, Rashi is a closed book. Yet, for ArtScroll's readers, Rashi's presence on the printed page reassures traditionally inclined Jews in the ways that Hebrew does for more liberally inclined Jews, as a patent of Jewish authenticity. The Rashi example is not a trivial one: Torah with Rashi was the heart of early childhood education for males in the late medieval/early modern periods. No fewer than three English translations of Rashi exist, and even in Plaut's Reform commentary, no one is cited more frequently.

PRESENCE IN THE PEWS

Contemporary Jews expect to find a Chumash waiting for them in synagogue. The Plaut, Stone, and Lieber Chumashim are lavish productions, with leather binding, a tassel to mark the place, and gold-embossed pages. As Gabriel Josipovici noted in *The Book of God*, the Bible in both Jewish and Christian cultures has always been given special handling; no other book gets produced with such careful attention to format. Once in synagogue, the Chumash may be used by those who find praying dull, but most frequently is used as a vehicle for reading along with the bar or bat mitzvah boy or girl and savoring their technical mastery or, perhaps, as something to read and reflect upon during the lengthy Torah service. Reassurance plays a role here. While most Jews own Bibles, many would be uncertain which volume to bring to worship, or how to navigate the book once there. The synagogue Chumash, often accompanied by a sheet (often colored, two-sided, and inaccurate) announcing the weekly portion and the aliyah honorees, gives the worshipper confidence that she or he has come to the right place and is well equipped. All Chumashim share the following technical aspects: weekly portion markings, the aliyah markings where the honoree comes up to the podium (*bima*) to bless on the Torah, the blessings before and after Torah and Prophetic readings printed out so the inexperienced can take a glance before coming up to the *bima*, and the Prophetic readings are present in all three American Chumashim. These features were missing from the Old World Chumash because they were not needed; they presume a ritual lack of expertise and existential distance from the text. To put it another way, the American Chumash today serves as a magnificent connector between contemporary Jews and an ancient text.[1]

THREE AMERICAN DENOMINATIONAL CHUMASHIM

Fred Greenspahn elegantly described today's American Chumashim as "denominationally vague" but "explicitly Jewish."[2] *The Torah: A Modern Commentary* came first, befitting the head start Reform Judaism enjoyed in America as an organized movement and liberal discomfort with the badly dated Hertz Chumash. Plaut's work served a modern Jewish audience that wanted to know the historical background of biblical narratives, practices, and terms. A German-born rabbi who carried a copy of Benno Jacob's *Genesis: Der Erste Buch das Tora* with him when he fled the Nazis, Plaut reflects the German liberal tradition in his positive attitude toward *parshanut* and in his lack of interdenominational hostility. (In Germany, rabbis continued to be employees of the community, not the individual synagogue.) In fact, all three American Chumashim would show this lack of intrapolemical spirit regarding the other two major denominations. The Orthodox Stone/ArtScroll does not slam Reform Judaism, nor does Plaut slam Orthodoxy. Even the most denominational of the three, David Lieber's Conservative *Etz Hayim*, displays its agenda via positive affirmations of Conservative halachah and historical method, not via denigration of Orthodoxy or Reform.

Although respectful of tradition, Plaut's Chumash was adamantly modern in orientation, illustrated by the fact that UAHC Press issued both "red" and "blue" editions, with the only difference being the direction in which the Chumash opened. (Hebrew books open from right to left; English books from left to right.) English dominated the volume visually. Although the Hebrew text was present, the font was small and the vowel and cantillation marks hard to read. In line with the idea that this would be a study Torah, Plaut broke the books up into interesting thematic units. This entirely justifiable procedure submerged awareness of the traditional breakdown into weekly portions, which were noted in the upper corner. Comparison with the ancient Near East was unambiguous, and discussion of other textual traditions also occurred. The "Gleanings" section at the back of each thematic unit represented Christian biblical scholars and literary giants like Milton; Jewish liberal or heterodox thinkers such as Buber and Rosenzweig, Benno Jacob, and Hermann Cohen; Jews who operated in an earlier era but got lost to the mainstream of tradition (e.g., Josephus and Philo); and, naturally, modern Jewish Bible commentators. The Jewish classical interpretive tradition was the best represented of all, but one often has to search the footnotes for specifics. One could contrast the prominence of Rashi in the Stone/ArtScroll Chumash, where Rashi serves as the ultimate touchstone of Jewish authenticity, with his appearance in Plaut's Chumash, where Rashi appears as just one voice among many. The most striking instance of Plaut's assumption that his readers did not demand specifics was his frequent citation "Midrash" in the "Gleanings" section. To someone deeply interested in Midrash, whether a particular comment came from the fourth century or the twelfth century, from a halachic midrash or a homiletic midrash, matters greatly. In Plaut, the reader seeking such information will need to go to the footnotes, and even these fall short, since the midrashim appeared in different volumes and with varying internal organization. Plaut represented the voice of the premodern Jewish tradition, but not its dynamism and penchant for dissent. I do not believe that a reader of Plaut would walk away knowing that earliest rabbinic sages and their medieval successors engaged in heated arguments over the exact meaning of Scripture.

American Reform's embrace of modern scholarship also found utterance in the brilliant introductory essays to each book by the noted Yale Assyriologist William Hallo (like Plaut, a German-Jewish émigré). Similar in tone to Hallo and Plaut, Bamberger's Leviticus commentary, while respectful of the original function of sacrifice and dietary purity laws, acknowledged that these practices were existentially distant from contemporaries. Finally, Plaut's introductory essay unambiguously described the Torah as "a human book composed by men." This bold statement, as the Bible scholar and Conservative rabbi Robert Gordis noted, "dispenses entirely with the concept of revelation in any form."[3] In brief, the Plaut Chumash Bible trumpeted its modernity more loudly than its adherence to Jewish tradition. This observation should be kept in mind as we take a brief glance at the 2005 reissue.

In the finest traditions of Madison Avenue, the revised Plaut was marketed by the Union of Reform Judaism (URJ) Press as "A Timeless Classic. A New Edition." This language revealed a distinctly ideological gesture toward "tradition," obvious even on the book cover, which featured the Hebrew word *Torah* on top, with the original "A Modern Commentary" demoted several font sizes. The URJ flyer announcing the revised edition listed eight improvements:

1. Newly designed running heads for easier navigation (Exodus 12: 17–26);
2. More accessible verse numbers in Hebrew text;
3. Cantillation marks and vowels now easier to read;
4. Aliyah markers;
5. Reorganized by Parashah; (note the proper vocalization of this word, often slurred in more traditional settings as "parsha");
6. New scholarly gender-sensitive language;
7. Changed God-language;
8. Gender-related adaptation of commentary.

With the exception of a more gender-sensitive approach, reflected in the new translation (mainly a gender-modified New JPS), the remaining changes were all aimed at facilitating interaction with the Hebrew text. Most prominent on the flyer was point 5, the reorganization by parashah, the organization being a point of considerable annoyance to rabbis and laypeople alike on those occasions when congregants using the original Plaut needed to flip through several pages, often more than once, to follow a single Torah reading. But there was more than convenience to this move. As David E. S. Stein explained in the official magazine of the movement, *Reform Judaism*, the function of the Plaut Chumash wound up exceeding original expectations: "Originally, the Torah commentary was designed for adult study groups and thus organized to topical sections—Rescue at the Sea, The Festival Calendar, etc. Soon after publication, however, the volume was placed in the pew because it was the best commentary available for congregational worship—and over time, the synagogue became the main setting in which it was read. But the topically oriented book was not easy to navigate for liturgical purposes."

Union of Reform Judaism president Eric Yoffie added an ideological note to the new publication, applicable to modern Jews in general, "The new edition [of Plaut] . . . will further our Movement's central goal of 'Torah at the center' as 'the best path and first step to securing the Jewish future.'"[4]

The second American Chumash to appear, the Stone/ArtScroll Chumash, can be called denominational, but it is not the product of Yeshiva University or the Rabbinical Council of America. The Stone/ArtScroll Chumash comes from the right-wing juggernaut known as ArtScroll or Mesorah Publications, which has produced individual Bible books, prayer books, and home prayer books, most of which have succeeded greatly. Much has been written about this publication giant—by Jewish standards—much of it hostile. The modern Orthodox rabbi B. Barry Levy has led the charge, and the following comment conveys the feelings stirred up by the ArtScroll approach. So Levy: "The pig is a deceptive animal, *Chazal* tells us, because when it rests it stretches forth its cloven hooves and gives the appearance of being kosher." What exactly does Rabbi Levy dislike? He enumerates his complaints concisely: ArtScroll is not modern, not scientific, not well organized, not scholarly, full of errors, and utterly right-wing.

It is undeniable that the Stone/ArtScroll Chumash was not as careful with the vocalizations and cantillation marks as it might have been. The ArtScroll Bible commentaries vary widely in quality: most of the experts I consulted find ArtScroll Genesis very poor, but Chronicles and Ezekiel much better, and in some respects more helpful than commentaries produced by the secular academy. One striking feature of the Stone/ArtScroll Chumash is that it provides a new translation, rather than using the New JPS, explicitly following Rashi's understanding in the case of difficult verses. Many find this procedure unpalatable. With the discovery of cognate languages, decoding of the Dead Sea Scrolls, and technological improvements in Masoretic studies, a more precise understanding of Hebrew text is possible today than was possible for Rashi. Archaeology finds no place in ArtScroll productions, and even the chronological tables and maps represent a curious blend of modern publishing techniques and medieval assumptions about the geography and chronology of the world. For some, the Stone/ArtScroll Chumash borders on Jewish fundamentalism. Levy concluded his damning assessment as follows: "ArtScroll will be a valuable primary source for the study of the East-Euromerican Orthodoxy of our age, and does make useful summaries of parts of many as yet untranslated works available in English. It is much less useful as a secondary source whose purpose is to explain the Bible. . . . Not every Hebrew sign in a butcher's window means that the meat sold inside is Kosher."[5]

Why, then, has the Stone/ArtScroll Chumash been widely adopted in Orthodox synagogues and found in many Jewish homes? I have already mentioned the presence of Rashi in the unique script designed for rabbinic works. This script, in my view, functions for its readership the way "regular" Hebrew does for a general Jewish readership—as a patent of authenticity. The Stone/ArtScroll does not incorporate, by name, any Christian, non-Orthodox Jewish, or even modern Orthodox figures who may be perceived as too left-wing, including Rav Joseph Soloveitchik or Nehama Leibowitz. Stone/ArtScroll does not confront biblical critical views at all. Neither did Mendelssohn or Hirsch, but by the 1990s the multivoiced nature of the Torah bothered increasingly few traditional Jews. In America, Soloveitchik explicitly denied multiple authorship of Torah, yet took the two creation narratives as the point of departure for his landmark essay, "The Lonely Man of Faith," arguing that the twofold and conflicted nature of the human being was appropriately reflected in Genesis. Stone/ArtScroll ignores Soloveitchik's biblical essays, though they are taught in numerous university Judaic studies and Jewish adult education classes. In Israel, Mordechai Breuer articulated an approach to the Bible that largely accommodated source criticism within a "Torah from Heaven" perspective. This, too, ArtScroll passes over in silence.

Stone/ArtScroll conveys a premodern Bible for the American Jew who would like to know what Judaism thought before the advent of modern critical biblical criticism. The Stone Chumash creates the impression of a traditional Chumash, even as it ignores the possibility, argued by Sarna and others, that Jewish tradition never shut the door on a potentially enlightening technique, or that tradition itself divided deeply on fundamental issues. This Chumash reports contradictory opinions, but rarely calls attention to these divisions or what they signify: that Jewish tradition has never been black and white. All the commentators sound the same, whereas anyone who reads Hebrew will find the styles of, say, Rashi and Ramban very different. This compounds the effect of downplaying difference: the traditional commentators sound like graduates of Flatbush Yeshiva. What attracts readers, I believe, beyond the beautiful leather binding and distinctive typeface, is the sense that there is nothing in the ArtScroll Chumash or multivolume Bible commentaries that would fail to pass muster in yeshiva circles. The notion of authority can be comforting in uncomfortable times—ArtScroll festoons its many products with rabbinic approbations, a curious reversion to the first modern Jewish Bible, Mendelssohn's, which did not make it into the "Bibliography of Sources Cited."

The third American Chumash, *Etz Hayim Torah and Commentary*, represents the Conservative movement's middle ground view of Torah as liable to critical scrutiny yet amenable to traditional illumination. This Chumash draws liberally from the five-volume *JPS Torah Commentary* and the JPS *Haftarah Commentary* by Michael Fishbane. The most striking feature of *Etz Hayim* is certainly its division of comments into *p'shat* (the plain or simple meaning), *d'rash* (the moral or homiletical meaning), and *halachah l'ma'aseh* (practical practice). One purpose of dividing *p'shat* and *d'rash* was clearly to allow critical biblical scholarship and traditional illumination a room of their own. Admirably, the medieval commentators often get cited as providers of critical scholarship, while modern masters, both nineteenth-century Hasidic authors and heterodox ones, provide the homiletic illumination. Still, the general rule is that the *Etz Hayim p'shat* renders the verse in the eyes of contemporary critical scholarship, while Midrash, Aggadah, and the more "moralistic" of the medievals do the principal speaking for Jewish tradition. Naturally, this division will be artificial at times. Determining what the Torah text actually says as opposed to what it merely implies is neither simple nor objective. Nevertheless, *Etz Hayim* has taken a bold stand here, and I think it has paid off: to synthesize traditional perspectives with critical ones in a single book without disorienting the reader, undesirable for a synagogue Bible, is no mean feat.

The third part of *Etz Hayim*, *halachah l'ma'aseh*, seems to me the most revealing. The introduction points out that halachah means something broader than law, its usual translation, and something other than the biblical commandment, since Jewish practice often varies from or elaborates the simple sense of Scripture. Marked in charcoal-colored bars, this section does exactly what it claims to, link Conservative halachic practice to the biblical text. *Etz Hayim* consistently forges this link through biblical verses and citations to the early sages, rather than medieval codes. This preference reflects an important intellectual distinction between Orthodox and Conservative Judaism. Orthodoxy sees the *Shulchan Aruch* and the codes succeeding it as the center of halachic practice; this is reflected in the curriculum of Yeshiva University and yeshivot further to the right. Conservative Judaism tends to privilege the early sages, and the Jewish Theological Seminary curriculum emphasizes Talmud study accordingly. Thus, this section of *Etz Hayim* represents a more ideological viewpoint than would be immediately obvious. More significantly, the editors link biblical verses to contemporary values on their own authority. Genesis 2:15, "To till it and to tend it," prompts this comment: "This requirement that we preserve nature even while we use it underlies classical and contemporary concern for ecology in Jewish law."[6] This comment is both praiseworthy and correct, but I do not think it is "halachah." Genesis 50:26, "Joseph died," prompts this: "we say of an individual we remember with love and respect 'May his or her memory be a blessing.'" Likewise, this custom is not legal, and so far as I know, is not derived from this verse. Many examples of moralizing or linking contemporary values to biblical texts which were *not* used to make halachic rulings could be cited in *Etz Hayim*. I cannot imagine a better example of my thesis: halachah, *l'ma'aseh* and otherwise, has been biblicized.

What are we to make of this tale of three Torahs? Can the contemporary Jewish reader benefit from a Chumash that treats the Torah as a book of historical, literary, and ethical gems, without the premise of God's involvement? The Plaut Chumash provides an affirmative answer, satisfying the large secular and religiously liberal population that it serves. Can the contemporary Jewish reader benefit from a Chumash that draws only from "Orthodox" sources, downplaying sharp disagreements between medieval commentators and ignoring other, indisputably Orthodox, commentators who do engage with the modern, secular academy? The Stone/ArtScroll Chumash provides another "yes," satisfying American Jews who would like to have a "traditional" Bible at hand, even if this concept of "tradition" causes some scholars to grit their teeth. Finally, *Etz Hayim*, with its dual commitment to biblical scholarship and grounding in tradition, also finds an audience, notwithstanding a middle ground position that necessarily involves compromise. As Greenspahn notes, the appearance of three American Chumashim in twenty years is a remarkable phenomenon, especially given the monopoly of the Hertz Chumash in the previous half century. Greenspahn takes this as an example of American Jewish creativity and so do I.

OF THE MAKING OF MODERN JEWISH BIBLES THERE IS NO END

What follows is neither an in-depth analysis of distinctly Jewish Bibles that do not fit my narrow definition of Chumash, nor a comprehensive survey of Jewishly inflected Bibles in America; this would require another book. It seems as if every month a new Jewishly inflected Bible appears—a new rendering by poet David Rosenberg, R. Crumb's graphic-novel version of Genesis, a Bible written in New York dialect, and so on. Mass market publishers like Bibles and Bible-related books, so do university presses, and so do Jewish presses, including the venerable Jewish Publication Society. Many Bible projects include Jewish participants, but do not attempt to express a Jewish sensibility. I will exclude all of them from consideration, as well as the Jewish Bibles produced for children, analyzed so well by Penny Shine Gold.[7] There remains an overwhelming list, and I will discuss only the following: Aryeh Kaplan, *The Living Torah*; Everett Fox, *The Five Books of Moses*; Richard Eliot Friedman's *Commentary on the Torah*; Robert Alter, *The Five Books of Moses*; Adele Berlin, Marc Zvi Brettler, and Michael Fishbane, eds., *The Jewish Study Bible*; and Elyse Goldstein, *The Women's Torah Commentary*.

Aryeh Kaplan, *The Living Torah* (1981) is still used in many Orthodox settings, non-Orthodox day schools, and synagogues. Kaplan (1934–1983) received a degree in physics as well as rabbinic ordination and wrote magnificently on the Jewish mystical tradition, but neither he nor his students, who finished *The Living Nach* after his death, exercised the rigor of subsequent Jewish Bible translations. Kaplan aimed at an "accurate, clear, modern and readable" translation by freely rendering units of meaning, abjuring a word-by-word approach, and conceding the distance separating the Torah and the modern reader:

> Many passages are highly ambiguous, and without help from the tradition, it is very difficult to picture these items [Tabernacle and Priestly vestments]. If the translator does not begin with a picture, the translation will be even more difficult to understand than the original. The reader will complete the text having little idea as to what is actually meant.
>
> On the other hand, if the translator has a good mental image of the Tabernacle, it will come across in translation. The ambiguities (which most probably stem from our lack of knowledge of biblical idiom) vanish, and a clear picture emerges.

The Living Torah includes useful diagrams, definitions, charts, and footnotes and provides the haftarah portions and their blessings, but eliminates any uncertainty in the biblical text, even when it belongs there. As Leonard Greenspoon noted, *The Living Torah* and its companion volume, *The Living Nach*, tend toward the hyperspecific. Kaplan's Exodus 20:10 specifies, "But Saturday is the Sabbath to God you Lord," a redundancy apparently aimed at Christianity. Kaplan's Leviticus 19:29 warns, "Do not defile your daughter with premarital sex," an activity without biblical terminological equivalent. Surely this commentary's title reflects a tendency which, were it in a Christian bookstore and named *The Living Bible*, would indicate a greater desire to reach the reader than to challenge him or her. Kaplan's cover is very attractive, purple and adorned with flowers, but I must admit that it is my least favorite modern Jewish Bible, largely because it seems less aware of the magnitude of its task. To quote Maimonides's letter to Shmuel Ibn Tibbon on the difficulty of translating overlooks the reality that Maimonides was referring to his own work, not the Torah.

Kaplan's *The Living Torah* may be seen as the ideological opposite of Fox's *The Five Books of Moses*. Fox came upon the works of Buber and Rosenzweig as a student and devoted a couple of decades to translating the Torah (and I and II Samuel) into English, following the Buber-Rosenzweig method, albeit with updates due to advances in scholarship. Still, the emphasis on Leitwörter, orality, Hebrew names, and the use of divine pronouns drew from Buber-Rosenzweig, as does the physical layout, which attempts to reflect the rhythms of actual speech (colometrics). The realization that the Bible was meant to be read aloud emboldens Fox to reproduce tone (emphasis, exhortation, panic, excitement) in ways that translations often underplayed. While Fox adds more commentary and footnotes than did Buber-Rosenzweig, these too are done in the spirit of bringing the reader and the text into dialogue. Fox's publisher, Schocken Books, embodies another connection to the German-Jewish tradition, as the company reproduced many Jewish classics and championed some original German-Jewish thinkers such as Agnon and Scholem. In the argot of translational theory, Kaplan displays a focus on "target language," while Fox displays a focus on "source language."[8]

The appearance of Richard Eliot Friedman's *Commentary on the Torah* (2001) possibly surprised those who knew him as the best-selling author of *Who Wrote the Bible?* and *The Hidden Book in the Bible*. The former was a breakthrough work, sometimes synthetic, sometimes original. Friedman connected the sources J, E, P, and D to actual writers and eras in a way that was comprehensible and free of Wellhausen's complex and extraneous theories of religious development. Even in his more debatable claims, Friedman laid out the issues, claims, and counterclaims reasonably. Overcoming the flaws and prejudices of earlier source criticism, especially the derogation of Judaism of the late biblical period, Friedman's book melted away much residual Jewish resistance to source criticism. Writing long after the advent of form criticism, canonical criticism, and literary criticism, Friedman did not argue that the source critical approach constituted the only way to read the biblical text, just that it was a useful one for someone interested in the particular questions it could answer. Friedman's conclusion explicitly contended that the Bible was more than the sum of its parts. While remaining agnostic on whether Genesis 1 and Genesis 2 were deliberately juxtaposed by the Redactor, Friedman argued that the cumulative effect of the two narratives was more profound than either one on its own. Friedman possessed a distinctly post-Buberian sense of wresting meaning from Scripture. As Friedman wrote in his closing sentence, "The question, after all, is not only who wrote the Bible but who reads it." Unlike Wellhausen, who felt a strong sense of conflict between his scholarship and the sacredness of Scripture and even resigned his teaching role preparing ministers, Friedman evinces no such anxiety: "The threat to religion never really materialized."[9]

Friedman's autobiographical comments in these two works reveal the dual loyalties of many modern Jewish Bible scholars. In *Who Wrote the Bible?* Friedman thanks the academics who trained him, especially Frank Moore Cross of Harvard.[10] The questions posed in *Who Wrote the Bible?* are fundamentally those of the academy, although Friedman did a wonderful job of making them accessible to outsiders. The chain of tradition in Friedman's introductory chapter includes Spinoza, Simon, and Wellhausen: a Jew, a Catholic, and a Protestant, but all renegades! In his *Commentary on the Torah*, however, the questions are set not only by what contemporaries now know, but also by what Jewish tradition taught. To wit, Friedman thanks his parents and his rabbi. As Jon D. Levenson noted, the field of Bible studies is highly self-selective. The people who are attracted to the arduous professional training needed to enter this field were probably interested from an early age, and so it seems in Friedman's case.

Friedman's goal of becoming a modern Rashi, while admirable, sequesters the fruits of his earlier source critical works from the more holistic treatment demanded by Torah commentary. Even with this suppression of source criticism accomplished, what would a "modern Rashi" signify? Friedman is too good a scholar not to allow a slew of modern questions answerable by comparative philology, archaeology, and alternative texts. Friedman's presumption that the Bible is humanly written, even if inspired in some manner, orients him to the biblical text in a way that Rashi would find foreign. Above all, Friedman cannot share Rashi's anthological stance toward the sages. The beauty of Rashi, in many ways, is his lack of sophistication and substantive creativity. Rashi, a pedagogue of genius, drew from the best of earlier rabbinic tradition and applied these teachings in a novel interlinear format. Rashi reads the Bible to deliver religious, even homiletical, lessons. For all his brilliance, Friedman's heuristic is unclear: sometimes his comment is literary, sometimes historical, and sometimes philological. Impressive as it is, Friedman's commentary appears to be caught between a Buberian desire to facilitate dialogue and a professional Bible scholar's desire to plumb the mysteries of the text.

The Jewish Study Bible (2004) announces itself as Jewish on four counts: (1) it views the Tanakh in its own terms, not part of a larger Bible, in other words, it is not a Christian Bible; (2) it takes cognizance of Jewish tradition; (3) it connects biblical passages and Jewish practice; and (4) it calls attention to passages that are meaningful in the life of the Jewish community. This is reflected in the numerous and learned notes in *The Jewish Study Bible*, but also in the roughly 150 pages of appendices, divided into "Jewish Interpretation of the Bible," "The Bible in Jewish Life and Thought," and "Backgrounds for Reading the Bible." Even this last category, putatively ecumenical, has the essay "The Development of the Masoretic Bible," hardly a "background issue" at all since Masoretic developments took place mainly in the postbiblical era. Here is as good a summary of what makes a *Jewish* Bible as any I have seen, and it could be applied to most the Bibles discussed in this chapter, including the five-volume *JPS Torah Commentary*, on which *The Jewish Study Bible* relies heavily. Written by four leading scholars trained between 1930 and 1975, the high point of modern Jewish Bible scholarship in Sperling's view, all four enjoyed some professional connection to the Jewish Theological Seminary. The *JPS Torah Commentary* courageously combines traditional Jewish exegesis and secular academic methods. Whether this results in a synthesis of these methods or merely juxtaposition will depend on the readers' understanding of these terms. Reviewers have noted the disparity of the entries' sizes and the different stances toward these approaches. (Sarna's Genesis-Exodus incorporates more traditional *parshanut*; Milgrom's Leviticus embraces secular academic methods more warmly.) That being said, the *JPS Torah Commentary* is unlikely to be surpassed anytime soon.

AMERICA'S VALIDATION OF THE MODERN JEWISH BIBLE: FOUR VARIATIONS ON A THEME

The range of the aforementioned Jewish Bibles indicates many things, one of which is that synagogue Bibles/Chumashim alone do not exhaust the interest in our subject, and that publishers think there are customers discerning enough to identify the differences in approach, utility, and target audience articulated by these Bibles. Since Alter's and Friedman's commentaries are produced by general publishers, not academic presses with modest expectations of reaching lay readers, one may conclude that the target audience includes non-Jews and/or Jewish laity. One last point: the use of the term Torah. A generation of Jewish studies/ Introduction to Judaism classes and the appearance in the pulpits of Christian spiritual leaders who know something about Judaism and relate to it sympathetically has overcome the foreignness of the term Torah—perhaps even made it attractive. Why are these prominent and able Jewish authors drawn to the genre of Torah commentary and translation? Because all know Scholem's dictum that commentary is the quintessential Jewish endeavor? Well, maybe in part. But allow me an even more simplistic question: Why write on the Torah at all? Deuteronomy, the swing door from Torah to Prophets, could be unhinged at either end. One could follow Gerhard von Rad and treat the Hexateuch (Pentateuch plus Joshua) as the most important biblical unit. Or, conversely, one could treat the Primary Narrative, the Tetrateuch (Genesis–Numbers), as the most important unit. This would be heresy from a traditional point of view, but Jewish dogma cannot be adduced as the explanation for this phenomenon. Richard Elliot Friedman is an avid source critic and Robert Alter, cagily agnostic.[11] Jewish liturgical needs also fail to provide an obvious answer to my rhetorical question, since all three denominations have distinguished synagogue Bibles (Chumashim) complete with prophetic readings and appropriate blessings at their disposal. In other words, Fox, Alter, and Friedman may or may not have produced Jewish Bibles, but they are not primarily synagogue Bibles. Actually, these works are not Bibles at all, they are Torah commentaries or Pentateuchs, although, as noted, Alter and Fox have translated I and II Samuel in separate volumes, and Kaplan's students rendered Nach. Not one of these authors, incidentally, bothers to make an argument for their selection, not even along the lines of scholarly consensus that the first five books of Moses come first in both Jewish and Christian Bibles, though the weight accorded that fact differs. Why a Pentateuch translation/commentary, then, instead of some other endeavor? I can think of only one reason: fidelity to Jewish tradition. And I think this is a perfectly adequate motive.

Do these Bibles indicate that American Jewish Bible scholars have learned to speak in a nonpolemic, nonapologetic manner? Has the academy liberated itself from two centuries of Protestant domination such that a Jewish term such as Torah can be employed without special pleading? Do these Bibles signal a Jewish consensus about what the Bible is today? I tend to think so, and in the preceding paragraphs, I have thus emphasized the "yes," but there are important "noes" too. Let us take a look at four areas of disagreement, or at least diversity, in the maze of modern American Jewish Bibles: (1) the role of biblical theology, (2) the role of feminist analysis, (3) the role of biblical historiography, and (4) the limits of literary criticism.

1. Biblical Theology and Jewish Biblical Theology: Jon D. Levenson

Do Jews do biblical theology? Jon D. Levenson has written most sophisticated analyses of the Protestant nature of Old Testament theology and staked out grounds for a Jewish response. From the beginning of modern critical scholarship, Levenson maintains, Protestant scholars were unwilling to accept that the task of historicizing the Bible would necessarily make it an ancient Near Eastern document rather than a Christian one, while the task of deriving a biblical theology could either be done from a frankly denominational point of departure (dogmatic theology) or aim at a purely objective perspective (biblical history), but not both. The construct Old Testament theology already constitutes an oxymoron, since none of the ancient Israelite writers were Christian or thought that they were preparing a theological supplement. The major quests of eighteenth- to nineteenth-century Old Testament scholarship—the search for the original Bible, analogous in New Testament scholarship to the quest for the actual words of Jesus, and the search for a theological center of the Old Testament—seemed either ill-conceived or uninteresting to Jews. Most Jewish scholars assumed the basic trustworthiness of the Masoretic Text, and most appreciated that Judaism was preserved by early sages who succeeded in applying the Bible to changing times. Protestantism, by contrast, was born from a hostile reaction to medieval Catholic tradition that had obscured, at least in the Protestant perspective, pristine Christianity. The attitudes of Protestants and Jews were antithetical on this point. In Torah, Jews already have a legal and liturgical center or heart; we do not feel the need for a theological one. Physically, Jews read scrolls until their end and then reread them, a more cyclical than teleological procedure, which lessens the need for a beginning, middle, and end. Exegetically, the traditional Jewish response to seeming contradictions in Hebrew Bible was to reconcile them, not to elevate one tradition over the other, which Protestant theology tended to do.

Nineteenth-century liberal Protestant Bible scholars operated in an echo chamber, unchallenged by either Jewish or Catholic scholars, who had little or no professional standing. Geiger offers an example of a Jew who tried to destabilize the regnant views and failed; the occasional dissenting Anglo-American voice such as George F. Moore was raised against gross misrepresentation of rabbinic literature, not against the bias of the entire enterprise. As Levenson put it in his witty "Why Jews Are Not Interested in Biblical Theology," modern Protestants steered awkwardly between an affirmation that all the commandments of the Torah (including circumcision and kashrut) were actually meant to be performed (running the risk of Judaizing), or that the Old Testament was metaphorically intended and had little to do with New Testament–based Christianity (running the risk of Marcionism). Jews and Judaism had their own issues regarding modern Bible scholarship, but were spared this particular Protestant dilemma. To the extent that traditional Judaism systematized, the preferred medium was the law code, not the theological summa.[12]

Jon D. Levenson's accessible *Sinai and Zion: An Entry into the Jewish Bible* (1985) directly challenged Protestant exclusivity in mainstream biblical scholarship. *Sinai and Zion* opens with a complaint: it seems as if modern Protestant Bible scholars have been looking for new ways to caricature Jewish legalism and to repeat Jesus's curse on the Temple. Modern Protestant "Biblical theology" thus appears as an extension of Christian theology rooted in the intra-Jewish polemics of the New Testament. This book's title signals the author's intent to defend the Sinai/Law and the Zion/Temple as unfairly maligned high points in ancient Israelite religion. Levenson's subtitle, while adamantly nonfundamentalist ("I make no claim that Rabbinic Judaism offers the correct understanding of the Hebrew Bible"), was polemically intended. "It is this willingness to consider rabbinic tradition on occasion and to highlight its relevance to Hebrew Bible and vice versa which makes this volume 'An Entry into the Jewish Bible.'"[13] Actually, the Jewishness of Levenson's approach goes well beyond using rabbinic traditions. His defense of Torah and Temple has already been mentioned. One can add his reliance on the modern "Jewish school," reflected even in the title, which is a homage to Buber's famous essay; his consistent criticism of Protestant scholarly bias; his locating performance of the commandments as the end point of the Exodus; his championing of Mosaic over Davidic covenant within the Hebrew Bible; his use of rabbinic liturgical units (the Shma) as a prism to illuminate the Bible; his often pointed subchapter title discussions (e.g., "Laws or Commandments?"); or asides, such as, the Christian Bible "includes within it a book of an alien religion." This last comment, duly protested by my undergraduate students in Baptist Oklahoma, begs for a parallel comment about the gap between biblical and rabbinic Judaism, but Levenson clearly does not think the leap from the Bible to Judaism was as great as the leap to Christianity.[14] His work exemplifies the sympathetic treatment now accorded to legal and ritual materials once routinely denigrated by Bible scholars.

Levenson's later works, *Creation and the Persistence of Evil* and *Death and Resurrection of the Beloved Son*, display a trend away from polemic and toward ecumenicism, understood by Levenson as ceding a legitimate interest to all Abrahamic faiths in biblical teachings, without, however, losing sight of their abiding differences. In *Creation and the Persistence of Evil*, Levenson sought to complicate the all-is-good viewpoint of the biblical view of creation (Genesis 1). Using many other creation references in the Hebrew Bible, Psalms, Prophets, and postexilic literature in particular, Levenson shows a much more complex, darker biblical conception of creation, which he feels is better adapted to address a post-Holocaust reality. (The presence of the Holocaust as a reference point in books on the Hebrew Bible is a common sign of Jewish or philosemitic authorship.) *Death and Resurrection of the Beloved Son* treats the theme of the imperiled younger son displacing the elder, most especially in the book of Genesis. As in *Creation and the Persistence of Evil*, Levenson gives a fair hearing to both Jewish and Christian traditions. The narrative message of the Akedah narrative, for Levenson, cannot be detached from legal text of Exodus 22:28–29, which sanctions a substitute for child sacrifice. Levenson rejects the popular view that Genesis 22 offers a simple polemical attack on Canaanite practices; child sacrifice was a "live option" in ancient Israel, to use William James's phrase, rejected only after considerable effort. Levenson's viewpoint varies from traditional interpreters, Judaic and Christian alike, yet he is not simply splitting the difference. Circumcision and redemption of the firstborn, two key life cycle events for Jewish boys, serve that original biblical intent, while, implicitly, Christianity lacks a comparably concrete act. Levenson has not shied away from polemics: he has savaged a major attempt at Jewish-Christian dialogue for its whitewashing of the fraught Jewish-Christian past, derided the shallow deployment of the exodus theme in liberationist theology, and attacked politically correct readings of figures such as Abraham. Nevertheless, Levenson's battle against mainstream Bible scholarship has subsided, and he himself holds the List Chair at Harvard Theological Seminary. Schechter wanted the Christian scholarly world to leave Judaism alone. The current generation has a more ambitious agenda, seeking a fairer appraisal of Judaism.[15]

2. Jewish Feminist Bible Scholarship: Tikva Frymer-Kensky

Parsing the respective and interconnected roles of feminism, Jewishness, and biblical studies is beyond the scope of my abilities. Each of these terms has many meanings, subsets, and constructs. To make matters even more complex, the conscious equation Jewish + feminist + Bible (the plus sign being preferable to the hierarchy-imposing hyphen) has a short history but a promising trajectory. As many of the contributors to *On Being a*

Jewish Feminist remarked, it was the latent antisemitism within feminism as well as the blatant sexism within Judaism that ignited Jewish feminism in the 1970s, a decade after Jewish women had already proven to be important figures in the American feminist movement in general. Despite a generation of ferreting out less patriarchal countertraditions, deploying anthropology to historicize gender divisions, and rereading biblical texts free from later rabbinic and Christian presuppositions, the male-oriented bias of the Hebrew Bible remains. Out of the approximately 1,100 named biblical characters only a little over one hundred are women; the textual life span of women generally runs from betrothal to weaning, while men are amply provided with birth and death narratives; and much of the Bible deals with public offices (kingship, priesthood, charismatic military leadership, prophecy), which offer either no or few female models. God is usually gendered male, even if most modern readers do not have an anthropomorphic view of God.[16]

Is the Bible a lost cause as a positive vehicle for Jewish + feminist identity? The question is a reasonable one, and some Jewish female scholars such as Esther Fuchs and Athalya Brenner have regarded the Bible as an unambiguous mandate for male superiority and therefore not attempted its rehabilitation. In this sense, Fuchs and Brenner and Judith Plaskow fall into what Nancy Fuchs-Kreimer, in a prescient article, called "the anthropological school." For this approach, the only correct equation is feminism versus Biblical Judaism; for Judaism to truly reflect the experiences of men and women equally (note: equality/egalitarianism alone does not meet that standard), Judaism must be rethought from the ground up. Or, is the Bible a God-given text and traditional Judaism, as its best embodiment, really in no fundamental need of "rehabilitation" from a gendered point of view? Reading the works of Nehama Leibowitz, or even, in this generation, Aviva Gottlieb Zornberg, many observers have been struck by the absence of sustained analysis along gender lines. This school also includes Judith Antonelli, a popular writer whose works proceed from frankly apologetic grounds. Certainly Fuchs-Kreimer intuited correctly that neither the "anthropological" nor the "literalist" positions would prove as attractive as the impulse to appropriate the Bible along feminist grounds, the "middle-grounders," in her phrase.[17]

Tikva Frymer-Kensky (1943–2006), arguably the outstanding female Bible scholar of our generation, advocated strongly for two propositions. One, the Bible does not have a gendered view of human behavior. In other words, men use persuasion, trickery, and violence to achieve their goals; so do women. Men seek wealth, power, and progeny; so do women. While social realities differed, human behavior differed according to the character of the individual, not the sex of the individual. While Frymer-Kensky's *In the Wake of the Goddesses* showed that Israel created a patriarchal culture and society, the ontological verdict on humans was not gender-based. Greco-Roman and rabbinic societies, held Frymer-Kensky, did enshrine the concept of innate gender differences. While Frymer-Kensky was not alone among Jewish scholars in placing the "blame" on Hellenistic society's misogyny for rabbinic Judaism's gender dichotomies, the result nevertheless cried out for rectifying.[18] Frymer-Kensky decided to develop a biblical theology responsive to gender equality to be used as the basis of a "reformed" Judaism. In her essay "The Emergence of Jewish Biblical Theologies," Frymer-Kensky writes, "The new interpretations of the Bible show that the rabbinic interpreters made choices and that other choices can be made."[19] Frymer-Kensky's call for biblical theology contradicts my claims that modern Jewish Bible scholarship generally accommodates rabbinic traditions. On the other hand, this exemplifies my overall claim that the Hebrew Bible has been regarded as essential for modern Jewish identity. Indeed, Frymer-Kensky elegantly explains the ways in which the Bible had been placed on a pedestal and ignored by previous generations. Along with her distinctly academic essays arguing these positions, Frymer-Kensky also produced *Reading the Women of the Bible*, which delineates female "Victors, Victims, Virgins, Voice."[20] Armed with an encyclopedic grasp of biblical narrative, a knack for close reading, and a deep empathy for these characters, she provides a reading of major female characters of the Hebrew Bible.[21]

Although there are many individual successes in Jewish + feminist Bible scholarship that considerations of space exclude,[22] the nature of the enterprise tends toward the collaborative. American feminism emerged out of a group consciousness that the opportunities afforded women did not match their abilities, aspirations, or range of interests. As Tamara Cohn Eskenazi and Andrea Weiss write, "We consider the Act of preserving a multiplicity of voices not only a defining feature of the Jewish interpretive tradition, but also an explicit feminist endeavor."[23] This collaborative spirit informs *Torah of the Mothers: Contemporary Jewish Women Read Classical Jewish Texts* (2000) and *The Torah: A Women's Commentary* (2008). The latter takes a fivefold approach to guiding the reader: "Central Commentary," "Another View," "Post-Biblical Interpretations," "Contemporary Reflection," and "Voices." All five reflect women's perspectives and creativity and the last, "Voices," invites poets, essayists, and assorted sages to respond creatively. *The Torah: A Women's Commentary* is distinguished by the number and quality of its contributors and the variety of its voices: scholarly, artistic, literary. While some might find the diversity of voices cacophonous, others will find this handsomely bound volume a wonderful menu of approaches to the Torah. As Judith Kates astutely notes, an assessment of the impact of gender analysis in modern Bibles would have to include sensitivity to this issue in Bibles that do *not* announce themselves as coming from a distinctly feminist perspective.[24]

Almost the opposite approach to Frymer-Kensky's efforts at reappropriation of the Bible grounded in ancient Near Eastern texts can found in the wide range of what might be called creative Jewish + feminist midrash. Jody Myers has argued that midrash enables a given author to take advantage of the findings of traditional biblical scholarship, but also offers a genre able to imagine areas of women's experiences that the Bible simply omits. Describing the reception accorded Anita Diamant's *The Red Tent*, Myers writes, "it is not surprising that her [Diamant's] book has filled a gap in the religious lives of modern Jewish women eager to connect to their biblical heritage." When it comes to Genesis 34, *The Red Tent* does more than fill in a gap: it retells the story of Dinah from her perspective, in contrast to the biblical narrative, which does not give her a single line of dialogue. This impulse to both connect with the Jewish tradition (Diamant herself uses the term midrash and several midrashim offer her novelistic points of departure) and also critique it. This central feature of Diamant's blockbuster animates both feminist and nonfeminist Jewish scholarship. Having taken a course with a prominent advocate/practitioner of creative biblical midrash, I can attest that this practice involves close reading of biblical texts, careful scrutiny of classical rabbinic midrash, and rich dialogue with the Bible itself. Critics may complain that contemporary midrash is not truly midrash; its practitioners fully realize the genre differences between classical rabbinic midrash and their own works. What contemporary creative midrash allows is a distinctly Jewish appropriation of the Bible, open to wide-ranging religious beliefs and practices. This approach differs from Frymer-Kensky philosophically in its refusal to choose eras (biblical over rabbinic) and a conviction that even the most meticulous ancient Near Eastern scholarship will never yield adequate feminist material—what Judith Plaskow called the limits of historiography in her seminal *Standing Again at Sinai*. Lastly, one should note the successful trade books produced by such diverse scholars and artists as Miki Raver, *Listen to Her Voice*; Vanessa Ochs, *Sarah Laughed*; Judith Baskin, *Midrashic Women*; Naomi Graetz, *Unlocking the Garden*; and the original poetry and translations of Marcia Falk and others. Feminism has proven a powerful tool for contemporaries to connect with the Bible, whether as a scholarly or as a creative endeavor.

3. Biblical Minimalism and Jewish Biblical Minimalism

Biblical minimalism may be defined as follows: the majority of the Hebrew Bible is fictional, was written with ideological purposes, was written principally in the Persian and Hellenistic worlds, and reflects a colonialist attitude to the Canaanites, which is mirrored in the colonialist attitude of Zionists toward Palestinians. Previous generations of biblical scholars have been largely uncritical of their primary source, doing little more than finding ways of restating the Bible's story; the Bible and its previous interpreters, therefore, deserve to be handled with a hermeneutic of extreme suspicion in which the presumption is that nothing in the Bible can be taken as true. This view, which the Israeli historian Sara Japhet angrily terms "revisionism at all costs," includes some famous names in the field, though more in Europe than in the United States: Philip Davies, Niels Peter Lemche, Thomas Thompson, John Van Seters, and Keith Whitelam. Although there is a strong anti-Zionist streak in this research, best captured by Whitelam's book *The Invention of Ancient Israel: The Suppression of Palestinian History*, the principal target of this group has been the Albright–G. E. Wright–John Bright school, which attempted to put archaeology in the service of proving the Bible. Although there were Jewish counterparts to Albright (Glueck, Yadin, Mazar), they are relative small-fry compared to the Protestant scholars named above. I highlight this in order to avoid giving the impression in what follows that this is another Jewish versus Protestant battle. Quite the contrary, as the "minimalists" represent a secularist agenda aimed against a neoconservative attitude that seeks to preserve the kernel of biblical history.

Still, there is a distinctly Jewish "edge" in some rebuttals of this minimalist school, and even where Jews have found minimalism academically persuasive, it has been articulated differently. A few examples will suffice. Sara Japhet, a master of Chronicles and the Persian period generally, comments that she originally greeted Philip Davies's *In Search of Ancient Israel* with a shrug, yet nobody has wielded a sharper skewer to the assumptions of the biblical minimalists. Davies differentiated three terms: biblical Israel, historical Israel, and ancient Israel. For Davies, the first is simply the Bible, a piece of historical fiction. The second is the scholarly construct recapitulating the first. Ancient Israel, which can only be derived from nonbiblical evidence, is probably best described as the short-lived, inconsequential state that existed from ninth century BCE to the Assyrian conquest of 722/721 BCE. In response, Japhet contends that Davies's chronological location of the Bible's authorship in the Persian period stems from a not very convincing process of elimination.[25] Since Davies refuses to consider that any of the Bible is preexilic, there are only a few eras in which the Bible could have been written—since there is so little external evidence about the Persian period, a relative dark spot in the entire first millennium BCE, it becomes Davies's default. Second, Japhet thinks the growing body of archaeological evidence confirms that there was an ancient Israel, even if the details do not precisely match the biblical account. The Tel Dan Inscription, which mentions the "House of David," and the Deir Alla Inscription, which mentions the prophet Balaam (Numbers 22–24), join a large body of older evidence including the Merneptah Stele, the Moabite Stone, the Sennacherib Prism, and so on. As Japhet notes, "It is this overwhelming harmony between the facts of the biblical story and extra-biblical written material that must form the basis for assessing the reliability of biblical historiography."[26] Finally, and this critique will sound familiar, Davies ignored the obvious stratification of biblical Hebrew. Israeli scholars have been able to differentiate tenth-century texts (e.g., "Song of the Sea," "Deborah's Song") from seventh- to sixth-century texts (e.g., Deuteronomy to II Kings) from Persian period texts (e.g., Chronicles). In the face of this "hard" philological evidence, Davies has no way to accommodate a view of the Bible as entirely a fifth-century fiction. This debate will be resolved by professional biblical scholars, although I think Davies's self-declared "theology of disbelief" cannot be sensibly applied to any ancient society. I am struck by Japhet's insistence on a kernel of historical reality. This turns out to be a common fallback position—conveniently supportive of either a national or an ethnic view of what makes the Bible Jewish.

History and historiography are not identical terms. Historiography suggests a methodology of writing history and an awareness of history-writing as a discipline. Until recently, the Greeks were acknowledged as the first historians, although Herodotus could be claimed by ethnographers and Thucydides by political scientists. As to the ancient Israelites, as long as the Bible was divine Scripture, consideration of biblical historiography was muted: after all, how could one question God's use of evidence? As the late Yosef Yerushalmi remarked in a celebrated study, "As a professional Jewish historian I am a new creature in Jewish history. My lineage does not extend beyond the second decade of the nineteenth century, which makes me, if not illegitimate, at least a parvenu within the long history of the Jews."[27] But Yerushalmi's portrayal of the absence of critical attitudes toward the Jewish past has been qualified, and on the other hand, Greek historiography has been reconceived as one of several ancient historiographical models. Consequently, to claim the Hebrew Bible, no longer construed as divine Scripture, as the oldest piece of human history writing, has been irresistible. This attempt to show that the Jews were the first historians, not the Greeks, falls into a once-deprecated mode called the "Jewish contribution" or the "Jewish factor," which has recently found some defenders. This rhetorical move also revives the Hebrews versus Hellenes dichotomy that we saw in Auerbach's *Mimesis*. In any event, Baruch Halpern in America and Yaira Amit in Israel have both made the argument with gusto that attention to sources and historical intent qualify the Bible writers as *ancient* historians. "But Herodotus did not manifest a desire to get at the truth any more than did the biblical narratives, nor did he seek to analyze and evaluate his sources; he too relied on popular traditions and theological explanations of events, which included the gods and could be categorized as miracles."[28] Once again, the national (Israeli) and the ethnic (American) Jewish stake in presenting the Bible as a repository of reliable history dovetail: in the spirit of

Schechter, these writers forward the Bible as one of the great contributions of Jews to Western civilization.[29]

Are there Jewish biblical minimalists? Of course. When Israel Finkelstein and Neil Asher Silberman published *The Bible Unearthed*, they did so to great fanfare and no small amount of outrage, and a similar reception greeted Ze'ev Herzog's deliberately provocative article in a leading Israeli newspaper.[30] Finkelstein, like Herzog an archaeologist at Tel Aviv University, seemed to be supporting a left-wing political agenda that minimized the importance of the ancient Israelite model for contemporary Israel, exactly the opposite of Ben-Gurion's agenda, treating the united kingdom of David and Solomon as a minor chieftaincy, revising a number of finds dated a century or two earlier by Yigael Yadin and Benjamin Mazar, and dismantling an image of a glorious Israelite past, first formulated by Heinrich Graetz, a German historian and a Jewish nationalist. On closer inspection, though, I find Finkelstein-Silberman quite different in tone from the so-called Copenhagen school or Sheffield school, beyond the absence of anti-Israel sentiment found in the latter. To begin with, much of Finkelstein-Silberman's work simply reported a consensus that the naive reading of David-Solomon's kingdom was hyperbolic—something that readers coming across the enumeration of Solomon's wives and harem girls in I Kings 11 probably assumed anyway. For Finkelstein, all Israel-Judah in the time of David probably contained about fifty thousand people; only about five thousand in Judah. There were no massive Solomonic building programs, as Yadin assumed on the basis of I Kings 9:15. On the other hand, they also write, "There is hardly a reason to doubt the historicity of David and Solomon."[31] Or again, regarding King Josiah and the reforms of the late seventh century BCE, they write, "To sum up, there is little doubt that an original version of Deuteronomy is the book of Law mentioned in 2 Kings. Rather than being an old book that was suddenly discovered, it seems safe to conclude that was written in the seventh century BCE, just before or during Josiah's reign."[32] Considering that Wilhelm De Wette forwarded this view as far back as 1805, this can hardly be considered revolutionary. Unlike many Jewish Bible scholars, including R. E. Friedman, Finkelstein-Silberman date P as postexilic, but their caption reads "Refashioning Israel's History," not "Inventing Israel's History," the Copenhagen school's view. Even with respect to the patriarchs, a lost cause for maximalists for decades, Finkelstein and Silberman consider these narratives full of monarchic realities from the seventh century BCE. No, Virginia, there was no great Davidic Empire. Was there an ancient Israel? *The Bible Unearthed*, the best-known Jewish biblical minimalist work, affirms this as obvious, as does a more recent article of Finkelstein's, revealingly titled "Archaeology and the Bible: Not Black and Not White."[33]

4. The Great Dissenter: James Kugel

My thesis has been that the makers of the modern Jewish Bible proceeded on the assumption that academic inquiry can deepen our appreciation of Torah; that Bible scholarship and Bible study are compatible; that objective inquiries and existential responses (religious, national, or ethnic) may be fruitfully married. But an intriguing exception to this rule comes from James Kugel's *How to Read the Bible: A Guide to Scripture Then and Now* (2007). Kugel, famed for his studies on biblical poetry and biblical interpretation, including *The Idea of Biblical Poetry, Early Biblical Interpretation, In Potiphar's House,* and *The Bible as It Was,* displays an unmatched mastery of the field of Bible studies. His Jewish loyalties have been expressed personally by his move from Harvard to Bar Ilan; academically, in his fine introduction *On Being a Jew*; and now online, defending himself against critics of this book from left and right at www.jameskugel.com. Clearly, publishing *How to Read the Bible* took considerable courage, and if I am critical of his conclusions and neglectful of his other works, that should not be taken as a lack of admiration for the person or the product. Although Kugel has been reviewed widely, his claims seem to have struck a special nerve with his Jewish readers, as an entire issue of the august *Jewish Quarterly Review* was given over to some passionate responses.[34]

In an early exchange with Jon D. Levenson and Michael Fishbane, Kugel agreed that Bible scholarship should broaden its menu of topics beyond those traditionally undertaken by Protestant scholars, and reappraise the worth of premodern interpreters.[35] Even in the 1980s, however, one could sense Kugel's discomfort with the moves made by his colleagues. In a review of Fishbane's *Biblical Interpretation in Ancient Israel*, Kugel reacted suspiciously to the former's conclusion that the basic categories of *biblical* exegesis were legal, narrative, and prophet. Kugel found it dubious that exactly the main categories of rabbinic exegesis already existed in the Bible. Kugel rightly perceived that Fishbane held that modes of interpretation in rabbinic Judaism were neither handed down by God at Sinai, nor borrowed from the Greco-Roman environment, but rather were developed autochthonously by Jews through the centuries. The very range of biblical interpretation from the Persian period to the Talmud, however, suggested a wavy line from biblical to rabbinic exegesis.

The anonymous, transdenominational scholars who flourished working from 300 BCE to 200 CE, whom Kugel called "the early interpreters," truly created the Bible. Kugel admits that the evolutionary chain of interpreting the Bible began in the Bible itself, and admits that selected biblical texts go back to 1000 BCE, if not further. But "the early interpreters" made the Bible by treating it as an eternally relevant, complex, divine, and esoteric source of meaning. Naturally, this perspective drove the process of canonization and drew strength from the creation of a biblical canon. But Kugel insists that this mode of reading, practiced by rabbinic Judaism, early Christianity, and many intertestamental works that made it into neither canon, was not inherent in Scripture. That is a shocking perspective for a self-defined Orthodox Jew; Kugel maintains that the reading strategy of the "early interpreters," while compatible with traditional Judaism or traditional Christianity, *is completely irreconcilable with modern biblical criticism.* Historical-critical inquiry cannot uncover "the true Bible," as Protestant scholars had hoped, *because ancient Israel had no Bible.*[36]

Kugel holds that that the historical quest for the original Bible and its meaning for contemporary Judaism are incompatible enterprises. Judaism has been defined by the rabbinic tradition and that the rabbinic tradition was just one of many competing understandings of the Hebrew Bible. Kugel employs the term "early interpreters," rather than sages or Tannaim, because that skews an accurate appraisal of authors who clearly precede formative rabbinic Judaism. This extraordinarily rich enterprise of the first few centuries BCE and CE includes Bible retellings, Bible rewritings, philosophical renderings (e.g., Philo), historical renderings (e.g., Josephus), sectarian appropriations (e.g., the Dead Sea Scrolls), Christian Gospels, and numerous early rabbinic texts. Kugel concludes that at the beginning of normative Judaism and Christianity, the "Bible" meant many different things to many different groups and had probably done so for quite some time. Does the Hebrew Bible, then, have meaning for Judaism? Yes, but that meaning is grounded in the early interpreters' belief that the Bible taught "service of God" above all. The Bible may yield a concept of service to God, but its elaboration is a clearly human enterprise. Or, to put it another way, biblical religion and Judaism are two different, albeit related, religious systems.

What does this have to do with how one reads the Bible? In Kugel's sweeping view, "Literary-Criticism Lite" attempts to save the Bible as a sacred text without making explicit theological claims. In an attack on literary criticism, Kugel accused scholars of attempting a "deep substitution" of textuality for divine authorship.[37] Taking aim at Erich Auerbach's phrase "fraught with background," Kugel doubted that biblical characters were characters at all in a literary sense, or that the Bible was "literature," as moderns would understand it. The Bible does *not* qualify as a literary masterpiece in the same league as Shakespeare, Dante, or Milton—contra the view of the literary scholar and avowedly secular Jew Harold Bloom. More radical still, while modern practitioners such as Sternberg and Alter explicitly assume that the Bible, whatever its authors' intentions, constitutes "literature," Kugel finds much of the Bible ill-described by that term. As to the artful placement of seemingly contradictory narratives by the Redactor (e.g., Genesis 1 and Genesis 2, or Genesis 38 in between 37 and 39, or Genesis 12, 20, and 26), Kugel finds this placement more simply explained by an ancient author's unwillingness to discard sacred traditions. In an interchange with Kugel, Adele Berlin perceptively notes that Kugel's skepticism toward the new literary readings derives in part from his own early research that cast doubt on the (modern) dogma of biblical parallelism.

Kugel was hardly the only Jewish scholar to consider historical and literary explorations incompatible: as Alan Cooper claimed in "Reading the Bible Historically and Otherwise," since Spinoza, one could be a historical reader or a literary reader, and both approaches could be equally rigorous. Cooper opts for the literary method without qualification or apology.[38] But Kugel challenges the second half of Cooper's claim. How can one be a rigorous literary analyst if the Bible was not meant to be literature, if one considers investigating the origin of the texts out of bounds (as belonging to historical source criticism versus literary criticism), and if one's methodology of assessing literary technique is nothing more than the intelligence of the interpreter given writ by the Bible's limited vocabulary and syntactical options? Although Kugel has not treated proponents of biblical historiography with the same withering criticism with which he has treated literary critics, and has opined that the Bible is generically closer to ancient historiography than literature, his implication is the same: *one can have modern biblical scholarship or the traditional Bible, but not both*. Kugel's position calls out for a more theologically sophisticated response than I am able to provide; Benjamin Sommer has responded accordingly in the *Jewish Quarterly Review* issue cited above. Kugel's radical compartmentalization of academic biblical scholarship and a devotional reading (loosely understood) of the Bible brushes against the grain of his Jewish contemporaries. For the makers of the modern Bible, that book holds the key to the modern Jewish experience—religiously, nationally, or ethnically. Kugel disagrees: "To put the matter, in I admit, rather shocking terms: since in Judaism it is not the words of Scripture themselves that are ultimately supreme, but the service of God (the 'standing up close') that they enjoin, then to suggest that everything hangs on Scripture might well be described as a form of fetishism or idolatry, that is a mistaking of the message for its Sender and the turning of its words into idols of wood or stone."[39]

CONCLUSION

My not very shocking conclusion to this chapter is that even today Jews speak in a shared idiom about the Bible. In the case of American Chumashim, denominational differences pale in comparison to what these synagogue Bibles have in common, beginning with the fact that the Chumash itself is a modern invention. These Chumashim illustrate what sociologist Lewis Coser called the "functional" nature of difference. One Chumash would not do, because American Jews hold a wide variety of beliefs about the Torah, even while agreeing on its centrality. *The Torah: A Modern Commentary*, the ArtScroll/Stone Chumash, and the Conservative *Etz Hayim* connect a contemporary American Jewish reading audience and an ancient Near Eastern text in a way that reflects the diversity of American Jewry. The same may be said for the many Jewish Bibles that do not aim at synagogue use, but intend to give American Jews an ownership stake in the Bible. I find it telling that *The Torah: A Women's Commentary* actually states "Jewish" as a goal, as if a Torah commentary could be anything but.

As to professional Bible scholars, I am struck by how much creative energy is still being generated by a desire to reformulate Bible studies in a non-Protestant key. (The positive response to this Jewish enterprise on the part of Christian scholars deserves a book of its own—by a competent authority.) But even where secularism (nihilism?) rather than Protestantism constitutes the challenge, in the case of biblical minimalism, for instance, Jewish scholars have tended toward dissent. Japhet and Halpern, respectively, stake claims to both the historicity and the historiography of the Hebrew Bible. Jewish Bible scholars tend to skew "early" on dating or "conservative" on historicity. Where Jewish minimalism is undeniable, it is either not so minimalist upon closer inspection (e.g., Finkelstein) or lacking in hostility to the Bible, Zionism, and modern Israel (e.g., Sperling).

Developments in modern Israel have also influenced the American Jewish Bible. Many Jewish scholars have spent time in Israel, whether as students, aspiring rabbis, archaeologists, or visiting faculty. The encounter with biblical lands and colloquial Hebrew has had a noticeable impact. Many American Jews have friends and family in Israel—so do Christian scholars, but surely in smaller percentages. As Jacob Neusner claimed in 1987, one expects that Jews in Jewish studies can read articles and books published in modern Hebrew. Sperling sums up the matter: "The rise of the State of Israel provided another commonality interaction between American and Israeli scholarship. United in their common knowledge of Modern Hebrew, Americans and Israelis studied and taught in each other's countries."[40] The making of the modern Jewish Bible has had a strong cosmopolitan component.

But the influences have been temporal-vertical as well as horizontal-spatial. Traditions of the Jewish past have exerted enormous impact. In Germany, Israel, and America, the Hebrew text provided the starting point of any translation or commentary. In all three sites, the relationship with the Jewish tradition (*parshanut ha-mikra*) influenced Jewish Bible scholars—sometimes more than they liked to admit. In contemporary America, Jews teach in colleges and universities; "professional" Jews teach Bible to a highly educated laity; Jewish authors write Bible books intended mainly for non-Jewish audiences. Some Jews, liberated from charges of special pleading common a generation ago, seek ways to reincorporate the rabbinic traditions back into the modern Bible. Some, including the late Tikva Frymer-Kensky, developed a Jewish Bible theology without recourse to rabbinic traditions, which, she contended, were more sexist than the Hebrew Bible. Others interested in a Jewish Bible theology, including Jon D. Levenson and Benjamin Sommer, consider rabbinic traditions, critically employed, a valuable way to flesh out theologies latent in the Hebrew Bible. Both external and internal pressures shape a Bible that "speaks" to contemporary American Jews.

Whether one surveys Jewish participation in biblical theology, feminism, historiography, or literature, all of which generate more scholarly work than they did a generation ago, it is rare in contemporary America to find a self-consciously Jewish Bible scholar doing what James Kugel has done: detaching this work from the ongoing concerns of contemporary Jewry. I suggest that the making of the modern Jewish Bible remains an important project for twenty-first-century American Jews. The last question I wish to address in this study is as follows: How coherent has this project been, and has its task been completed? Or, to put it differently, is there a Jewish school of modern biblical scholarship?

Conclusion

Is There a "Jewish School" of Modern Bible Study?

The making of the modern Jewish Bible, I believe, is an intellectual achievement on par with the Jewish Enlightenment, the scientific study of Judaism, the revival of Hebrew, or the Zionist ideology. Contrary to popular deprecations of Jewish modernity, the last two centuries have constituted the acme of Jewish Bible study. The ceremonial role assigned the Bible, the Torah in particular, has often been a liturgical metaphor for the displacement of the greater intellectual energies poured into talmudic works by Jewish scholars, always male. Developments since Mendelssohn's day have restored the Bible to actual preeminence within many quarters of the Jewish world, and in recent decades, have allowed women to contribute to the explication of Torah within both devotional and academic contexts. Several factors have contributed to suppressing acknowledgment of the Bible's comeback, including (1) the ministerial nature of Torah commentary and translation (i.e., these endeavors look less original since they attend to an ancient text); (2) generic considerations (i.e., Bible scholars tend to focus on the Bible itself, not the development of the field; modern historians look for more explicitly "modern" developments; prose and poetry inspired by the Bible gets handled by scholars of literature); and (3) the spatial and temporal dimension of these endeavors, stretching over three continents and a couple of centuries.

PROFESSIONALS AND PROFESSIONS

Like any great achievement, the making of the modern Jewish Bible created tensions and fissures. One of these has been between "pure" scholarship and more explicitly Jewish approaches. The late Michael Signer differentiated *biblical scholarship* from *biblical studies*, arguing that within Judaism an objective, nondenominational, discipline-driven enterprise always coexisted with a more homiletic, religious one. Following Signer, one could claim we simply are watching the natural divide of these two approaches, with biblical scholarship finding its home in the university and biblical studies in homes, pulpits, synagogues, and study groups. But I do not find this dichotomy persuasive. One expects to find articles in the *Journal of Biblical Literature* to be written in a different style than in the *Jewish Study Bible*, but many of the concerns, issues, orientations, and even authors are the same.[1] Similarly, and despite his remarkable erudition, I resist Sperling's view of a "Jewish school" as too guild-oriented. Popular interest fuels academic inquiries: Bible studies seem no more removed from these influences than any humanistic endeavor.[2] From the perspective of the twenty-first century, one may doubt the reality of a Jewish school altogether. Jewish scholars hold eminent positions in originally Christian denominational institutions and have trained a generation of students—Jewish and non-Jewish. The mushrooming of Jewish studies programs in the last generation, with efforts to establish Jewish studies as a rigorous discipline, has led to many more Jews teaching courses on Bible, on Bible as literature, or on the Bible's interpretive history and contemporary use and abuse.

The Protestant monopoly on the Bible in the university, never uniform in any event, no longer exists. One can identify Christian scholars sufficiently influenced by Jewish teachers and peers to write works cognizant of Jewish tradition. While I have been presenting Jewish efforts as partly motivated by anticolonialist impulses, the subalterns have found plenty of sympathizers among the ruling caste. One can adopt a Jewish perspective without being Jewish, and one sees scholars sufficiently alienated from Judaic traditions such that they would never display Jewish tendencies. To an outsider looking in, the vestigial differences between Jews and Christians appear trivial compared to the rift between contemporaries and their predecessors on such issues as the basic historicity, the prevalence of critique as a mode of scholarship, or the acceptance of "strong readings" of the Bible, which an earlier era would have denigrated as "eisigesis," reading into the text.

To reiterate, I am observing *the construction* of Jewish readings of the Bible. Such tendencies may result organically from a particular scholar's early education and ethnoreligious background, but also may result from a conscious tendency to cultivate an approach recognized as Jewish by the academy and the marketplace. These tendencies reflect the Jewish experience, and attempt to shape this experience and the community that lives it out. I have spared the reader the usual quotation marks around Jewish because I accept that wrestling with the Bible, just as Buber claimed, has been a constant in Jewish history—the modern era included. Conventional wisdom holds that the founders of Jewish studies preferred to neglect the Bible as a text and the biblical period as history. For many reasons, this salutary neglect was a pipe dream; Zunz himself, whose "Concerning Rabbinic Literature" limned Jewish studies as postbiblical, turned to the Bible late in life—the emergent scholarship proved too interesting to ignore. What transpired, instead of benign neglect, was the creation of a modern Jewish Bible that speaks to the religious, national, and ethnic needs of the Jewish people. The modern Jewish Bible continues to engage scholars and laypeople, believers and agnostics, practitioners of Judaism and avid secularists, and in greater numbers than ever before in our long, long history. Possibly I should conclude here. But I would like to briefly underscore four commonalities of the modern Jewish Bible that cut across era, denomination, gender, and country of origin.

POLEMIC AND APOLOGETIC

In religious studies, "polemic" is an attack on another religion, "apologetic" is a defense of your own, and neither is good. But the polemic against source criticism has proven very fruitful. Some Jewish authors entered into the fray to admit its scientific importance, but correct its biases. Yehezkel Kaufmann devoted much ink to dating the Torah before the first exile. Kaufmann, an ardent nationalist, sought a national past created in the national homeland. He needed P in Jerusalem more than he needed Moses at Mount Sinai. Kaufmann had plenty of company: not every Jewish scholar dated P as preexilic, but many of the most influential did. The defense of P, like the defense of Ezra, often identified as R, already undertaken by Mendelssohn, constituted a pronounced tendency, as did the defense of characters deemed "Jewish" by source critics, such as Esther and Tamar, Jacob/Israel, and Judah.

Others attacked the validity of source criticism altogether. David Zvi Hoffmann presented Leviticus from a traditionalist perspective, demonstrating how much better one could understand the roles of worship and ritual if one knew a little law—which Wellhausen did not. Benno Jacob also rejected source criticism as speculative; his commentaries on Genesis and Exodus, which included counting verses, word repetitions, and nuances of the same word in different contexts, offered a different approach. No fundamentalist, Jacob believed that he had demonstrated a coherent voice, an author, where source critics saw only J, E, P, and D.

Still others responded to the source critical challenge indirectly, most famously Martin Buber and Franz Rosenzweig. Their posture was that the traditional Jewish text remained the only possible starting point for understanding God's Word, in their perspective the ultimate goal of responding to the Bible. While Buber had a deep interest in academic scholarship, his end goal, in Steven Kepnes's words, "was nothing less than the restoration of the role of the Hebrew Bible in the intellectual religious and practical life of the Jewish people."[3] Scholars such as Erich Auerbach (implicitly) and Robert Alter (explicitly) consider source criticism overly focused on the parts at the expense of the whole. Their respective approaches, while focusing on literary issues, invite a more than "literary" relationship with the Bible, as do the putatively historical works of Nahum Sarna. Even today, source criticism continues its "sand in the oyster" role, for instance, in Ilana Pardes's exposure of the Protestant biases in some feminist scholarship for uncritically assigning J and P the labels "sexist" and "egalitarian," respectively.[4]

This Jewish polemic against source criticism, arguably lasting long after it had given way to other academic approaches, yielded many constructive results. A simple observation emerges: a century-long polemical impulse on the part of Jewish Bible scholars aimed at the biases of Protestant-dominated Bible studies led to some wonderful scholarship, and largely cured the biblical mainstream of its latent antisemitism. Should somebody at the Society of Biblical Literature today start talking about "Late Judaism," that person would be enlightened, and not necessarily by a Jewish conference participant. If one believes in scholarly progress in the humanities, here is a sterling example.

PRESENCE OF RABBINIC INTERPRETATIONS

The quintessential form of Jewish creativity, according to Gershom Scholem, is commentary, and the linear commentaries of the medieval rabbis contained the sort of analysis useful to modern Bible scholarship.[5] One of Nehama Leibowitz's great insights was that even midrashic reflections—generally less rigorous than those of the medieval *pashtanim*—reflect extreme sensitivity to the biblical text. Most of the key figures in modern Jewish Bible scholarship, even the heterodox ones, were traditionally trained and had spent considerable time mastering Rashi and company. The use of rabbinic literature was by no means limited to the Orthodox. Benno Jacob held many source critical emendations unnecessary, and held that medieval exegetes had already "solved" a particular problem.

Scholars debate the indebtedness of Martin Buber to traditional Jewish commentators, but he demonstrably cited them in letters, principally to Rosenzweig, to support his translational choices, and felt validated when he could cite rabbinic tradition in support of his renderings. In Buber and Jacob's era, proximity to the academy inhibited acknowledgment of this debt to the Jewish tradition. Ludwig Feuchtwanger offered a more neutral (neutered?) view of how some German Jews hoped to see the discipline of Bible studies develop: "A Jewish, Catholic or Protestant Bible scholarship is completely untenable in terms of the nature and concept of scholarship. For this reason, the only possible locus and framework for the study of the Old Testament is not the theological faculty but rather Semitic philology, ancient history and the comparative study of religion."[6]

In a secular context, Jewish indebtedness to rabbinic commentaries came out of the closet only recently. But even before this turn of events, Jewish Bible scholars such as Cassuto, Schechter, Kohler, Jacobs, David Zvi Hoffmann, and so on took their cues from the rabbinic sources in subterranean fashion. Robert Alter entered the field with a spirited defense of midrashic insights in his *Art of Biblical Narrative*, while Michael Fishbane's *Biblical Interpretation in Ancient Israel* proved that the Bible contained the exegetical techniques later used by rabbinic Judaism. While an admittedly shallow measure, the ubiquity of "Torah" and "midrash" in the titles of scholarly and popular books, by Jews and Christians, legitimizes a Jewish view of the Bible and its commentaries. Most generally, this recourse to tradition is a way of articulating a "Jewish" voice in an academic discipline open to all, but by dint of sheer numbers, at least outside Israel, necessarily dominated by others.

PREEMINENCE OF THE HEBREW TEXT

No matter their denominational orientation or country of origin, Jewish Bible scholars have emphasized the *Hebrewness* of the Bible, often manifested as a paean to the importance of sounding the text aloud, whether in Hirsch's *Lautverwandshaft*, Buber's emphasis on theme words, or even Leibowitz's predilection for students acting out particular narrative scenes. Often this emphasis on Hebrew*ness* accompanied a preference for the Masoretic Text. Although the Septuagint, the Samaritan Pentateuch, and the Dead Sea Scrolls were all originally produced by Jews and for Jews, these texts, along with their variant readings, were adopted mainly by communities that left the Jewish world. The Masoretic Text alone remained as the basis for later exegesis, and adherence to it has been one marker of Jewish Bible scholarship. Ahad Haam's footnotes to Jeremiah and Moshe Greenberg's comments on the New English Bible Deuteronomy, described above, reveal fidelity to the most basic conservative impulse: the conviction that contemporaries do not necessarily know better than their predecessors.

Spinoza sought to deflate the Bible's influence, yet he shared the fascination with Hebrew, and insisted that analyzing the New Testament required understanding the Jewishness of the early Christian environment. Moses Mendelssohn could dismiss both lower and higher textual criticism as ephemeral. Mendelssohn's confidence in the Masoretic Text was great, and his belief in Hebrew as the original language of humankind, frankly medieval. Jewish scholars continued to defend the superiority of the Traditional Text, despite scholarly agreement regarding the presence of numerous variant readings within the Masoretic traditions. The New JPS Tanakh, still the most widely used Jewish Bible in North America, assured its readers on the front page and on the book's spine that the translation follows the "Traditional Hebrew Text." Intimately connected with this deprecation of all translations—even as they are furiously produced—is the modern credo that the Torah is to be read in Hebrew, or at least glanced at in that ancient tongue, as the American Chumash demonstrates.[7] The *Hebrewness* of the Bible and the concomitant view of the scholarly inferiority of those working in another language resonated even in Israel, where Ahad Haam could "undo" Karl Marti's emendations of Jeremiah and the Orthodox Nehama Leibowitz could reproach the Orthodox Mordechai Breuer for taking source criticism seriously. Those "scholars," she reminded him, did not know Hebrew.

PLURIFORMITY

Ahad Haam, better than anyone, expressed the inevitable malleability of the Bible: "The Holy Scriptures are not immanently holy. What have men not found in the Holy Scriptures from the time of Philo until the present day? In the Holy Scriptures they all sought only the truth, each his own truth, and they all found what they sought, found it because they were compelled to, for if not, the truth would not be the truth and the Holy Scriptures would not be holy."[8] Ahad Haam accepts the Bible's ever-varying meaning as the thread connecting every era of Jewish history. In the instance of Jewish modernity, I would insist that context has played a predictably decisive role. German Jews created a religious Bible dignified, learned, aesthetic, and linguistically elevated, even in translation. While Mendelssohn wanted to raise the cultural, and Buber the spiritual, levels of their contemporaries, both saw their projects as the elevation of the human spirit: a fundamentally religious task. National Jews created a national Bible: their fundamental secularization of a holy text destabilized both the Bible's authority and its Jewishness—Ahad Haam attempted to prop up both. Ben-Gurion's generation succeeded in making the Bible a key to unity, but this success could only have been partial, since his contemporaries often looked at the Bible's message differently than he did, even within the Labor mainstream, and certainly beyond it. In America, a fierce desire to connect with the past as a means of imparting contemporary identity, what I consider an ethnic impulse, has encouraged the appropriation of the Bible as literature, as history, as devotional and study text, but always in a modern, American, and Jewish idiom. The making of the modern Jewish Bible constitutes an impressive achievement and I will be gratified if I have forwarded its appreciation.

Notes

INTRODUCTION

1. On how the Bible became the Bible, start with James Kugel, *How to Read the Bible* (New York: Free Press, 2007) and the forceful responses in *Jewish Quarterly Review* 100, no. 1 (Winter 2010).

2. Jonathan Sheehan, *The Enlightenment Bible* (Princeton, NJ: Princeton University Press, 2005), xiv.

3. Ahad Haam, *Al Parashat Derakhim* [At the Crossroads] (Berlin: Jüdischer Verlag, 1921, 1930), 1:138.

4. Jacob Neusner and Ernst Freirichs, *Judaic Perspectives on Ancient Israel* (Philadelphia: Fortress Press, 1987), xii.

5. Michael Morgan, ed., *The Jewish Thought of Emil Fackenheim* (Detroit, MI: Wayne State, 1987), 223–34.

6. Lawrence Schiffman, *From Text to Tradition* (Jersey City, NJ: KTAV, 1991), 266–67.

7. Ephraim Karnafogel, "The Role of Bible Study in Medieval Ashkenaz," in *Frank Talmadge Memorial Volume*, ed. Barry Wallfish (Haifa: Haifa University, 1993).

1. SPINOZA AS *JEWISH* BIBLE CRITIC

1. Bertrand Russell, *A History of Western Philosophy* (New York: Simon and Schuster, 1945), 569.

2. Michah Gottlieb, "Defending Spinoza?" *AJS Review* 30, no. 2 (November 2006): 427–33.

3. The three translations are Samuel Shirley, 1989; Martin Yaffe, 2004; and Jonathan Israel, 2007.

4. Leo Strauss, *Spinoza's Critique of Religion* (New York: Schocken, 1965), preface, 29, 165, and 191–92.

5. Wolfson, *From Philo to Spinoza: Two Studies in Religious Philosophy* (West Orange, NJ: Behrman House, 1977), 64.

6. Spinoza, *Tractatus*, Jonathan Israel translation, 55.

7. Yirmiyahu Yovel, "Spinoza, The First Secular Jew," *Tikkun* 5, no. 1: 40–42, 94–96.
8. Steven Nadler, *Spinoza: A Life* (Cambridge: Cambridge University Press, 1999), 292.
9. Rebecca Goldstein, *Betraying Spinoza: The Renegade Jew Who Gave Us Modernity* (New York: Schocken, 2006), 3.
10. Alan Cooper, "On Reading the Bible Critically and Otherwise," in *The Future of Biblical Studies: The Hebrew Scriptures*, ed. Richard Elliott Friedman and H. G. M. Williamson (Atlanta: Scholars Press, 1987), 61–79.
11. Spinoza, *Tractatus*, Jonathan Israel translation, 112.
12. Spinoza, *Tractatus*, chap. 7.
13. Spinoza, *Tractatus*, Jonathan Israel translation, 122.
14. Steve Smith, *Spinoza, Liberalism and the Question of Jewish Identity* (New Haven, CT: Yale University Press, 1997); Steve Smith, *Spinoza's Book of Life* (New Haven, CT: Yale University Press, 2003).
15. Richard Popkin, "Spinoza and Bible Scholarship," in *The Cambridge Companion to Spinoza* (Cambridge: Cambridge University Press, 1996), 407n39.
16. Spinoza, *Tractatus*, Jonathan Israel translation, 154.
17. Nancy Levene, *Spinoza's Revelation* (Cambridge: Cambridge University Press, 2004), 126.
18. Thomas Hobbes, *Leviathan: A Critical Edition*, ed. G. A. J. Rogers and Karl Schumann, 2 vols. (Bristol, UK: Thommes Continuum, 2003), 296, 303, and 410.
19. Hobbes, *Leviathan*, 412.
20. Hobbes, *Leviathan*, 303.
21. Hobbes, *Leviathan*, 413.
22. Levene, *Spinoza's Revelation*, 240.
23. Adam Sutcliffe, *Judaism and Enlightenment* (Cambridge: Cambridge University Press, 2003), 133.

2. MENDELSSOHN'S BIBLE: THE IDEAL OF JEWISH SELF-SUFFICIENCY

1. Alexander Altmann, *Moses Mendelssohn: A Biographical Study* (Tuscaloosa: University of Alabama, 1973); Altmann, "Moses Mendelssohn: The Archetypal German Jew," in *The Jewish Response to German Culture*, ed. Jehuda Reinharz and Walter Schatzberg (Hanover, NH: University Press of New England, 1985).
2. David Sorkin, "The Mendelssohn Myth and Its Method," *New German Critique* 77 (1999): 7–28; Sorkin, *The Religious Enlightenment: Protestants, Jews and Catholics from London to Vienna* (Princeton, NJ: Princeton University Press, 2008), 167–213.
3. Allan Arkush, *Moses Mendelssohn and the Enlightenment* (Albany: State University of New York Press, 1994).
4. Werner Weinberg, ed., *Moses Mendelssohn, Hebräische Schriften*, 15:1 (Stuttgart: Friedrich Frommann Verlag, 1971), "Or L'Netivah," 241.
5. Moses Mendelssohn, cited in Sorkin, *Moses Mendelssohn*, 81; Sorkin, *The Religious Enlightenment*, 191; Edward Breuer, *The Limits of Authority: Jews, Germans and the Eighteenth-Century Study of Scripture* (Cambridge, MA: Harvard University Press, 1996). Please note: I prefer "Traditional Text" to "Masoretic Text" since the latter misleadingly suggests that only one Hebrew version existed.
6. W. Gunther Plaut, "German-Jewish Bible Translations" (LBI Memorial Lecture 36, New York, 1992), 9.
7. Naomi Seidman, *Faithful Renderings* (Chicago: University of Chicago Press, 2006), 176.
8. Jonathan Sheehan, *The Enlightenment Bible* (Princeton, NJ: Princeton University Press, 2006), 180.
9. Steven Lowenstein, "The Readership of Mendelssohn's Bible Translation," in *The Mechanics of Change* (Atlanta, GA: Scholars Press, 1992), 33n8.

10. Weinberg, *Moses Mendelssohn, Hebräische Schriften*, 15:1, 241.
11. Lowenstein, "The Readership of Mendelssohn's Bible Translation," 44.
12. Yosef Yerushalmi, *Zakhor* (Seattle: University of Washington Press, 1982), 69.
13. Moses Mendelssohn, "Kohelet Mussar," trans. Edward Breuer and David Sorkin, *LBI Yearbook* 48 (2003): 8.
14. "Alim L'Trufah," in *Moses Mendelssohn, Hebräische Schriften*, ed. Weinberg, 15:1, 323–31, especially pp. 326–28.
15. Cited in Weinberg, *Moses Mendelssohn, Hebräische Schriften*, 15:1, 84.
16. Franz Rosenzweig, "The Eternal: Mendelssohn and the Name of God," in *Scripture and Translation*, ed. Rosenwald and Fox (Bloomington: Indiana University Press, 1987), 99–101. Sorkin, *Moses Mendelssohn and the Religious Enlightenment* (Berkeley: University of California Press, 1996), 55–65; Allan Arkush, translator, Moses Mendelssohn, *Jerusalem* (Hanover, NH: Brandeis University Press-University Press of New England, 1983), 209n94.
17. Cited in Altmann, *Moses Mendelssohn*, 383.
18. Weinberg, *Moses Mendelssohn, Hebräische Schriften*, 15:1, 91; Altmann, *Moses Mendelssohn*, 383; Sorkin, "The Mendelssohn Myth and Its Method," 15.
19. Spinoza, *Tractatus Theologico-Politicus*, 7:12, 9:19–20; Sorkin, *Moses Mendelssohn*, 71.
20. Ze'ev Weintraub, *Targumei ha-Torah L'lashon ha-Germanit* (Chicago, 1967), 93–94, 226–27.
21. See Adam Sutcliffe, *Judaism and Enlightenment*, passim.
22. Sorkin, *Moses Mendelssohn*, 78; Breuer, *The Limits of Authority*, 221.
23. Franz Rosenzweig, "The Eternal: Mendelssohn and the Name of God," in *Scripture and Translation*, 99.
24. Abigail Gillman, "Between Religion and Culture," in *Biblical Translation in Context*, ed. Frederick Knobloch (Bethesda: University of Maryland Press, 2002), 114.
25. Michael Meyer, "Moses Mendelssohn: The Ephemeral Solution," in *The Origins of the Modern Jew* (Detroit: Wayne State, 1967).
26. Ismar Elbogen, in Weinberg, *Moses Mendelssohn, Hebräische Schriften*, 15:1, 82.

3. SAMSON RAPHAEL HIRSCH: THE CHIMERA OF SELF-EXPLANATORY SCRIPTURE

1. Max Wiener, ed., *Abraham Geiger and Liberal Judaism* (Philadelphia: JPS, 1962), 86. See also Ken Koltun-Fromm, *Abraham Geiger's Liberal Judaism, Personal Meaning and Religious Authority* (Bloomington: Indiana University Press, 2006), 12. For German Orthodoxy's varied stances toward Wissenschaft des Judentums, see Mordechai Breuer, *Modernity within Tradition* (New York: Columbia University Press, 1992), 184–202.
2. Ismar Schorsch, *From Text to Context* (Waltham, MA: Brandeis University Press, 1994), 320.
3. Nahum Sarna, "Abraham Geiger's Contribution to Bible Scholarship," in *New Perspectives on Abraham Geiger*, ed. Jakob J. Petuchowski (Cincinnati: HUC Symposium, 1976).
4. Susannah Heschel, *Abraham Geiger and the Jewish Jesus* (Chicago: University of Chicago Press, 1998).
5. Henry Wasserman, *False Start: Jewish Studies at German Universities during the Weimar Republic* (New York: Humanity Books, 2003).
6. Max Wiener, *Abraham Geiger and Liberal Judaism*, 216.
7. Koltun-Fromm's *Abraham Geiger's Liberal Judaism* champions Geiger's relevance to contemporary Jews as a model of synthesizing authority and personal meaning. While I am sympathetic to Koltun-Fromm's approach, the gap between "authority" and "personal meaning" in the nineteenth century was not easily bridged; Geiger's contemporaries sought an objective "essence of Judaism," validated by history.

8. Morris Margolies, *Samuel David Luzzato: Traditionalist Scholar* (New York: KTAV, 1979), 96.

9. Schorsch, *From Text to Context*, 319–22; Michael Meyer, *Response to Modernity: A History of the Reform Movement in Judaism* (New York: Oxford University Press, 1988), 89–99.

10. Eliyahu Klugman, *Samson Raphael Hirsch* (Brooklyn, NY: Mesorah Publications, 1996), 334.

11. Klugman, *Samson Raphael Hirsch*, 331.

12. Jay Harris, *How Do We Know This?* (Albany: State University of New York Press, 1994).

13. Hirsch, *Commentary to the Pentateuch*, Exodus 21:2. All translations from Hirsch follow Isaac Levy, ed., *Samson Raphael Hirsch, Commentary to the Pentateuch*, second revised edition (London: Soncino, 1962–1967).

14. Scholars have speculated about *Moriah*'s nonappearance. Grunfeld believed that the journal *Jeschurun* reflected Hirsch's views on the Bible; Rosenbloom believed that Hirsch backed away from an enormously difficult task. I am gratified that Shlomo Chertok, in *Kankan Yashan Maleh Hadash* (Tel Aviv: Ha-Kibbutz ha-Meuchad, 2010), entertains the idea that Hirsch's Chumash is his *Moriah*, which I think provides the best solution.

15. Isidore Grunfeld, trans., *Horeb: A Philosophy of Jewish Laws and Observances*, edited by Samson Raphael Hirsch, vol. 1 (London: Soncino Press, 1962), cxli–cxlv.

16. Hirsch, *Horeb: A Philosophy of Jewish Laws and Observances*, lvi.

17. Noah H. Rosenbloom, *Tradition in an Age of Reform* (Philadelphia: JPS, 1976), 192.

18. Hirsch, "A Basic Outline of Jewish Symbolism," in *Timeless Torah* (Philipp Feldheim, 1957), 365.

19. Hirsch, *Horeb*, 207.

20. Menachem Elon, "Codification of Law," in *Encyclopedia Judaica*, first edition, 5:628–56; Menachem Elon, *Jewish Law* (Philadelphia: JPS, 1994), 3:1138–1452. I would like to thank my "Codes" teacher Rabbi Michael Pitkowsky for bringing Elon's works to my attention.

21. Hirsch, *Horeb*, lxx.

22. See Ephraim Avigdor Speiser, *The Anchor Bible Genesis* (New York: Doubleday, 1964), xxxi–xxxiv, 150–52.

23. Breuer, *Modernity Within Tradition*, 65.

24. Breuer, *Modernity Within Tradition*, 80; Altmann, "Moses Mendelssohn as the Archetypal German Jew."

25. Rosenbloom, *Tradition in an Age of Reform*, 198.

26. Sara Japhet, "Revisionism at All Costs," in *The Jewish Past Revisited*, David Myers and Ruderman, eds. (New Haven: Yale University Press, 1998), 224.

27. Joseph Gugenheimer, "Die Hypothesen der Bibelkritik," *Jeschurun* 13 (1867), 14 (1868), and 15 (1886).

28. Arnold Eisen, "Divine Legislation as Ceremonial Script," *AJS Review* 15 (1990): 239–67.

29. Robert Liberles, *Religious Conflict in Social Context: The Resurgence of Orthodoxy in Frankfurt am Main* (Greenwood, CT: Greenwood Press, 1985).

30. Hirsch, *The Nineteen Letters*, 1836, Letter 18.

31. Hirsch on Genesis 3:17–19.

32. Hirsch on Genesis 9:27.

33. Hirsch on Genesis 17:1.

34. Hirsch on Genesis 17:1.

35. Hirsch, "Lessons from Jacob and Esau," *The Collected Writings*, vol. 7 (New York: Feldheim, 1984), 319–31. See also Hirsch on Numbers 22–24 and on Numbers 31:2.

36. Hirsch on Genesis 25:27.

37. Hirsch on Genesis 33:4. See also "Lessons from Jacob and Esau," *Samson Raphael Hirsch, The Collected Writings* (New York: Feldheim, 1984), 7:317–331.

38. Hirsch on Genesis 22:11.

39. Hirsch on the Forgotten Sheaf in Nehama Leibowitz, *Studies in Devarim/Deuteronomy* (Jerusalem: Hemed Press, 1980), 246–47.

4. BENNO JACOB AND THE CALL FOR A "JEWISH" BIBLE SCHOLARSHIP

1. In this book I have consistently used "source criticism" rather than "documentary hypothesis," or "higher criticism," or "literary criticism." Solomon Schechter, "The Higher Criticism—Higher Antisemitism, in *Seminary Addresses and Other Papers* (New York: The Burning Bush Press, 1959); Schechter, "The Study of the Bible," in *Studies in Judaism, Second Series* (Philadelphia: JPS, 1908), 32–54. For the complicated publication history of Wellhausen's work, see Douglas Knight, foreword to *Prolegomena to the History of Israel*, by Julius Wellhausen (Atlanta: Scholars Press, 1994), v–x.

2. Benno Jacob, *The Jewish Quarterly Review* 26 (1935–1936): 189. Yakov Shavit and Gideon Aran, *The Hebrew Bible Reborn* (Brill, 2007); Ran ha-Cohen, *Reviving the Old Testament* (Tel-Aviv: Hakibbutz Hameuchad, 2007).

3. Michael Brenner, *The Renaissance of Jewish Culture in Weimar Germany* (New Haven, CT: Yale University Press, 1991), 103–10; Hans-Joachim Bechtholdt, *Die Jüdische Bibelübersetzungen im 19: Jahrhundert.* (Stuttgart: W. Kohlhammer, 1995).

4. Kurt Wilhelm, "Benno Jacob, A Militant Rabbi," *LBI Yearbook* 7 (1962): 75–94.

5. Benno Jacob, *Das erste Buch der Tora-Genesis. Übersetzt und erklärt* (n.p.: Schocken Verlag, 1934).

6. Rabbi Ernest Jacob, Benno Jacob's son, collaborated on *Genesis*.

7. See Jacob's "Quellenscheidung" in *Das Erste Buch der Tora: Genesis*, 949–1049.

8. Walter Jacob, "Life and Works of Benno Jacob," in *The Second Book of the Bible: Exodus* (Hoboken, NJ: Ktav, 1992), xix.; on Maybaum see Ran ha-Cohen, *Reviving the Old Testament*, 204–218; on David Hoffmann see Alan Cooper in Jeremy Cohen and Martin Goodman, eds., *Perspectives on Judaic Studies* (Oxford: 2004).

9. Yaakov Elman, "Benno Jacob in Historical Context," *Die Exegese hat das erste Wort* (Stuttgart: Calwer, 2002), 114; Shuly Rubin Schwartz, *The Emergence of Jewish Scholarship in America: The Publication of the Jewish Encyclopedia* (Cincinnati: HUC Press, 1991), 134–45.

10. Brenner, *Renaissance of Jewish Culture*, 106–7.

11. Benno Jacob to Gershom Scholem, cited in Brenner, *Renaissance of Jewish Culture*, 107.

12. Christian Wiese, *Challenging Colonial Discourse: Jewish Studies and Protestant Theology in Wilhelmine Germany* (Leiden-Boston: Brill, 2005), 223.

13. Ruth Maren Niehoff, "Bibelkritisches Elements in der Exegese Benno Jacobs," in *Die Exegese hat das erste Wort*, 97.

14. "The theory that Genesis is composed from various sources, which can be separated, has been refuted." Jacob, *Das erste Buch der Tora: Genesis*, 1048, cited in Ernest Jacob, "The Torah Scholarship of B. Jacob," *Conservative Judaism* 15, no. 4 (1961): 1–62.

15. Jacob, *Das erste Buch der Tora: Genesis*, 10.

16. Jacob, *Das erste Buch der Tora: Genesis*, 35.

17. Jacob, *Genesis*, 261, as cited by Walter Jacob, ed.

18. Jacob, *Das erste Buch der Tora: Genesis*, 711–24; Jacob, *Mischehen* (Berlin: Philo Verlag, 1930), a comparative study of Esau and Tamar.

19. Jacob, *Das Erste Buch der Tora*, 9–10; 711–24.

20. Jacob, *Das erste Buch der Tora: Genesis*, 930–31.

21. Jacob, *Exodus*, 1052.

22. Jacob, *Exodus*, 1053.

23. Henry Wasserman, *False Start* (Amherst, NY: Humanity Books, 2003), 28.

24. Jacob, *Genesis*, 40.

25. Jacob, *Genesis*, 148.

26. Jacob, *Genesis*, 13.

27. Jacob, *Exodus*, 1074.

28. Jacob, *Das Erste Buch der Tora: Genesis*, 83.

29. Jacob, "Vorwort," *Das Erste Buch der Tora: Genesis*, 11.
30. Jacob, "Hexateuch," *Jewish Encyclopedia* 6:377.
31. Jacob, cited in Wiese, *Challenging Colonial Discourse*, 225.
32. Jacob, *Das Erste Buch der Tora: Genesis*, 83.
33. Schwendemann, review of *Die Exegese hat das erste Wort*, in *Beiträge zu Leben und Werk Benno Jacobs* (Stuttgart: Calwer Verlag, 2002), 7.
34. Jacob, *Genesis*, 63, 69.

5. THE MARTIN BUBER–FRANZ ROSENZWEIG BIBLE: CULTURE OR RELIGION?

1. On Buber and the Bible, see Paul Schilpp and Maurice Friedman, eds., *The Philosophy of Martin Buber*, Library of Living Philosophers (La Salle, IL: Open Court Publishing Company, 1967), esp. Nahum Glatzer, "Martin Buber as an Interpreter of the Bible," 361–80, and James Muilenburg, "Buber as an Interpreter of the Bible," 381–402; Grete Schaeder, *The Hebrew Humanism of Martin Buber* (Detroit: Wayne State University, 1973), esp. 339–80; Nahum Glatzer and Paul Mendes-Flohr, eds., *The Letters of Martin Buber* (Syracuse, NY: Syracuse University Press, 1996).
2. Everett Fox and Lawrence Rosenwald, *Scripture and Translation* (Bloomington: Indiana University Press, 1994).
3. Fox and Rosenwald, *Scripture and Translation*, 7.
4. Seidman, *Faithful Renderings*, 183.
5. James Kugel, "Literary Criticism Lite," Appendix 1 of *How to Read the Bible* (New York: Free Press, 2007); Gershom Scholem, "Martin Buber's Judaism," in *Jews and Judaism in Times of Crisis*, ed. Werner Dannhauser (New York: Schocken, 1976).
6. Franz Rosenzweig, "'The Eternal': Mendelssohn and the Name of God," in *Scripture and Translation*, 104; Fox, "Franz Rosenzweig as Translator," *LBI Yearbook* 34 (1989); Fox, *The Five Books of Moses* (New York: Schocken, 1983), xxix–xxx.
7. Steven Kepnes, *The Text as Thou* (Bloomington: Indiana University Press, 1992), 41–60.
8. Muilenburg, "Buber as an Interpreter of the Bible," 402.
9. Ernest Wolf, "Martin Buber and German Jewry," *Judaism* 1, no. 4 (1952). See the essays of Steven Weitzman and Mara Benjamin in *Prooftexts* 27, no. 2 (2007).
10. See Buber, *I and Thou*, part 3, and "The Words on the Tablets" for his view of revelation.
11. Chaim Potok, "Martin Buber and the Jews," *Commentary*, March 1961, 1–5.
12. Martin Buber, *On the Bible* (New York: Schocken, 1968), 1.
13. Franz Rosenzweig, "The Unity of the Bible," in Rosenwald and Fox, *Scripture and Translation*, 23.
14. Buber in "The How and Why of Our Bible Translation" (1938), in Rosenwald and Fox, *Scripture and Translation*.
15. Brenner, *The Renaissance of Jewish Culture*, 104.
16. Niehoff, "The Buber-Rosenzweig Translation," *Journal of Jewish Studies* 44, no. 2 (1993): 258–79.
17. Niehoff, "The Buber-Rosenzweig Translation," 279.
18. Mara Benjamin, *Rosenzweig's Bible* (New York: Cambridge University Press, 2009), 12–15.
19. Franz Rosenzweig, "It Is Time," in *On Jewish Learning* (Madison: University of Wisconsin Press, 2002), 36.
20. Alan Levenson and Jeffrey Schein, "Will the Real Franz Rosenzweig Stand Up?" *Journal of Jewish Education* 76, no. 2 (2010): 151–63.
21. Rosenzweig, "It Is Time," *On Jewish Learning*, 30.
22. Nahum N. Glatzer, ed., *Franz Rosenzweig: His Life and Thought* (New York: Schocken, 1953), 269.

23. Glatzer, *Franz Rosenzweig: Life and Thought*, 262, 268.
24. Glatzer, *Franz Rosenzweig: Life and Thought*, 275.
25. Nahum Sarna, *Genesis*, The JPS Torah Commentary, xviii; Mara Benjamin, "Buber-Rosenzweig and Robert Alter," *Prooftexts* 27, no. 2 (Spring 2007): 254–74. See also Benjamin Harshav in *Religious Studies Review* 34, no. 4 (2008): 310.
26. "The place of Scripture in Rosenzweig's writing is an overlooked and significant dimension of his work." Benjamin, *Rosenzweig's Bible*, 5. See also Benjamin Britt, *Walter Benjamin and the Bible* (Lewiston, NY: Edwin Mellon, 2003).

PART II INTRODUCTION: THE BIBLE IN MODERN ISRAEL

1. Even socialists such as Nachman Syrkin (1867–1924) identified elements in Russian populist socialism with prophetic utopianism. See Ehud Luz, *Parallels Meet* (Philadelphia: JPS, 1988), 192.
2. My characterization of nationalism relies on the classic works of Benedict Anderson, Ernst Gellner, and Eric Hobsbawm.
3. Hazaz's "The Sermon" is translated in Joel Blocker, ed., *Israeli Stories* (New York: Schocken, 1965), 84; Hazaz, "Ha-Derasha," *Sippurim Nivrachim* (Dvir, n.d.), 184–202.
4. Among the many works on the revival of Hebrew, I recommend Benjamin Harshav, *Language in Time of Revolution* (Berkeley: University of California Press, 1998).
5. Benedict Anderson, *Imagined Communities* (London: Verso, 1991), 78.
6. On the relationship of Bible and archaeology, see Israel Finkelstein and Neil Asher Silberman, *The Bible Unearthed* (New York and London: Free Press, 2001), 4–24.
7. Even revisionist positions rely on a reading of the Bible. The ancient historian Moses Finley put this well in his classic *The Use and Abuse of History* (London and New York: Penguin, 1971), 22: "Unless a generation is captured on paper and the framework of its history fixed, either contemporaneously or soon thereafter, the future historian is forever blocked. He can reinterpret, shift the emphases, add and deduct data, but he cannot create the framework *ex nihilo*. That is why we can write the history of the Persian wars, thanks to Herodotus, and the history of the Peloponnesian War, thanks to Thucydides, but not the history of the intervening fifty years, not for all the writers of tragedy and comedy and all the inscriptions and material objects unearthed by modern archaeologists."
8. Jonathan Brown and Laurence Kutler, *Nelson Glueck* (Cincinnati: Hebrew Union College Press, 2006), 62–64.
9. Neil Asher Silberman, *A Prophet from Amongst You: The Life of Yigael Yadin* (Reading, MA: Addison-Wesley, 1993), 24–27; Amos Elon, "Politics and Archaeology," in *The Archaeology of Israel: Constructing the Past, Interpreting the Present*, ed. Silberman and David Small (JSOT Press, 1997).
10. Silberman, *A Prophet from Amongst You*, 3.
11. Elon, "Politics and Archaeology," 45.

6. EARLY ZIONISM AND THE BIBLE: AHAD HAAM AND HIS OPPONENTS

1. The term "Zionismus," though coined by Nathan Birnbaum, did not come into common use until the Hovevei Zion and Hibbat Zion organizations (1880s). For Graetz and Smolenskin, Jewish nationalist is a better designation than Zionist.
2. Heinrich Graetz, "Memoirs," in *History of the Jews*, ed. Philipp Bloch and Heinrich Graetz, vol. 6 (Philadelphia: JPS, 1898), 84–86.
3. Max Soloveitchik's "Outline of Academic Biblical Scholarship" [Hebrew] (Odessa, 1915), cited in David Engel, "Hebrew Nationalism and Biblical Criticism," in *Ki Baruch Hu: Festchrift in Honor of Baruch Levine* (Winona Lake, IN: Eisenbrauns, 1999), 484n2.

4. This story has been well told by Menachem Haran, "Fifty Years of Biblical Research in Israel" (Jerusalem: Goldberg, 1968); David Myers, *Reinventing the Jewish Past* (New York: Oxford University Press, 1995), 102–8; Shavit and Eran, *The Hebrew Bible Reborn*, 384–98; and Engel, "Hebrew Nationalism and Biblical Criticism," 486–87.

5. Shavit and Eran, *The Hebrew Bible Reborn*, 386.

6. Menahem Haran, *Biblical Research in Hebrew* (Jerusalem: Magnes Press, 1970).

7. Alfred Gottschalk, "Ahad Haam as Biblical Critic," *Hebrew Annual Review* 7 (1982): 105–19.

8. Shavit, *The Hebrew Bible Reborn*, 149–55. Ahad Haam's comments ("Literary Observations," in "Yalkut Katan," *Kol Kitvei Ahad Haam* [Tel Aviv: Dvir, 1956], 288n2) on Avraham Kahana's *Perush Mada'i* (Zhitomir and Tel Aviv, 1904–1930) are the former's most positive on biblical scholarship in general.

9. Steven Zipperstein, "Symbolic Politics, Religion and Ahad Haam," in *Zionism and Religion*, ed. Shmuel Almog, Jehuda Reinharz, and Anita Shapira (Waltham, MA: Brandeis University Press, 1998), 66n21. "It is unlikely that Ahad Haam, a Bible scholar, was unaware of the passage and its midrashic implications, particularly in view of the extensive notes that he took (much later to be sure, in England) on nearly every passage of the Bible in preparation for the writing of a never-completed book on biblical literary style. Interestingly the index card devoted to Genesis 26 skips the passage."

10. Ahad Haam adored the verse, "This was the word of the Lord to Zerubavel: not by might and not by power, but by spirit (*ruah*)" (Zechariah 4:6). But Zechariah, as many prophets, was also a priest, and cannot be used to uphold a dichotomy between these two roles.

11. Anita Shapira, *Land and Power: The Zionist Resort to Force* (New York and Oxford: Oxford University Press, 1992), 22.

12. Shapira, *Land and Power*, 28.

13. Yael Zerubavel, *Recovered Roots* (Chicago: University of Chicago Press, 1995).

14. Jacob Golomb, *Nietzsche and Zion* (Ithaca and London: Cornell University Press, 2004), 123.

15. Golomb, *Nietzsche and Zion*, 132–33.

16. This dichotomy of Shem and Japhet reflected a rabbinic idiom for talking about the relationship of Jewish and general culture.

17. Shmuel Almog, *Zionism and History: The Rise of a New Jewish Conscience* (Jerusalem: Hebrew University/Magnes Press, 1987), emphasizes the common ground shared by Ahad Haam and Berdichevsky, both champions of reconfiguring Jewishness as cultural rather than religious.

18. Cited in Shapira, *Land and Power*, 211.

19. Shapira, "The Bible and Israeli Identity," *AJS Review* 28, no. 1 (2004): 11–42, 18–19; Shavit and Eran, *The Hebrew Bible Reborn*, 44–45.

20. Shavit and Eran, *The Hebrew Bible Reborn*, 41.

21. Ahad Haam's "Priest and Prophet" shares an affinity with Buber's sharp distinction between "religiosität" and "Religion" as the inspirational versus the institutional manifestations of religion.

22. Gottschalk, "Ahad Haam as Biblical Critic," *Hebrew Annual Review* 7 (1982): 113.

23. Brenner, cited in Laurence Silberstein, *The Postzionism Debates* (New York: Routledge, 1999), 43.

24. "And proceeding from this [the relationship to the Holy Tongue] the relationship to the Scriptures the believers see in them the book of books revealed by God, that is not liable to literary criticism and bears no likeness between this Book and to other books and no question of literary value. However, even the non-believer, if he is a national Jew, does not have a merely literary relationship to the Scriptures—but rather, literary and national alike/as one." Ahad Haam, "Torah M'zion," in *At the Crossroads*, 3:127.

25. Cited in Menahem Brinker, "Brenner's Jewishness," *Studies in Contemporary Jewry* 4 (1988): 235.

26. Almog, *Zionism and History*, 130.

27. Mossinson taught Tanach in four parts, corresponding to German practices and the canon of the Christian Bible. He thus ignored the Jewish canon of "the twenty-four," and demoted Torah to the last part of the Bible instruction. Ahad Haam wrote that a student could reconstruct Mossinson's lectures using Karl Marti's *Commentary on the Old Testament* (1897–1903), but not the Tanach. See Alfred Gottschalk, "Ahad Haam as Bible Critic," 105–18; see also Steven Zipperstein, *Elusive Prophet* (Berkeley: University of California Press, 2000), 240–44.

28. Mossinson, "The Tanakh in the School," in *The Bible in Israeli Education*, Jacobus Schoeneveld (Assen and Amsterdam: Van Gorcum, 1976), 27–38.

29. Ahad Haam, "The Hebrew Gymnasium," in *At the Crossroads*, 4:144–54.

30. Shavit, *The Hebrew Bible Reborn*, 378.

31. Ahad Haam, "The Hebrew Gymnasium," in *At the Crossroads*, 4:153.

32. Schoneveld, *The Bible in Israeli Education*, 27–38.

33. Menachem Haran, "Fifty Years," 12–13.

7. THE BIBLE AS NATIONAL LINCHPIN: DAVID BEN-GURION AND HIS OPPONENTS

1. Dan Kurzman, *Ben-Gurion: Prophet of Fire* (New York: Simon and Schuster, 1983), subdivided his biography into three sections (Moses, Joshua, and Isaiah), titled each chapter from a verse of Scripture, and explicitly described the Bible as Ben-Gurion's inspiration from youth onward. Shabtai Teveth, *Ben-Gurion. The Burning-Ground, 1886–1948* (Boston: Houghton Mifflin, 1987), 12–13, noted that Ben-Gurion attended a reformed primary school and presumably learned Bible and Hebrew.

2. Teveth, *Ben-Gurion*, xi–xv.

3. Shavit and Eran, *The Hebrew Bible Reborn* (Berlin: Walter de Gruyter, 2007), 494n44. By 1956 the Bible in state-secular Israeli middle schools occupied four to five hours per week, thirty weeks per year.

4. Michael Keren, *Ben-Gurion and the Intellectuals: Power, Knowledge and Charisma* (DeKalb: Northern Illinois University Press, 1983), 105.

5. Anita Shapira, "The Bible and Israeli Identity," *AJS Review* 28, no. 1 (2004): 11–42; Shapira, "Ben-Gurion and the Bible: The Forging of an Historical Narrative?" *Middle Eastern Studies* 33, no. 4 (October 1997): 645–74; Shapira, *New Jews/Old Jews* [In Hebrew] (Tel Aviv: Am Oved, 1997), and Shapira, *The Bible and Israeli Identity* (Jerusalem: Hebrew University Press, 2005).

6. Shapira, "The Bible and Israeli Identity," 21n41.

7. Ben-Gurion found the Bible relevant to America's racial question: "Had the Americans heeded Amos, they never would have adopted slavery and would be avoiding all the racial tensions at present in America." Jews had it easier than African-Americans: "Thanks to our Bible, the Jewish reinsertion into a creative stream of human history, as realized by the return to Israel, has been relatively easy." Ben-Gurion, *Recollections* (London: Macdonald, 1970), 125–28.

8. Ben-Gurion, *Recollections*, 121.

9. Arthur Hertzberg, *The Zionist Idea* (Philadelphia: JPS, 1997), 559–70. On Jabotinsky, see Michael Stanislawski, *Zionism and the Fin de Siècle* (Berkeley: University of California Press, 2001), 116–238.

10. Jonathan Kolatch, ed., *Ben Gurion Looks at the Bible* (Middle Village, NY: Jonathan David, 1972), 49. See also Mordechai Kogan, ed., *Ben-Gurion and the Tanach* (Beer Sheva, 1989).

11. *Ben-Gurion Looks at the Bible*, 198–99. Ben-Gurion resorted to the Midrash about God offering every nation the Torah before Israel accepted it. Perhaps he forgot that this story is not in the Bible.

12. *Ben-Gurion Looks at the Bible*, 4.
13. Both Ben-Gurion and Ahad Haam regarded Moses as a positive model. Arnold Band, "The Ahad Ha-Am and Berdyczewski Polarity," in *At the Crossroads: Essays on Ahad Haam*, ed. Jacques Kornberg (Albany: State University of New York Press, 1993), 49–59.
14. Nur Masalha, *The Bible and Zionism: Invented Traditions, Archaeology and Post-Colonialism in Israel-Palestine* (London and New York: Zed Books, 2007), 21. While Zionism did lean on the Bible, the Jewish debate was principally internally directed, at least before 1967.
15. Ben-Gurion, *Recollections*, 19.
16. Mitchell Cohen, *Zion and State: Nation, Class and the Shaping of Modern Israel*, 2nd ed. (New York: Columbia University Press, 1992).
17. Shapira, "Ben-Gurion and the Bible," *Near Eastern Studies*, 670.
18. *Ben-Gurion Looks at the Bible*, 238.
19. Ben-Gurion, *Recollections*, 125–28.
20. "Uniqueness and Destiny," in *Ben-Gurion Looks at the Bible*, 108–35.
21. *Ben-Gurion Looks at the Bible*, 44.
22. *Ben-Gurion Looks at the Bible*, 53.
23. *Ben-Gurion Looks at the Bible*, 13.
24. Ben-Gurion and Hazaz, "Dialogue on State and Literature," in Shapira, *The Bible and Israeli Identity*, 139–57.
25. Ben-Gurion and Hazaz, "Dialogue on State and Literature," 144.
26. "Uniqueness and Destiny," *Ben-Gurion Looks at the Bible*, 1–43.
27. Thomas Krapf, *Yehezkel Kaufmann* (Berlin: Institut Kirche und Judentum, 1990).
28. Nahum Sarna, "From Wellhausen to Kaufmann," *Midstream* 7, no. 3 (1961): 64–74, 68.
29. Yehezkel Kaufmann, *The Religion of Israel*, trans. Moshe Greenberg (Chicago: University of Chicago, 1960), 153. An abridgement of *Toldot Ha-Emunah Ha-Yisraelit* (Tel-Aviv: Bialik, 1937).
30. Jon D. Levenson, "Kaufmann and Mythology," *Conservative Judaism* 36, no. 2 (1982): 35–43.
31. Kaufmann, *The Religion of Israel*, 200.
32. Shavit and Eran, *The Hebrew Bible Reborn*, 459.
33. Ben-Gurion, "The Eternality of Israel," Government Annual 1953, cited in Shavit and Eran, *The Hebrew Bible Reborn*, 484.
34. Keren, *Ben-Gurion and the Intellectuals*, 100–103; Shavit and Eran, *The Hebrew Bible Reborn*, 455–59.
35. Paul Mendes-Flohr, *A Land of Two Peoples* (Oxford: Oxford University Press, 1983) offers a good starting point.
36. Stanislawski, *Zionism*, 223–36, who cautions against overinterpreting Jabotinsky's fiction; Shlomo Avineri, *The Making of Modern Zionism* (New York: Basic Books, 1981), 173–75.
37. James Diamond, *Homeland or Holy Land? The Canaanite Critique of Israel* (Bloomington: Indiana University Press, 1986); Ratosh, "Ha-Nefesh," in *The Penguin Book of Hebrew Verse*, ed. T. Carmi (New York: Penguin), 544–45.
38. Ehud Luz, *When Parallels Meet*, passim. See also Arthur Hertzberg, *The Zionist Idea* (Garden City, NY: Doubleday, 1959), who interprets Zionism as secular messianism.
39. *The World of Rav Kook's Thought* (Jerusalem: Avi Chai, 1985) offers a good starting point on Abraham Isaac Kook; on Zvi Yehuda Kook, begin with the many essays of Gideon Aran.

8. NEHAMA LEIBOWITZ'S BIBLE: RETURNING TRADITION TO THE TEXT

1. Leibowitz's weekly questions (*gilyonot*) are available online at Mofet JTEC-Jewish Portal of Teacher Education, The Lookstein Center, and Gilyonot Nechama: The Gilyonot Nechama Website (Keren Keshet Sinunit).

2. Marla Frankel, *Teaching the Bible: The Philosophy of Nehama Leibowitz* (Tel Aviv, 2007), 22–23. Leibowitz corrected and returned well over 20,000 *gilyonot*.

3. Hayuta Deutsch, *Nehama* (Tel Aviv: Yediot Ahronot, 2008); Yael Unterman, *Nehama Leibowitz: Teacher and Bible Scholar* (Jerusalem and New York: Urim Publications, 2009).

4. On her Berlin-Marburg years, see Deutsch, *Nehama*, chap. 2, and Unterman, *Nehama Leibowitz*, 28–34.

5. Jacob Katz, *With My Own Eyes* (Hanover, NH: Brandeis University Press, 1995).

6. Hillel Goldberg, *Between Berlin and Slobodka: Jewish Transitional Figures from Eastern Europe* (Hoboken, NJ: KTAV, 1989).

7. Shapira, "The Bible and Israeli Identity," *AJS Review* 28, no. 1 (2004): 34. Shapira is right in seeing the gradual decline in the Bible's influence in the 1970s, relative to the Holocaust, but this is hard to correlate in any way with Leibowitz, who made aliyah in 1930.

8. Yaira Amit, "Some Thoughts on the Work and Method of Nehama Leibowitz," *Immanuel* 20 (Spring 1986): 7–13.

9. Eliezer (Ed) Greenstein has related Leibowitz to postmodern literary approaches in two essays, "A Pragmatic Pedagogy of Bible," *Journal of Jewish Education* 75 (2009): 290–303, and "The Many-Faceted Interpretation of Nehama Leibowitz and Post-Modernist Interpretation," *Limmudim* 1 (2002): 21–33.

10. My characterization of New Criticism relies on William Spurlin, "What Is Criticism?" in *The New Criticism and Contemporary Literary Theory*, ed. William Spurlin and Michael Fischer (New York: Garland Press, 1995), and Howard Adams and Leroy Searle, *Critical Theory Since 1965* (Tallahassee: University Press of Florida, 1986).

11. It is always hard to prove a negative—in this case, Leibowitz's relative lack of interest in women as full-blown biblical characters. To take three instances of discussions that beg for attention to the issue of gender: In her discussion of Miriam's and Aaron's criticism of Moses (Numbers 12), Leibowitz acknowledges the unequal punishments accorded Moses's siblings, but passes on quickly to the issue of gossip (*lashon ha-rah*). In her discussion of Jephtah and his daughter (Judges 11), Leibowitz is most concerned with the issue of whether the sacrifice was actual or figural, meaning that Jephtah's unnamed daughter was consigned to a life of virginity. Leibowitz deals with Judah and Tamar (Genesis 38) in her *gilyonot*, but focuses mainly on Judah's admission (Genesis 38:26), and does not include a discussion of this chapter in her *Studies in Bereshit/Genesis*.

12. Vanessa Ochs, *Words on Fire* (New York: Harcourt, Brace, Jovanovich, 1990), 263–86.

13. My sketch is drawn from Shmuel Peerless, *To Study and to Teach: The Methodology of Nehama Leibowitz* (Jerusalem: Lookstein Center/Urim Publications, 2004), from notes on a *parshanut ha-mikra* class taught by Dr. Walter Herzberg, and from discussions with two colleagues, Dr. Ron Brauner and Dr. Moshe Berger.

14. Nehama Leibowitz, *Active Learning in the Teaching of History* (Chicago: Torah Education Network, 1989).

15. Moshe Arend, Rut Ben-Meir, and Gavriel Chaim Cohen, eds., *Pirkei Nehama: Professor Nehama Leibowitz Memorial Volume* (Jerusalem: The Jewish Agency, 2001), 648.

16. Leibowitz, *New Studies in Bereshit/Genesis*, 17.

17. Leibowitz, *New Studies in Shmot/Exodus*, 652.

18. Leibowitz, *New Studies in Devarim/Deuteronomy*, 295.

19. Leibowitz, *New Studies in Devarim/Deuteronomy*, 302.

20. Howard Deitcher, "Between Angels and Mere Mortals: Nechama Leibowitz's Approach to the Study of Biblical Characters," *Journal of Jewish Education* 66, nos. 1–2 (Spring/Summer 2000), 9.

21. Leibowitz, *New Studies in Shmot/Exodus*, 389, 485–86.

22. Leibowitz, *New Studies in Genesis*, 366.

23. Deitcher, "Between Angels and Mere Mortals," 11.

24. Deitcher, "Between Angels and Mere Mortals," 10.

25. Rivka Horwitz, "Nehama Leibowitz and German-Jewish Parshanut in the 19th–20th Centuries," in *Pirkei Nehama*, 212–14.

26. Leibowitz, *New Studies in Devarim/Deuteronomy*, 226.
27. Leibowitz, *New Studies in Devarim/Deuteronomy*, 226.
28. Leibowitz, *New Studies in Devarim/Deuteronomy*, 226–27.
29. Leibowitz, *New Studies in Devarim/Deuteronomy*, 226–27.
30. Leibowitz, *New Studies in Bereshit/Genesis*, 376.
31. This exchange of letters between Bergman and Leibowitz may be found in Leah Abramowitz, *Tales of Nehama* (Jerusalem: Gefen Publishers, 2003), 275–79, and in *Pirkei Nehama*, 659–61.
32. Leibowitz, *New Studies in Bereshit/Genesis*, 36–37.
33. Leibowitz, *New Studies in Bereshit/Genesis*, 150.
34. Leibowitz, *New Studies in Bereshit/Genesis*, 150.
35. Benno Jacob, *Quellenscheidung und Exegese im Pentateuch* (Leipzig: Kaufmann, 1916).
36. Leibowitz, *New Studies in Bereshit/Genesis*, 439–42.
37. Leibowitz, *New Studies in Bereshit/Genesis*, 448–49n2.
38. Greenstein, "Pragmatic Pedagogy," 33, for Leibowitz's antiracialist comments on Ruth and Naomi. On the German academy's capitulation to racism in the 1930s, see Max Weinreich, *Hitler's Professors* (New York: YIVO, 1946); Robert Ericksen, *Theologians Under Hitler* (New Haven, CT: Yale University Press, 1985); Ericksen and Heschel, eds., *Betrayal* (Minneapolis: Fortress Press, 1999); and Alan Steinweis, *Studying the Jew* (Cambridge, MA: Harvard University Press, 2006).
39. Leibowitz, *Studies in Shmot/Exodus*, 312–13.
40. Leibowitz, *Studies in Shmot/Exodus*, 688n5.
41. Leibowitz, *Studies in Devarim/Deuteronomy*, 196, where she sided with Rashi, Old JPS, and Buber-Rosenzweig in their rendering of *ki* in Deuteronomy 20:19 as an interrogative.
42. Leibowitz, *New Studies in Shmot/Exodus*, 399.
43. Leibowitz, *New Studies in Shmot/Exodus*, 486.
44. Leibowitz, *Studies in Vayikra/Leviticus*, 532.
45. Leibowitz occasionally commented on the prophetic readings. It is worth noting that these passages are linked, in traditional Jewish fashion, to the weekly Torah readings.
46. Leibowitz, *Studies in Devarim/Deuteronomy*, 361, 362n7. See Lou Silberman's "Buber's Job and His Generation," in *Judaic Perspectives on Ancient Israel*, ed. Neusner and Freirichs (Philadelphia: Fortress Press, 1987).
47. Leibowitz, "Note to Teachers," cited in Unterman, *Nehama Leibowitz*, 428.
48. Amit, "Some Thoughts on the Work and Method of Nehama Leibowitz," 7–13.
49. Abramowitz, *Tales of Nehama*, 178.
50. Yeshayahu Leibowitz, *Judaism, Human Values and the Jewish State* (Cambridge, MA: Harvard University Press, 1992), 11.

PART III INTRODUCTION: AMERICA AND THE JEWISH BIBLE

1. Jonathan and Nahum Sarna, "Jewish Bible Scholarship and Translations in the United States," in *The Bible and Bibles in America*, ed. Ernst Freirichs (Atlanta: Scholars Press, 1988), 83–116; Frederick Greenspahn, "The Beginning of Judaic Studies in American Universities," *Modern Judaism* 20, no. 2 (2000): 209–25; Penny Shine Gold, *Making the Bible Modern: Children's Bible and Jewish Education in Twentieth-Century America* (Ithaca, NY: Cornell University Press, 2004); S. David Sperling, *Students of the Covenant* (Atlanta: Scholars Press, 1986); Sperling, "Major Developments in Jewish Biblical Scholarship," in *Hebrew Bible/Old Testament: The History of Interpretation*, ed. Magna Saebo (Göttingen: Vandenhoek & Ruprecht, forthcoming).

2. Lance J. Sussman, "Another Look at Isaac Leeser and the First Jewish Translation of the Bible in the United States," *Modern Judaism* 5, no. 2 (May 1985): 159–90; Lance J. Sussman, *Isaac Leeser and the Making of American Judaism* (Detroit, MI: Wayne State, 1999).

3. Shalom Goldman, ed., *Hebrew and the Bible in America* (Waltham, MA, and Hanover, NH: Brandeis and Dartmouth, 1993), and *God's Sacred Tongue: Hebrew and the American Nation* (Chapel Hill: University of North Carolina Press, 2004).

4. Daniel Radosh, "The Good Book Business," *New Yorker*, December 18, 2006, 54–59.

5. Naomi W. Cohen, "The Challenges of Darwinism and Biblical Criticism to American Judaism," *Modern Judaism* 4, no. 2 (May 1984): 121–51.

6. Preface to Old JPS (1917).

7. Sussman, "Another Look at Isaac Leeser," 161.

8. Sussman, "Another Look at Isaac Leeser," explains that the Leeser Bible appeared in stages: an English-only translation of the Pentateuch in 1845, a vocalized Hebrew text in 1848, and the whole *Twenty-four Books of the Holy Scriptures* in 1853–1854.

9. Sussman, "Another Look at Isaac Leeser," 172.

10. Sussman, "Another Look at Isaac Leeser," 168, 181; Harry Orlinsky, "Jewish Biblical Scholarship," in *Essays in Biblical Culture and Bible Translation* (New York: KTAV, 1974), 294; Joseph Hertz, "Jewish Translations of the Bible in English," in *Sermons, Addresses and Studies*, vol. 2 (London: Soncino, 1938), 70–93.

11. Robert Fierstien, *A Different Spirit. The Jewish Theological Seminary in America, 1886–1902* (New York: JTS, 1990), 72.

12. David J. Fine, "Solomon Schechter and the Ambivalence of Jewish Wissenschaft," *Judaism* 1997: 4–24.

13. Harvey Meirovich, *A Vindication of Judaism: The Polemics of the Hertz Pentateuch* (New York and Jerusalem: JTS Press, 1998).

14. Joseph H. Hertz, ed., *Pentateuch and Haftorahs*, 2nd ed. (London: Soncino, 1981), vii.

9. FINDING A JEWISH VOICE: NAHUM SARNA AND ROBERT ALTER

1. Sarna, *Understanding Genesis*, xv.

2. Jeffrey Tigay, introduction, *Studies in Biblical Interpretation* (Philadelphia: JPS, 2000), x–xxii.

3. Sperling, "Major Developments in Jewish Biblical Scholarship."

4. See the JPS Torah Commentaries by Baruch Levine, "Leviticus," and Jeffrey Tigay, "Deuteronomy," which highlight the prominence of these books in Jewish tradition.

5. Samuel Sandmel, "The Haggadah Within Scripture," *Journal of Biblical Literature* (1961): 105–22.

6. Sarna, "The Authority and Interpretation of Scripture in Jewish Tradition," in *Studies in Biblical Interpretation* (Philadelphia: JPS, 2000), 69.

7. For a helpful distinction between canonical criticism inner-biblical interpretation, see Bernard M. Levinson, *Deuteronomy and the Hermeneutics of Legal Innovation* (New York: Oxford University Press, 1997), esp. 13–17.

8. Bernard Bamberger, *The Bible: A Modern Jewish Approach*, A Hillel Little Book (New York: B'nai Brith Foundations, 1955).

9. Sarna, *Understanding Genesis*, xv.

10. Bamberger, "Introduction to Leviticus," in Plaut, *The Torah: A Modern Commentary*, (New York: Union of American Hebrew Congregations, 1981), 813.

11. H. L. Ginzberg, Arnold B. Ehrlich, and Harry Orlinsky all worked in Jewish institutions, had traditional Jewish educations, and championed source criticism. Sandmel, Bamberger, and Plaut were all ordained Reform rabbis.

12. Nahum Sarna, "The Authority and Interpretation of Scripture in Jewish Tradition," 72–73. Emil Fackenheim, "New Hearts and Old Covenant," in Michael Morgan, *The Jewish Philosophy of Emil Fackenheim* (Detroit: Wayne State Press, 1987), 223–34.

13. Sarna, *Understanding Genesis*, xxii; cf. Sarna, *JPS Genesis Commentary* 1:5. See also Sarna's essays in *Studies in Biblical Interpretation*, especially "Hebrew and Bible Studies in Medieval Spain" and "Abraham Ibn Ezra as Exegete."

14. Sarna, *Encyclopedia Judaica*, 4:819.

15. Sarna, *Encyclopedia Judaica*, 4:828–30.

16. Sarna, *Understanding Genesis*, 25.

17. Sarna, *Exploring Exodus*, 5.

18. See Gabriel Josipovici, *The Book of God* (New Haven: Yale University Press, 1987) on the respective preferences of Jews for scrolls and Christians for codices. Frederick Greenspahn, "Do Jews Have a Bible?" In *Sacred Text, Secular Times: The Hebrew Bible in the Modern World*, ed. Leonard Greenspoon and Brian LeBeau, 1–12 (Omaha, NE: Creighton University Press, 2000); Nahum Sarna, "Geiger and Biblical Scholarship," in *New Perspectives on Abraham Geiger* (Cincinnati: Hebrew Union College, 1976), 24.

19. Robert Alter, *The World of Biblical Literature* (New York: Basic Books, 1992), 136.

20. Sarna, *Understanding Genesis*, preface.

21. Sarna, *JPS Genesis Commentary*, xvi.

22. Sarna, *Exploring Exodus*, xix.

23. Sarna, *Exploring Exodus*, 3–5.

24. Sarna, *Understanding Genesis*, xxi; Sarna, "From Wellhausen to Kaufmann," *Midstream* 7, no. 3 (1961): 64–74, 68; Sarna, "Ruminations of A Jewish Bible Scholar," *Bible Review* (June 1988): 4–5; Stephen Geller, "Wellhausen and Kaufmann," *Midstream* (December 1985): 38–48.

25. Shavit and Eran, *The Hebrew Bible Reborn*, 390–94.

26. Ellen Frankel, obituary for Nahum Sarna, *Los Angeles Times*, June 30, 2005.

27. Sarna, *Understanding Genesis*, 59.

28. Sarna, *Understanding Genesis*, 43.

29. Sarna, *Understanding Genesis*, xxv.

30. Sarna wrote in *Exploring Exodus*, "I am not addicted to parallelomania" (xxix).

31. Sarna, *Understanding Genesis*, xxvii.

32. Sarna, "The Decalogue," *Studies in Biblical Interpretation* (Philadelphia: JPS, 2000), 234–35.

33. Sarna, *Understanding Genesis*, 226.

34. Robert Alter, The Art of Biblical Poetry (New York: Basic Books, 1985), 20–21; Alter, World of Biblical Literature, 1–24, 40–46.

35. Steven Weitzman, ed., "After *The Art of Biblical Narrative*," *Prooftexts* 27, no. 2 (2007).

36. Susanne Klingenstein, *Enlarging America* (Syracuse, NY: Syracuse University Press, 1998), acknowledges Alter's biblical works as his most influential, yet devotes only three pages of a very lengthy chapter to the subject, 300–302.

37. Erich Auerbach, *Mimesis* (Princeton, NJ: Princeton University Press, 1953), 13. On Auerbach and Bloom, see Susan Handelman, *Slayers of Moses* (Albany: State University of New York Press, 1982), 179–83. Against Auerbach, see Vassilis Lambropoulos, *The Rise of Eurocentrism* (Princeton, NJ: Princeton University Press, 1993), 3–96.

38. Auerbach, *Mimesis*, 23.

39. Mara Benjamin, "The Tacit Agenda of a Literary Approach to the Bible," *Prooftexts* 27 (2007): 254–74. See Alter's comments on secondary canonicity in Alter, *Canon and Creativity* (New Haven, CT: Yale University Press, 2000).

40. Alter, "Introduction," *The Five Books of Moses*, cxxiii.

41. Alter, *WBL*, 206. Compare Martin Buber, "The Person Today and the Jewish Bible," to whom Alter is clearly indebted.

42. Alter, *World of Biblical Literature*, 161.

43. Alter, *The Five Books of Moses*, xvi–xxii.

44. Alter, *The Five Books of Moses* (New York: W. W. Norton, 2004), xix.

45. Benjamin, "The Tacit Agenda of a Literary Approach to the Bible," *Prooftexts* 27 (2007): 254–74.

46. Alter, *World of Biblical Literature*, 22 and 76–77.

47. Alter and Kermode, introduction to *The Literary Guide of the Bible* (Cambridge, MA: Harvard University Press, 1987).
48. Alter, *World of Biblical Literature*, 11.
49. Alter, *World of Biblical Literature*, 76.
50. See Alter's comments on the difference between the testaments' "diachronic dimension of this literary corpus" in *World of Biblical Literature*, 76.
51. Alter, *The Art of Biblical Poetry* (New York: Basic Books, 1985), 206.
52. Alter, *The Five Books of Moses*, xxix.
53. Alter's translation of 25:30a in *The Five Books of Moses*.
54. Jack Kugelmass, *Key Texts in American Jewish Culture* (New Brunswick, NJ: Rutgers University Press, 2003), 4.

10. SEEKING AN AMERICAN JEWISH BIBLE

1. Palestinian Talmud, Sanhedrin 10:1, is the earliest reference to Chumash that I could locate. The term does not appear frequently in early rabbinic sources.
2. See Frederick Greenspahn, "How Jews Translate the Bible," in *Studies and Texts in Jewish History and Culture* X, ed. Bernard D. Cooperman (College Park: University of Maryland Press, 2002), 41–61; Greenspahn, "Does Judaism Have a Bible?" 1–12; Greenspahn, "Why Jews Translate the Bible," in *Biblical Interpretation in Judaism and Christianity*, ed. Isaac Kalimi and Peter Haas (New York and London: T & T Clark International, 2006), 179–95.
3. Robert Gordis, "The Torah and Modern Man," in *Judaism* 24, no. 3 (1975): 348, in review of Plaut.
4. Eric Yoffe, "*The Torah: A Modern Commentary*," in *Judaism* (Spring 2005): 51–53.
5. B. Barry Levy, "Judge Not a Book by Its Cover," *Tradition* 19, no. 1 (Spring 1981): 89–95.
6. *Etz Hayim Torah and Commentary*, xix, 15.
7. Penny Shine Gold, *Making the Bible Modern* (Ithaca, NY: Cornell University Press, 2004).
8. Everett Fox, *The Schocken Bible*, vol. 1, *The Five Books of Moses* (New York: Schocken, 1983–1995), especially ix–xxv.
9. Richard Elliot Friedman. *Who Wrote the Bible?* 243.
10. Friedman, *Who Wrote the Bible?* 31.
11. Alter, *The Five Books of Moses*, xi.
12. Jon D. Levenson, "The Hebrew Bible, The Old Testament, and Historical Criticism," in *The Future of Biblical Studies*, ed. Richard Elliot Friedman and H. G. M. Williamson (Atlanta: Scholars Press, 1987). On Levenson, see Marvin Sweeney, "Why Jews Are Interested in Biblical Theology," *Jewish Book Annual* 55/56 (1997–1998): 134–68; Isaac Kalimi, *Early Jewish Exegesis and Theological Controversy* (Assen, The Netherlands: Royal Van Gorcum, 2002), 107–134.
13. See Levenson's comments on Hertz, *Sinai and Zion* (San Francisco: Harper and Row, 1988), 4–6.
14. Levenson, *Sinai and Zion*, 216–17.
15. Assessing the impact of the Jewish critique on Bible scholarship would require an insider's expertise.
16. Gender-sensitive translations such as *The Torah: A Modern Commentary*, 2nd edition; *The Torah: A Women's Commentary*; and Fox, *The Five Books of Moses*, render "Lord" as "Eternal" or simply leave the letters, YHVH.
17. Nancy Fuchs-Kreimer, "Feminism and Scriptural Interpretation," *Journal of Ecumenical Studies* 20, no. 4 (1983).
18. See Tikva Frymer-Kensky's introduction in *Studies in Bible and Feminist Criticism* (Philadelphia: JPS, 2006), xxi. Several Protestant feminists had made a similar rhetorical move with the Old Testament and New Testament, blaming Judaism for patriarchy and upholding Jesus as the true protofeminist.

19. Frymer-Kensky, "The Emergence of Jewish Biblical Theologies," in *Jews, Christians, and the Theology of the Hebrew Scriptures*, ed. Alice Bellis and Joel Kaminsky, Symposium Series 8 (Atlanta: Society of Biblical Literature, 2000), 365–79, 368.

20. Frymer-Kensky, *Reading the Women of the Bible* (New York: Schocken, 2002).

21. Frymer-Kensky, *In the Wake of the Goddesses* (New York: Macmillan, 1992); Frymer-Kensky, *Studies in Bible and Feminist Criticism* (Philadelphia: JPS, 2006).

22. Among my favorites who either explicitly term themselves feminists or apply gender analysis fruitfully: Ilana Pardes, Adele Berlin, Yaira Amit, and Susan Niditch.

23. *The Torah: A Women's Commentary* (New York: Union for Reform Judaism, 2008), xxxv. See also Ellen Frankel's *The Five Books of Miriam*, and Athalyah Brenner's impressive companion series to the entire Bible.

24. Judith Kates, review of *The Jewish Studies Bible*, *Nashim: A Journal of Jewish Women's Studies and Gender Issues* (2005): 253–58.

25. Sara Japhet, "Revisionism at All Costs," in *The Jewish Past Revisited*, ed. David Myers and David B. Ruderman (New Haven: Yale University Press, 1998), 220–21, 225–26.

26. Japhet, "Revisionism at All Costs," 224.

27. Yosef Yerushalmi, *Zakhor*, 81.

28. Yaira Amit, *History and Ideology: An Introduction to Historiography in the Hebrew Bible* (Sheffield, UK: Sheffield Academic Press, 1999), 23.

29. Baruch Halpern, *The First Historians* (San Francisco: Harper and Row, 1988). See also William Dever, *What Did the Bible Writers Know and When Did They Know It?* (Grand Rapids, MI: Eerdmans, 2001).

30. Israel Finkelstein and Neil Asher Silberman, *The Bible Unearthed: Archaeology's New Vision of Ancient Israel and the Origins of its Sacred Texts* (New York: Touchstone, 2001).

31. Finkelstein and Silberman, *The Bible Unearthed*, 142.

32. Finkelstein and Silberman, *The Bible Unearthed*, 281.

33. Israel Finkelstein, "Archaeology and the Bible: Not Black and not White," in *The Controversy Over the Historicity of the Bible*, ed. Lee Levine and Amihai Mazar (Jerusalem: Yad ben Zvi—Dinur Center, 2001), 141–52.

34. *Jewish Quarterly Review* 100, no. 1 (Winter 2010): 139–89. Kugel's book has also been reviewed by Jeremy Dauber, *Ha'aretz* (October 2010), and by Abraham Socher, *Commentary* (December 2007), as well as in non-Jewish publications, for instance, Peter Steinfels, *New York Times* (December 2007).

35. James Kugel in *AJS Newsletter* 36 (1986): 16–24.

36. James Kugel, *How to Read the Bible*, 9–10, 28–29, 40–45, 79–80, and 679–82.

37. James Kugel, "On the Bible and Literary Criticism," *Prooftexts* 1 (1981).

38. Alan Cooper, "Reading the Bible Historically and Otherwise," in *The Future of Biblical Studies*, ed. R. E. Friedman and H. G. M. Williamson (Atlanta: Scholars Press, 1987).

39. Kugel, *How to Read the Bible*, 685; Kugel, "Bible Criticism. Literary Criticism Lite," www.jameskugel.com. See also Yeshayahu Leibowitz, *On Just About Everything*, 5th ed. (Jerusalem: Hebrew University Press, 1988), 104–6; Yeshayahu Leibowitz, *Judaism, the Jewish People and the State of Israel* (Tel Aviv, 1977), 348.

40. Jacob Neusner and Ernst Freirichs, eds., preface to *Judaic Perspectives on Ancient Israel* (Philadelphia: Fortress Press, 1987); Sperling, "Major Developments in Jewish Biblical Scholarship."

CONCLUSION: IS THERE A "JEWISH SCHOOL" OF MODERN BIBLE STUDY?

1. Michael Signer, "How the Bible Has Been Interpreted in Jewish Tradition," *New Interpreters' Dictionary of the Bible*, vol. 1 (Nashville, TN: Abingdon, 1994), 65–82.

2. Sperling, "Major Developments," restricts his inquiry to North America, but most of the figures in this book (Mendelssohn, Hirsch, Ahad Haam, Ben-Gurion, and Leibowitz) would be excluded by his standards—as is Robert Alter, whose works have exerted such enormous influence.

3. Steven Kepnes, *The Text as Thou* (Bloomington: Indiana University Press, 1992), 53.

4. Ilana Pardes, *Countertraditions in the Bible: A Feminist Approach* (Cambridge, MA: Harvard University Press, 1992), 13–59.

5. The Jewish rehabilitation of rabbinic exegesis also had a polemical dimension: the Christian tradition tended to be more theological and less philological. Christian commentators often worked in translation: for all his brilliance, Augustine knew neither Hebrew nor Greek.

6. Ludwig Feuchtwanger, in Ismar Schorsch, "The Ethos of Modern Jewish Scholarship," in *From Text to Context: The Turn to History in Modern Judaism* (Hanover, NH: University Press of New England, 1994), 165.

7. Solomon Schechter, "The Study of the Bible," *Studies in Judaism*, 2nd Series (Philadelphia: JPS, 1908), 37, expressed a widely held view when he jibed that, "The dread of partiality for the Masoretic text is so great in certain circles that the notion seems to gain ground that the best qualification for writing on the Old Testament is ignorance of Hebrew."

8. Ahad Haam, *At the Crossroads*, 1:138.

Selected Bibliography

Abramowitz, Leah. *Tales of Nehama*. Jerusalem: Gefen Publishers, 2003.
Almog, Shmuel. *Zionism and History: The Rise of a New Jewish Conscience*. Jerusalem: Hebrew University/Magnes Press, 1987.
Alter, Robert. *The Art of Biblical Narrative*. New York: Basic Books, 1981.
———. *The Art of Biblical Poetry*. New York: Basic Books, 1985.
———. "The Bible as Secondary Canon." In *Insiders/Outsiders*, edited by David Biale, Susannah Heschel, and Michael Galchinsky. Berkeley, CA: Berkeley, 1998.
———. *Canon and Creativity*. New Haven, CT: Yale University Press, 2000.
———. *The Five Books of Moses*. New York: W. W. Norton, 2004.
———. *The World of Biblical Literature*. New York: Basic Books, 1992.
Altmann, Alexander. *Moses Mendelssohn: A Biographical Study*. Tuscaloosa: University of Alabama Press, 1973.
———. "Moses Mendelssohn as the Archetypal German Jew." In *The Jewish Response to German Culture*, edited by Jehuda Reinharz and Walter Schatzberg. Hanover, NH: University Press of New England, 1985.
Amit, Yaira. *History and Ideology: An Introduction to Historiography in the Hebrew Bible*. Sheffield, UK: Sheffield Academic Press, 1999.
———. *Reading Biblical Narratives*. Minneapolis, MN: Fortress Press, 2001.
———. "Some Thoughts on the Work and Method of Nehama Leibowitz." *Immanuel* 20 (Spring 1986): 7–13.
Arend, Moshe, Rut Ben-Meir, and Gavriel Chaim Cohen, eds. *Pirkei Nehama: Professor Nehama Leibowitz Memorial Volume*. Jerusalem: The Jewish Agency, 2001.
Arkush, Allan. *Moses Mendelssohn and the Enlightenment*. Albany: State University of New York Press, 1994.
Auerbach, Erich. *Mimesis*. Princeton, NJ: Princeton University Press, 1953.
Bach, Alice, ed. *Women in the Hebrew Bible*. New York and London: Routledge, 1999.
Bamberger, Bernard. *The Bible: A Modern Jewish Approach*. A Hillel Little Book. New York: B'nai Brith Foundations, 1955.
Bechtoldt, Hans-Joachim. *Die jüdische Bibelkritik im 19. Jahrhundert*. Stuttgart: W. Kohlhammer, 1995.
———. *Jüdische deutsche Bibelübersetzungen*. Stuttgart: Kohlhammer, 2005.

Benjamin, Mara. *Rosenzweig's Bible*. Cambridge: Cambridge University Press, 2009.

———. "The Tacit Agenda of a Literary Approach to the Bible: Buber-Rosenzweig and Robert Alter." *Prooftexts* 27, no. 2 (2007): 254–74.

Berlin, Adele. "On the Use of Traditional Jewish Exegesis in the Modern Literary Study of the Bible." In *Tehillah le-Moshe*. Winona Lake, IN: Eisenbrauns, 1997.

Berlin, Adele, and Marc Zvi Brettler, eds. *The Jewish Study Bible*. Oxford and New York: Oxford University Press, 2004.

Brenner, Michael. *The Renaissance of Jewish Culture in Weimar Germany*. New Haven, CT: Yale University Press, 1991.

Brenner, Yosef Chaim, cited in Laurence Silberstein. *The Postzionism Debates*. New York: Routledge, 1999.

Brettler, Marc Zvi. "Biblical History and Jewish Biblical Theology." *The Journal of Religion* 77 (1997): 563–83.

Breuer, Edward. *The Limits of Authority: Jews, Germans and the Eighteenth-Century Study of Scripture*. Cambridge, MA: Harvard University Press, 1996.

Breuer, Edward, and David Sorkin, translation and commentary to Moses Mendelssohn, "Kohelet Mussar." In *Leo Baeck Institute Yearbook* 48 (2003): 3–23.

Breuer, Mordechai. *Modernity Within Tradition*. Translated by Elizabeth Petuchowski. New York: Columbia University Press, 1992. Originally published as *Jüdische Orthodoxie im deutschen Reich, 1871–1918*.

Brinker, Menahem. "Brenner's Jewishness." *Studies in Contemporary Jewry* 4 (1988): 235.

Broka, Michael. "Targumei ha-Miqra shel Yehudai Germania." In *Proceedings of the Tenth World Congress of Jewish Studies*, division C, vol. 2. Jerusalem, 1989.

Buber, Martin. *Darko shel Mikra*. Jerusalem: Mossad Bialik, 1964.

———. *Moses: The Revelation and the Covenant*. New York: Harper & Brothers, 1958.

———. "On the Interpretation of the Bible." In *The Philosophy of Martin Buber*, edited by Paul Schilpp and Maurice Friedman. Library of Living Philosophers. La Salle, IL: Open Court, 1967.

———. *The Prophetic Faith*. New York: Macmillan, 1949.

Cassuto, Umberto. *Biblical Scripture and Canaanite Scripture*. [Sifrut mikrait v'sifrut k'nanit]. Jerusalem: Hebrew University Press, 1983.

———. *The Documentary Hypothesis*. Jerusalem, 1972.

Cogan, Mordechai. *Ben Gurion v'haTanakh. Am v'Artzo*. Be'er Sheva: Ben Gurion University, 1989.

Cohen, Naomi W. "The Challenges of Darwinism and Biblical Criticism to American Judaism." *Modern Judaism* 4, no. 2 (1984): 121–57.

Cooper, Alan. "Biblical Studies and Jewish Studies." In *The Oxford Handbook of Jewish Studies*, edited by Martin Goodman and Jeremy Cohen, 14–25. Oxford: Oxford University Press, 2002.

Deitcher, Howard. "Between Angels and Mere Mortals: Nechama Leibowitz's Approach to the Study of Biblical Characters." *Journal of Jewish Education* 66 (Spring/Summer 2000): 1–2.

Deutsch, Hayuta. *Nehama: Sippur shel Hayehah*. Tel Aviv: Yediot Ahronot, 2008.

Dever, William. *What Did the Biblical Writers Know and When Did They Know It?* Grand Rapids, MI: William Eerdmans, 2001.

Eisen, Arnold. "Divine Legislation as Ceremonial Script." *AJS Review* 15 (1990): 239–67.

Engel, David. "Hebrew Nationalism and Biblical Criticism." In *Ki Baruch Hu: Festchrift in Honor of Baruch Levine*, 483–507. Winona Lake, IN: Eisenbrauns, 1999.

Fackenheim, Emil. "New Hearts and Old Covenant." In *The Jewish Philosophy of Emil Fackenheim*, Michael Morgan, 223–34. Detroit: Wayne State Press, 1987.

Fine, David J. "Solomon Schecter and the Ambivalence of Jewish Wissenschaft." *Judaism* 1997: 4–24.

Finkelstein, Israel, and Neil Asher Silberman. *The Bible Unearthed: Archaeology's New Vision of Ancient Israel and the Origins of Its Sacred Texts*. New York: Touchstone, 2001.

Fishbane, Michael. *Biblical Interpretation in Ancient Israel*. Oxford: Clarendon Press, 1985.
Fox, Everett. *The Five Books of Moses*. New York: Schocken, 1995.
——. "Franz Rosenzweig as Translator." *Leo Baeck Institute Yearbook* 34 (1989).
——. *The Schocken Bible*. Vol. 1, *The Five Books of Moses*. New York: Schocken, 1983–1995. *In the Beginning* appeared first (1983); the entire *Five Books of Moses* in 1995.
Fox, Everett, with Lawrence Rosenwald. *Scripture and Translation*. Bloomington: Indiana University Press, 1994.
Fraade, Steven. "Comparative Midrash Revisited: The Case of the Dead Sea Scrolls and Rabbinic Midrash." In *Agendas for the Study of Midrash in the Twenty-first Century*, edited by Marc Lee Raphael. Williamsburg, VA: College of William and Mary, 1999.
——. "Interpreting Midrash 2: Midrash and Its Literary Contexts." *Prooftexts* 7, no. 3 (1987).
Frankel, Marla. *Teaching the Bible, The Philosophy of Nehama Leibowitz*. Tel Aviv: Yediot Ahronot, 2007.
Friedman, Richard Elliot. *Commentary on the Torah*. San Francisco: Harper & Row, 2001.
——. *Who Wrote the Bible?* New York: Simon & Schuster, 1987. 2nd ed. San Francisco: Harper and Row, 1997.
Friedman, Richard Elliot, and H. G. M. Williamson, eds. *The Future of Biblical Studies*. Atlanta: Scholars Press, 1987.
Frymer-Kensky, Tikva. "The Bible and Women's Studies." In *Feminist Perspectives on Jewish Studies*, edited by Lynn Davidman and Shelley Tennenbaum. New Haven, CT: Yale University Press, 1994.
——. "The Emergence of Jewish Biblical Theologies." In *Jews, Christians, and the Theology of the Hebrew Scriptures*, edited by Alice Bellis and Joel Kaminsky, 109–21. Symposium Series 8. Atlanta: Society of Biblical Literature, 2000.
——. *In the Wake of the Goddesses*. New York: Macmillan, 1992.
——. *Reading the Women of the Bible*. New York: Schocken, 2002.
——. *Studies in Bible and Feminist Criticism*. Philadelphia: JPS, 2006.
Fuchs-Kreimer, Nancy. "Feminism and Scriptural Interpretation." *Journal of Ecumenical Studies* 20, no. 4 (1983).
Geiger, Abraham. In *Abraham Geiger and Liberal Judaism*, ed. Max Wiener. Philadelphia: JPS, 1962.
Gillis, Michael. "Midrash and the Narrative Mode of Thought: Some Implications for Teaching Bible and Midrash." Melton Center for Jewish Education, The Hebrew University of Jerusalem, March 2001.
Glatzer, Nahum, and Paul Mendes-Flohr, eds. *The Letters of Martin Buber*. Syracuse, NY: Syracuse University Press, 1996.
Goitein, Shlomo Dov. *Omanut ha-Sippur ba-Mikra*. Jerusalem: Jewish Agency, 1956.
Gold, Penny Shine. *Making the Bible Modern*. Ithaca, NY: Cornell University Press, 2004.
Goldberg, Hillel. *Between Berlin and Slobodka: Jewish Transitional Figures from Eastern Europe*. Hoboken, NJ: KTAV, 1989.
Golomb, Jacob. *Nietzsche and Zion*. Ithaca, NY, and London: Cornell University Press, 2004.
Goshen-Gottstein, Moshe. "Christianity, Judaism and Modern Bible Study." *Supplements to Vetus Testamentum* 28 (1974): 69–88.
Gottschalk, Alfred. "Ahad Ha-am as Biblical Critic." *Hebrew Annual Review* 7 (1982): 105–19.
Graetz, Heinrich. "Memoirs." In *History of the Jews*, edited by Philipp Bloch and Heinrich Graetz, vol. 6. Philadelphia: JPS, 1898.
Greenberg, Moshe. *Al ha-Mikra ve-al Yahadut*. Tel Aviv: Am Oved, 1984.
——. "Ha-yitachen mada Mikra bikorti ba'al ofi yehudi? [Can Modern Critical Jewish Scholarship Have a Jewish Character?] *Proceedings of the Eighth World Congress of Jewish Studies*, vol. 1, 95–98. Jerusalem: 1983. Reprinted in *Studies in the Bible and Jewish Thought*, Moshe Greenberg, JPS Scholars of Distinction Series. Philadelphia: JPS, 1995.
——. *Studies in the Bible and Jewish Thought*. Philadelphia: JPS, 1995.
——. *Understanding Exodus*. New York: Behrman House, 1969.

Greenspahn, Frederick. "Does Judaism Have a Bible?" In *Sacred Text, Secular Times*, edited by Leonard Greenspoon and Brian LeBeau, 1–12. Omaha, NE: Creighton University Press, 2000.

———. *Essential Papers on Israel and the Ancient Near East*. New York: New York University Press, 1991.

———. *The Hebrew Bible: New Insights and Scholarship*. New York: New York University Press, 2008.

Greenspoon, Leonard. "Jewish Translations of the Bible." In *The Jewish Study Bible*, 2005–2020. Oxford: Oxford University Press, 2004.

———. "How Jews Translate the Bible." In *Studies and Texts in Jewish History and Culture* X, edited by Bernard D. Cooperman, 41–61. College Park: University of Maryland Press, 2002.

———. "Why Jews Translate the Bible." In *Biblical Interpretation in Judaism and Christianity*, edited by Isaac Kalimi and Peter Haas. New York and London: T & T Clark International, 2006.

Greenstein, Edward. "A Pragmatic Pedagogy of Bible." *Journal of Jewish Education* 75 (2009): 290–303.

———. "Theories of Modern Bible Translation." *Prooftexts* 3 (1983): 9–39.

———. "The Many-Faceted Interpretation of Nehama Leibowitz and Post-Modernist Interpretation." *Limmudim* 1 (2002): 21–33.

Grunfeld, Isidore, trans. *Horeb: A Philosophy of Jewish Laws and Observances*, edited by Samson Raphael Hirsch, vol. 1. London: Soncino Press, 1962.

Gugenheimer, Joseph. "Die Hypothesen der Bibelkritik." *Jeschurun* 13 (1867), 14 (1868), and 15 (1886).

Haam, Ahad. *At the Crossroads* [Al Prishat Drachim]. 4 vols. Berlin: Jüdischer Verlag, 1921.

Ha-Cohen, Ran. "Hitmoddidut Hokhmat Yisrael." PhD diss., Tel Aviv University, 2002.

———. *Renewing the Old Covenant*. Tel Aviv: Ha-Kibbutz HaMeuchad, 2006.

Halpern, Baruch. *The First Historians*. University Park: Penn State University Press, 1996.

Handelman, Susan. *The Slayers of Moses*. Albany: State University of New York Press, 1982.

Haran, Menachem. *Biblical Research in Hebrew*. Jerusalem: The Magnes Press, 1970.

Harris, Jay. *How Do We Know This?* Albany: State University of New York Press, 1994.

Hartman, Geoffrey, and Sanford Budick, eds. *Midrash and Literature*. New Haven, CT: Yale University Press, 1986.

Heschel, Susannah. *Abraham Geiger and the Jewish Jesus*. Chicago and London: University of Chicago Press, 1998.

Jacob, Benno. *The First Book of the Bible, Genesis*. New York: KTAV, 1974. A translation of *Das erste Buch der Tora*. Berlin: Schocken, 1934.

———. *Quellenscheidung und Exegese im Pentateuch*. Leipzig: Kaufmann, 1916.

———. *The Second Book of the Bible, Exodus*. New York: KTAV, 1992.

Josipovici, Gabriel. *The Book of God*. New Haven, CT: Yale University Press, 1987.

Kalimi, Isaac. *Early Jewish Exegesis and Theological Controversy*. Assen, The Netherlands: Royal Van Gorcum, 2002.

Kalimi, Isaac, and Peter Haas, eds. *Biblical Interpretation in Judaism and Christianity*. New York and London: Frank Case, 2006.

Kaplan, Aryeh. *The Living Torah*. New York and Jerusalem: Moznaim Publishing, 1981.

Kaufmann, Yehezkel. *The Religion of Israel*. Translated by Moshe Greenberg. Chicago: University of Chicago, 1960. An abridgement of *Toldot Ha-Emunah Ha-Yisraelit*. Tel-Aviv: Bialik, 1937.

Keren, Michael. *Ben Gurion and the Intellectuals*. De Kalb: Northern Illinois University Press, 1953.

Klingenstein, Susanne. *Enlarging America*. Syracuse, NY: Syracuse University Press, 1998.

Klugman, Eliyahu. *Samson Raphael Hirsch*. Brooklyn, NY: Mesorah Publications, 1996.

Knobloch, Frederick. *Biblical Translation in Context*. Bethesda: University of Maryland Press, 2002.

Kohler, Kaufmann. "The Attitude of Christian Scholars Toward Jewish Literature." In *Studies, Addresses and Personal Papers*. New York: Bloch Publishing, 1931.

Kolatch, Jonathan, ed. *Ben-Gurion Looks at the Bible*. Middle Village, NY: Jonathan David, 1972.

Koltun-Fromm, Ken. *Abraham Geiger's Liberal Judaism, Personal Meaning and Religious Authority*. Bloomington: Indiana University Press, 2006.

Kugel, James. *AJS Newsletter* 36 (1986): 16–24.

———. *The Bible as It Was*. Cambridge, MA: Harvard University Press, 1998.

———. "The Bible in the University." In *The Hebrew Bible and Its Interpreters*, edited by William Henry Propp, Baruch Halpern, and David Noel Freedman. Winona Lake, IN: Eisenbrauns, 1990.

———. *How to Read the Bible: A Guide to Scripture Then and Now*. New York: Free Press, 2007.

———. *In Potiphar's House*. San Francisco: Harper, 1990.

———. "On the Bible and Literary Criticism." *Prooftexts* 1 (1981).

Küsche, Ulrich. *Die unterlegene Religion: Urteil deutscher Alttestamentler*. Berlin: Institüt Kirsch und Judentum, 1991.

Lambropoulos, Vassilis. *The Rise of Eurocentrism*. Princeton, NJ: Princeton University Press, 1993.

Leibowitz, Nehama. *New Studies in Genesis–Deuteronomy*. 7 vols. Jerusalem: Hemed Press, 1954–1996.

Leibowitz, Yeshayahu. *Judaism, the Jewish People and the State of Israel*. Cambridge, MA: Harvard University Press, 1992. Originally Tel Aviv, 1977.

———. *On Just About Everything*. 5th ed. Jerusalem: Hebrew University Press, 1988.

Levenson, Alan, and Jeffrey Schein. "Will the Real Franz Rosenzweig Stand Up?" *Journal of Jewish Education* 76, no. 2 (2010): 151–63.

Levenson, Jon D. *Creation and the Persistence of Evil*. San Francisco: Harper & Row, 1988.

———. *Death and Resurrection of the Beloved Son*. New Haven, CT: Yale University Press, 1993.

———. "The Hebrew Bible and Historical Criticism." In *The Future of Biblical Studies: The Hebrew Scriptures*, edited by Richard Elliot Friedman and H. G. M. Williamson. Atlanta: Scholars Press, 1987.

———. *Sinai and Zion: An Entry into the Jewish Bible*. San Francisco: Harper & Row, 1988.

Levine, Lee, and Amihai Mazar. *The Controversy Over the Historicity of the Bible*. Jerusalem: Yad ben Zvi—Dinur Center, 2001.

Levy, B. Barry. "Judge Not a Book by Its Cover." *Tradition* 19, no. 1 (Spring 1981): 89–95.

Levy, Isaac, ed., *Samson Raphael Hirsch, Commentary to the Pentateuch*, second revised edition (London: Soncino, 1962–1967).

Liberles, Robert. *Religious Conflict in Social Context: The Resurgence of Orthodoxy in Frankfurt am Main, 1838–1877*. Greenwood, CT: Greenwood Press, 1985.

Lieber, David, ed. *Etz Hayim: Torah and Commentary*. Philadelphia: JPS, 2001.

Lowenstein, Steve. "The Readership of Mendelssohn's Bible Translation." In *The Mechanics of Change*. Atlanta: Scholars Press, 1992.

Margolies, Morris. *Samuel David Luzzato: Traditionalist Scholar*. New York: KTAV, 1979.

Meirovich, Harvey. *A Vindication of Judaism: The Polemics of the Hertz Pentateuch*. New York: Jewish Theological Seminary, 1998.

Meyer, Michael. *Response to Modernity: A History of the Reform Movement in Judaism*. New York: Oxford University Press, 1988.

Myers, David N. *Reinventing the Jewish Past: European Jewish Intellectuals and the Zionist Return to History*. New York: Oxford University Press, 1995.

Neusner, Jacob, and Ernst Freirichs, eds. *Judaic Perspectives on Ancient Israel*. Philadelphia: Fortress Press, 1987.

Niehoff, Maren Ruth. "The Buber-Rosenzweig Translation of the Bible." *Journal of Jewish Studies* 44, no. 2 (1993).

Ochs, Vanessa. *Words on Fire*. New York: Harcourt, Brace, Jovanovich, 1990.

Orlinsky, Harry. *Essays in Biblical Culture and Bible Translation*. New York: KTAV, 1974.
Pardes, Ilana. *The Biography of Ancient Israel: National Narratives in the Bible*. Berkeley: University of California Press, 2000.
———. *Countertraditions in the Bible: A Feminist Approach*. Cambridge, MA: Harvard University Press, 1992.
Peerless, Shmuel. *To Study and to Teach: The Methodology of Nehama Leibowitz*. Jerusalem: Lookstein Center/Urim Publications, 2004.
Plaut, Walter Gunther. "German-Jewish Bible Translations." LBI Memorial Lecture 36, New York, 1992.
Potok, Chaim, ed. *The JPS Torah Commentary*. Genesis–Deuteronomy. Jerusalem, New York, and London: JPS, 1984–1989.
Rosenbloom, Noah H. *Studies in Literature and Thought*. Jerusalem: Rubin Mass, 1989.
———. *Tradition in an Age of Reform*. Philadelphia: JPS, 1976.
Sarna, Nahum. "Abraham Geiger's Contribution to Bible Scholarship." In *New Perspectives on Abraham Geiger*, edited by Jakob J. Petuchowski. Cincinnati: HUC Symposium, 1976.
———. "The Authority and Interpretation of Scripture in Jewish Tradition." In *Studies in Biblical Interpretation*. Philadelphia: JPS, 2000.
———. "Bible." In *Encyclopedia Judaica*, 4:814–76.
———. *Exploring Exodus*. New York: Schocken, 1986.
———. "From Wellhausen to Kaufmann." *Midstream* 7, no. 3 (1961): 64–74.
———. "Geiger and Biblical Scholarship." In *New Perspectives on Abraham Geiger*, 24. Cincinnati: HUC, 1976.
———. "Ruminations of a Bible Scholar." *Bible Review* 4, no. 3 (June 1988).
———. *Understanding Genesis*. New York: JPS, 1966.
Sarna, Nahum, and Jonathan Sarna. "Jewish Bible Scholarship and Translations in the United States." In *The Bible and Bibles in America*, edited by Ernst Freirichs, 83–116. Atlanta: Scholars Press, 1988.
Schaeder, Grete. *The Hebrew Humanism of Martin Buber*. Detroit: Wayne State University, 1973.
Schechter, Solomon. "Higher Criticism—Higher Antisemitism." In *Seminary Addresses and Other Papers*. New York: The Burning Bush Press, 1959.
Scholem, Gershom. "Martin Buber's Judaism." In *On Jews and Judaism in Times of Crisis*, edited by Werner Dannhauser, 126–71. New York: Schocken, 1976.
Schorsch, Ismar. *From Text to Context: The Turn to History in Modern Judaism*. Hanover, NH: Brandeis University Press, 1994.
Segal, Moshe Z. *The Pentateuch: Its Composition and Its Authorship*. Jerusalem: Magnes Press, 1967.
Seidman, Naomi. *Faithful Renderings*. Chicago: University of Chicago Press, 2006.
Shapira, Anita. "Ben-Gurion and the Bible: The Forging of an Historical Narrative?" *Middle Eastern Studies* 33, no. 4 (Oct. 1997): 645–74.
———. "The Bible and Israeli Identity." *AJS Review* 28, no. 1 (2004): 11–42.
———. *Ha-Tanach v'zehut Yisraelit*. Jerusalem: Magnes Press, 2005.
———. *Land and Power: The Zionist Resort to Force, 1881–1948*. New York and Oxford: Oxford University Press, 1992.
Shavit, Yaacov, and Mordechai Eran. *From Holy Scriptures to the Book of Books*. Berlin and New York: De Gruyter, 2007.
Sheehan, Jonathan. *The Enlightenment Bible*. Princeton, NJ: Princeton University Press, 2005.
Signer, Michael A. "How the Bible Has Been Interpreted in Jewish Tradition." In *The New Interpreters' Dictionary of the Bible*, vol. 1, 65–82. Nashville: Abingdon, 1994.
Silberman, Lou. "Buber's Job and His Generation." In *Judaic Perspectives on Ancient Israel*, edited by Jacob Neusner and Ernst Freirichs. Philadelphia: Fortress Press, 1987.
Simon, Uriel, ed. *Scripture and Us* [Ha Mikra V'Anahnu]. Tel Aviv: Dvir, 1979.
Soloveitchick, Max, and Zalman Rubasheff. *Toldot Biqqoret HaMikra*. Berlin: Dvir, 1925.

Sommer, Benjamin. "Two Introductions to Scripture: James Kugel and the Possibility of Biblical Theology." *The Jewish Quarterly Review* 100, no. 1 (Winter 2010): 153–82.
Sorkin, David J. "The Mendelssohn Myth and Its Method." *New German Critique* 77 (1999): 7–28.
———. *The Religious Enlightenment: Protestants, Jews and Catholics from London to Vienna.* Princeton, NJ: Princeton University Press, 2008.
Speiser, Ephraim Avigdor, ed. *The Anchor Bible Genesis.* New York: Doubleday, 1964.
Sperling, S. David. "Major Developments in Jewish Biblical Scholarship." In *Hebrew Bible/Old Testament: The History of Interpretation,* edited by Magna Saebo, vol. 4. Göttingen: Vandenhoek & Ruprecht, forthcoming.
———. *Students of the Covenant.* Atlanta: Scholars Press, 1992.
Stern, Elsie. "Teaching Torah in the Twenty-First Century." *Prooftexts* 25, no. 3 (2005): 376–402.
Sternberg, Meir. *The Poetics of Biblical Narrative.* Bloomington: Indiana University Press, 1985.
Sussman, Lance J. "Another Look at Isaac Leeser and the First Jewish Translation of the Bible in the United States." *Modern Judaism* 5, no. 2 (May 1985): 159–90.
Sweeney, Marvin. "Why Jews Are Interested in Biblical Theology." *Jewish Book Annual* 55/56 (1997–1998): 134–68.
Tigay, Jeffrey, ed. Introduction to *Studies in Biblical Interpretation,* x–xxii. Philadelphia: JPS, 2000.
The Torah: A Women's Commentary. New York: Union for Reform Judaism, 2008.
Unterman, Yael. *Nehama Leibowitz: Teacher and Bible Scholar.* Jerusalem and New York: Urim Publications, 2009.
Weinberg, Werner, ed. *Moses Mendelssohn, Hebräische Schriften.* 15/1. Stuttgart: Friedrich Frommann Verlag, 1971.
Weintraub, Ze'ev. *Translations of the Torah in the German Language* [Targumei ha-Torah L'lashon ha-Germanit]. Chicago, 1967.
Weitzman, Steven, ed. "After *The Art of Biblical Narrative.*" *Prooftexts* 27, no. 2 (2007).
Wiener, Max. *Abraham Geiger and Liberal Judaism.* Cincinnati: Hebrew Union College, 1996.
Wiese, Christian. *Wissenschaft des Judentums und protestantische Theologie im wilhelminischen Deutschland.* Tübingen: Mohr Siebeck, 1999.
Wolf, Ernest. "Martin Buber and German Jewry." *Judaism* 1, no. 4 (1952).
Zerubavel, Yael. *Recovered Roots: Collective Memory and the Making of Israeli National Tradition.* Chicago: University of Chicago Press, 1995.
Zipperstein, Steven. *Elusive Prophet: Ahad Haam and the Origins of Zionism.* Berkeley: University of California Press, 2000.
———. "Symbolic Politics, Religion and Ahad Haam." In *Zionism and Religion,* edited by Shmuel Almog, Jehuda Reinharz, and Anita Shapira. Waltham, MA: Brandeis University Press, 1998.

Name Index

Abraham (the Patriarch), 38, 61, 73, 85. *See also* Genesis, book of
Abraham Ibn Ezra, 16, 39; Ahad Haam (Asher Zvi Ginsburg), 2, 97, 100, 105–114, 214; background and education, 105–106; Brenner's criticism of, 109, 111; contrasted with Berdichevsky and Brenner, 105–109; essays referencing Bible, 108–111; Herzliya Gymnasium, 111–113; legacy on teaching Bible, 114; polemics against Protestant Bible scholars, 111–113; positions regarding Mossinson and Marti, 112–113; Nietzsche's influence on, 108
Albright, William Foxwell, 100–101, 166
Alter, Robert, 172–180,193; background and education, 173–175; criticized, 172–173; Hebrew nature of Bible, 178–179; influence, 173, 176, 179; literary study of Bible, 172–180; preceded by Erich Auerbach, 174–175
Altmann, Alexander, 29–30
Amit, Yaira, 142, 149, 201
Arkush, Allan, 30–31
Artom, Shmuel Elia, 167
Auerbach, Erich, 174–175

Bamberger, Bernard, 159
Ben-Gurion, David, 115–132, 214; between Ahad Haam and Berdichevsky, 118–122; attitude toward rabbinic Judaism, 124–125, 130; background and education, 115, 117; influenced by Yehezkel Kaufmann, 125–130; on Joshua, 121–122; legacy of, 130–132; opposed to Kookism, 132; preference of First Temple over Second Temple, 125
Benjamin, Mara, 90, 92, 175, 177–178
Ben Yehuda, Eliezer, 99–100
Berdichevsky, Micha Yosef, 97, 105–109
Berlin, Adele, 205
Bloom, Harold, 176–177
Brenner, Yosef Chaim, 97
Breuer, Edward, 32
Breuer, Mordechai, 55, 93
Buber, Martin, 81–94; background and education, 83; Bible translation, with Rosenzweig, 86–90; "Der Mensch von heute" ("The Person of Today"), 82–85; *I and Thou (Ich und Du)*, 82; legacy of, 86–90

Cassuto, Umberto, 104, 139, 167
Cooper, Alan, 14, 24, 205

Delitzsch, Friedrich, 65–66, 75, 166
Dever, William, 100
De Wette, Wilhelm, 18

Eichhorn, Johann Gottfried, 32
Elman, Yaakov, 69
Ezra the Babylonian, 1–2, 18–19, 39, 51

Fackenheim, Emil, 6
Fishbane, Michael, 203
Fox, Everett, 86, 190–191
Friedman, Richard Elliot, 191–192, 193
Frymer-Kensky, Tikva, 196–199, 207

Geiger, Abraham, 45–49, 165
Geller, Stephen, 65, 126
Gillman, Abigail, 33–35
Ginsberg, H. L., 155
Graetz, Heinrich, 103
Greenberg, Moshe, 168–169
Greenspahn, Frederick, 183
Greenspoon, Leonard, 190

Halpern, Baruch, 201
Harris, Jay, 18
Hazaz, Hayim, 99, 100; opposed to Ben-Gurion's biblicism, 124
Hertz, Joseph, 155–156
Herzl, Theodor, 96
Heschel, Susannah, 46
Hirsch, Samson Raphael, 45–46, 48–63, 93–94; background and education, 52; *Horeb* (1837), 51–54; legacy, 49; *The Nineteen Letters* (1836), 51–54; Orthodoxy debated, 49, 55
Hobbes, Thomas, and *Leviathan*, 21–22

Jabotinsky, Vladimir, 130–131; pragmatism before Peel Commission, 117; *Samson*, 130
Jacob, Benno, 65–80, 211–212; *Babel und Bibel* controversy, 65–66; background and education, 67–68; legacy of, 70–71, 78–79; non-Orthodox maximalist, 69; polemics against Protestant Bible scholars, 67–69; political views, 68; verdict of Wasserman, 74
Japhet, Sarah, 200–201
Joseph, 58, 72–73, 76–77, 139, 146, 172. See also Genesis, book of
Josiah/Josian, 202

Kaplan, Aryeh, 189–191; *The Living Torah*, 189–190
Kariv, Avraham, 124
Kaufmann, Yehezkel, 125–130, 165, 168, 211; polemics against Protestant Bible scholars, 211
Kepnes, Steven, 86
Keren, Michael, on Ben-Gurion, 116
Kugel, James, 172, 203–205; *How to Read the Bible: A Guide to Scripture*, 203

Leeser, Isaac, 153–154
Leibowitz, Nehama, 133–150, 197, 212; background and education, 134–136; contrasted to Yeshayahu Leibowitz, 150; influence of Buber-Rosenzweig on, 147–149; influence of Hirsch on, 143–146; legacy of, 133, 136–138; Orthodoxy of, 133–150, esp. 137, 140; reading of Deuteronomy, 141; against source criticism, 142; Zionism of, 134–135, 140
Leibowitz, Yeshayahu, 150
Lessing, Ephraim Gotthold, 30
Levene, Nancy, 23
Levenson, Jon D., 194–196, 207; *Creation and the Persistence of Evil*, 196; *Sinai and Zion*, 195
Levy, B. Barry, 186–187
Lowenstein, Steven, 34–35
Luzzato, Shmuel David, 48, 62

Maimonides (Moses ben Maimon, also Rambam), 9, 31, 54
Mendelssohn, Moses, 29–44, 54–57, 214; Bible work *Sefer Netivot ha-Shalom*, 37–43; bibliocentrism, 42; compared with S. R. Hirsch, 55; evaluation of philosophy, 29–32; *Jerusalem* (1782), 30; legacy of, 43–44; opposed to Luther, 42–43; views on history, 39–40; Yiddishims in, 32–33
Mossinson, Benzion, 111–113. See also Herzliya Gymnasium, debate at
Muilenberg, James, 85–86

Nachmanides (Moses ben Nachman, also Ramban), 38
Neusner, Jacob, 3–4
Niehoff, Marin Ruth, 70–71, 89
Noah, 60–61, 79–80, 169. See also Genesis, book of

Plaut, W. Gunther, 183–185
Potok, Chaim, 86–87

Ramban (Rabbi Moshe ben Nachman), 38
Rashbam, 42, 162–163
Rashi (Rabbi Shlomo Yizhak), 35, 49, 71, 91, 118; criticized by Ben-Gurion, 118; presence in American Chumashim, 182; presence in Friedman's *Commentary*, 192
Ratosh, Jonathan, 131
Rebecca (the Matriarch), 62, 74
Rosenbloom, Noah, 52

Rosenzweig, Franz, 81–94; background, 81–82; debt to Mendelssohn, 43; *It Is Time (Zeit Ist)*, 90–91; views on Hebrew, 90–93

Sandmel, Samuel, 158
Sarna, Nahum, 157–172; background and education, 157; *Exploring Exodus*, 161; *Understanding Genesis*, 157
Schechter, Solomon, 154–155
Schliemann, Heinrich, 101
Scholem, Gershom (Gerhard), 41, 47, 85, 87, 90, 177, 191, 193
Seidman, Naomi, 32–33, 69
Segal, M. H., 104
Shapira, Anita, 121
Shavit, Yaacov, 5
Sheehan, Jonathan, 1, 5, 152
Smith, Steven, 16, 20
Smolenskin, Peretz, 104

Sorkin, David Jan, 30, 39
Speiser, Ephraim Avigdor, 160, 176
Sperling, S. David, 4, 172, 192, 206
Spinoza Benedict (Baruch), 9–27, 54; background and education, 9–10; evaluation of philosophy, 10–11; *Tractatus Theologico-Politicus*, 13–22
Strauss, Leo, 11–12, 20, 22
Sutcliffe, Adam, 21

Wellhausen, Julius, 65, 70, 94, 105, 125–126, 155, 191
Wessely, Naftali Hartwig, 35
Wise, Isaac Mayer, 154
Wolfson, Harry Austrin, 11–12

Yadin, Yigael, 101, 130, 202
Yovel, Yirmiyahu, 12

Zunz, Leopold Lipmann, 26, 46, 211

Subject Index

American Bible, 152–156
archaeology, 100–102
Authorized Version (King James Bible), 17, 22, 36, 88, 153–154, 160, 179

Babel-Bibel controversy, 5, 65–66, 166. *See also* Delitzsch, Friedrich
Bible: creation narratives in, 17, 58, 70, 75, 160, 167, 169–170; criticism of, 45, 77, 103–105; eisigesis/exegesis of, 4, 22, 32, 47, 57, 60, 69, 71, 78–79, 84, 139, 158–159, 203; feminist evaluations of, 196–199; Hebrew language nature of, 40–42, 57, 89, 99–100, 213–214; historiography, 39–40, 199–202; interpretation of, 15, 18, 47, 57, 77, 79, 84–86, 92, 120, 140–142, 145–146, 158–159, 169, 174, 180, 198, 203, 212–213; minimalism, 199–202; narrative style, 172–177; oral nature, 57, 83–84, 87–88; religion, 194–196, 197–199; translation, 32–33, 37, 91–92, 183–189, 189–192
bibliocentrism, also bibliolatry, 42, 150, 158

Canaanites (New), 108
chosenness, doctrine of, 12
Christianity, 1, 7, 14, 18, 19–21, 36, 60, 78–81, 84–87, 90, 120, 142
Chumash, 2–3, 5, 39, 155, 180–189, 205–206
Code of Hammurabi, 75

Commandments (also Mitzvot), 29, 31, 38, 50–52, 54, 62, 195
conversos (or Marranos or *anusim*), 12

darshan (expositor), 43
Deir Alla Inscription, 200
Deuteronomy, book of (*Sefer Devarim*), 2, 17, 19, 22, 55, 59, 128–129, 148, 193, 202
Documentary Hypothesis. *See* source criticism
Dutch Republic, 9

Eastern Europe, 103–104, 106
Enlighteners/Enlightenment (*Aufklärer/Aufklärung*), 1, 13, 31, 42, 113, 121
Enuma Elish, 75
Etz Hayim Torah and Commentary, 187–189
Exodus, book of (*Sefer Shmot*), 22, 42, 51, 58–59, 71, 73–74, 85, 147–148, 163–165, 168–170

Genesis, book of (*Sefer Bereshit*), 6, 17, 38, 54–56, 58–59, 60–62, 71–74, 84, 106, 120, 145–146, 160–164, 169–170, 191, 195

Haifa Technion, debate at, 111–113
halachah (Jewish law, Jewish way), 46, 50, 52–55, 104, 135, 149, 188
haskalah/maskil(im), 26, 32, 209
Hebrew University, 104
Herzliya Gymnasium, debate at, 111–113

Israel (British Palestine), 123

J, E, P, D. *See* source criticism

Karaite(s), 45, 109
keri/ktiv (Torah as read/Torah as written), 59. *See also* scroll(s)
King James Bible (1611). *See* Authorized Version

Lavon Affair, 116
law code. *See* halachah
leitwort/leitwörter, 57, 85, 88, 138, 190
Leviticus, book of (*Sefer Vayikra*), 67–68, 148, 159

marrano. *See* conversos
masoretes/Masoretic Text. *See* Traditional (Torah) Text
midrash, 6, 16–17, 57, 59, 61–62, 72, 77, 85, 89, 110, 114, 122, 124, 139, 161, 173, 184, 199, 212–213
minimalism (or Copenhagen School, Scheffield School). *See* Bible, minimalism
Mishnah, 31, 40, 42, 59–60, 100, 124–125
Mishneh Torah (of Maimonides, also *Yad Ha̱zakah*), 31
Mitzvoth (or Mitzvot). *See* Commandments

Near East, ancient, 71, 75, 101, 127
new Canaanites, 131
new literary criticism, 139, 147, 173–177
New JPS, 185–186, 214
Numbers, book of (*Sefer Bemidbar*), 22, 58, 148

Old and New Testaments, compared, 15, 18, 20–21, 86, 88, 111, 113, 152, 178–179
Old JPS, 147, 153–154, 181
Oral Torah and Written Torah compared, 6, 41, 49–51, 59–60, 69, 93–94, 150, 212–213
Orthodox Judaism, 49

parashah (sing.)/*parashot* (pl.), 58, 148, 183
parshanut or *parshanut ha-Mikra*. *See* Bible, interpretation
pashtanim, 42
Peel Commission, 97, 117, 156
Pentateuch. *See* Chumash
Pesach/Passover, 96, 128
Pharisaic, 46, 109
Philippsohn-Herxheimer Bible, 26

pilpul, 52
Priestly Code ("P"), 68, 128–129
prophets (*Neviim*), 2, 5, 90, 106–107, 110, 119, 127–129, 148
Protestant Bible scholarship: biases of, 15, 26, 32, 66–70; dominance of, 26, 210
p'shat. *See pashtanim*

Redactor/Redacted ("R") Text, Redactor (also *Verfasser* [B. Jacob] or Narrator [N. Sarna]), 19, 58, 69, 72, 87, 163, 170–171, 176, 191, 204
Reform Judaism, 46–48
rua̱h (spirit/breath), 84, 110

scripture, 2, 5–6, 13–15, 22, 40–41, 49, 53–54, 59, 67, 76–78, 85, 158–159, 162–163, 191, 205, 214
scroll(s), 2, 16, 18, 33, 59, 73, 77–78, 163, 194
Second Aliyah, 38
Second Temple Judaism, 212
secularism, 12
Sefer ha-Chinuch, 54
Septuagint (Greek translation of Bible), 5, 69, 74, 94, 112, 213
shimeni atzeret, 29
shma (central affirmation in Judaism), 59, 195
Shulchan Aruch (16th law code), 54
sidra (weekly Torah portion). *See parashah*
soteriological, 23, 182
source criticism/source critics (also J, E, P, D), 2–3, 5, 56–57, 128–129, 164–165, 176, 191–192, 193, 211
Stone, The/ArtScroll Chumash, 186–187, 189
supersessionist, 20, 76

Tanakh (or Tanach). *See* Bible
Tel Dan Inscription, 200
Tetragrammaton, 37, 56, 85–86
The Torah: A Modern Commentary, 183–186, 189
Traditional (Torah) Text, 40–42, 69, 74, 87, 114, 163–164, 192, 213–214

Vulgate (Latin translation of Bible), 22, 74, 88

War for Israeli Independence, 123
Weimar Republic, 11, 66, 70, 134–135
World Wars, 7, 26

Zionism, 4, 47, 96–100, 104, 107–109, 119–120, 122, 129, 209

About the Author

Alan T. Levenson, BA/MA, magna cum laude, Brown University, and Ph.D., Ohio State University, is Schusterman/Josey Professor of Jewish Intellectual and Religious History at the University of Oklahoma. Before taking this position, he taught history, thought, and Bible at Siegal College in Cleveland, Ohio, for eighteen years. He has been a visiting professor at the College of William and Mary and at Case Western Reserve University. He is the author of three books: *Modern Jewish Thinkers: An Introduction* (Jason Aronson, 2000; second edition, Rowman & Littlefield, 2006); *Between Philosemitism and Antisemitism: German Defenses of Jews and Judaism* (2004); and *The Story of Joseph: A Journey of Jewish Interpretation* (2006), and many essays on German Jewry, modern Jewish thought, and pedagogy. He has received fellowships from Tel Aviv University, the American Council of Learned Societies, the German Academic Exchange Program the Memorial Foundation of Jewish Culture, and the Littauer Foundation.

Since arriving in Oklahoma, Levenson has published several essays including "George Eliot's *Daniel Deronda*" (*Prooftexts*); "New York: The Cosmopolitan Jewish City" (*The Reconstructionist*); "Will the Real Franz Rosenzweig Please Stand Up?" (*Journal of Jewish Education*); and "The Mantle of the Matriarchs: Ruth 4:11–15" (*The Jewish Bible Quarterly*). He is currently editing a one-volume history of Jews and Judaism. He lives in Norman, Oklahoma, with his wife, Hilary, and their son, Benjamin Ze'ev.